HAIL TO THE REDSKINS

ALSO BY ADAM LAZARUS

Best of Rivals: Joe Montana, Steve Young, and the Inside Story Behind the NFL's Greatest Quarterback Controversy

Super Bowl Monday: From the Persian Gulf to the Shores of West Florida—The New York Giants, the Buffalo Bills, and Super Bowl XXV

Chasing Greatness: Johnny Miller, Arnold Palmer, and the Miracle at Oakmont (with Steve Schlossman)

HAIL TO THE REDSKINS

Gibbs, the Diesel, the Hogs,
AND THE GLORY DAYS OF
D.C.'S FOOTBALL DYNASTY

ADAM LAZARUS

wm

WILLIAM MORROW
An Imprint of HarperCollins*Publishers*

HarperCollins books may be purchased for educational, business, or sales promotional use. For information please e-mail the Special Markets Department at SPsales@ harpercollins.com.

A hardcover edition of this book was published in 2015 by William Morrow, an imprint of HarperCollins Publishers.

FIRST WILLIAM MORROW PAPERBACK EDITION PUBLISHED 2016.

Library of Congress Cataloging-in-Publication Data has been applied for.

ISBN 978-0-06-237576-6

HB 03.13.2023

For Aaron and Benjamin,
the two newest members of the *Lazarus* Fun Bunch

Contents

Author's Note

Several months ago, when the controversy surrounding the Washington Redskins' nickname hit full stride, my editor, Peter Hubbard, suggested taking on the issue in a prefatory note. Tensions over such prominent, widespread use of a team name—believed by many to be derogatory of Native Americans—have become too large and omnipresent to ignore.

A 2014 Langer Research poll conducted for ESPN's investigative program *Outside the Lines* found that the number of Americans who supported the Redskins' nickname had decreased considerably: 71 percent (of the 1,019 Americans polled) approved of keeping the name. Twenty-two years earlier, a similar poll found that 89 percent favored keeping the name.

Recently, the federal government has also entered the debate. In May, fifty members of the United States Senate wrote letters to NFL commissioner Roger Goodell, endorsing a name change. A month later, the United States Patent and Trademark Office canceled the Washington Redskins' trademark, declaring it "disparaging to Native Americans."

Even the president of the United States weighed in on the issue.

"If I were the owner of the team and I knew that there was a name of my team—even if it had a storied history—that was offending a sizeable group of people, I'd think about changing it," Barack Obama told the Associated Press in October 2013.

As I started reviewing my own stance on the name, I thought of an exchange between two characters from one of my favorite television shows, *The West Wing*.

Early in the episode entitled "The State Dinner," the fictional presidential administration's press secretary, C. J. Cregg (played by Allison Janney), learns about a public relations matter that crops up. At nearby Lafayette Park a group had protested the White House's sizeable collection of eighteenth- and nineteenth-century vermeil tableware made of silver and gold. In explaining the protestors' cause to the White House press corps, Cregg says that the workers who crafted the vermeil "were blinded by the mercury while making these pieces. Louis XV would melt them down to pay for his wars against his people. So, in general, they're seen in some circles as a symbol of a government's bloody and tyrannical oppression of its own people."

Later, Cregg approaches the administration's First Lady, Abbey Bartlet (Stockard Channing), hoping to defuse the minor situation. Mrs. Bartlet responds to Cregg's inquiry by saying, "It's our history. Better or for worse, it's our history. We're not going to lock it in the basement or brush it with a new coat of paint; it's our history."

Essentially, this is how I feel about the Redskins' name.

At the simplest level I think the name is problematic, if not offensive. The spirit behind the name is not hateful or racist; it's just a remnant of an era and worldview that have both passed.

Furthermore, a large number of citizens believe the name is degrading or ugly and, therefore, it should be changed. Many of those people are intelligent, respected members of the media, who don't have anything to gain or lose based on the nickname of a sports team.

I can certainly empathize with those who believe there are more important issues in this country than the name of a football team. And I can equally empathize with those who believe political correctness and sensitivity have run amok in our society. There's truth to both of those claims.

Personally, I think a name change is the right thing to do, but I'm not a vehement, passionate supporter. This issue will never go away unless the team name "Redskins" is abandoned, so I'm in favor of ending the controversy, not necessarily changing the name.

A smart, rational debate over this topic could fill up every single page of this book. But I think these pages are better used for celebrating and remembering the glory days of the franchise.

Doing so without use of the word "Redskins," however, would be historically inaccurate, clumsy, and ultimately absurd. During the years in which this true story takes place, roughly 1981 through 2007, the professional football team in Washington was known as the Redskins, so I refer to that team and those players as "Redskins."

To do otherwise would be locking a piece of history in the basement or brushing it with a new coat of paint.

Adam Lazarus
September 2014

March 1981

I have resigned my position of fullback for the above corporation, effective one o'clock p.m., Sunday July 27, 1980. Happy trails to you, until we meet again.

—John Riggins, mailgram to Washington Redskins front office

TWO MONTHS on the job, Joe Gibbs had finally heard enough.

From the moment the Redskins named Gibbs their new head coach on January 13, 1981, countless people he encountered inside and around the nation's capital gave him the same unsolicited advice: "You need to get Riggins back here."

John Riggins, the Redskins' eccentric yet gifted running back, sat out the previous season. He left Redskins training camp in July 1980 in protest of his contract: the front office refused to grant him a $200,000-per-year raise following a second consecutive 1,000-yard season. But during an exhausting, lengthy, and very public discord between Riggins and the Redskins, the thirty-one-year-old admitted that money wasn't the reason for his absence.

"For some reason or another, I haven't been able to get in a football frame of mind this year," he told Paul Attner of the *Washington Post* in August. "I could come back now and collect my $200,000, but I'd be doing them a disservice the way I feel. I have more integrity than that. I hope. I'm not just going to do that.

"I thought more money would help out. A new contract is like a new baby being born. It represents revitalization, life to come. It's a good feeling, it could pick me up. I figured maybe the Redskins could try to help me out. But maybe I was wrong to ask them to help me solve my problem, so I am taking them off the hook."

Instead of playing football, Riggins returned home to Lawrence, Kansas. For $135 in enrollment fees, he attended a four-hour-per-week money management economics course at the University of Kansas. But he quickly bored of drinking beer, hunting and fishing with his buddies, and the occasional home repair, such as painting his house.

"I took the whole year, I'm a slow worker," he later said.

Riggins missed football and the camaraderie. He even drove to St. Louis in late December to visit his former teammates after a game against the Cardinals. But he had no intention of returning to the NFL and ignored the phone calls from both Redskins personnel and other teams that showed an interest in trading for him.

"When I left, I wanted out," he later said. "At that point, football wasn't that much fun. I'd achieved a certain amount of success and I guess it wasn't a challenge. I'd had my best year the year before I quit."

Joe Gibbs knew that as well. So on his way back from the NFL's annual spring meetings in Hawaii, he made a detour to Kansas. The forty-year-old, first-time head coach rented a car and drove to Lawrence. On a chilly day in the college town, he stopped at a corner gas station and asked the first person he saw to help him find Riggins.

"Everybody in Lawrence, Kansas, knows where John Riggins lives," Gibbs learned. "This guy is famous."

Following the local's directions Gibbs drove across the flat, scenic terrain to a nearby dirt road, and pulled up to the entrance of a 160-acre estate that featured "a barn with seven stalls for horses . . . a stretch of pastureland meant for corn and alfalfa . . . and row upon row of neatly baled hay for cattle." Riggins never bought the horses, never planted the crops, and sold the cattle years earlier.

Gibbs exited the car and knocked on the front door of the farmhouse.

"Right away I knew I had a chance to get John Riggins to come back because Mary Lou, his wife, answered the door, hair's up in rollers, the kids are running through the house. She told me she wanted to come back . . . so I said, 'Mary Lou, you got to get an appointment for me.'"

The next morning at his motel Gibbs received a message inviting him back to the house for a ten a.m. breakfast meeting. He put on his best suit, drove to the farmhouse, and spotted Riggins strolling through the courtyard, decked in camouflage hunting gear, and carrying for his guest twelve ounces of hospitality.

"I meet him at the back door. I've got a Budweiser in each hand," said Riggins, who did not know the Redskins' coach abstained from alcohol. "I drank my beer and I drank Joe's and we sat down and we had breakfast and then we discussed a few things."

While Mary Lou served the two, Gibbs tried to coax Riggins out of retirement, promising an offense that would feed him the ball "every down." But ten minutes into his sales pitch, Gibbs noticed Riggins looked disinterested, even bored.

"I'm not getting anything from him," he recalled decades later.

After a brief moment of awkward silence, Riggins leaned over the table, and with his trademark self-confidence made his pitch to Joe Gibbs.

"You need to get me back there: I'll make you famous."

Gibbs would become famous, and in short order. Twenty-two months later, he gave the championship-starved fans in and around the nation's capital their first NFL title in forty years. By the end of his seventh season in Washington he'd capture a second Super Bowl victory, and a third by the end of his eleventh. When he stepped down as Redskins coach, almost exactly twelve years after his brief visit to Lawrence, Kansas, Gibbs's 140 total victories earned him the highest winning percentage (.683) of anyone in NFL history to coach at least 200 games.

John Riggins's breakfast-table prophecy, however, wasn't entirely on point. He didn't make Joe Gibbs famous. Joe Gibbs made *him* famous. And Riggins wasn't the only man to become a legend under Gibbs's watch. Throughout those twelve seasons, a handful of stars—some rare football talents, others unforgettable personalities, still others an equal mix of both—wore the burgundy and gold and fought for old D.C.

But none—not John Riggins, Joe Theismann, Doug Williams, Dexter Manley, Art Monk, Darrell Green, the Hogs, or even Joe Gibbs himself—became icons or made others icons all on their own. Quintessentially egalitarian, the Washington Redskins of the 1980s and early 1990s were the model team, the model dynasty. They were all famous, and they were all champions, together.

CHAPTER 1

Joe Who?

BRASH, INTIMIDATING, and always sharply dressed to project an old-fashioned elegance, Jack Kent Cooke fit in perfectly with the Washington, D.C., aristocracy. But what separated the business tycoon who cherished classical music, Brooks Brothers, as well as impeccable elocution from the rest of the city's elite was a flair for success in the plebeian world of professional sports.

In 1951, he purchased a floundering minor league baseball team, the Toronto Maple Leafs, and turned them into the International League's top drawing club within a year. The former door-to-door encyclopedia salesman who built a television broadcasting and newspaper empire sold the team in 1964, and then purchased the Los Angeles Lakers a year later. Despite paying a whopping $5.2 million (close to twice as much as anyone had ever spent on an NBA team) Cooke again flashed his Midas touch. He oversaw the acquisitions of Wilt Chamberlain and Kareem Abdul-Jabbar, won six Western Conference titles and an NBA championship in 1972, built the Fabulous Forum in Inglewood, and in 1979, sold the club (and the Kings, the local NHL team he founded) for a substantial profit.

Cooke—who in 1971 was the chief financier of the "Fight of the Century" between Muhammad Ali and Joe Frazier—also owned a piece of the Washington Redskins. On the advice of his friend, famed New York City attorney Bill Shea (namesake of the Mets' stadium), Cooke had purchased a 25 percent stake in 1961. Over time, as his fellow shareholders, including majority holder George Preston Marshall, either died or were pushed out, Cooke consolidated ownership. By 1974, he had obtained roughly 85 percent of the team.

Cooke viewed these sports ownerships as a lark, not a passion, and certainly not as a livelihood.

"We were in other businesses besides the Washington Redskins," Cooke's son, John, recalled decades later. "The Washington Redskins were always a hobby to the Cooke family. He used to tease Joe [Gibbs] and anyone else who would overhear us, that he had to go back from Redskin Park to make enough money to pay for all this."

As had been the case with the Maple Leafs, the Lakers, and the Kings, Cooke did not interfere with the day-to-day operations of the Redskins. He trusted and relied on the people he hired to run his team.

But by 1981, with the completion of Cooke's sale of the Lakers as well as his own relocation from Southern California first to Upperville, Virginia, then later Middleburg, he felt compelled to make a significant change. He fired his head coach, Jack Pardee.

"The reason he was let go is that Pardee was very secretive," recalled John Kent Cooke, the team's executive vice president. "The atmosphere at Redskin Park at that time was not good."

"There was a wonderful man named Nate Fine, who was the photographer for the Washington Redskins . . . Dad said to him 'How are things down there?' "

"Not very good, Mr. Cooke."

"What do you mean?"

"Everything's secretive. You walk down the hall, they slam the door shut, right away. Nothing's open. There's dissension in the players, the front office, everywhere."

That news caused Cooke to investigate, and after a series of inquiries and discussions, he met with Pardee to talk about the status of the organization.

"In those meetings, Jack Pardee was terrible in presenting and talking to Dad," John Kent Cooke said. "Usually around my dad, people would be very nervous, no matter who the hell you are. You have to sit on the edge of your seat, pay attention because he was so quick. But that had no bearing with poor Jack and Jack just made a miserable presentation. Finally, Dad said, 'I gotta get rid of this guy.'"

Although Pardee had won the NFL's Coach of the Year award in 1979 and was well respected throughout the league, his firing was not a surprise: Washington did not reach the postseason in his three-year tenure, posting a .500 record.

Pardee played for George Allen, who practically hated rookies and had little interest in developing talent. Allen's "Over the Hill Gang" of veterans guided the Redskins to their first Super Bowl in 1972, but the championship window began to shut. Pardee, a linebacker on that team, played eight seasons for Allen, and he, too, built a heavily veteran roster. He gave little playing time to or simply cut promising youngsters that the club's forward-thinking general manager, Bobby Beathard, found in the draft or signed as college free agents.

The forty-three-year-old Beathard, an easygoing Californian, ran out of patience.

"I can't stay with the Redskins under the present conditions," he told his wife, Christine, in December 1980. "If Mr. Cooke decides to keep both Jack and me, I'm going to have to look for another job."

Beathard had been hired as the Redskins' general manager in 1978, the same year Pardee succeeded George Allen. His plan to rebuild the aging roster depended on draft choices and young players, a difficult task given that Washington's first pick that spring came in the sixth round.

"They did a great job, the previous [staff]," Beathard recalled, "but after a while, when you don't believe in the draft, things get old."

Just after the 1980 season ended, Beathard won his power struggle: Pardee was fired.

"It became apparent to me that Beathard and Pardee held divergent views of how to produce a winning team for Washington," Cooke told the press. "After careful consideration, I have decided to endorse Mr. Beathard's program of a winning future for the Redskins. The search for the new head coach will begin at once."

Cooke, who always craved star power, had two candidates in mind: George Allen, the fiery former Redskins head coach, and John Madden, who retired two years after winning a Super Bowl in 1976. The former Oakland Raiders head coach had been Beathard's college roommate at Cal-Poly, San Luis Obispo.

"What [Cooke] was hoping is that we landed a big name, someone, not necessarily a *big* name but somebody recognizable," Beathard said in 2014. "Mr. Cooke believed in making a splash and would have liked to have had a name, [given] his background in newspaper business and all that."

Beathard didn't care nearly as much about name recognition. Through eighteen years in professional football, he knew that great head coaches were made, not born, and in January 1981 he assured Jack Kent Cooke, "I've got the right guy, if you just hang with me."

A defensive back for the AFL's San Diego Chargers in 1960, Beathard played on the Sid Gillman coaching staff that included Chuck Noll and Al Davis. His playing career over following that one season, Beathard soon became a scout for Hank Stram's Kansas City Chiefs, then the Atlanta Falcons, and in 1972 the director of player personnel for the Don Shula–led Miami Dolphins. So when time came to hire his first head coach as a general manager, Beathard knew exactly the man he was looking for. He was after Joe Gibbs.

Given endorsements from Chargers head coach Don Coryell and wide receivers coach Ernie Zampese, Beathard alerted his boss that Gibbs, San Diego's offensive coordinator, was the choice. Cooke had just one comment for his general manager.

"Who in the heck is Joe Gibbs? They'll crucify me!"

HOURS BEFORE BEATHARD CALLED the candidate that his boss had never heard of, a weary, defeated Joe Gibbs wolfed down a few slices of pizza, returned to his car, and continued the drive toward his house in La Costa, California.

Earlier that January day, Gibbs and the Chargers narrowly missed out on a chance to play in Super Bowl XV, losing the 1980 AFC Championship Game to the Oakland Raiders, 34–27. When Gibbs returned home after the quick dinner with his wife and children, he was stunned but thrilled to answer Beathard's telephone call.

Following a brief condolence on the loss, Beathard asked Gibbs to meet him that evening in San Clemente. Together, they drove to Los Angeles International Airport and took the red eye to New York City, where the next evening they would meet with Jack Kent Cooke in the owner's suite at the Waldorf Towers.

During part of the flight, Beathard coached Gibbs on how to address and respond to Cooke, but even the tutorial couldn't prepare Gibbs for the frequently combative owner who personally called up local newspapers to berate reporters for everything from vocabulary to content.

Well before they were supposed to meet Cooke, as Gibbs put on his best pinstriped suit, the phone in his room rang. It was Cooke, who impatiently said, "Get up here right now, young man."

Petrified, Gibbs tracked down Beathard and they hurried upstairs to Cooke's office suite, which overlooked the Chrysler

Building, one of his consolation prizes in the sale of the Lakers. Cooke's intimidation tactics continued throughout the three-and-a-half-hour interview. In addition to frequently correcting Gibbs's grammar and word choices, Cooke read the sports page aloud during the sit-down; he wanted to inform Gibbs that a football coach was not a genius, no matter what the reporters had written.

Although clearly uneasy and self-conscious because of the sophisticatedly dressed, ultra-successful businessman in front of him—"I had never felt more like a PE major"—Gibbs did not fold under the pressure. Glancing at a yellow notepad with questions and a list of the necessities he would need to succeed, Gibbs convinced Cooke that he was someone "with as much intensity as I have."

Soon they were discussing terms of a contract as well as a strategy for hiring the best assistant coaches. Every question that Cooke fired at Gibbs—who had interviewed for only two previous college head coaching jobs—he answered with a thoughtful, measured reply.

"Joe and I were both pretty nervous," Beathard later said, "but it ended up that Joe was so well-prepared, Mr. Cooke loved him. There wasn't one thing he asked that Joe wasn't prepared for. We'd already pretty much put the staff together, and Mr. Cooke hired him."

Gibbs didn't exactly think up each of his responses on the fly, nor did he conceive them the night before during his cross-country flight. He had been formulating these answers for nearly two decades.

"I was forty years old and had been pursuing a head coaching job all my adult life," he wrote years later. "It was all I wanted, all I thought about."

THE SON OF A NORTH CAROLINA deputy sheriff, Joe Jackson Gibbs began to dream about becoming a head coach in the early 1960s.

Although he had never played organized football until his family moved to Southern California—"all the gear they gave me I was putting everything on wrong"—Gibbs eventually became a fine quarterback at Santa Fe High School. An honorable mention All-Conference player for nearby Cerritos (California) Junior College, Gibbs accepted a partial scholarship and transferred to San Diego State University in 1961. For Aztecs head coach Don Coryell, who would became a Division II coaching star by posting three undefeated seasons between 1966 and 1969, Gibbs played center, guard, tight end, and linebacker. As a senior, he was named the team's "Most Inspirational Player."

"Probably because I wasn't any good," he later joked.

Gibbs's grit and determination, coupled with a country twang, a polite nature, and a dash of naiveté endeared the six-foot-tall, 190-pound lineman to people he met on campus.

"He was a tough guy [but] he wasn't one of these guys who said, 'I'm a big, bad football player,'" remembered San Diego State's student equipment manager Bill Bell. "He carried a briefcase for his books, he wore glasses."

But his limited speed kept him from any postcollege future as an athlete, and because he wasn't a great student, the physical education major saw only one option after graduation.

"I was interested in math and science. But I discovered I wasn't very good at math and I wasn't smart enough in other areas. I wanted to play pro ball, but I wasn't good enough. If I couldn't play, I thought I could coach."

His first crack at coaching came in a familiar environment: in 1964, Don Coryell hired him as a graduate assistant at San Diego State, mostly working with the offensive line. In addition to learning how to be a coach (for $125 per week) and earning a master's degree in physical education—ironically, his thesis entitled "The Adaptability of the 5-2 Defense to Modern Offensive Football" cited George Allen's *Complete Book of Winning Football Drills*—Gibbs ran the coaching staff's errands and even chauffeured John Madden, the team's defensive coordinator.

"I'd drive Madden on Wednesday nights all the way to Riverside to a class he taught and he'd sit over there and smoke his cigarettes," he said decades later. "I'd sit in the class with him. He'd teach the class and I'd drive him all the way back. I was his gofer. I was all of those guys' gofer. I went and got the hamburgers."

At the end of Gibbs's two-year apprenticeship, while eyeing a full-time position with his other alma mater, Cerritos College, Coryell offered him a job as offensive line coach. He served just one season on the staff—the Aztecs went undefeated for the first time in school history—before embarking on a coaching odyssey in which he moved his wife (and later his young children) several times. But in each place he landed, Gibbs found a coaching mentor.

From San Diego State, Gibbs and his high-school-sweetheart-turned-wife, Patricia Escobar, headed east to Florida State University (FSU). In Tallahassee, he worked with a program that had been invited to bowl games four of the previous five seasons, but more important, he worked with head coach Bill Peterson.

Although Peterson's backward way with words later provided Gibbs endless storytelling material to entertain his assistants—he once tried to assemble the team picture by shouting "pair up in threes and line up in a circle"—the FSU head coach possessed a keen eye for finding smart young assistants. By the time he left Florida State in 1970, Peterson already had a list of protégés that included Don James, Bill Parcells, and Bobby Bowden, the coach who would eventually shatter all of his Florida State coaching records. Just as those future coaching legends did, Gibbs absorbed every bit of Peterson's approach.

"Bill Peterson was totally devoted to football. Great work ethic. He tortured you, worked your rear end off," Gibbs later said. "Bill also had an amazing sense of people. Dan Henning was a substitute school teacher when Bill hired him on the spot."

During Gibbs's two years under Peterson, FSU continued to rise. They went 15-4-1 during that span and played in the Gator Bowl in 1967 and the Peach Bowl in 1968. Transforming the Seminoles into a ranked team was only part of Peterson's record. In addition to inventing the "hot receiver" (a pre-snap adjustment to counter a defense showing blitz), Peterson produced Florida State's first consensus All-American in 1964, wide receiver and future Super Bowl MVP Fred Biletnikoff.

In an era of college football marked by Woody Hayes's "three yards and a cloud of dust" mentality, Peterson was widely considered an innovator of the passing game. The next two coaches under whom Gibbs studied were the exact opposite.

On January 22, 1969, Gibbs agreed to leave Tallahassee for Los Angeles, where he would become John McKay's offensive line coach at the University of Southern California (USC).

Despite a slight pay cut, the job offered several fringe benefits: not only would the growing Gibbs family (Pat was pregnant) be closer to both Joe and Pat's roots, but USC featured the best running offense in all of college football and they routinely attracted top-tier recruits.

In the four years prior to Gibbs's arrival, the McKay offense churned out two Heisman Trophy–winning ball carriers, Mike Garrett in 1965 and O. J. Simpson in 1968. Both would be playing on Sundays by the time Gibbs arrived on campus, but the Trojans' ground attack remained college football's gold standard. With Clarence Davis, Sam Cunningham, and quarterback Jimmy Jones— dubbed the All-Black Backfield—USC pounded opposing Pac-8 defenses, averaging nearly 250 rushing yards per game.

Teaching USC's offensive linemen the specifics and nuances of McKay's offense came naturally to Gibbs, and not just because he had been a guard and center for nearby San Diego State. Don Coryell invented the I-formation, and upon taking a job as an assistant at USC in 1960, he taught John McKay the entire scheme.

"You think of 'Air Coryell' and all those things," John Madden said eulogizing Coryell in 2010. "Don Coryell invented the I-formation. And we look at pro football today and if you use two-back, every one is still using the I-formation. . . . There was a time where he was all about I-formation, power, and running."

Coryell may have created the offensive formation that McKay used to win two national championships, but, as Joe Gibbs quickly realized, the Trojans' rugged, overpowering ground game reflected their head coach's personality.

"John McKay: Extremely bright. Great wit. Tough, hardnosed guy," Gibbs recalled. "He could make you laugh. But, hey, everyone was afraid of him."

Despite finding the ideal setting for both his personal and professional lives—Gibbs considered sunny California home and the Trojans were loaded with young talent on offense—Gibbs left USC after the 1971 season. Don Breaux, a former coaching colleague at Florida State who joined the University of Arkansas, halted a duck-hunting trip in southeast Arkansas with Razorbacks defensive coach Harold Horton to call Gibbs and gauge his interest in coming to Fayetteville. Breaux used a simple yet effective pitch to lure Gibbs to Fayetteville.

"A lot of coaches that came through Arkansas at that time saw that they had a good chance of becoming a head coach," Horton said later. "At that time there were a lot of people—like Doug Dickey, Johnny Majors, Jimmy Johnson, Hayden Fry, Raymond Berry, Jim Mackenzie—come through here, had become head coaches. I think that's one of the things that enticed him to come to Arkansas, he felt like it was a good stepping-stone to a head coaching position."

Intrigued by the opportunity, Gibbs spoke with the Razorbacks' head coach, Frank Broyles.

"Frank Broyles was far and away the best salesman I was ever around," Gibbs said. "If Frank believed it, he could sell you. He was the most organized, too, the most polished."

But there was more to Broyles than efficiency and southern charm. A fine quarterback at Georgia Tech in the mid-1940s—his Orange Bowl passing record lasted for fifty-five years—Broyles turned Arkansas into a top ten team by 1959, his second season. Six years later, the Razorbacks won the national championship, with a steady, conservative ground attack.

Given his knowledge and experience from his time at USC, Gibbs was hired in order to add to that rich running game legacy. But he also brought with him several intangibles, especially on the recruiting trail.

"[Gibbs] was really very personable, and he could be very, very serious. He was not a yeller or a screamer or a guy that tried to intimidate you into getting better. It was more of a teaching style. Fairly quiet guy, was not a yeller, you could just tell he knew every aspect of the game," recalled offensive tackle John Boozman, who later became a United States senator from the state of Arkansas. "We were young and trying to decide what we wanted to do in the future and he was very stable, always a good example. . . . He was very much a good role model, as we were in a pretty formative period of our lives. Very competitive though."

On at least one occasion, that competitiveness and passion burst through Gibbs's placid exterior. At the end of the 1971 Liberty Bowl, two inexplicable penalties late in the fourth quarter cost the Razorbacks an upset victory over Tennessee, infuriating Arkansas's thirty-one-year-old offensive line coach.

"The referees had to run off the field. There was this huge twelve-foot[-tall] chain-link fence, and they ran through the gate and then they immediately locked it after themselves or somebody locked it," recalled Boozman. "And I can remember Coach Gibbs literally halfway up the fence, trying to get at them. He was that upset."

Once again, Gibbs's hunger for a head coaching job—he believed it would only come once his coaching profile was strong enough—made his stay at Arkansas comparatively short. An offer to coach in the NFL, where Don Coryell had been named head coach of the St. Louis Cardinals, meant Gibbs, Pat, and their two boys were on the move again. Just like each previous coaching pit stop, Gibbs's new job meant a different set of responsibilities: Coryell asked him to coach the running backs. Wanting to collect another marketable skill, Gibbs accepted the job even though he had only previously coached offensive line.

"You want the best people you can get," Coryell said fifteen years later. "People you know and trust. We had to get Joe."

The position change proved a seamless one for Gibbs. Featuring several strong young offensive linemen, including Conrad Dobler and Dan Dierdorf, the Cardinals' running game improved every season. Bruising fullback Jim Otis and quick tailback Terry Metcalf provided consistency for a St. Louis offense that had been plagued by turnovers in previous seasons. In 1974, Coryell's squad won a division title for the first time in twenty-six years, and the next season, they repeated as NFC East champs. In 1975, both Metcalf and Otis, who led the conference in rushing, received Pro Bowl nominations.

"Even in those early years, we used to say he's going to be a head coach someday—that's the kind of personality, the kind of person Joe Gibbs was. And it filtered down to the [running back] position and to the team, that if we run [the offense] the correct way, we can be successful," Metcalf remembered years later. "A lot of people felt that way because he stuck to details. He was pretty much the offensive coordinator, he pretty much had the offense in his hands, directed of course from Coryell, but I don't think Coryell would have given him that position if he didn't have trust and confidence that Joe Gibbs could handle that."

A tumultuous 1977 season, however, undercut the Cardinals' rise to the top of the conference, and when Coryell was fired—he had publicly blasted the fans and team management after a December loss to Washington—Gibbs was out of a job. Another one of Gibbs's mentors soon called to offer him work. John McKay, who left USC in 1975 to take over the NFL's expansion team in Tampa, wanted Gibbs as his offensive coordinator. But Gibbs's second tenure under

McKay was far less fruitful than the first: the entire Buccaneers organization was mired with injuries, inconsistency, and incompetence. Tampa Bay finished 5-11, gained the fewest yards of any team in the league, and even in the middle of the season their offense occasionally failed to simply deliver the play call from the sideline into the huddle. McKay—who told Gibbs, "Joe, I don't think you're really comfortable on the sideline"—moved him up to the coaches' box, where he radioed in plays to an assistant, who relayed them to a player, who relayed them to the team's rookie quarterback, Grambling State star Doug Williams.

"I'm here to tell you, there were about three plays in the next game that I didn't even recognize," Gibbs said.

Once the "miserable" season was over, Gibbs left Tampa Bay and returned to the staff of Don Coryell, who had been hired by the San Diego Chargers following his ousting in St. Louis. Again, convinced he "had to get Joe," Coryell asked Gibbs to be his running backs coach. Within a few weeks the Chargers' offensive coordinator Ray Perkins left to take over as head coach of the New York Giants. Gibbs was promoted.

Thirteen years and six coaching stops later Gibbs was right back where he started: in gorgeous San Diego working under Don Coryell. But all his hard work, all his absorbing of different offensive schemes and philosophies, was about to pay off.

Coryell's teams achieved great success by running the ball (usually from the I-formation that he invented), but now his offensive brilliance and creativity sparkled through the passing game. Coryell developed a "passing tree" that detailed route running, revolutionized the use of the presnap motion, and popularized personnel shifts, frequently switching from two-back sets to four-receiver sets, then back to the I-formation.

"It's an attitude of attack," Chargers quarterback Dan Fouts said in 2010. "We're going to attack every part of that field—width, length—and then we're going to attack every weakness in that defense. It's like [fast breaks in] basketball. Three-on-two, then it comes down to a two-on-one, and then it's a one-on-none. Throw the ball to the one-on-none. It was the attitude of, 'Look for the bomb first, and then work your way back to the line of scrimmage. . . . He believed in scoring and scoring a lot and as often as possible. Nothing pleased him more than a touchdown pass. That was his baby."

But Coryell's significance could not be confined to simple route combinations or offensive formations.

"He showed tremendous intensity. He got ready for every game just like he was going to play in it," Gibbs said in 1986. "I watched him from being run-oriented in college to passing almost every down in the pros. Don could adjust to his talent. He'd try anything, make any change. It was a quality I learned from him. I used to be so strict, so absolute. He was the opposite."

Prior to Gibbs joining the Chargers' staff, the San Diego offense was improving but not yet dynamic. In 1978, Dan Fouts threw more touchdowns than interceptions for the first time in his seven-year career, and Coryell's club finished 9-7, their only winning record since the AFL-NFL merger eight seasons earlier. Once Gibbs assumed the role of offensive coordinator, however, the Chargers' offense exploded. They tied a franchise record with twelve wins and scored the second most points in the NFL, while Fouts became just the second quarterback in history to throw for more than 4,000 yards in a season.

"Our greatest day would be on Wednesday, when we'd get the game plan," Fouts said. "We'd come out of that offensive meeting, and when we hit the practice field, we'd be sky high because we knew, 'Oh, this one's going to score. . . . Oh, yeah, that one will get us a first down. . . . Oh, boy, can't wait for that opportunity.' And we'd carry on like that Wednesday, Thursday, Friday, and Saturday. Then, on Sunday, it was like, 'Hey, we've scored on this play four times already.' "

The following year, the offense now dubbed "Air Coryell" was even better. Fouts's 4,715 yards shattered his own single-season record and the trio of Kellen Winslow, John Jefferson, and Charlie Joiner became the first in history to each amass more than 1,000 yards receiving. As a group, the unit led the NFL in total yards, scored the most points in franchise history, and for a second straight season they torched the vaunted Pittsburgh Steelers "Steel Curtain" defense.

"San Diego has a super offense," two-time Super Bowl MVP Terry Bradshaw said after his Steelers lost to San Diego in the final week of the 1980 season. "I would like to pick Coach Gibbs's brain for about two weeks and find out what's going on with him and his strategies."

Two weeks later, despite Fouts's tenth 300-yard passing day of the season, the Chargers fell to Oakland in the AFC Championship Game, putting Joe Gibbs on a plane to New York City to appear before Jack Kent Cooke.

"I loved that team and the coaching staff, and I owed a lot to Don Coryell," Gibbs later wrote. "But I wanted a head coaching job, and I could hardly wait."

WITH DETAILS OF HIS new deal having been hammered out the day before, Gibbs and Redskins general manager Bobby Beathard gathered before a pack of reporters at Redskin Park on January 13, 1981, to announce the hiring.

Described by the *Washington Post*'s Ken Denlinger as "stylish and articulate . . . instantly likeable . . . an apparent motivator," Gibbs made a strong first impression. Still, his coaching résumé won him far more fans than his personality.

Washington's offense scored the fourth-fewest points of any team in the NFL the previous season and had been shut out twice in 1980. Given his tremendous success in San Diego and a reputation as an inventive, hardworking assistant, Gibbs was expected to improve upon those numbers. Jack Kent Cooke told reporters that he wanted the new regime to make the games "fun for the fans" by bolstering the offense, especially the passing game, which prompted Redskins quarterback Joe Theismann to call the news "like Christmas and New Year's wrapped up in one announcement."

Still, Beathard and Gibbs made sure that the press (as well as Redskins fans) knew of the first-time head coach's pedigree. Gibbs cited and praised Don Coryell, John McKay, Frank Broyles, and Bill Peterson, but also introduced one caveat.

"If there is one thing I have learned from each of these successful men," he said, "it is to be a success you have to be your own man."

As for his new boss—a businessman, not a football coach—Gibbs also had a message.

"I feel a tremendous sense of responsibility and gratitude to Mr. Cooke," he told the press. "I want him to look back on this and say it was the best decision he ever made."

With his first press conference behind him Gibbs turned his attention toward building a coaching staff. Employing an interview process that one participant later compared to a "CIA [background] check," Gibbs managed to hire nearly all of the assistant coaches whom he and Bobby Beathard had targeted.

Prior to Gibbs's arrival, Washington's defense had been fairly solid, finishing tenth or higher in points allowed during each of Jack Pardee's three years. Looking to retain some continuity, Beathard and Gibbs not only kept the team's well-trained secondary coach Richie Petitbon, they promoted him to defensive coordinator. Petitbon, a player and assistant under George Allen a few years earlier, tabbed LaVern "Torgy" Torgeson and Larry Peccatiello to fill out the defensive staff.

As a first-time head coach with an exclusively offensive background, however, Gibbs would be judged by his ability to revamp the league's twenty-fifth-ranked offense. And to help him, he brought in coaches whom he trusted, men he'd worked with for years.

For assistant head coach, Gibbs hired Dan Henning, the Miami Dolphins' passing game coordinator. An innovative, decisive football mind, Henning had been on the Florida State offensive staff with Gibbs in 1968. Don Breaux, the former Arkansas assistant who talked Gibbs into joining Frank Broyles's staff in Fayetteville, became the Redskins' new backfield coach. And Wayne Sevier, the quarterback during Gibbs's junior season at San Diego State, was given a spot on the staff as special teams coach. Personable and smart—he graduated with distinction in mathematics and was tinkering with computers as early as the 1970s—Sevier coached in both St. Louis and San Diego under Don Coryell.

But Warren "Rennie" Simmons knew Gibbs longer than anyone on the staff, longer than even Pat Gibbs knew her husband. One of Gibbs's first friends after his family moved to Southern California in 1955, Simmons played on the same varsity football team at Santa Fe High with Gibbs, the team's quarterback. They were teammates again at Cerritos Junior College as well as San Diego State. Simmons also joined the coaching profession following college and by 1978 was coaching at Cerritos. Both living in Southern California, the Gibbs and Simmons families became close: Rennie and his wife, Carol, drove Gibbs to meet Bobby Beathard in San Clemente the night before his interview with Jack Kent Cooke. By the end of the month, Gibbs paid back his knowledgeable, ultra-professional friend, hiring Simmons as the Redskins' tight ends coach.

The only offensive assistant whom Gibbs hadn't previously worked with—they'd never even met—was Joe Bugel. A stout, fiery western Pennsylvanian, Bugel became the offensive line coach of the Houston Oilers in 1977. Along with the arrival of University of Texas Heisman Trophy winner Earl Campbell, Bugel eventually transformed Houston's running game into the best in the NFL. The Oilers, however, fired their head coach, Bum Phillips, right after losing in the 1980 playoffs, creating an opening for Washington and Bobby Beathard to offer Bugel the job as Redskins offensive line coach.

"Everything I had heard about Bugel was what we wanted: a guy that was a great, great teacher," remembered Beathard, who had reached out to Bugel two weeks before officially hiring Gibbs. "We really wanted a guy who would develop kids out of college."

For Bugel, and indeed the entire Redskins' staff, doing just that occupied much of their attention. When the Redskins completed training camp on September 1, the roster included twelve players (more than one-quarter of the team) who had never played a down in an NFL regular-season game. And five weeks into the 1981 NFL season, that inexperience showed.

THE REDSKINS OPENED UP with four consecutive divisional games, one against each of their NFC East foes: the Cowboys, Giants, Cardinals, and Eagles. They lost them all.

Nobody expected the previously 6-10 team with a rookie head coach to best their nemesis, the perennial playoff-caliber Cowboys, or Philadelphia, who reached the Super Bowl the previous season. But they allowed 40 points to previously winless St. Louis and mustered only one scoring drive in a 17–7 home loss to the New York Giants, a team that hadn't posted a winning record since 1972.

"Everybody didn't know their role and those first five games we had to learn on the fly, the entire team, coaches, players, how to work together," remembered Gibbs's former Cardinals star Terry Metcalf, who was acquired by the Redskins that April following three seasons in the Canadian Football League. "It was disheartening because we knew we were a good team, we knew we had talent. We just weren't putting it together the correct way."

An increasingly impatient Jack Kent Cooke phoned his general manager on the Monday after the second loss.

"I want you down at my office," Cooke demanded.

"I can't, I have to go on my scouting trip," Bobby Beathard replied.

"Do you own the team?"

"No, sir."

"Then you get out to my office."

Beathard canceled his trip to a variety of colleges and drove the half hour to Cooke's Upperville, Virginia, office.

"Boy he chewed me out," Beathard recalled decades later. "Then we lose another one, same deal. Get chewed out . . . He said, 'You get *your* coach.' I go into the office and told Joe. . . . He said, 'I can't, it's game plan day!' I said, 'We gotta go to Mr. Cooke's.' So we go out there. That was after the third loss. So then we go out after the fourth loss and he said, 'I should fire both of you.'"

The first meeting was vintage Jack Kent Cooke.

"Mr. Cooke has this book open on his desk, and it's got some paragraphs highlighted with a yellow marker," Beathard recalled. "He started reading out loud about General MacArthur and the element of surprise. He said, 'I don't see a damned bit of surprise in this offense. Everyone in the stadium knows what you're doing. I could call the plays myself.'"

The second episode, however, wasn't nearly as chilling. Cooke reiterated an impulse to fire the GM and coach, telling them, "I'm getting letters from people, but because I like you both so much, I won't do it." But he also delivered a measure of encouragement.

"You're going to turn this around," Cooke said. "You're going to do it. You've got what it takes. Now, get back to work."

Privately, however, Cooke had run out of patience early in that 1981 season.

"Dad said to me, as we were driving back from the park, 'I think I'm going to get George Allen back,'" John Kent Cooke remembered. "And I said, 'Oh God, Dad, you can't do that—all hell will break loose! . . . He thought about it. And he decided not to do it."

Despite sensing his owner's frustration—"I told myself, 'Hey, I'm getting fired,'" he said years later—Gibbs remained unflappable in front of his players.

"He kept his cool no matter how bad things got," safety Mark Murphy said. "He handled a most difficult situation very well. People were already asking him about his job security, but he stayed calm. That impressed a lot of players. Sure, he got upset sometimes and we were chastised, but nothing out of the ordinary. I'd say he earned our respect during that period. And I think that's essential before a coach can do anything with a team."

In addition to the losing streak, his owner's tirade, and repeated bad luck on the field—"Injuries are no excuse, but I have never seen anything like this," he told the press—Gibbs had just overcome another frustrating administrative issue.

Three years earlier, as a prime example of the Jack Pardee–era Redskins' penchant for sacrificing draft choices for aging veterans, Washington acquired defensive end Coy Bacon from the Cincinnati Bengals in exchange for their first-round draft pick. Bacon, entering his eleventh season, was one of the league's premier pass rushers, and he would lead the club in sacks each of the next three years. But by the start of the 1981 season he was thirty-eight years old. He missed two voluntary workouts that spring and once training camp opened he skipped or was late to several team meetings. Fines didn't improve his attendance, and when he was tardy to the Thursday practice before the game against St. Louis, Gibbs sent him home after a heated exchange. The next day, Bacon was released.

But even more frustrating for Gibbs than cutting a player with 38 sacks over the previous three seasons or the ripping he had received from the owner and the Washington press was his offense's performance.

On the stat sheet, the Redskins' offense looked promising, even successful, in September. Not only had the offense averaged 382 yards per game, but it was balanced. Twice they rushed for over 100 yards, and they averaged 21 first downs during that stretch, all with a first-year starter, Jeff Bostic, at center and three rookies starting elsewhere on the offensive line. Injuries had been the catalyst of the youth movement upfront, and even Gibbs admitted after Week One that he only played rookies Mark May, Melvin Jones, and Russ Grimm "because they were the best we had."

Despite the yardage totals, the Redskins were winless through the first month, and a rash of turnovers significantly contributed to their losing streak. Through four games, they turned the ball over fifteen times.

"This is the hardest thing I've ever gone through in eighteen years of coaching," Gibbs told the press after the fourth loss.

Bobby Beathard, who months earlier had been confident enough to recommend Gibbs to the team's demanding owner, now began to worry.

"I can't imagine a worse situation for a new head coach," he later said. "Here was a guy with great expectations still trying to get his first win in a town that's really serious about their football team. I thought he would break, but he didn't come close."

Even another disastrous loss, in Week Five against San Francisco, could not break Gibbs. On the game's opening possession, the 49ers drove the length of the field for a touchdown. Then their defense forced a Redskins fumble that was returned 80 yards for a touchdown. The crowd at Robert F. Kennedy Stadium (RFK) thoroughly booed the home team, and some even donned paper bags over their heads.

Sitting in his private box located in the mezzanine, Jack Kent Cooke tried to remain optimistic when a friend gave him a message from R. Sargent Shriver (John F. Kennedy's brother-in-law) saying, "Don't forget, Yale was down, 12–0, in the first quarter and we won."

"Oh I'm not giving up," the owner replied.

Some locals had given up on him. Longing for the days when D.C. super-lawyer and new Baltimore Orioles owner Edward

Bennett Williams controlled the franchise, a few fans hung a banner reading "Go Back Home Cooke We Want EBW," from the upper deck of RFK.

Cooke's hope for a redemptive comeback soon vanished. The Redskins turned the ball over 5 more times, and late in the third quarter they trailed by 27. At the end of the 30–17 defeat, Washington was the only winless team in the NFL. Joe Gibbs's team had matched the club's worst start in sixteen seasons.

"For every two things we do right, we do five or six things wrong," said quarterback Joe Theismann. "We have many new players, but our problems aren't of a youth nature. You can't blame experience. It is just mistakes at key times, and it's not just one man or some players not functioning. It's all the units. The new system isn't difficult, but adapting to new people has had its problems."

A fifth straight loss rendered Joe Gibbs and his offensive philosophies the lightning rod for those problems. Installing an "Air Coryell" offense three thousand miles west of San Diego resembled shoving a square peg into a round hole. And the press and all his critics made sure everyone knew it.

In Monday's *Washington Post*, one columnist referred to the loss as another "weekly humiliation," spoke of Gibbs's "coaching panic," and asked if "Gibbs has failed Theismann by asking him to execute too much."

Gibbs cut out that article, entitled "Forget Parity: This Team Needs Charity—and Faith," and carried it around with him for years, until it was faded and wrinkled.

"I want to remember that feeling," he later said. "I don't ever want to forget what that felt like. Those were days when you go back and question everything you've done."

CHAPTER 2

The Birth of a Dynasty

LATE SUNDAY EVENING, several hours after his second interception prompted a benching in Week Five's loss to San Francisco,
Redskins' quarterback Joe Theismann jumped into his car. Heading west through comparatively light traffic for the D.C. area, he
reached Vienna, Virginia, around eleven o'clock, pulled into a quiet
neighborhood, and knocked on a suburban family's door. Pat Gibbs
opened it, and then retrieved her half-asleep husband.

"He was the most stunned person in the world to see me.... The
look on his face was priceless. It was one of fatigue, of shock; we'd
[just] lost another football game," Theismann remembered decades
later. "You could call it a 'come to Jesus meeting.'"

Although it wasn't exactly a secret, Gibbs had repeatedly heard
the gossip about Theismann: he spent too much time being a celebrity, not enough time being a football player.

Handsome and charismatic, the former All-American and Aca-
demic All-American at Notre Dame—where sports information

director Roger Valdiserri tweaked the pronunciation of his last name from *THEES-man* to rhyme with "Heisman"—had endured a long wait to become a starting NFL quarterback.

A contract dispute in 1971 persuaded Theismann to forgo a professional career with the Miami Dolphins. He joined the Toronto Argonauts of the Canadian Football League, where the undersized but athletic quarterback became a two-time All-Star.

"I loved the city of Toronto, loved playing up there," he said. "It was a game that was built for my skills when it came to moving around and making plays with your legs."

Another contract impasse ended his stay north of the border. Redskins head coach and general manager George Allen acquired Theismann's rights in exchange for a first-round draft choice because "he has just enough experience to help us in 1974."

No one, not even Allen, knew at the time that Theismann would make an impact as a punt returner, not a passer. After an injury to All-Pro defensive back and returner Ken Houston, Theismann talked his way onto the field during a game against the Giants—he took advantage of a distracted head coach—and gained a spot as the Redskins' return man. But at the quarterback position, Allen trusted veterans Sonny Jurgensen and Billy Kilmer far more. Theismann didn't start a single game until the middle of his third season in Washington and he wouldn't become the team's opening day starter until Jack Pardee's arrival in 1978.

When he did finally earn the job outright, however, he didn't give it up. And over the next three years, as the face of the franchise, Theismann became a star within the nation's capital.

The father of three young children—he frequently attended his eldest son's Little League games and rode horses with his daughter—Theismann owned two restaurants, invested in real estate, and gave a few dozen motivational speeches (for a $5,000 fee) per year. He also did local advertisements for banks and a furniture company, national ads for Canon cameras, and regularly hosted local television and radio talk shows.

His public appearance schedule was even busier. In addition to being a spokesman for the Heart Association, the Veterans' Administration, and the United Way, Theismann served as honorary chairman of the Special Olympics and on the board of D.C.'s Children's Hospital. He also made ample time for his fans.

"He knew who he was, but he also knew what he wanted. He wanted to maximize his opportunities at that time, in terms of endorsements, in terms of everything, and I think he sought that stuff out aggressively," remembered *Washington Post* beat writer Gary Pomerantz. "[But] Joe was better with autographs and with kids—and particularly kids who had physical disabilities or were even dying—than any athlete I've ever seen. He gave more of himself in that way than people ever knew. And when people knew about it they thought, 'Oh, that's just Joe looking for attention.' He didn't look for attention. He did that out of an authentic heart. It was real."

In between businesses, philanthropy, family, and football, he found time to take acting lessons and audition for roles. By 1981, the actor, self-described as a "cross between Clint Eastwood and Burt Reynolds," had landed minor roles on the television series *B.J. and the Bear* and in the movie *The Man with Bogart's Face*, in which he played a bodyguard who has his jaw broken by the title character.

"Evidently someone had told [Joe Gibbs] that I wasn't dedicated to football and that I had other interests and that football wasn't a priority for me. And it certainly was a priority for him," Theismann said. "Being the starting quarterback of the Washington Redskins was important to me, and I wanted him to know how important."

During their two-hour conference after the 1981 loss to San Francisco, Gibbs was blunt and honest with Theismann about his concerns.

"You have a lot of interests," Gibbs said. "I need someone who is totally dedicated to playing quarterback for me."

"Joe, I'll do this," Theismann replied. "I will get out of every contract, every obligation I have away from the game of football if that's what it takes for you to believe in me. But I would like to have the opportunity to prove to you that I can do the things you need me to do without doing that."

"I had my doubts," Gibbs later admitted. "I wasn't sure that Joe had his priorities straight, that he might have been too busy with the other things he was doing to concentrate on the job. I wasn't sure."

Gibbs's uncertainty carried over into the next week. Prior to the trade deadline, which was eight days away, he and the front office discussed dealing Theismann to Baltimore, Detroit, and the Los Angeles Rams.

Theismann's stalled contract negotiations—he would be a free agent in February and the two sides stood very far apart—as well as his 9 interceptions in five games were reasons for the inquiries. Gibbs also wanted to find the right signal caller for his offensive system, which Dan Fouts had mastered in San Diego during the previous two seasons.

"I wasn't Joe's [quarterback]," Theismann later said. "There's a little saying I use: a new broom sweeps clean. He wanted *his* quarterback."

But Washington did not make a deal. With rookie Tom Flick and journeyman Mike Rae as the only other quarterbacks on the roster, Gibbs and Theismann were stuck with each other, at least until the end of the 1981 season.

Gibbs may not have been sold on Theismann as the Redskins' quarterback of the future, but the sit-down between the two did produce results.

"It just so happens that our meeting coincided with Joe's philosophy of being a run-based football team, and that's really when our fortunes changed," said Theismann, who averaged 275 yards passing during the five-game losing streak. "Around that fifth game, we changed from being the San Diego Chargers of the east. I led the league in attempts, completions, and interceptions, every passing category you could, because that's what they basically did in San Diego."

Although Gibbs and his staff didn't tear up their playbook or start from scratch, they did adapt their game plan more to fit their personnel. The Redskins didn't have a big pocket-passer like Dan Fouts, nor did they have a veteran possession receiver like future Hall of Famer Charlie Joiner, an acrobatic wideout like John Jefferson, or a singular talent at tight end like Kellen Winslow, the NFL's leader in receptions.

"If you have a Kellen Winslow, you do one thing," Gibbs later said. "If you don't, you do other things."

Gibbs did, however, have John Riggins.

ON JUNE 11, 1981, Riggins strolled onto the practice field at Redskins minicamp and announced to the media, "I'm bored, I'm broke, and I'm back."

"What did I miss the most?" he told reporters. "Besides the money, I guess I missed the little kiddie atmosphere. I'd have to grow up if I quit football. Actually, all the coyotes had the mange and the mules ran off, so I had to do something. The money I can make here is so much better than what I was doing in Kansas. I got a 'B' in money management at [the University of] Kansas, but then I didn't have any money to manage."

His March meeting with Gibbs had a surprising effect on the somewhat rudderless thirty-one-year-old.

Mary Lou Riggins had wanted her husband back at work instead of hunting and drinking every day. They were also both troubled by the "definite cash-flow problem" caused by retirement: Riggins misread his contract and thought the deferred payments Washington still owed would begin in 1981, but they did not until 1983.

"You didn't realize," Riggins later told Joe Gibbs, "you were the second appointment that day, the banker was there first."

But the new Redskins head coach extending an olive branch to his retired yet still valuable commodity had made the difference.

"I really thought John was done with football at the time," his brother Billy said. "When Gibbs came out to the house he made John feel like they really needed him."

Although the Redskins' refusal to increase his salary and his flickering desire to play football keyed Riggins's retirement in 1980, feeling unappreciated by Washington's coaching staff clinched his decision.

"Jack [Pardee] called me a couple of times in the off-season to say things like, 'Do you have a mandatory weight program? You've got to learn to make better decisions in upfield situations. You're not getting off the ball quick enough,'" Riggins later admitted. "If he had said just once, 'Gee, you had a good year. . . .' What's wrong with a little common courtesy, rather than 'Here are the films, work on 'em.'"

Two days after Gibbs left Lawrence, Riggins called Redskin Park to say he wanted to play football in 1981. Gibbs's euphoria—he welcomed the option of dealing away the "egomaniac" for a high draft pick—dissipated when Riggins then demanded a no-trade clause.

Riggins won the right to veto any trade, but he didn't secure the $200,000 raise, the request that sparked his holdout the previous summer. Assured that he would be playing for the team he wanted, Riggins focused on winning the Redskins' starting running back job.

During the sit-down with Gibbs in Lawrence, Riggins had promised that, were he to return, he'd do so in peak condition. And he kept his word: despite a year away from football and a diet that called for beer at ten o'clock in the morning, Riggins demonstrated his athleticism the day he arrived.

"He showed he was in great physical shape. He went through the physical drills bang, bang, bang," Gibbs said in August. "He was a little lost out there sometimes. But that's understandable. He came around very quickly."

At training camp in Carlisle, Pennsylvania, a few weeks later, he again wowed the new coaches and general manager Bobby Beathard, who stood by the track with a stopwatch as Riggins ran quarter-miles in between two-a-day practices.

"He was running ten quarters in about seventy-five seconds each," said Beathard. "It was just incredible. Then he'd shower and have lunch. And in the afternoon he'd be out there giving his best with the other players."

But when the regular season opened, his stamina and durability became a problem, and it was obvious that he wouldn't last as the every-down, every-series stalwart his reputation carried.

"John Riggins looked awful for about three or four weeks into camp and after," Gibbs said. "There was a Philadelphia game—he was hurt, he'd taken a year off—when he ran, he looked like . . . molasses. He just didn't look good. And he had on those high-heel, high-top boots. I wasn't used to that. . . . The whole time I'm going, 'My gosh, we've got this guy.' Everybody said he was a phenom, and he just didn't look good to me."

Riggins unusual fashion sense—every straight-laced NFL coach knew he had worn his hair in a mohawk and afro and once painted his toenails green as a member of the New York Jets—didn't trouble the Redskins' staff nearly as much as his work ethic. He didn't practice aggressively and was not a great student of the game, explaining that "I don't thrive on work, but I know what I have to do on Sunday and I know what I have to do during the week to be able to do it on Sunday."

"I can't practice what I do," he later said. "I don't study films because I don't know what to look for. To me, being an effective runner is a matter of using every sensory organ you have. You have to hear and smell and feel and taste, and the finer you can hone those senses, the better runner you'll be."

The staff grew concerned by his performance.

"I think the coaches had to get used to his style," running backs coach Don Breaux later said. "We had never had him before and you look for something flashy, but he's not flashy."

Although the coaches questioned whether their expensive, free-spirited, big-name ball carrier possessed the same skills and passion to be a 1,000-yard running back, they weren't discouraged. The two-back scheme that Joe Gibbs installed during training camp did not demand an every-down workhorse. Both running backs would split the carries and block for one another.

Through the first five weeks of the 1981 season Riggins barely contributed. He shared playing time with fellow running backs Joe Washington, Terry Metcalf, and Wilbur Jackson; and with Joe Theismann throwing passes as frequently as Dan Fouts, there weren't many carries to go around anyway. Riggins had rushed the ball just 36 times for 122 yards entering Week Six. Relegated to a role-player, Riggins lost interest and his productivity waned.

"I have to run the ball at least twenty times a game to be effective," Riggins once said. "It takes a bit for me to get the feel of how the defense is going to react, who's doing what."

Four months after he returned to the Redskins, having given in on his contract demands, Riggins was no longer willing to compromise on his playing time. On the plane ride home from the loss to Philadelphia, he approached Joe Bugel.

"You know, Coach, playing two backs in the backfield isn't working," Bugel recalled Riggins saying. "Joe Washington don't like to block for me, and I don't like to block for him."

Neither Bugel nor Gibbs had a very strong counterargument, especially after the next Sunday's turnover-filled loss to San Francisco. So, on October 5, just a few hours after Joe Theismann knocked on his head coach's door late the previous evening, the Redskins' coaching staff arrived at Redskin Park to prepare a game plan for the Chicago Bears. Together Gibbs, Bugel, Dan Henning, Don Breaux, and Rennie Simmons gathered in their windowless office nicknamed "the Submarine" to consider Riggins's request.

Within those long hours, as they gobbled down caffeine and candy—Breaux ate several bananas and drank gallons of Coca-Cola

he poured into a giant plastic bag filled with ice while Gibbs preferred chocolate candies—the staff realized Riggins had a point.

"When I first got here," Gibbs explained a few years later, "I
thought we'd have the ideal backfield with both Riggins and Joe
Washington back there. But then I thought about it, and it didn't
make sense to have 180-pound Joe Washington blocking a 250-
pound outside linebacker when Riggins was carrying the ball. And
when Washington was carrying the ball, you'd have Riggins tiring
himself out blocking for him. I'd rather have one fresh back in there
and let the [second] tight end block the linebackers."

Heavily advised by Bugel, Gibbs redesigned the base offense to
feature one, not two running backs, and two tight ends.

"I came from Houston where Earl [Campbell] was running the
ball, and Joe came from San Diego where [Dan] Fouts was throwing
the ball out of this setup," Bugel later said. "Joe was smart enough to
adapt this to his personnel so we can do both."

Bugel had schemed the plays and coached the line that allowed
Campbell to win rushing titles each of the previous three seasons and
that propelled the Oilers to three consecutive playoff berths. After
watching Campbell, a bowling ball of a runner, Bugel learned that
Houston's one-back offensive machine depended on a specific cog.

"You have to have that big, punishing bull of a back," Bugel said.

That description perfectly fit John Riggins, and when the Redskins debuted their new offense that Sunday against the Chicago
Bears, the 235-pound Riggins reminded anyone who had forgotten
that he was one of the game's unique talents.

THREE TURNOVERS FORCED BY the Redskins' defense, including
Neal Olkewicz's interception-turned-touchdown of a screen pass
intended for Walter Payton, built a 17–0 halftime advantage over
the Bears. Supplied with their biggest lead of the season, the visiting Redskins leaned on Riggins to close out the 1-4 Bears. During

one stretch in the fourth quarter the offense ate up nine minutes of clock, capping off a 69-yard drive with a short touchdown run by Riggins. On that one possession alone, he carried the ball 10 times for 62 yards.

By the end of the 24–7 victory, Riggins had amassed 126 yards and 2 touchdowns on 23 carries. And with Joe Washington adding 88 more yards on 21 carries when Riggins needed a break, the new one-back approach's debut was a rousing success.

"This was the first time both Riggins and Washington have been healthy at the same time since the first game," Gibbs said that afternoon at Soldier Field. "We gave John a chance for some heavy ball carrying for the first time. He showed how well he can hold up when you give him a chance. We needed him and he came through."

Having waited eighteen years to become a head coach, then enduring a losing streak in which he feared for his job, Joe Gibbs was so bubbly in his postgame press conference that he apologized to the media.

"This is a different feeling for me, the first time around," he said. "I'm happy, happy, happy."

Even after he returned to practice the next day, Gibbs's mood was palpable.

Prior to the start of the season, Gibbs had planned to select one "outstanding player" from the team's first win. Six weeks of pent-up frustration caused him to splurge. Not only did he honor Riggins and four others with state-of-the-art portable TVs, Gibbs gave several additional players prizes, including watches, sports coats, shirts, and free dinner coupons.

"Things are a lot more relaxed today," he said on the Monday after the victory. "We can laugh and have some fun for a change."

But not everyone inside the Beltway was as cheerful following the Redskins' first win in six tries.

"We've heard about 'game plans,' but how many armchair quarterbacks had this one figured out?" a skeptical *Washington Post* editorial entitled "So on to the Super Bowl" declared the next morning.

"By concentrating on the sixth game instead of the first five Coach Joe Gibbs has succeeded in throwing off the planning of every opposing coach for the remainder of the season. In addition, in one fell swoop the Redskins have jumped from the worst team in the league in wins and losses to one of the six worst—with five others not much loftier at two wins and four losses.

"Clearly," the member of the *Post*'s editorial board continued, sarcastically, "we're witnessing the birth of a dynasty."

NO TELEVISIONS, DRESS CLOTHES, or fashion accessories were awarded to Redskins players the following Monday. A fourth-quarter field goal gave Miami a 13–10 win and Washington fell to 1-6. But to close observers, a narrow road loss to Don Shula's first-place Dolphins revealed further progress. The Redskins defeated the Patriots a week later—Gibbs's first victory before the crowd at RFK—then reeled off three more wins, two of which came against NFC East foes St. Louis and the Giants.

"To win here [at Giants Stadium], to beat a good team, like this, well it's one of the biggest wins of my career," said Joe Theismann, who threw 7 touchdown passes during the winning streak.

At 5-6, the Redskins were tied for the NFC's last wild card spot: the "on to the Super Bowl" sentiment wasn't quite as ridiculous now.

"Who would have thought we'd be even talking about playoffs at this point after the way we lost our first five games?" Gibbs said. "I thought we would straighten ourselves out and start winning, but no one could have guessed this, not even the coaches."

More important than having an outside shot at a once-unthinkable playoff berth, Redskins players' confidence had grown. So did their standing among the rabid locals, who had bought up every seat at RFK Stadium each of the previous sixteen seasons.

Safety Mark Murphy could now walk through his neighborhood with his head held high.

"The kids made fun of me and the dogs barked at me," he said. "Now the kids want to play catch and the dogs show me all their tricks."

The team's first-round pick in the previous draft, offensive tackle Mark May, had become "tired of hearing people say 'There's one of the Deadskins.'" Now he could return to eating meals in public, rather than reheating frozen pizzas at home.

And when Joe Gibbs and Joe Bugel left the office together, they didn't have to stealthily move about the city.

"We'd drive home at night with our headlights out so no one would see us," Bugel remembered years later about the 0-5 start. "We had a lot of enemies. It was pretty upsetting."

Consecutive road losses to playoff teams, Dallas and Buffalo, dropped Washington from the postseason hunt, but they closed out the 1981 season with another winning streak, defeating the Eagles (the defending NFC Champions) as well as the Colts and Los Angeles Rams. Eight wins in their final eleven games boosted the once shameful record to a very respectable 8-8.

During the resurgence, the new one-back offense blossomed. Joe Washington and John Riggins rotated as the primary ball carriers— Washington gained 144 yards on 27 attempts in a win over the Detroit Lions—and Joe Theismann threw the ball more effectively. And despite a winter of more Theismann trade rumors, the free agent quarterback's contentious contract negotiation, an 0-4 exhibition schedule, and a knee injury to Joe Washington, *Sports Illustrated* noted, prior to the start of the 1982 regular season, that "there's great optimism along the Potomac." The drafting of hard-hitting cornerback Vernon Dean in the second round and a preseason trade for veteran pass rusher Tony McGee sparked the positive outlook, as did the growth—both literal and figurative—of many younger players. Dan Riley, the team's recently hired full-time weight and conditioning coach (a novelty among most NFL staffs), implemented a one-on-one, supervised weightlifting program that quickly showed results. The offensive line's average weight increased to an impressive 273-pound mark, and Joe Gibbs noticed that John Riggins's "muscles were just rippling" during training camp.

But more than any single off-season upgrade or acquisition, the fabulous recovery and finish to the previous year ignited excitement within the organization.

"I knew that next season, they were going to the Super Bowl, based on the last half of the prior season, because we were unbeatable then," remembered running back Terry Metcalf, who suffered a career-ending concussion during a pickup basketball game that off-season. "We knew who we were, we knew what each person brought to the table . . . we knew what we could do when we put our heads together."

TWO WEEKS INTO THE SEASON, they looked every bit the Super Bowl contender. Playing on the road, Washington defeated Tampa Bay and Philadelphia, both playoff participants the previous January. And in those two victories, the Redskins showcased versatility.

In the 37–34 overtime win over the Eagles, Joe Theismann had a career game—28 completions, 382 yards passing, and 3 touchdown passes—and he directed a 13-point fourth-quarter comeback. A week later, Washington forced four Buccaneer fumbles while John Riggins bested one of the NFL's stingiest defenses. Shouldering most of the load with Joe Washington still sidelined and the field at Tampa Stadium a sloppy quagmire, Riggins rushed for 136 yards on 34 carries in the 21–13 win.

The Redskins had proved they could win the offensive shootout as well as the slow-paced slugfest. The next two months, however, would curb the Redskins' budding dominance.

The day after the Redskins' plane returned from Tampa, the National Football League Players Association executive committee voted (eight for, one against) to walkout on the season in protest of the league's revenue sharing structure. One member of the committee was Redskins safety Mark Murphy, the team's leading tackler each of the three previous seasons.

"[The owners are] not taking our association seriously," he told the *Chicago Tribune*. "They're making a big mistake. They're greatly underestimating the players' strength. [The Redskins] are 2 and 0, and our fans are excited, and we're sorry it came to this, but we have to take a stand to show the owners we're serious."

Undrafted out of Colgate University, Murphy became a George Allen favorite in 1977 after turning down a financial management position with General Electric. Five years later, the former economics major was one credit shy of finishing his master's degree at nearby American University. In negotiations with the league's owners and their representatives, his background and intelligence served the union well during frequent sixteen-hour workdays. He received so many calls from reporters and fellow players that he eventually disconnected his phone and got an unlisted number.

"It was hard," recalled Murphy later. "It was a long strike and it went on and on, but I was very proud of the way we stayed together as a team."

A few NFL players, including future Hall of Famers Lynn Swann, John Stallworth, Steve Largent, and Ray Guy, chose not to side with the union and vowed to report to their respective teams' headquarters, but not nearly enough showed up to play their scheduled Week Three game. Teams considered retooling their rosters with scabs—teams had invited additional players to training camp so that "replacement players" could be quickly assembled should the players strike—then changed their minds. Coaches such as the Eagles' Dick Vermeil and the Bears' Mike Ditka had publicly condemned the idea.

"Grabbing a bunch of people and trying to put a team together is not a viable solution," Joe Gibbs told the press.

Television mogul and owner of Major League Baseball's Atlanta Braves, Ted Turner, disagreed. The Players Union joined with Turner to field a series of All-Star football games that would conclude with a championship game in Hawaii. The first, held at RFK on October 17, drew few fans (far less than the 8,760 paid attendance) and fewer stars.

"I guess I'll do just about anything for money," John Riggins commented after signing up for the $2,500 payday.

Along with twelve other Redskins, Riggins received an additional $500 winner's share thanks to a late field goal by Mark Moseley.

Joe Theismann did not participate in the game and had no plans of doing so in any future exhibitions. The veteran quarterback, who as a rookie had angered teammates by reporting to training camp during a preseason players strike in 1974, now fought to keep the team unified.

With contact between the coaches and players forbidden, Theismann routinely gathered players for team practices at places such as neighborhood parks or South Lakes High School in Reston, Virginia.

"It was the first time I had actually tried to assume a leadership role," he later wrote. "Those six weeks made up one of the most important periods of my life . . . if [Joe Gibbs] had any last doubts about my commitment to football, they should have been erased during the strike."

Although Theismann found a silver lining in the work stoppage, as the number of weeks of canceled games grew, the entire season appeared in danger of being lost.

"I am very pessimistic," Joe Gibbs said on November 10. "Maybe they can work out something and the season can be played. But common sense dictates that you have to reorder your priorities. We've done about as much as we can watching film."

Within a week, Gibbs's boredom and frustration halted. The strike came to an end as a tentative agreement (greatly favoring the owners) was reached: although the league minimum and several player bonuses increased slightly and players won severance

packages, the owners made few concessions to their original proposal. All twenty-eight teams returned to their practice facilities to
begin a seven-game schedule that would close out the 1982 regular
season. Upon learning that Theismann and many of his players had
practiced together during the strike, Gibbs was encouraged.

"I feel good that they did try to keep working on the passing
part," he said before the schedule resumed with a road game against
the Giants. "We'll just have to see how much good that did, but it
couldn't hurt. I just feel optimistic about things. I hope I feel the
same way tomorrow."

That Sunday afternoon at the Meadowlands, Joe Theismann
threw 2 first-half touchdowns in a 27–17 victory. A week later, in
their first home game of the season, the Washington defense suffocated Philadelphia, forcing 5 turnovers during a 13–9 win.

"There is something about this team that enables them to come
up with a play every time they need it," Gibbs told the press after
the win. "But we sure want to bring every game right down to the
wire. What ever happened to runaways?"

Near the end of the third quarter of their next game, Gibbs
remembered the feeling of being on the losing end of a blowout. Penalties, turnovers, and an inability to handle blitzes put Washington
in a 17–0 hole against Dallas. Reawakening the RFK Stadium crowd,
the Redskins narrowed the gap to 7 points in the fourth quarter, and
expected to get the ball back, but a Cowboys fake punt thwarted the
comeback effort and they fell, 24–10.

The first defeat of the season, particularly to a team that barely
lost that January's NFC Championship Game (still famous for the
Dwight Clark back-of-the-end-zone "Catch"), did not destroy the
team's confidence. At 4-1 they were tied atop the NFC East. Their
remaining schedule included three games against St. Louis and
New Orleans—clubs that finished last in their division the previous
year—as well as the Giants, whom Washington had defeated in late
November.

But the loss to Dallas still stung.

Enemies since before the Cowboys even played their first game in 1960—the two clubs' owners quarreled prior to Dallas being officially granted an expansion team—the teams' two annual showdowns only fueled animosity between the organizations, the players, and their fans. And when George Allen, who despised the Cowboys as early as his tenure with the Rams, became head coach in 1971, he forged a permanent culture of Dallas-hatred inside Redskin Park. In addition to referring to "America's Team" as "the damn Cowboys," he once physically demonstrated his plan to kick Tom Landry at midfield, and even ordered the hot water shut off in the visiting locker room at RFK so that Dallas's players had to take cold postgame showers.

By the start of the Joe Gibbs Era in Washington, the disdain for Dallas had become irreversible. And it showed at the end of Week Five of the 1982 season.

"We really can't stand Dallas," third-year receiver Art Monk said after the loss. "Nothing against them personally—we just don't like them. We just really wanted to beat them and I think we can. We can't get down because there is a possibility we can meet them in the playoffs, so we don't want to lose any more."

THE REDSKINS WON OUT. Victories in the final four contests of the regular season pushed Washington's record to 8-1, the best in the NFC. In previous years, that record would have earned Gibbs's squad a coveted first-round playoff bye, but upon settling the strike and implementing a special truncated schedule, the league increased the number of playoff teams from the customary ten (five per conference) to an unprecedented sixteen (eight per conference), meaning the eventual conference champions would have to play three rounds before making the Super Bowl. (The league returned to a ten-team playoff field the following year, then expanded to the current twelve-team format in 1990.)

The "Super Bowl Tournament," as it was dubbed, began on January 8, 1983, and Washington's hot streak continued. Three touchdown passes from Joe Theismann and a steady running game built a 31–0 third-quarter lead over Detroit, who had no offensive solutions to Washington's top-ranked scoring defense and turned the ball over 5 times.

A week later, the Redskins toppled Minnesota 21–7 to advance to the NFC Championship Game for the first time in ten years. Another fine day by Theismann along with a stout defensive effort that shut the Vikings out during the second half were both overshadowed by the performance of John Riggins.

Riggins had sat out the final two games of the regular season to nurse a bruised thigh; the coaching staff wanted him at full strength for the postseason. On the eve of the showdown with Detroit, only the second playoff game of his eleven-year career, Riggins approached Joe Bugel to insist that he was ready.

"I'm really getting down the road," he told Joe Gibbs, after Bugel sent him to the head coach. "I don't have many of these left. I've been out two weeks and I'm ready. Give me the ball."

In Washington's two playoff victories, that's exactly what Gibbs did: Riggins carried the ball 62 times.

"Thank God we have John Riggins," Gibbs told the press following the win over Minnesota. "He's stupendous. It's really remarkable when you think about it. Here's a guy thirty-three years old, but when he says he is going to do something, he is going to do it. And he says he's going to carry the ball for us."

Far surpassing his stoic effort against the Lions, Riggins carried the ball 37 times for 185 yards (both career highs) against the Vikings. As he excited the field, Riggins bowed to the RFK fans, many of whom blew diesel truck horns they had brought to the game. Late that season, WMAL-AM supplemented their radio broadcast trio— Frank Herzog, Sam Huff, and Sonny Jurgensen—with a diesel-horn sound effect after each powerful Riggins run. The blend of speed and power that Riggins routinely showcased made for a perfect, evocative analogy and soon one of the iconic nicknames in NFL history, "the Diesel," was born.

"In my memory, it was Sam Huff who came up with the nickname because he loved the way Riggins plowed through defenses," Herzog recalled decades later. "I don't remember which game it was but I think bad weather was involved and Sam was saying in the pregame show that 'the Redskins better fire up their diesel,' John Riggins, for this one."

Following the crowd-pleasing effort against Minnesota, "The Diesel" characteristically ignored all interview requests, donned his customary camouflage pants and shirt, and then walked into the parking lot. There he autographed a female fan's shoe, tossed back a shot of tequila, washed it down with half a can of beer that an old friend handed him, and drove home.

"John's a living representation of an old Hank Williams Jr. song," offensive tackle George Starke told one of the reporters whom Riggins spurned. "Hard-drinkin', hard-fightin', ornery. That's what makes him a good runner."

As Riggins exited the parking lot—first removing the "Run on Diesel Power, High Octane" banner that fans placed on his car—he did not know who Washington would play the following week. Neither did his teammates or coaches; that was to be determined the next afternoon, when the Packers and Cowboys played that weekend's other NFC Divisional Playoff game in Irving, Texas. But they all rooted for one team.

Although it went against thirty-two years of tradition, tens of thousands of fans—once the defeat of Minnesota had been secured—began hoping the Cowboys would win. Chants of "We want Dallas. We want Dallas" filled RFK, then poured onto East Capitol Street, and continued into the nearby Stadium-Armory Metro station.

Redskins fans' wish came true: the Cowboys defeated Green Bay and would play Washington at RFK the next Saturday. And while the upstart Redskins had no shortage of motivation—they were playing a hated rival who had beaten them in six consecutive contests, with a Super Bowl berth on the line—Dallas provided a bit more.

Late in the week, a report surfaced that the Cowboys were leaving Texas on Friday with their suitcases packed for ten days, not just the weekend; the strike had changed the postseason schedule and there would no longer be a bye week before the Super Bowl, so Dallas was preparing for the lengthy trip to the Rose Bowl in Pasadena, California, site of Super Bowl XVII.

"We were angry at these guys. It was a little more personal in that game because of what they had said. The arrogance of this football team to have one of their coaches make a statement that they're going to pack and then they're going to fly from D.C. to California was an absolute and total insult and we talked about that the whole week," defensive tackle Darryl Grant recalled years later. "That day, everybody was in the locker room on time and everybody was focusing, there was very little chatter in that locker room. Guys would just look each other in the eyeball and just nod. That's all we did. We were getting taped up, guys with their bubble gum, drinking their coffee, wasn't nobody listening to music, or jumping around."

Redskins players didn't need to supply the intensity; the sellout crowd of 55,045 inside RFK Stadium was amped up enough.

"The fans were screaming like they were going to come down there and physically do harm," Grant said. "The intensity that I saw in the fans that day, the stadium rocking, and being in that tunnel, hearing them call out the other team, sends chills down my spine."

The pandemonium remained well after the opening kickoff, even as the two-point home underdog surrendered a field goal on Dallas's first possession. From there, the Redskins' offense—which made several adjustments that week to avoid another underwhelming performance against Dallas's Doomsday Defense—took control of the game.

"We changed some stuff for this game," said guard Russ Grimm, who was matched up most of the day with six-time All-Pro defensive tackle Randy White. "We were zone blocking last time and not coming off quickly. We went more man-to-man, more double-teams this time. We decided to take them on, be physical and let the best man win."

The new blocking scheme, coupled with a new formation that flexed out one tight end (Rick Walker) and frequently put the other (Donnie Warren) in motion was an instant success. Chewing up both the clock and small chunks of yardage, Riggins pounded through the aggressive offensive line, setting up a first-quarter touchdown pass from Theismann to Charlie Brown. After a great special teams hit and fumble recovery from linebacker Monte Coleman put Washington inside the Dallas red zone, Riggins added to the lead. Having already far surpassed his yardage total from the meeting back in early December, he dove across the goal line for a one-yard touchdown run with less than three minutes remaining in the half.

"I went up to John before the game," explained center Jeff Bostic, "and said, 'We need a big game from you.' He said, 'You take care of the guys up front and leave the rest to me.'"

Behind 14–3 at halftime, the Cowboys narrowed the gap, despite the absence of All-Pro quarterback Danny White, who had been knocked out of the game following a brutal hit. Seldom-used backup Gary Hogeboom tossed a pair of third-quarter touchdowns to pull Dallas within 4 points. The display of life only further incited the riotous crowd.

"I've been around the NFL and athletics for years and I have never been around a more electric, intense stadium than that day," Mark Murphy said in 2014. "I distinctly remember looking behind our bench—and it was the old baseball stands—and our fans standing up, just jumping up and down on the stands. And you could see the bleachers just going up and down. It's probably a miracle that they didn't collapse. The atmosphere of the stadium was just unbelievable."

"This is the most exciting game I was ever at in my life in any sport," Charley Casserly, the team's assitant general manager at the time, recalled decades later.

Amid the hysteria, Washington's defense regained command midway through the fourth quarter. Linebacker Mel Kaufman smoothly intercepted Hogeboom's sideline pass, setting up a Washington field goal that increased the lead to 24–17 and on the ensuing kickoff they pinned Dallas deep in their own territory. At the 10-yard line, Hogeboom tried to loft a screen pass over Dexter Manley, but the defensive end who gave Danny White a concussion two quarters earlier, batted the ball in the air. Defensive tackle Darryl Grant, a San Antonio native raised by Cowboys fans, grabbed the interception and ran through two tacklers into the end zone for the game-clinching score.

"Of course Dexter doesn't read nothing but pass. . . . Dexter just took off. And when he did, I just started back-tracking; and he took that ball and I just happened to be in the right place at the right time," said Grant, who appeared on the cover of the next week's edition of *Sports Illustrated*, violently spiking the football after the touchdown. "Any other time I might not have thrown the ball down, but I was just so revved up with the emotions."

The crowd who shook the foundations of RFK Stadium with jumping, cheering, and a cacophonic rendition of the team's fight song, "Hail to the Redskins," hardly noticed Dallas's next, futile possession: they were too busy counting down the final six minutes and fifty-five seconds. The Cowboys ignored the final twelve seconds and headed into the locker room early, only to be forced to return for one more play. Then the celebration began.

Fans stormed the field, some tearing down a goal post, others shoving the dirt and grass from the playing field into their pockets and cups. Many of them chanted "We beat Dallas, we beat Dallas!"

The architect of the 31–17 triumph, Joe Gibbs, was hoisted onto the shoulders of several Redskins players who carried him off the field and into the winning locker room. While veteran defensive tackle Dave Butz passed out cigars, Gibbs was handed a telephone. On the other end was President Ronald Reagan, calling from the Aspen Lodge at Camp David, Maryland.

"I just want to congratulate [you] and all that great gang of yours. What an afternoon this has been!" Reagan said. "Well, listen, I just wanted to say if the fellows feel like, when the season is over . . . I could use them helping me up there with the Congress."

"This has been a team effort here as you know," replied Gibbs, who could barely hear the president inside the boisterous locker room. "Everybody in Washington deserves the credit. Everybody."

The short conversation ended and Reagan turned his attention back to preparing for the following Tuesday's State of the Union address.

"This was the way it was supposed to be," Gibbs said. "I haven't even thought about the Super Bowl. This is our Super Bowl, this was everything rolled into one. The Redskins versus Dallas, the team we wanted to beat the most. How can you top that?"

"The Super Bowls are great, but the atmosphere for conference championships is so good, it's unique, it's a difference setting. Especially the way that season played out. People thought the season was going to be canceled," Mark Murphy added. "It was an exciting time for Redskins fans."

The absence of a bye week before the Super Bowl cut the players' and coaches' celebrations short. And in addition to the usual hassle of travel arrangements, obtaining tickets for family and friends, and media requests and public appearances (which were heightened by the Los Angeles venue), the distractions mounted throughout the week.

"I think this is good for the team," Joe Washington said midweek. "If you needed to get pinched about being at the Super Bowl, this will pinch you. It will get your mind off Dallas and onto this week. Besides, these players deserve the recognition they are getting. Everyone finally is getting some publicity."

The one player getting more attention and notoriety than any of his teammates was John Riggins. Following the win over Dallas, the veteran who ceased speaking to the media a year earlier ended his silence. During an impromptu press conference in the shower he told reporters that after the strike ended two months earlier, he was so mentally drained that he considered retiring again.

"I was ready to pack my bags and head for Kansas. Boy, what a mistake that would have been.

"I've waited a long time for this," he added.

Riggins intended to savor the moment.

Before an eager audience at Tuesday's press event he regaled dozens of reporters with his insights into the D.C. limelight, explaining, "If you're a public figure in Washington, you're just a piece of toilet paper: you know you're going to get smeared, the trick is not to get flushed down."

The next evening, with Riggins as their Pied Piper, a handful of Redskins players took advantage of Gibbs's no-curfew policy. Exploring the Los Angeles nightlife, they partied throughout Newport Beach, and then returned to the team hotel to deliver early-morning wakeup calls.

"We hit the town and got in about three o'clock," Russ Grimm said. "We drank a few beers, had a few shots here and there. We weren't staggering drunk but we had a little buzz on. . . . We came back to the hotel and figured if we were up, we'd wake somebody else up."

And for Jack Kent Cooke's hastily organized Friday night team party at the Westin South Coast Plaza hotel—where the 350 guests were told to dress casual—Riggins arrived wearing a top hat, tuxedo, white tie, white vest, and white gloves. It wasn't the ideal attire to eat the "lucky ribs" that Sam Legard—a Loudoun County, Virginia, restaurateur who had driven to Pasadena—cooked for the team as part of a weekly ritual.

"I wouldn't call [my behavior] crazy," he told an inquiring journalist that night. "I'm just expressing myself. I like to do what I like to do at the moment. I'm spontaneous, but I like to think I'm always in control of the situation."

Off the football field, few would have agreed with his assessment. But on the field, Riggins made everyone a believer, especially that Sunday night at the Rose Bowl.

The Redskins' Super Bowl opponent was Don Shula's Miami Dolphins, a veteran club lacking in offensive firepower but replete with skilled, solid defenders, dubbed "the Killer Bees," because seven of its regulars' last names began with the letter "B." They yielded an average of only 208 yards per game in their three playoff wins and shut out the New York Jets in the AFC Championship Game, prompting Las Vegas to install Miami as three-point favorites.

Given the two stout defenses—Washington and Miami allowed the fewest and second fewest points in the league that year, respectively—and a slightly rainy forecast, Super Bowl XVII figured to be a slow, plodding affair. Midway through the first period, however, a 76-yard touchdown from David Woodley to Jimmy Cefalo, who had burnt the Washington secondary, gave the Dolphins a 7–0 lead. Even worse than the early deficit was the disappearance of the rhythm and consistency that Washington used to overpower the Dallas Cowboys a week earlier.

"In our first couple of offensive series, I think we were just caught up in playing in the Super Bowl," offensive lineman Joe Jacoby wrote. "It was hard not to be excited. Theismann was probably a little hyper, but I'd say that was true for all of us. We moved the ball pretty well, but we were forced to punt when we let them sack Theismann a couple of times on third down. Then all of us calmed down and we began to play much better."

Behind 10–3, the Redskins combined a string of short Riggins runs with timely passing from Theismann to cover 76 yards. On a third-and-one from the Miami 4-yard line, wide receiver Alvin Garrett hauled in a perfectly placed pass lofted from Theismann to the back right corner of the end zone. But the glee from Washington's first-ever offensive touchdown in a Super Bowl evaporated. On the ensuing kickoff, Dolphins defensive back Fulton Walker sprinted past the Washington sidelines for a 98-yard touchdown return.

Although a few Redskins were shocked—"I almost swallowed my tongue when I saw Walker's run," linebacker Larry Kubin said—the group remained confident as they headed off the field at the end of the first half. The locker room was so calm that kickoff returner Mike Nelms fell asleep.

"The coaches were more shook than we were at halftime," offensive tackle George Starke said. "We knew we were moving the ball in the first half. We just weren't scoring."

At the start of the third period, that did not change. A sack ruined the first drive, and despite a well-timed 44-yard reverse to Alvin Garrett, the best they could do from Miami's 3-yard line was a field goal. The next three possessions included a listless three-and-out, two interceptions, and another near-interception that Miami would have easily returned for a touchdown had Theismann not alertly knocked the ball out of linebacker Kim Bokamper's hands. The Redskins entered the final period trailing for the first time since their midseason loss to Dallas. Switching sides of the field did nothing to cure the offensive woes: a doomed flea-flicker early in the fourth quarter resulted in Washington's second turnover in less than six minutes.

Much like John Riggins had during the team's dismal 0-5 start a year earlier, then again on the eve of the postseason, left tackle Joe Jacoby approached Redskins offensive line coach Joe Bugel.

"Hey, [Buges,] let's stop running that trick stuff and let's start trying to run the ball," Jacoby told him on the sidelines.

And as he did twice for Riggins, Bugel took Jacoby's suggestion to Joe Gibbs.

"We're not the smartest guys in the world," Bugel said. "Sometimes you have to understand that the coaches aren't out there playing. The players are. You should listen to what they say."

Aided by excellent field position, the Redskins gave the ball to Riggins on back-to-back plays on the next series, gaining 8 yards. But on third down, running back Clarence Harmon was barely able to get beyond the line of scrimmage. Facing fourth-and-one at the Miami 43-yard line, Joe Gibbs made the biggest decision of his young coaching career.

"There comes a time in a game there's a gut decision. You have to make it and live with it," he said later that evening. "If we lost the game, I wanted to lose it by being physical."

Assistant head coach Dan Henning recommended to Gibbs a play that would become the most famous in Washington Redskins history: goal-line, I-left, tight-wing, fake-zoom, 70 Chip. The off-tackle run into the right side of the defense had become a staple of the Washington ground attack, one that Joe Bugel and his linemen delighted in refining. To achieve perfection, during practices the Redskins ran 70 Chip against a defense with thirteen, not eleven, defenders.

Following a Dolphins time-out, the Redskins broke the huddle and lined up in an I-formation featuring Riggins in the tailback spot and Otis Wonsley as the fullback. With tight end Clint Didier motioning from the left side of the formation to the right, then reversing back to where he began (i.e., "fake zoom"), Joe Theismann took the snap from Jeff Bostic. And although he considered faking the handoff and rolling the opposite way on a naked bootleg—"I seriously needed my head examined," he later admitted—Theismann turned around and placed the ball in Riggins's stomach.

Spying a huge gap between Didier and Rick "Doc" Walker, Riggins surged toward the hole.

"You can't have eleven offensive players blocking eleven defensive players because of the quarterback. So it's eleven to ten for the defense. We tell John there's one man you're going to be looking at," Joe Bugel explained. "We disguised it real good. [Don] McNeal slanted to Didier, and it put McNeal on the other side. McNeal was the guy we couldn't account for in the blocking, and he slipped and fell."

McNeal not only had the misfortune of slipping before the snap—as he mirrored Clint Didier's motion—but after regaining his footing he was also the last man standing between Riggins and the end zone. The 192-pound cornerback from Alabama could not slow down the 235-pound running back, who plowed through a failed arm-tackle.

"I was tiptoeing through there and the only guy left was the corner, McNeal," Riggins said. "But I had the feeling—and you get this in a game—that I was going to hit a big one. I have a notorious reputation for not being fast enough. But I was a sprinter in high school. Once I get past the linebackers, I can go."

With no one left to catch him, Riggins covered the remaining 39 yards for the go-ahead touchdown. Washington's sideline erupted, as did tens of thousands of Redskins fans at the Rose Bowl, including an exuberant Jack Kent Cooke, who once again owned the team that was winning a championship in Southern California.

Washington now led 20–17, but ten minutes remained on the clock, and Miami had already twice shown they could score quickly and from anywhere on the field. Still, the Redskins held the momentum, and everyone in the stadium knew it.

"I felt that was the game right there," Jeff Bostic said. "That broke their backs. It wasn't so much what it did for our team, it was what it did to their team. It took all the emotion out of them."

There was no 98-yard touchdown return of the kickoff, no 76-yard bomb down the sideline. Instead, Miami ran three plays, and punted the ball away. And any remaining doubt over which team would leave Pasadena with the Lombardi Trophy was soon erased by Riggins and the Washington offensive line.

Earlier in the week, Riggins pulled aside Don Breaux to ask if the running backs coach knew the Super Bowl rushing record, which the Steelers' Franco Harris set at 158 yards eight years earlier.

"He said he just felt like he could maybe get it," Breaux said. "Here's a guy with so much confidence, and that's what he gave this football team. He felt he was unstoppable, and so did they."

Riggins's 43-yard fourth-quarter touchdown run nudged him to within 14 yards of Harris's mark. Five consecutive runs not only pushed him well past the record, they drained the clock down to the two-minute warning. And having earned a much-needed break after 8 rushes on that one drive, Riggins watched as Joe Theismann rolled out of the pocket and hit Charlie Brown for a 6-yard touchdown pass that sealed the win.

"Two years ago, just about this time, I was camping out at my farm in Kansas," the game's MVP told reporters that evening. "I was listening to the coyotes howl every night and I decided I wanted to come back and play football again. If you had told me I'd be playing in the Super Bowl twenty-four months later, and winning the dog-gone thing, I'd find that very hard to believe. But here I am."

Finished with his philosophical, road-less-traveled reflections, Riggins returned to his familiar spontaneous, unpredictable persona. Responding to the news of President Reagan's second congratulatory phone call to Joe Gibbs in as many weeks, Riggins explained that, "at least for tonight, Ron's the President, but I'm the King." Then he shared his thoughts on the future.

"I can still walk away," he told reporters in the locker room. "It's still possible. You guys know me, I'm like the wind. I change my mind every five minutes."

John Riggins was always in control of the situation.

CHAPTER 3

Hog Heaven

JOHN RIGGINS'S 166 yards and 38 carries against the top-ranked Miami defense were not the only Super Bowl records set that late January evening in Pasadena.

Fulton Walker's 98-yard runback before halftime was the first kickoff ever returned for a touchdown in the Super Bowl. Not to be outdone, the Redskins' Mike Nelms also set a Super Bowl record for special teams excellence, returning 6 punts for a combined 52 yards. And despite the 76-yard touchdown reception that gave Miami an early lead, Washington set a Super Bowl standard for pass defense, allowing just 4 completions, none in the second half.

The most unusual (albeit unofficial) first in Super Bowl history set that day, however, came courtesy of Redskins owner Jack Kent Cooke and Dolphins owner Joe Robbie. Earlier in the week, they agreed to share the cost of the traditional "winners'" party, and invite both teams' players, coaches, and fans.

"Dad knew [former Chargers owner Barron Hilton] because

they shared offices at the Beverly Hilton when Dad first came to L.A.," John Kent Cooke said. "So he called him up and said, 'We want to have this party after the game, but we don't have any money—neither Joe Robbie nor I can afford to do this.' And Barron said, 'Tell you what, I'll provide the banquet hall, and you guys pay for the food and the booze, and you guys split it.' "

Apparently, a Super Bowl title wasn't high enough stakes for the two exceedingly wealthy entrepreneurs, so Cooke and Robbie made a wager on the game: the owner of the losing team would pick up 75 percent of the tab.

Cooke won the game and the bet, but many of Robbie's players still showed up to the Beverly Hilton's International Ballroom.

"It was dreadful," John Kent Cooke said, "because we were all elated and they were totally depressed."

Unlike his counterpart, Don Shula—who congratulated Redskins general manager Bobby Beathard and admitted, "You got a pretty good little fullback there"—Joe Gibbs did not attend that awkwardly divided party of two thousand. During his first few hours as a world championship head coach, Gibbs scoured the tunnels and rooms beneath the Rose Bowl Stadium looking for his wife.

"I lost her," Gibbs said the next day. "I thought she was going to wait for me, but when she saw everyone get on team and staff buses, she panicked and got on one, too. I didn't know it. I came out of the locker room and couldn't find her."

Even with assistance from several police officers remaining at the stadium, Gibbs still hadn't found Pat. Hours later, he considered filing a missing person's report.

"During the week, they had told me something about a Super Bowl celebration party after the game, but you know me, I'm in a cloud thinking about the game, and I couldn't remember where the party was. I didn't know what was going on but that is where she was," he said with a grin.

Exhausted and starving, Gibbs turned his search toward food and wound up at a nearby Bob's Big Boy restaurant, where he ordered a hamburger.

"Everyone was saying, 'Isn't that Joe Gibbs, the coach who just won the Super Bowl?'"

Around two a.m., Gibbs finally found Pat and the couple reveled in the first championship of their nineteen-year journey. Invigorated by the reunion with his wife, his players, and his staff—"I haven't been to bed and I'm enjoying it"—Gibbs celebrated until after eight the next morning. At a press conference inside the Los Angeles Marriott, the second-youngest head coach ever to win a Super Bowl answered questions about the Redskins' performance and his newfound reputation as a football "genius."

"[I'm] a very average person who loves what I do and works hard at it," Gibbs said. "But I get embarrassed at being called a genius or anything like that. People who are a success in this business are the ones who have been in for ten years. My goal is to be one of those people. If ten years from now I'm standing here, then maybe I'll feel I'm a success."

With his final obligation of Super Bowl XVII completed, Gibbs boarded an elevator, where an awestruck woman had recognized him from the previous night's Super Bowl broadcast on NBC.

"Can I have your autograph, Coach Shula?" she asked.

"I told you we don't get any respect," Gibbs said to his friends inside the elevator.

By that evening, however, Gibbs realized he was wrong.

At 6:41 p.m. the team's chartered DC-10 landed at Dulles Airport, where it and the passengers sat on the tarmac. Ten minutes later Marine One touched down near a fire engine (always present when the presidential helicopter lands) draped with a hand-painted banner that read "Welcome, World Champions." President Ronald Reagan and his wife, Nancy, stepped out, each wearing a Redskins button on the lapel of their heavy winter coats, as the temperature was below freezing. They walked to the base of the airstairs, the signal that Jack Kent Cooke could begin to deplane.

Also dressed in a trench coat, as well as his customary houndstooth Brooks Brothers walking hat, Cooke handed the president the Lombardi Trophy. The two California transplants chatted, and over the next seventeen minutes—Marine One took off by 7:08 p.m.—the cavalcade of players, coaches, staff, and family members exited the plane. Each received a presidential greeting and congratulations. One person handed Reagan a Redskins baseball cap, which he put on.

"Congratulations," Reagan yelled into Joe Gibbs's ear, above the roaring noise of jet and helicopter engines. "You really brought the city together."

Reagan meant the Redskins had figuratively brought the city together. But by Wednesday the president's words could also be taken literally.

On Wednesday, 500,000 people gathered for a rally by the District Building on Pennsylvania Avenue—Reagan and D.C. mayor Marion Barry had granted federal and city employees a two-hour paid hiatus, and most local schools allowed students to skip class if they brought a signed note from their parents.

Ignoring a light, cold rain, the delirious crowd shrieked as Redskins players and coaches arrived.

"I don't think the day could be a greater testimony to the fact that there's no other fans in the world that would come out on a day like this, except in Washington, D.C.," Joe Gibbs announced as he raised the Lombardi Trophy into the air. "And I want you to know that each one of you has a small piece of this trophy today."

Not all of the heroic faces from the Super Bowl appeared on the stage or in the buses that passed south on Fourteenth Street, then east onto Constitution Avenue, before stopping at Third Street NW. Practicing for the annual Pro Bowl in Hawaii, five Redskins, including Joe Theismann, were not there.

Neither was John Riggins. He did not fly back with the team, staying in Pasadena for a luncheon to honor the Super Bowl MVP. And despite returning home late Tuesday evening, Riggins missed the next day's rally, claiming he overslept. He phoned a local television station to explain, "I didn't reset my watch."

Fearing they would miss wonderful footage—the game's biggest star drawing the biggest cheers—WDVM-TV sent a limousine to pick him up at his home near Fairfax Circle. They rushed Riggins downtown just as the parade ended, but in time to attend the private after-party at the Hyatt Regency. Fans swarmed him, his eight-year-old son, Krafton, and three-year-old daughter, Portia, as they all walked inside.

"[And] I thought 'The Killer Bees' were tough," Riggins said as he signed autographs for twenty minutes, only briefly stopping to ask the crowd if his children were still present, which they were.

One of the team's longest-tenured, most popular, and best players, Riggins became the symbol of their first championship in forty years. His absence from the local Super Bowl celebration would have been both conspicuous and disappointing.

"It's like seeing the Macy's Thanksgiving Day parade without a Santa Claus," a congressional aide said prior to Riggins's surprise appearance at the Hyatt.

But after the team's championship run, Riggins was no longer the Redskins' only idolized entity. By now, the oft-anonymous men who thanklessly blocked for running backs like John Riggins—a motley collection dubbed "the Hogs"—had become the darlings of D.C.

BEHIND EVERY ONE OF the 610 rushing yards that John Riggins collected during the 1982 playoffs—against Detroit and Minnesota, then the hated Cowboys, and finally Miami in the Super Bowl—was an aggressive, fearless offensive line who repeatedly pounded and exhausted opposing defenses.

"We knew their tendencies," said Dolphins defensive coordinator Bill Arnsparger. "For the most part, they did what we expected them to do. When they did it, we just didn't stop it. Their offensive line made it possible for Riggins to have a game like that."

Keenly aware that his offensive line paved the way for a historic postseason—averaging 153 yards and 34 carries over four games remains the greatest ever playoff stretch for a running back—Riggins rewarded his blockers. During the summer of 1983, the same time Riggins permanently moved his family from Kansas to Washington, the avid hunter gave each offensive lineman a .460 Mark V Weatherby Magnum rifle and a lone round.

"That's the biggest, toughest gun there is," Riggins told *Sports Illustrated*'s Paul Zimmerman. "They can fire it once and then put it over the fireplace."

That unit, along with significant contributions from a trio of fine blocking tight ends, allowed Washington to wear down opposing defenses late in each postseason showdown. And although the praise given to Riggins peaked with his record-setting Super Bowl performance, the young group had already started to gain a reputation as one of the best in the league, even among their opponents.

"From the way they played today," Dolphins defensive end Kim Bokamper said hours after the Super Bowl, "I have to say they are as good as any offensive line we faced."

Other great offensive lines had existed prior to Washington's 1982 playoff run. The Baltimore Colts, Green Bay Packers, and most recently the Oakland Raiders won multiple NFL championships by assembling offensive lines that reliably opened running lanes and protected the passer. Yet each of those excellent units, packed with Pro Bowlers and future Hall of Famers, remained almost totally eclipsed by their "skill position" teammates.

Apart from league insiders and the media, few football fans appreciated the intricacies of offensive line play: precise footwork, quickness off the snap, proper alignment. No offensive line—regardless of their dominance or the championships they forged—had yet broken free from their dull, nondescript stereotype to become mainstream.

That changed with one spontaneous, casual term of endearment uttered by offensive line coach Joe Bugel on a cold and wet morning during Redskins training camp in the summer of 1982.

Looking over his unit just as they began a drill, Bugel noticed guard Russ Grimm.

"Russ, of course, is a little bit portly, so his stomach is kind of peeking out from underneath his jersey and he's getting ready to go first," George Starke recalled years later. "And Joe Bugel looks down at Russ there on the ground with his stomach sticking out, he said, 'Jesus, Russ, you're like a big ol' hog laying there on the ground.' And that's where the name 'Hog' came from."

The label quickly caught on. Inside the locker room, the offensive linemen became known as Hogs. And once the public learned of the nickname in August—wide receiver Alvin Garrett shared it with the *Washington Post*—it snowballed.

After the midseason players' strike, newspaper articles addressing the offensive line included pig-related headlines and puns, some clever, some not-so-clever. Prior to the NFC Championship Game, during a joint WRC-AM radio interview with Joe Gibbs, former president Richard Nixon lauded the Hogs by name. And later that year, a CBS Sports pregame show segment on Joe Bugel and the Hogs featured *The NFL Today* anchor Irv Cross tossing into a muddy pen a Dallas Cowboys jersey, which pigs then chewed up.

Fans across town now wore T-shirts, sweatshirts, and buttons reading "I Love Them Hogs," as well as rubber pig snouts over their noses. And beginning late in the 1982 season, several more passionate, committed Hogs' supporters gained notoriety of their own.

For Halloween that year, Redskins fan Michael Torbert—a nuclear engineer who worked on the staff of United States Navy Admiral Hyman G. Rickover—trick-or-treated with his young children in suburban Fairfax, Virginia, wearing his grandmother's black-and-white polka-dotted dress, a cheap yellow wig, a hand-made white leather hat, and a rubber pig snout.

"That was a Q-test for me to see if people got a kick out of it," Torbert recalled. "Then I recruited a bunch of guys to go to the Eagles game in November."

Directly behind the Redskins' bench, in Section 108 at RFK Stadium, Torbert and ten other similarly dressed fans stood out from the other members of the fast-growing Hogs' fan base. Soon, "The Hogettes," as the group became known, were local and even national celebrities, attracting crowds within the crowd when they traveled to road games.

"They treated us like kings in Dallas, we had a great time down there. . . . The Eagles Stadium and the Giants Stadium, the fans were a little bit rougher, so we had to be a little more careful up there," said Torbert, who rarely missed a Redskins home game throughout the next thirty seasons. "The Hogs were vital to the success of the Redskins, so we thought they deserved their own cheerleading squad. That's why we suited up."

Aware that others were making money and drawing attention off their likeness and nickname, George Starke, Mark May, Don Warren, and Rick Walker formed an incorporated company to sell licensed merchandise.

Based in D.C., Super Hogs Inc. started with three full-time employees and in less than a year was selling forty different products (posters, bumper stickers, coloring books, buttons, balloons, hats, T-shirts, and rubber pig snouts) and organizing public appearances.

In 1983, its first year in existence, Super Hogs Inc. grossed $150,000. They donated 15 percent to Martha's Table, a local soup kitchen for homeless children.

"It's something we did not to make a profit off of," Russ Grimm said. "We just did it to bring the team together and bring the Washington fans together. But now it's a term we have to live up to."

Inside Redskin Park, members of the pack were punished for not wearing the "official" T-shirt (featuring a cartoon pig in between two goal posts) at least once a week: the five-dollar fine went to Joe Bugel, aka Boss Hog, to fund a plentiful dinner at his house after the season.

But just playing offensive line did not automatically christen a player as a member of the Hogs.

"[Rookie offensive tackle] Don Laster wanted to buy a shirt but we wouldn't sell him one," Bugel said in November. "This is an exclusive group. You only get in on a majority vote. Riggo wanted in since this summer, but they are tough. They kept saying no, but on Monday at the team meeting, we gave him a shirt. He stood up and put it on immediately and the whole place went wild."

Letting Riggins join the Hogs was only fair; he had let them join *his* exclusive group: "the 5 O'Clock Club."

Besides "the Lombardi Sweep" and the axiom that "only perfect practice makes perfect," Vince Lombardi brought with him another tradition to Washington when he took over as head coach in 1969. As he did in Green Bay, Lombardi and reporters gathered for cocktails and an informal press conference after training camp practices, at an old Victorian house across the street from Dickinson College in Carlisle, where the Redskins practiced.

Lombardi died less than a year after taking over in Washington, but several of his players continued the postpractice social hour. According to Redskins historian Michael Richman, the players-only incarnation of the 5 O'Clock Club started under defensive tackle Diron Talbert during the mid-1970s. Talbert and the other "charter members," including Billy Kilmer, Sonny Jurgensen, Ron McDole, and Len Hauss, drank a few cold beers and chatted with each other, not reporters or coaches.

Those seasoned veterans invited Riggins into their inner circle after he joined the Redskins in 1976. Years later, Riggins was now the grizzled old veteran.

"Riggo carried over the 5 O'Clock Club from the old group," Russ Grimm said. "And we looked up to Riggo, he was like the mentor."

Several of the Hogs needed a mentor: aside from veterans George Starke and Fred Dean, the Redskins' offensive linemen were green.

"Most of us were fresh out of college," tackle Joe Jacoby remembered. "We all enjoyed our beverage, and then that bond formed out there, because we're hanging out there with offensive linemen and we're in there with our running back."

Before ending his retirement in 1981, Riggins hadn't known Jeff Bostic, Joe Jacoby, Russ Grimm, and Mark May, the four cornerstones of the Hogs. Grimm, Jacoby, and May were rookies that year, and although Bostic was on the roster, Riggins was still in Kansas listening to the coyotes howl during the 1980 season.

Bostic, an undrafted, undersized center from Clemson, was released from the Philadelphia Eagles' 1980 training camp. On his drive home to Greensboro, North Carolina, he stopped at Redskin Park to ask for a tryout. Within a year, he became the "quarterback" of the offensive line, identifying the defensive alignments and calling out blocking assignments for his linemates.

Jacoby, by far the biggest Hog, also went undrafted and, like Bostic, arrived in Washington with little fanfare. Despite a strong career at the University of Louisville, teams thought he lacked the upper-body strength to play in the NFL. Redskins scout Charley Casserly encouraged him to hit the weights after his senior season and just before the draft Jacoby's bench press increased to 405 pounds.

Casserly convinced Bobby Beathard to sign Jacoby—who was also being courted by the Cowboys—but Joe Gibbs knew nothing about their pet project.

"I sat in [Gibbs's] office for twenty minutes, and he was telling me what great opportunities I had as a *defensive* lineman," Jacoby said. "I didn't want to blow it, so I didn't tell him I played offense. He found out later and wanted to get out of the contract."

The miscommunication proved to be a happy accident. With his improved strength Jacoby became indispensable from the outset of training camp.

"How can you pass up a guy who is six foot seven and weighs 300 pounds?" Joe Bugel said that July. "You'd be nuts not to give him a shot. Maybe with this guy, we got real, real lucky."

Jacoby had the opportunity to shine during minicamp after that year's first-round draft pick, Mark May, held out. May signed a $650,000 contract the next week, but remained behind Jacoby on the depth chart. With George Starke at the other tackle spot, May was sidelined early that season. But the next year, the release of guard Melvin Jones won "May Day," as he was known, a regular spot in the lineup along with veteran Fred Dean.

In their NFC Championship Game win over Dallas, May provided the Redskins with the ideal size to neutralize six-foot, seven-inch defensive tackle John Dutton and gigantic defensive end Ed "Too Tall" Jones. And much to the dismay of one his fellow linemates, he also provided the relatively tight-lipped Hogs with a formidable trash-talker.

"I used to yell at Mark all the time because he was always bickering back and forth with [the Cowboys'] Randy [White]," Russ Grimm said years later. "I'd be coming back to the huddle and I'd say 'May Day, why don't you shut up? I'm the guy who has to block him. Why don't you talk to Dutton or Too Tall, who's on your side. Leave my side alone.'"

Grimm had heard May talk for years, far longer than anyone else on the roster; the two had been college teammates for four seasons before both were selected in the 1981 draft. A linebacker and quarterback at Southmoreland High outside of Pittsburgh—Woody Hayes personally visited his home, asking him to play quarterback at Ohio State—Grimm chose to attend Pitt, where head coach Jackie Sherrill moved Grimm to center. At first, Grimm hated the switch and wanted to transfer, but he eventually discovered the benefits of his new position.

"I forgot who said it," Grimm explained in 1982, "but I always remember one thing about being on the line: What better satisfaction is there than to move a man from one spot to another against his will?"

Grimm, and his knack for displacing defensive linemen, was obscured by teammate Mark May, who won the Outland Trophy his senior season and was selected seventeenth overall in the 1981 NFL Draft. But the Redskins noticed and traded into the third round to select him. The coaching staff moved Grimm to left guard, and by the end of his rookie season, his football knowledge and technique won him a starting job.

"Grimm makes me bubble all over. He's so sound. He never makes a wrong step," Bugel said the next year.

Grimm's ability to play through pain also helped win over his offensive line coach. A summer construction worker who once fell off a thirty-foot scaffold, received nineteen stitches, then returned to work within an hour, Grimm prided himself on gritting through aches and pains. He simply loved to play football—"I play because it is fun and if you get paid for it, fine," he said in his second year.

"I'm more your construction-type worker," he said. "Just work outside, have a few hot dogs and hamburgers for lunch, go back and work for a few more hours, pick up your lunch box, go to a bar for a few beers, then go home and get something to eat."

Grimm's ideal workday became reality once he and his fellow Hogs were invited to join John Riggins in the 5 O'Clock Club.

After practice ended, those select few—a mixture of defensive players, linemen, tight ends, and occasionally a player whose recent display of toughness warranted temporary access—met in a dilapidated equipment shed in the corner of the practice field. Inside, there was no air conditioning, no lighting, no bathroom, and only one rule: nothing said in the shed, left the shed.

"I would doubt if it was more than twelve [feet] by twelve [feet]," recalled defensive tackle Dave Butz, the club's sergeant-at-arms. "It was so old it was full of leather dummies, that's how old the equipment was in there. A lot of the boards on the outside had rotted out over the years, so we put cardboard around the base and we had a kerosene heater in there. The old Redskin Park did not have lights so when it became four thirty or five o'clock it was already dark."

Inside, while discussing a variety of subjects and drinking beers that the equipment staff put on ice during practice, the 5 O'Clock Club unwound before heading home.

"Traffic up in D.C. was horrible, so you got finished with practice at four thirty, five, you were just going to sit in traffic, so we would sit out there. It became like a fraternity," Jeff Bostic remembered. "We solved a lot of world problems out there in that shed. We started a bond of brotherhood out there in that shed."

In time, as the Redskins and specifically the Hogs became more successful, the legend of the 5 O'Clock Club grew. They too had their own hats, T-shirts, and jackets; Riggins wearing his during an informal Super Bowl press conference only added to the mystique. Beer distributors clamored to supply the club with their brands. And the week of the NFC Championship Game against Dallas, a surprise guest visited after hearing about the private hotspot.

Before leaving Redskin Park for the Cowboys hotel, where he planned on meeting players and coaches to prepare for the CBS broadcast of the game, John Madden burst through the door to the shed.

"He opened up and he goes 'Hey! Is this the 5 O'Clock Club!?,' kind of like Rodney Dangerfield," Butz recalled. "We all said, 'Come on in, John.'"

Madden sat down, launched into a few hilarious stories that captivated the club, and helped the group finish off the beer. Hoping to keep the party going, Madden pulled out a bulky early-1980s cell phone, called the driver of his personal bus—he drove everywhere due to his fear of flying—and instructed him to bring to the shed all the beer aboard the early incarnation of the famed "Madden Cruiser."

"I thought that was cool," said Butz. "John Madden just ordered us beer."

While the 5 O'Clock Club drank beers, played cards, and hobnobbed with celebrities, Joe Gibbs and his coaching staff convened a few hundred feet away inside Redskin Park. And unlike the players' club, which closed down from winter until the team returned from training camp in August, there was no break for the coaches. They studied film, scouted prospects, and systemically graded every player in the league. Winning a Super Bowl in his second season at the helm only drove Gibbs to work harder.

"The owner demands that you win, and everyone on down demands that you win. This will be a tough act to follow," Gibbs said the morning after the Super Bowl victory over Miami. "We realize we're not a dominant team. . . . We definitely need additions to our team."

That off-season the Redskins would make two acquisitions—one on offense, one on defense—that made them a dominant team in 1983 and well into the next decade.

IN LESS THAN TWO YEARS, Joe Gibbs—greatly aided by assistant head coach Joe Bugel—had built the biggest, strongest, and most intimidating running game in football. By the end of the 1982 season, it was so efficient and so reliable that opposing defenses knew exactly where John Riggins was headed and were still incapable of stopping him.

But the scheme that Gibbs designed relied on more than just a punishing runner and massive blockers at the line of scrimmage. Washington's offense was the perfect blend of brute and brains.

From the day he arrived in Washington in January 1981, Gibbs believed in confusing defenses as much as he believed in outmuscling them.

"I have one basic philosophy," he said at his introductory press conference. "Don't slow down for the defense. You attack the defense."

To do so, Gibbs employed an endless combination of offensive formations and pre-snap motions from wide receivers, backs, and especially tight ends.

"Obviously, we're not the first team to move around so much," Gibbs said. "The difference is the degree with which we do it. We do it a lot more than most teams. It's a constant evolution of formations. You change as much as 30 to 40 percent per year. With one back and four receivers, it gives us a lot of flexibility."

"They had so much movement that sometimes we got confused," Dolphins All-Pro linebacker A. J. Duhe said after the Super Bowl. "Their double motion was very good. . . . They had a good mixture of snap counts and formations. It wasn't a case of too much Riggins, but he's an awfully good runner."

The presnap motions and a smattering of trick plays—which had so irritated Joe Jacoby during the fourth quarter that he confronted Joe Bugel—laid the foundation for Riggins to physically and mentally exhaust Miami's front seven.

"I told my players that this game will be won by John," Gibbs said after the win. "But all the things that go with it—the flea-flickers, the reverse—all those will help John. We've go to keep them off him."

That spirit of deception and trickery motivated Gibbs to develop a play that would become one of the most famous in NFL history: the counter.

Although "70 Chip" became synonymous with the Redskins' Super Bowl win over Miami, Washington relied far more on the use of "50 Gut" to wear down opponents. A simple, up-the-middle run with no complex, nuanced blocking techniques, 50 Gut was used so often during that postseason run (specifically against Dallas) that Gibbs feared he'd slowed their "constant evolution."

He wanted a play that, to defenders, looked like 50 Gut, forcing them to overcommit to their diagnosis and, as a result, be out of position when they realized the ball was headed in the opposite direction. Footage of a college powerhouse provided Gibbs exactly what he was looking for.

"The whole counter started when we saw some film on Nebraska in the early eighties," Gibbs admitted decades later. "Tom Osborne was doing some really innovative things with his line up front, and we were watching it and thought, God, that's good stuff. So we stole it. We had no pride whatsoever, and really, nobody does in this game. We all steal things."

Stealing a play that helped running back Mike Rozier win the Heisman Trophy later that year, Gibbs and the coaching staff locked themselves in the Submarine and toyed with the counter during the months after Super Bowl XVII. At summer practices he taught the play to his offense.

By design, the quarterback (Joe Theismann) and running back (usually John Riggins, but occasionally Joe Washington) took the same initial steps they would as if the play call was 50 Gut. With the defense biting on the action, Theismann pivoted around and handed the ball to Riggins, who had also changed directions. With Theismann's back turned to the defense, they couldn't see that he no longer had the ball and he ran away from Riggins, pretending he was the ball carrier.

"Joe and John have to be good actors on this," Joe Bugel explained. "Usually Joe will take two [defenders] with him on the rollout."

The Redskins' offensive line also employed misdirection. The center, along with the guard and tackle that began the play on the side where Riggins was headed (known as the "front side") also stepped as if the call was 50 Gut. This, too, fooled defenders who used the offensive line as their key.

But the most decisive blow came by way of the other guard and tackle. At the snap, those "backside" linemen turned and ran parallel to the line of scrimmage, toward the "front side," where Riggins was headed and where the ball was ultimately intended to go. Known as the "pulling" guard and tackle, these two blockers had a full head of steam as they targeted a specific defender. The lineman closer to the ball, the guard, cleared out the first man he saw. The trailing lineman, the tackle, headed upfield and became the de facto lead blocker for Riggins.

Although the play could also be run to the left side, the coaching staff recognized it was most effective to the right, the side that tackle Joe Jacoby and guard Russ Grimm pulled toward.

"Watching a 290-pound guard (Grimm) and a 310-pound tackle (Jacoby) pulling over," Bugel said, "well, it's just an awesome sight."

"If you're a 180-pound defensive back and you see Jacoby coming at you, you start shaking in your boots," Jeff Bostic said.

Their size—Jacoby was by far the Redskins' biggest lineman—was a major reason why they ran the counter to the right so often. But the duo also had chemistry and instincts for finding the right defenders to block and not hesitating even for a second.

"I guess I always had the ability as far as pulling and running and getting to that place," Jacoby remembered years later. "My job was easy, those guys were blocking the defensive front, I'm turning up and sometimes hitting a linebacker, most of the times it was hitting the secondary."

If all the pieces of this carefully timed system—Theismann's fake, Riggins's false step to mimic 50 Gut, the backside linemen decisively plowing into defenders—operated correctly, the result was a huge hole for the ball carrier to run through.

"It's a play that makes the linebackers have to move laterally, so they're not coming downhill toward the line of scrimmage," Grimm said. "The right side is all blocking angles down. Jacoby and I pull. I got the kickout block. If the guy closes flat then Joe has to go around me. If he goes up the field a little bit then I kick him out then Joe turns up inside. It's a play where you can't be too fast as a running back. John would just give you that little pause, that little counter step, and take it and he would read it from there. You get defenders moving sideways, and he's hard enough to tackle if you're coming straight at him, let alone if you get him from the side."

And, just to add another wrinkle of confusion for his opponents, Gibbs designed the play to be run out of several different formations, with several different motions. With a tight end in motion, the play was called "counter trey"; without a tight end in motion, it was known as "counter gap."

The Redskins offense practiced the new play throughout training camp, and by Week Four of the 1983 season, the counter was ready for debut against the Seahawks.

Inside Seattle's Kingdome, Riggins rushed for 83 yards and a touchdown. Despite his advanced age of thirty-four and the pounding he'd taken over the years—that afternoon he passed Joe Perry for sixth on the all-time rushing list—Riggins was once again the Redskins' bell cow during the 27–17 win. He totaled a season-high 30 carries, which allowed Washington to control the football for just under twenty minutes during the second half.

The Hogs, however, knew they could do better.

"I'm disappointed Riggo didn't get more [yards]," tight end Rick Walker said. "We'll have to work harder. You wait. In November and December, he'll be stronger, we'll be better, and those 80-yard rushing days will turn into 100."

Even with Riggins's comparatively low numbers—he'd averaged 153 yards in four postseason games that January—the Redskins' offense flourished. And the unveiling of the counter was largely responsible.

Still searching for ways to attack the defense, Gibbs and the staff devised a play-action pass based off the counter. And late in the second period, with the Redskins ahead by four, Joe Theismann faked the counter to Riggins, whirled around, and heaved a pass downfield. Alvin Garrett nabbed the ball for a 47-yard touchdown, Theismann's second long touchdown pass of the quarter.

"Those TD passes were the result of [the defense] concentrating on John Riggins," the quarterback explained.

Already boasting the top line and the top power runner in the game, the defending Super Bowl champions now possessed a new weapon, the counter package, that suggested invincibility.

"Washington is the best team we've played," Seattle head coach Chuck Knox said after his team lost. "They have everything."

And that was just on offense.

CHAPTER 4

Coming Up Short

KIRK MEE served in the Washington Redskins' front office for a quarter century, a stretch that began well before Joe Gibbs's arrival and lasted far after. Hired just prior to the death of Vince Lombardi in 1970, Mee left a year later to be the head coach at Earlham College, but returned in 1974. The energetic, self-described "free spirit" from Wilmington College coached on both George Allen's and Jack Pardee's staffs, and beginning in 1978 also worked as director of pro scouting, the post at which he remained throughout Gibbs's tenure.

As he did for Allen and Pardee, Mee assisted Gibbs and his staff by breaking down film, scouting (in person) future opponents, and compiling detailed grades of hundreds of players throughout the league during the off-season. But his most valuable role was as a college scout, a task he approached with passion, commitment, and a touch of healthy paranoia.

"I flew all the way to Los Angeles and back just to time a guy in the 40-yard dash," Mee said in 2014. "Even though you had friends that were scouts with the Giants, Denver, and all over—'cause you're on the road with them, you see them, you talk to them—you were never going to trust what they say when it comes to certain things. He's not going to tell you that he was at a timing and [a player] ran a 4.4 or a 4.6 or a 4.75, and if they did tell you, you wouldn't believe them. Any time there was a timing, you had your own people there, so you saw it on your own watch, that the guy, how fast he was."

"I flew all the way out there to time one guy," he continued, "because we didn't have a good time on him and we wanted to make sure. It had been real easy to say, 'Oh, I know so-and-so at the San Diego Chargers, he's going to be there, he's going to time him, we can take his time.' Uh-uh. It's not your watch. And it's the same way with height and weight."

In August 1982, near the end of training camp, each Redskins scout left Washington to check out a handful of college players throughout the country. Mee's territory was southern Texas. One of the first cities he stopped in was Kingsville, roughly 130 miles from the Mexican border; a fellow scout had told him to keep tabs on a defensive back at the Division II school there, Texas A&I.

"This is the first or second school I visited since I left training camp, so it's really early [in the college season], so the only thing I could look at is film, 'cause they hadn't played any games yet and they're just starting practices. . . . I was there for two practices, and in between practices you watch film. And the only film I had was [the previous year's] film," Mee remembered.

"I couldn't believe my eyes. I could not believe my eyes. I had never seen a guy on film, his feet were so fast, so quick. He could accelerate. He could do everything. And on top of that, they had him running kickoffs and punts back. Any time he touched the ball . . . it was like [he was gone.]"

The prospect who amazed that coach and professional scout of twenty years was Darrell Green.

The son of a Maxwell House Coffee lab technician and a deli

cook who divorced when he was in fifth grade, Green grew up in Houston. He tried out for the football team as a junior at Jesse H. Jones High School in South Park, and weighing 120 pounds, his mother's advice was, "Don't let them big boys hurt you now."

"My mother, bless her heart, did not want me to play football," he said. "My father said I could be the best player out there. But he was concerned about my size."

By his senior year, up to a comparatively robust 145 pounds, Green was an All-City cornerback, but the only serious collegiate offers he received were from track coaches, not football coaches. Texas A&I promised that he could play both sports. A week after arriving at Kingsville, however, he became homesick and ran across campus to catch a friend who was driving back to Houston for the Labor Day weekend. He missed his ride and returned to his dorm in tears.

"I'm sitting there at school crying about not going home, and then I found out they'd had a wreck and my friend got killed," Green said years later. "I was supposed to be in that car. If I had caught up with them, I might not be here today."

Braving that first semester, Green remained shaken by the tragedy. Still missing his family, he went home to Houston to work as a furniture deliveryman and attend night school. During that year and a half, he "grew up a little bit," then returned to Texas A&I. Endowed with incomparable speed, he developed a reputation as the "fastest guy in the state of Texas," both on the football field and on the track.

"I saw him line up for a 100-meter race one time where every single guy defaulted out of just fear of running against him. He ended up running the race by himself," remembered college teammate tight end Jack Bechta. "I saw him run against Southwest Texas State, where he was the last leg of a mile relay, and he got the baton and Southwest had almost a three-eighths to a half-track lead and Darrell caught them right at the wire. I've never seen anything like it. They think it was one of the fastest [quarter miles] ever run in the mile relay anywhere in the country. . . . He has a chase gear that has no ceiling on it. We've seen it in track, we've seen it in football."

As a junior, Green won both the 100- and 200-meter 1982 NCAA Division II individual championships. For the Javelinas' football team he was equally marvelous. A part-time wide receiver, fabulous return man, and the Lone Star Conference's Player of the Year at corner, Green won a spot on the Associated Press's "Little All-American" team for Division II and Division III players.

Upon returning from his Texas scouting trips, Kirk Mee informed Washington's general manager that "this kid's a hell of a player, fast as lightning." Bobby Beathard was curious enough to also make the long trek to Kingsville to scout Green in person and see if he warranted using the team's first-round (twenty-eighth over-all) draft pick. Just like Mee, Beathard wanted to time Green with his own watch.

"I'd never seen anybody run from there to here that fast. I can't believe this," Beathard recalled thirty years later. "I thought, 'God, I don't want anybody to know about this guy.' I'm sure some teams knew about him, but I thought there's no way this guy's going to last till the twenty-eighth pick."

In April 1983, two weeks after Green ran the fastest 100-meter dash in the world that year (10.08) at the Angelo State University Invitational, the Redskins spurned several trade offers to select him in the first round. Despite Green's mythical speed—many knew about the unofficial, wind-aided 9.9 he ran in the 100 meters—the selection of a five-foot, seven-inch defender brought out several detractors, including one on his new team.

"They would send us out to scout players before the draft, and I never scouted Darrell Green," Redskins defensive coordinator Richie Petitbon said. "Had they sent me to scout Darrell Green I don't think I would have recommended drafting him. When I saw Darrell Green, I thought he was very, very small, and I worried about that . . . until I saw him run. And once you saw him run, you realized this was a special talent."

Green won over more than just one person with a single sprint.

"The only question was, you look at him and you say, 'God, he's so small. Can he really line up and play a physical brand of NFL football?'" said Redskins scout and future NFL general manager Billy Devaney. "It didn't take very long in minicamp to see that he was so genetically gifted. . . . Everything that goes into playing corner: the athletic arrogance, the competitiveness, Darrell had it. It was like he's from Texas A&I and he strolled in like he belonged from day one. He wasn't in awe of anything."

"In those days, there was a real off-season. You'd have a three-day minicamp and then the players were gone," Devaney said. "At the end, the way Coach Gibbs had it structured is there'd be mini-camp practices and then the last day it was timing and testing, everybody ran their forties and all that. Usually at that point veterans just can't wait to get out—they've had it, they've got vacation plans. As soon as their testing is over, they can take off. Well, the defensive backs were always running last. All the veterans stayed around because they wanted to watch Darrell run his forty . . . offensive line, everyone, you name it, the whole team. It was so special."

Just the folklore attached to Green had a considerable impact on several veterans. Cornerback Joe Lavender retired one day after the draft. Pro Bowl kick returner Mike Nelms—aware of Green's special teams abilities—soon ended a lengthy holdout and took far less than he had reportedly wanted. Nelms's agent, Rick Bennett, also completed negotiations for Redskins safety Tony Peters prior to the start of minicamp.

But incumbent cornerback Jeris White, the veteran Green would directly challenge for a starting job, didn't come to that minicamp. He held out all summer, looking for a better deal. Beginning with training camp in late July, Green's speed had practically made the coaches forget about the team's coleader in interceptions the previous year.

"You're talking about a guy [Green] who could run in the Kentucky Derby," Petitbon said later that season, "versus a guy [White] who couldn't run in the third race at Bowie."

White's holdout carried over into the preseason, during which time Green—now nicknamed "MX," after the United States Air Force's new MX intercontinental ballistic missile—continued to make an impression on the Washington coaches.

In the team's opening exhibition game against Atlanta, he returned the first punt he fielded for a 61-yard touchdown. Two weeks later, he suffered through a miserable evening against the Miami Dolphins, giving up several long passes and failing to tackle opposing ball carriers.

"Darrell made enough mistakes to last a lifetime," Petitbon said after losing the preseason Super Bowl rematch 38–7. "If he keeps missing tackles—that scares me more than anything."

But in his very first NFL game, Green not only stopped missing tackles, he made one of the most famous tackles in history.

The Redskins opened the 1983 NFL season at home on *Monday Night Football* against the Cowboys. Trailing 10–0, Dallas handed off to Tony Dorsett, the three-time Pro Bowl running back who had set an NFL record in January by rushing for a 99-yard touchdown against the Minnesota Vikings. From his own 17-yard line, the former Heisman Trophy winner squeezed through the middle of the Redskins' front seven, shifted to the sideline, and bolted for the end zone.

"That was my fault," remembered defensive tackle Darryl Grant, the star from Washington's victory over Dallas eight months earlier. "The guard pulled, and he took a few little steps and came back where I was. I was green coming into the game and [Tom] Landry knew it; he knew I was hungry, hungry, hungry. So as soon as that guard pulled I was gone. You should have heard me yelling 'Go get 'em, Darrell!' "

Green couldn't have been in a worse position to get Dorsett. As the team's left cornerback, he began the play on the opposite sideline from where Dorsett was running, leaving Redskins in his wake. But Green did not give up on the play. He recognized where Dorsett was headed, calculated the perfect angle, and soared across the field—"This missile goes by me," linebacker Mel Kaufman said—through a mass of both Cowboys and Redskins players.

"At the time, there wasn't a faster player in the NFL than Tony Dorsett and no one caught him from behind," Mark Murphy said. "Darrell and I were both chasing him, and I joked that I think I would have caught him by the Anacostia [River]."

The play—later ranked by NFL Films as the seventh greatest tackle in the league's first seventy-five years—ultimately saved the Redskins four points: the defense held the Cowboys to a field goal. But Green's touchdown-saving effort wasn't enough to stave off defeat. Not long after ABC's Howard Cosell inadvertently ended his career on *Monday Night Football* by calling Redskins receiver Alvin Garrett "that little monkey," Dallas proceeded to score four second-half touchdowns. Washington lost the game, 31–30, but they had found a game-changer.

Aided by the national television primetime broadcast, the twenty-three-year-old Green made a name for himself practically overnight.

"It was kind of a coming out for him on national TV," recalled Neal Olkewicz, another defensive player who was cheering Green on from well behind the pack. "People all of a sudden noticed, 'Where did this guy come from? He's something special.'"

Green's uncanny speed and a cocky-but-never-abrasive self-confidence, masked by a "baby face" atop an admittedly "itty-bitty" frame, made him ripe for stardom. But so too did his place on the Washington roster.

The two biggest personalities on the Redskins, Joe Theismann and John Riggins, were both in their mid-thirties. Riggins had just begun his seventh year in Washington, Theismann his tenth. And while the Hogs had certainly grabbed a large share of the local appeal, they were a collective group, with only a nickname and a cartoon pig as their public face.

Green's career may have been short, he may have come from a

tiny school, and he may have been exceptionally small in stature, but even as a rookie he was impossible to overlook.

"Yeah, I feel young. I don't have to be around Joe Theismann or George Starke to feel young," he said two months into his NFL career. "I feel honored to be around here. I'm learning every day. My speed? That will be with me for another twenty-five years."

THE WEEK ONE LOSS, the team's first in nearly nine months, had been difficult for delirious Redskins fans to swallow. Even Jack Kent Cooke, who spoke of "sheer, unadulterated, uncompromising ecstasy" in the locker room after the Super Bowl, couldn't relax as he sipped white wine in the owner's box.

"I came here tonight, heaving so many sighs, I may throw a hernia," he said two hours before kickoff. "I'm worried, I'm tense. I am on a diet of worry. Never mind that we won the Super Bowl. I want to win consistently. Whoever said consistency is the hob-goblin of little minds surely did not [have] winning a Super Bowl in mind."

Cooke's insatiable hunger for victories did not entirely mir-ror the expectations of the 1983 Redskins around town and among the national media. In classic coach-speak, Joe Gibbs pointed to a myriad of factors—tougher schedule, more *Monday Night* games, complacency, and opponents' eagerness to knock off the world champions—that made repeating as Super Bowl champions difficult. He even admitted during training camp that "we're not the kind of football team that can physically dominate you, like some of the [championship] teams of years ago, we need the total team effort, everybody playing together." Harsher skeptics suggested their title the previous season had been a fluke, even worthy of an asterisk, due to the shortened regular season and unusual playoff format forced by the players' strike.

"I don't think people like to accept us so fast because of the way

Joe Gibbs came in here and beat all those teams in just two years," wide receiver Charlie Brown said in the preseason.

"Do we have respect?" Mark Murphy asked rhetorically that August. "Judging from the preseason polls, I'd say we don't. Nobody is picking us to win the division."

Losing at home to their division rival—blowing a 20-point halftime lead in the process—further stalled the club's Super Bowl bandwagon. But beginning the next week with a decisive victory in Philadelphia, a five-game winning streak restored Washington's luster. And by early October, they were once again considered, along with Dallas, the class of the NFL. The high point of the streak was a dramatic home win over the undefeated Los Angeles Raiders, who held a 15-point fourth-quarter lead before the Redskins roared back. With thirty-three seconds remaining, Joe Theismann's touchdown pass to a diving Joe Washington, who snagged the ball just beyond the fingertips of linebacker Rod Martin at the goal line, lifted the Redskins to a 37–35 win.

Adding the counter to the game plan a week earlier had again given Washington's offense a huge boost that day against Los Angeles. John Riggins rushed for 91 yards and a touchdown and, as was the case against Seattle, the extra defensive attention he warranted opened up the passing game. Theismann threw for a career-high 417 yards and notched his 11th touchdown pass in just five games.

The next month's cover boy for Gentlemen's Quarterly—"[the photo] was pretty ugly . . . but we were so happy to get a straight man on the cover," the editor later said—Theismann was now playing the best, most consistent football of his career. Always his greatest asset, Theismann's accuracy gave Washington the most reliable arm in the NFL. And at thirty-four years of age, his deceptive mobility in the pocket allowed Redskins receivers time to find soft spots in opposing defenses.

Even Cowboys hero and Theismann's onetime rival Roger Staubach asked a reporter to "tell Joe, I've never seen a quarterback so perfect before," following a game that October.

"My career has come full cycle," he said late in the season. "It really is nice to be appreciated for what you do."

No one appreciated Theismann more than his pass catchers.

The longest-tenured Redskins' receiver, Art Monk, sat out the first month of the 1983 regular season due to a knee injury. The twenty-five-year-old, who also missed the Redskins' world championship run eight months earlier due to a broken foot, came back for the win over Los Angeles, nabbing 3 passes for 59 yards.

The return of the six-foot, three-inch, 210-pound receiver gave Theismann back the huge target he'd relied heavily on since 1980. But during each of Monk's prolonged absences, Theismann and the Redskins air attack thrived, thanks to a trio that, by comparison, made Art Monk look like one of the Hogs.

During the four playoff wins that culminated with a victory in Super Bowl XVII, Charlie Brown and Alvin Garrett horded catches, including both of Theismann's touchdown passes against Miami. Together, the two combined for 32 receptions, 486 yards, and 7 touchdown catches on a team devoted to running the football.

Garrett, a running back from Angelo State University whom the Giants cut the previous year, caught 3 touchdowns in the playoff win over Detroit. Before filling in for Monk, Garrett was primarily a special teams player with a toughness and willingness to hit that led that Joe Gibbs to call him "a human spear. . . . He's looking to kill guys." During the off-season, Garrett's route-running and receiver skills improved.

In the Week One loss to Dallas, he collected 101 yards on 10 passes, one of which incited Cosell's infamous comment. And, against Seattle, when Joe Gibbs unveiled his play-action corollary to the counter, Garrett streaked by a bewildered Seahawks secondary for a long touchdown.

But in the weeks that followed, as Theismann's arm heated up, Charlie Brown solidified his place as the Redskins' most dangerous receiver.

An eighth-round pick from South Carolina State in 1981, Brown flashed brilliance in the preseason only to spend his entire rookie year on the injured reserve with a knee injury. He made up for lost time in his first pro game, scoring a 78-yard touchdown in a season-opening win over Philadelphia. Using a distinctive running style—"It looks like he's ice skating," Dan Henning explained—Brown excelled in the open field.

In the strike-shortened 1982 season he led the club in yards and the NFC in both yards-per-catch and receiving touchdowns, giving rise to the nickname "Downtown" Charlie Brown. Entering the 1983 season, the admittedly "cocky" Pro Bowl receiver with a South Carolina license plate that read "All-Pro," successfully held out during the preseason, securing a lucrative new contract, worth reportedly $980,000 over four years. He quickly proved worthy of the raise.

Following 3 touchdowns in the opening month of the season, Brown lit up the Raiders' top-ranked defense for 11 catches, 180 yards, and a critical fourth-quarter touchdown in the Redskins' Week Five shootout victory.

Outstanding statistics mounted for Garrett and Brown that year, even after Art Monk's knee healed. By season's end, Brown broke the team record with 78 receptions and was named to a second straight Pro Bowl. But despite the accolades and numbers collected by Brown and Garrett, along with the speedy Virgil Seay, the receiving corps' short stature appealed most to fans and the media.

Even before the Hogs nickname flooded the city, the Redskins' pass catchers also rallied around a cute, playfully disparaging moniker. Each well under six feet tall, they called themselves "the Smurfs," an homage to the popular children's cartoon that debuted on NBC in 1981. Veteran running back Terry Metcalf—also vertically challenged and therefore accustomed to locker-room ribbing—claimed credit for the nickname.

"I started calling them Smurfs last year," he said in 1982. "I just happened to be watching the Looney Tunes one day and saw the

Smurfs, those little people in the cartoons. And that's what Virgil and Alvin are, little people."

At five feet, seven inches, Garrett was considered the smallest Smurf. Just slightly taller, the five-foot, eight-inch Seay explained that, "I'm Papa Smurf and Alvin's just Smurf."

"The funny thing about it, they would argue about who's the tallest," Charlie Brown said.

Brown was initially exempt from the Smurfs, but at five feet, ten inches, he was often lumped in with Garrett and Seay. Beginning with the 1982 playoffs, the threesome formed another, slightly more inclusive club that also competed with the Hogs for the spotlight.

As a salute to Art Monk, who watched the postseason game against Detroit in a cast on the sideline, Alvin Garrett and a few teammates planned a hand-slapping celebration should one of them score. Garrett forgot the choreography on his first 2 touchdown catches, but following the third, he remembered. In the end zone, Garrett, Seay, Brown, Otis Wonsley, Clarence Harmon, and Rick Walker formed a circle, jumped as high as possible and—completely out of sync—tried to execute a high-thirty.

"The Fun Bunch," as the group became known, completed the ritual following every touchdown catch during the playoffs and well into the 1983 regular season. Art Monk, the inspiration for the end zone party, naturally joined upon his return to the field: similar to the 5 O'Clock Club, the Fun Bunch had rolling membership. And with a quarterback at his peak and a fine group of receivers, the Redskins had plenty of opportunities to initiate new members.

"I would go into games not even questioning whether we'd win," Theismann later said. "The only question that I had on my mind was how many points we were going to score."

Theismann was mistaken prior to the Redskins' *Monday Night Football* showdown in Green Bay on October 17. Washington scored 5 touchdowns but fell to the Packers 48–47.

After that one-point loss in Green Bay, Washington won their next nine games to claim the top seed in the NFL playoffs for the second consecutive year.

When the regular season was over, the Redskins had six First-Team All-Pros (Charlie Brown did not justify his vanity plate) and seven Pro Bowlers on their roster, in addition to the league's MVP in Joe Theismann and a handful of new NFL record-holders.

John Riggins—who set new personal bests for attempts and yardage—scored 24 rushing touchdowns, surpassing the NFL record. The defense, tops in the league against the run, forced 61 turnovers, the most in league history. Even Mark Moseley—who became the only special teams player in league history to win the NFL MVP the previous year—set a single-season kicking record with 161 points.

But the offense as a collective body earned the most praise. A year after finishing the 1982 regular season with a pedestrian 21.1 points per game, the Hogs, the Smurfs, the Fun Bunch, the Diesel, and Theismann shattered the NFL single-season points record. In sixteen games, Washington scored 541 points, an average of 33.8 per game.

The reigning league MVP quarterback, the reigning Super Bowl MVP running back, the NFL's best offensive line, a record-setting kicker, and a fine collection of receivers, won the Redskins mounds of adulation. But their head coach drew even more.

Once again, the press could not help but anoint Joe Gibbs—winner of the NFL's Coach of the Year award for the second straight season—a coaching virtuoso.

"And I was starting to believe a little bit of it myself," Gibbs later admitted.

ACROSS THE SPAN OF the first seven quarters, the Redskins breezed through the 1983 NFC playoffs. After a much-deserved bye week,

Washington routed the Los Angeles Rams 51–7. In what he called "probably the most complete football game we've played," Joe Theismann carved up the Rams secondary with his usual precision; John Riggins outplayed his counterpart, rookie phenom Eric Dickerson; and the defense forced 4 turnovers. Three came from Washington's group of defensive backs, which now also sported a self-deprecating nickname.

Surrendering 3 touchdowns and 403 yards through the air in October's 48–47 regular season loss to Green Bay led to a torrent of criticism, particularly from their defensive coordinator. That evening Richie Petitbon told the press, "We really stunk. . . . I don't think anybody was without sin."

"The secondary is now called 'the Pearl Harbor Crew' since everybody, the fans, the media, keeps bombing us," safety Mark Murphy explained. "Oh, sure. Our T-Shirts will come out soon."

The youngest and smallest member of the Pearl Harbor Crew, Darrell Green, was also its biggest star, and against the Rams he demonstrated why. Green notched a team-high 7 tackles, knocked down 6 throws, and early in the final period snatched a pass bobbled by Dickerson at the Redskins' 28 and raced into the end zone, high stepping the final 45 yards.

"Everybody knows that I don't brag," Green told the press. "The good Lord blessed me with a lot of speed, and I knew no one would catch me. No, I wouldn't call it showboating."

One week after scoring an NFL-record 38 first-half playoff points against the Rams, Washington managed only 7 in the opening two quarters of their NFC Championship Game matchup with the San Francisco 49ers. A rushing touchdown from John Riggins followed by a 70-yard scoring strike from Joe Theismann to Charlie Brown then gave the Redskins a 21–0 fourth-quarter lead that seemed to lock up a trip to Tampa, Florida, for Super Bowl XVIII.

But San Francisco's passing game also boasted a mobile, accurate former Notre Dame quarterback with a Super Bowl championship victory. Joe Montana rallied the 49ers back with 3 touchdown passes in an eight-minute span, reminding everyone how the Pearl Harbor Crew first got its nickname. Montana even bombed "MX": the 49ers Freddie Solomon caught Darrell Green "by surprise, flat-footed . . . then he just took off" for a 76-yard touchdown.

"There was a time late in the game when I thought it was all slipping away," said Russ Grimm. "They just kept coming at us. This was the hardest game I have ever played in my life."

Their lead now gone, Grimm and the Hogs opened up running lanes for John Riggins, who extended his record streak of consecutive 100-yard playoff games to six. Following Riggins's ninth carry of the drive, the Redskins reached San Francisco's 8-yard line. With forty seconds remaining they sent Mark Moseley out to attempt the game-winner on an RFK Stadium surface that he declared "atrocious": the league ordered that green-painted sand be sprinkled onto the chewed up parts of the field prior to the playoffs.

The last of a dying breed of straight-ahead kickers, Moseley had already missed 4 field goals from inside 45 yards that day. John Riggins offered him a "blindfold and a cigarette after the last one he missed."

"He didn't have time to do that," Moseley said. "He was too busy sucking up oxygen."

From the hold of Joe Theismann, Moseley's 25-yard attempt sailed through the uprights with just twenty seconds remaining, and when Vernon Dean intercepted Montana's next throw Washington had prevailed, 24–21.

Unlike the previous year's win over Dallas, which ended with players carrying Joe Gibbs off the field and the head coach answering a congratulatory phone call from President Reagan, the end of this NFC Championship Game brought about a few sighs of relief among the shouts of joy.

"We were the best team in football all year, and yet I was scared, afraid that perhaps it was not meant to be," Joe Washington said.

"When Mark went out there for that last field goal, I didn't know whether to look or not. I wanted to go back to the Super Bowl, and I was afraid this time we weren't going to make it. I guess it's our turn again—twice in a row is hard to believe."

From the 49ers' perspective, losing to Washington was even harder to believe. Penalties plagued both teams—a Darrell Green kickoff return for a touchdown had been called back due to an illegal lateral—but San Francisco drew two flags at the worst possible time. On the Redskins' game-winning drive, cornerback Eric Wright was called for pass interference on a throw to Art Monk that 49ers head coach Bill Walsh said, "could not have been caught by a ten-foot Boston Celtic."

The 27-yard penalty pushed Washington into field goal range. Another flag in the secondary, against safety Ronnie Lott, again gave the Redskins a first down, allowing them to drain even more time off the clock. Neither penalty was blatant.

"If the Redskins are so mighty, so overpowering and invincible, then how come they can't just take the damn ball in the end zone?" Lott asked reporters afterward. "How come they gotta get help from some damn referees?"

The complaints from Lott, Walsh, Wright, and a handful of other 49ers may have sounded like sour grapes. They had just lost an intense, emotional game and with it, a trip to the Super Bowl. But squandering a 3-touchdown fourth-quarter lead at home and needing a bailout from the referees to squeak by with a win hardly fit the profile of a team that had won thirty of its previous thirty-three games. And although plenty of fans celebrated in Georgetown bars, car horns honked across Capital Avenue, and singing of "We're on our way / to Tampa Bay!" filled the locker room, the day aroused doubts in some observers' minds.

"The Washington Redskins proved something Sunday in their narrow 24–21 win over the San Francisco 49ers in the NFC title game—they are not invincible," Stan Goldberg of Maryland's

Frederick News-Post wrote. "To say they are, for the use of a better term, is hogwash. The Redskins also are not awesome nor the best team in the history of pro football. They also do not walk on water. No sports team is invincible. . . . Football teams are made up of human beings and they make mistakes—a lot of them."

The NFC Championship Game collapse, however, was greatly overshadowed by the place in NFL history that stood before the Redskins in Super Bowl XVIII. With a victory over the three-point underdog Los Angeles Raiders—a franchise that had won two championships in the previous seven years—the 1983 Redskins could lay claim to the title of greatest team in NFL history: repeat Super Bowl champions, owners of the most prolific offense and most opportunistic defense of all time, their only blemishes during the regular season two early-season one-point losses.

"I think that team was one of the best teams to ever play in the NFL," Gibbs said in 2014. "[But] one thing you learn in coaching is you're never more than six days away from a disaster, so I think it keeps you humble."

THE REDSKINS DIDN'T JUST lose Super Bowl XVIII; they were annihilated.

Minutes into the game, a rematch of October's exciting showdown with the Raiders, 3 Joe Theismann incompletions forced the Redskins to send out punter Jeff Hayes. His punt was tipped and didn't get beyond the line of scrimmage. An all-out pressure overloaded the Redskins' blockers and the Raiders' Derrick Jensen surged through. He blocked the punt, the ball rolled backward, three Raiders followed it into the end zone, and Jensen pounced on it for an easy touchdown.

"I thought it was a big factor," said Clint Didier, a member of the Redskins' punt team. "It started us wondering what was happening."

Defensive coordinator Richie Petitbon felt that same sense of uncertainty several hours earlier while the team drove to the game.

"For some reason the bus got lost," he said years later. "We got to the stadium just in time to get dressed and get on the field to warm up. And that throws you off, that was a very tiring effect for us. Not that that was the main reason we didn't play good, but it looked like it was just not your day today."

Long before the blocked punt and the late arrival to Tampa Stadium, plenty had gone wrong for the defending world champions.

During that week, the team stayed at an airport Holiday Inn, while their counterparts stayed at the Hilton; apparently Jack Kent Cooke didn't want to impose on his friend Barron Hilton a second time. Leaving their dingy, cramped hotel rooms for daily practices and media sessions didn't offer Redskins players and coaches much relief. A small lobby made it very difficult to exit the hotel without being bothered by drunken fans and autograph seekers who knew where the team was staying.

The practice facilities were even worse. While the Raiders held their practices at the Tampa Bay Buccaneers headquarters, the Redskins prepared for the game at the University of South Florida. The school had no football team and therefore limited resources. Worse yet, four men were caught taking photographs from a nearby building during the team's Thursday practice. That day's film was confiscated by NFL security officials.

"Bad week, we had a horrible hotel, we had a horrible practice facility," Jeff Bostic remembered. "You couldn't get in and out of the lobby, you couldn't get any peace. . . . The facilities and stuff were awful, we were right along the highway. I'm convinced [Raiders owner] Al Davis had us spied on."

Spartan accommodations and covert surveillance didn't concern John Riggins, who once again entertained reporters throughout the week with his smile, his stories, and, as usual, his attire.

At Thursday's press conference Riggins sauntered to a podium in front of 1,200 reporters, dressed in cowboy boots, a white silk pilot's scarf around his neck, and an olive-colored paratrooper suit, with blue and yellow patches and a nameplate that read, "John Riggins, Commander, Riggo's Rangers." The Washington, D.C., Air National Guard had presented it to him.

"You're all probably wondering why I'm dressed like a clown," he said. "Well, last year the 'Skins marched on Miami and this year we're going to fly over L.A. The bombs will be hot and heavy in the first half, which allow our ground troops to carry us to victory in the second half."

By that point in the season, however, despite his showmanship and animation, Riggins was drained. Addressing the crowd noticeably hoarse, he explained that after each of Washington's playoff games he was "quite exhausted . . . for some reason or another." Asked for a guess as to why, Riggins first pointed to the sandy terrain through which he collected 242 yards on 61 carries during the two postseason wins.

"I can't help but think that playing on that RFK beach had something to do with it," he said. "Either that or I'm getting old."

Age hadn't yet slowed down Riggins before. Neither had the wear and tear from 749 total rushes since the start of the 1982 season, nor had his notorious love of beer. But even John Riggins couldn't barrel past the flu.

After admitting Riggins was sick earlier in the week—which explained the hoarse voice on Thursday—a Redskins official denied press reports that he missed the team's final walk-through practice on Saturday due to illness. Riggins later told reporters, "I'm just lazy, I don't like to practice on Saturday." His fellow 5 O'Clock Club veteran Dave Butz discovered the truth the next morning.

"I went into his room to get him to get on the bus and everything had water on it," said Butz, who also missed practice early in the week due to the flu. "He had run the hot water all night long. The TV, the desktop, the dresser, everything had standing water on it, because he was trying to be able to breathe enough to get to the game."

Riggins made it through warm-ups and carried the ball three straight times for 11 yards to open up Washington's first possession of Super Bowl XVIII, the series that ended with the blocked punt. As the game wore on, the Redskins leaned on Riggins, who was repeatedly hemmed in by the Raiders 3-4 defensive front.

"Reggie Kinlaw, their nose tackle, was the best player on their defense," Theismann said. "He just controlled the line of scrimmage. We were a run-based football team. We couldn't run the football tackle-to-tackle. We couldn't block Reggie Kinlaw."

They also couldn't block the Raiders' linebackers, who used superior sideline-to-sideline lateral speed that, as Riggins said, "amazed me because they were playing so close."

Their running game stifled, Washington was forced to throw the ball much more than the game plan had called for. But twenty-mile-per-hour winds blowing in from the Gulf of Mexico, an off-day from their MVP quarterback, and the Raiders' pair of All-Pro cornerbacks, hampered the passing game. By halftime, all that the highest scoring offense in NFL history could muster was 2 field goal attempts, only one of which Mark Moseley made.

"With Lester Hayes and Mike Haynes, there were two lock-down corners," Theismann said. "And all of our adjustments—any [audibles] that were called—were fades and I just couldn't hit 'em. I played a bad football game. I look back at that football game on many different occasions, and I see opportunities in my mind that I just didn't execute."

Neither did many of his teammates.

Apart from the special teams blunder that led directly to 7 points and the Hogs' inability to move the Raiders front seven, Washington's defense was overwhelmed.

Although the Pearl Harbor Crew's repeatedly blown coverages had caused the Redskins to allow huge chunks of yards and points that year, great plays against the run frequently rescued the defense. The key to Washington's top-rated run defense was a pair of stout defensive tackles, Dave Butz and Darryl Grant. Early in the game, however, as Grant lunged to make a tackle, his helmet came off as he collided headfirst with another player. The resulting concussion sent him to the sideline for much of the first half.

"That took away half the center of the line by having him gone," Butz said. "Darryl Grant had a fantastic motor and he made my job so much easier because he was an outstanding player. . . . We worked in tandem together and when he went down that just made me say 'Oh my, it's gonna be a long game now.'"

Early in the second quarter, the Raiders needed just three plays to march 65 yards—wide receiver Cliff Branch ran right by Anthony Washington and Darrell Green for a 50-yard completion—for the game's first offensive touchdown. In the third quarter, after the offense finally pieced together a touchdown drive of their own, cutting the lead to 21–9, Washington's defense could not stop the Raiders' attack. Short completions from Jim Plunkett and the running of Marcus Allen covered 70 yards in eight plays to give the Raiders a 28–9 lead midway through the third quarter.

By the time Allen delivered his transcendent, field-reversing 74-yard touchdown run, the Redskins' will had already started to fade.

"We always thought we could win," Mark Murphy said, "but when they came right back and scored after we scored to open the second half [that] was pretty discouraging."

Eventually the game came to a merciful end with Washington losing the biggest blowout in Super Bowl history, 38–9.

"We could make excuses, I guess," Russ Grimm said. "But they beat us, offensively, defensively, and with the special teams. That's all there is, isn't it?"

Joe Theismann found some comfort in the final score, explaining, "If it was closer I might feel worse."

But whether or not the margin of victory had been 1 point or 29, the way in which Washington lost Super Bowl XVIII was especially painful.

Exactly fifty-one weeks after he phoned the winning locker room beneath the Rose Bowl Stadium, President Ronald Reagan made the same congratulatory call to the winning locker room beneath Tampa Stadium. Raiders head coach Tom Flores—who would the next day have to assure reporters, "I'm not a genius"—answered the call.

"That was a wonderful win tonight," Reagan told Flores. "I just think you ought to know that you've given me some problems. I have already had a call from Moscow. They think that Marcus Allen is a new secret weapon, and they insist that they dismantle it. Now, they've given me an idea about that team that I just saw of yours. If you turn them over to us, we'd put them in silos and we wouldn't have to build the MX missile."

A year earlier, it had been John Riggins whom Reagan fawned over, telling Joe Gibbs during his congratulatory phone call, "I'd like to know if your team would now like to help me on Capitol Hill. . . . Also, do you think Riggins would mind me changing the spelling of my name to add an 'I' and a couple of 'G's?"

Not only did Allen steal the president's corny, pandering adulation he also erased Riggins's place in the record books. Allen's 191 yards blew past the 166 total Riggins set against Miami.

Carrying the ball 26 times, Riggins gained just 64 yards, for a paltry 2.46 yards-per-carry average. The Redskins' 90 total rushing yards against the Raiders was their lowest figure in twenty-six games.

Those rushing statistics were a bit misleading. Washington fell behind early, and throughout most of the second half they trailed by 3 touchdowns; they had to largely abandon the running game. Still, the Raiders' front seven owned the line of scrimmage.

"We got tired of hearing about the Hogs," the Raiders' future Hall of Fame defensive end Howie Long said. "I never had Hog before. It tasted good."

That night in Tampa, Long and the Raiders declared themselves "the Slaughterhouse Seven." Their butchering of the Hogs, Riggins, and in the end, the Redskins' offense, was best exemplified by one play in the second half.

Faced with a fourth-and-one on the Raiders 26-yard line late in the third quarter and their chances of an unprecedented comeback rapidly deteriorating, the Redskins eschewed a field goal try and turned to Riggins and 70 Chip, just like they had in a similar moment against the Dolphins.

"That's bread and butter for us. We won the Super Bowl with it last year out of the near formation instead of the I," Joe Gibbs said. "We were going with our best shot there."

Riggins headed for the same spot—off-tackle, in between two tight ends' blocks—which he burst through a year earlier before bowling over Don McNeal. But against Los Angeles the hole collapsed. Raiders linebacker Rod Martin slipped by Rick Walker, wrapped up Riggins behind the line of scrimmage, and with an assist from safety Mike Davis brought the Diesel to the ground, well short of the first-down marker.

"I felt there was some daylight to the outside, but when I got there, I just couldn't see it," Riggins explained. "I didn't have 20-20 vision today. I made some bad reads, and I was guessing on their defense. Unfortunately I was guessing wrong almost all day."

Joe Gibbs's decision making was no better that day. And much more so than the failed fourth-down run, one disastrous call in particular, near the end of the first half, doomed Washington's title hopes.

Following the blocked punt and the Raiders' touchdown pass to Cliff Branch, the Redskins trailed Los Angeles 14–0 early in the second period. But on the ensuing drive Joe Theismann picked up four first downs through the air, pushing Washington near the Raiders' goal line, where Mark Moseley's 24-yard field goal snapped the offense's scoreless skid. Offering more encouragement that they could rebound from the sloppy start, the Redskins' defense halted a promising Raiders drive that had reached Washington territory.

They forced a punt, which rolled dead at the Redskins' 12-yard line with only twelve seconds remaining before halftime.

Given their field position and the time on the clock, no one expected the Redskins to do anything other than take a knee or at the very most run the ball. Joe Gibbs had another plan.

"Joe was upset at the fact that we hadn't scored [enough] points," offensive coordinator Jerry Rhome remembered. "He wanted to get something on the scoreboard before the halftime."

To take one last shot at doing so, Gibbs called "Rocket Screen," a slow-developing screen pass to running back Joe Washington. Five months earlier, against the same Los Angeles Raiders team, Washington had been a hero of the Redskins' regular-season win, catching 5 passes for 99 yards and 2 touchdowns, including the game-winner in the final minute. Gibbs hoped to recapture some of that magic and spark another double-digit comeback victory.

"With [twelve] seconds left in the half, you have two choices: you can either fall on the ball or try to get something," Gibbs explained. "I wanted to run something safe. It got us a 67-yard gain in the first game [against the Raiders]. I was hoping we'd get 20 or 30 yards and maybe get a field goal. . . . I didn't like the idea of falling on the ball."

Joe Theismann wasn't nearly as optimistic. Uneasy about the decision to run a play and especially a screen pass, he double-checked the call with his head coach.

"I'm at the sidelines, I'm talking to Joe and . . . I said, 'I just don't feel good about putting the ball up in the air this far backed up with hardly any time left.' He says, 'We have two time-outs.' And I'm thinking, 'So what? There's no time left.'

"But I think, 'Well, Joe's a great coach. We're in the Super Bowl. I'll listen to him.' I started walking away and I get about five feet away, and I turn around. I'll never forget, he points at me and says, 'Run it.'

"So now I'm jogging on the field, and I just don't feel good about this. I don't like this. It doesn't make sense. . . . But it didn't matter.

The sovereign Lord has made the decision, so I'm just going to go with it."

Theismann called the play in the huddle, took the snap from Jeff Bostic, retreated into the pocket to draw defenders with him, looked right, then off his back foot flung the ball to the left. At the 5-yard line, Joe Washington waited arms-open for the ball; it never came. Reserve linebacker Jack Squirek—who was told by Raiders assistant coach Charlie Sumner to "watch for the screen"—stepped in front of Washington, caught the ball, and hopped into the end zone for a touchdown.

Instead of going into halftime down 14–3, still well within striking distance after a nightmarish first half that began with the blocked punt, the Redskins now trailed 21–3 with all the momentum in the Raiders' favor.

"If I had had the luxury to stop the world at that point, right before the interception and return for a touchdown and called for an impromptu opinion poll on what I should have done, the majority of the people would have told me to go for it," Gibbs said. "But after it failed so terribly and with everybody watching it happen, I guarantee nobody would have had the guts to say it was a good idea. I guess you just have to know when to hold 'em and when to fold 'em. That was a time I should have put 'em away. And that's a time I'll have to answer for the rest of my life."

"But I wonder about it all now, and that's one of the things I'll always have to deal with. I keep going back and saying why did that happen? Why? Why?"

Many more asked that same question. And as a result, Joe Gibbs and his Rocket Screen—not the blocked punt, the blown coverages, the failure on fourth-and-one, the frequent missed blocks of the Raiders front seven, or repeatedly whiffing on Marcus Allen during his 74-yard touchdown run—became the symbol of the Redskins' Super Bowl XVIII humiliation.

"For one brief instant at the end of the half," *Washington Post* beat writer Gary Pomerantz explained in the next morning's edition, "the Redskins' offensive genius lapsed into buffoonery."

Gibbs did not appreciate the article. Four months after the column ran, he approached Pomerantz about it.

"He was not happy with me," Pomerantz remembered. "And it obviously stuck in his craw all those months later."

It stuck in his craw far longer than a few months.

"True story," Gibbs said several years later. "I went from being a pretty bright, sharp guy to being called in the *Washington Post* the next day a buffoon. What that taught me was this: if you fail in the world's eyes, the world will turn on you."

CHAPTER 5

Second Chances

"I'VE NEVER had a worse feeling after a game than when we lost Super Bowl XVIII," Joe Gibbs recalled years later. "You'd think it would be enough to get to the Super Bowl, but it wasn't. That was a bitter plane flight home."

Gibbs cheered up a little upon returning to Washington, D.C., on Monday afternoon. Even without the Lombardi Trophy to show off, he and his team again received a warm welcome home. At least 150 people braved twenty-nine-degree cold to cheer the team on as they arrived at Redskin Park the day after their loss to the Raiders. As he walked off the team bus, fans that did not think he was a buffoon cheered, "We want Joe Gibbs! We want Joe Gibbs!"

Gibbs shook hands with many among the crowd, chatted with several more, signed a few autographs, and even accepted a Redskins helmet cake that one fan had made for him.

"I just want to say thank you all for coming today," he said. "We feel for everybody. It's just unbelievable that you all are here. You are number one!"

The condolence tour continued on Wednesday as Gibbs and many of his players signed autographs and thanked a crowd of 100,000 that showed up for a parade that started on Pennsylvania Avenue.

"In our Redskins family, we have the fans. . . . It doesn't matter what the weather is. It doesn't matter what happens in the stadium. You are here," Gibbs announced during a rally held in the shadow of the Washington Monument.

Six weeks later, Gibbs would return to another nearby D.C. landmark and symbol of American democracy, this time to rally around a far different cause.

On February 29, 1984, he appeared on Capitol Hill, before a United States House of Representatives' Republican study committee. Beside a handful of sports and entertainment stars—including his rival, Dallas Cowboys head coach Tom Landry—Gibbs shared with the panel his stern advocacy for returning prayer to public schools, in order "to put God back in His rightful place in our life."

"Marxist doctrine and pornographic presentation are allowed in our society as freedom of speech," said Gibbs, who that same month had publicly supported and donated $150 to the local group Citizens Against Pornography. "Yet we deny to our youth in schools the freedom to make any statement to and on behalf of God."

Despite strong support from President Reagan, who said that "the Supreme Court [had] expelled God from America's classrooms," the movement failed. In late March, the Senate struck down the bill, fifty-six to forty-four, preventing it from being sent to the House.

"The issue of free religious speech is not dead as a result of this vote," Reagan told reporters in the White House Briefing Room. "We have suffered a setback, but we have not been defeated. Our struggle will go on."

For Joe Gibbs, it would as well.

A TRUE ANOMALY IN the gruff, macho, stressful world of competitive football, Joe Gibbs never swore. He ordered, he disciplined, he became angry, and he yelled—although when he did, Gibbs's voice sometimes reached a high-pitched squeal that resulted in muted laughter, not fear—but he would not use profanity.

"There were guys on the team that wanted to see Joe curse for the first time," defensive end Charles Mann said. "They just wanted to hear him curse, when he gets angry just throw out one of those F-bombs so we can know you're real. But he never did."

The closest Gibbs came was an occasional substitute for the word "ass," which led players to refer to him as "Coach Buns."

Aware that most of his colleagues believed it was as much a part of football as the goal post and hash marks, Gibbs didn't ban swearing in Redskin Park. Most of the team's coaches and players appreciated that, especially Joe Bugel, whose choice of vocabulary could make a drill sergeant uncomfortable.

"I was kind of a rough-and-tumble guy," recalled special teams ace Pete Cronan. "I used to address the special team before every game, animated, excited—it was more for me than for them. And [Gibbs] pulled me aside. He says, 'Are you going to talk to the team today?' I said, 'Yeah, sure, Coach, why, what's up?' He says, 'Good, I want you to, I want you to keep that up. By the way, you know the rules, right? . . . You can't take the Lord's name in vain.' That meant everything else was good!"

But Gibbs hadn't always been so virtuous, so admittedly "boring," enjoying a glass of whole milk with cookies before bed, and considering an ideal Saturday night "sitting at home with his wife, Pat, and two sons, eating hamburgers and watching TV."

Born in Mocksville, North Carolina, Joe Gibbs grew up in Enka, North Carolina, a sleepy, rural town on the western side of the state, near the Tennessee border. His father, Jackson Cephus "J.C." Gibbs, was the deputy sheriff of the nearby city of Asheville. He often chased down bootleggers, and according to folklore set a state-record by confiscating 2,800 gallons of moonshine in 1942. J.C.'s eldest boy, two years old at the time, eventually discovered the dangers of his father's job.

"We would bring in narcotics addicts and drunks, and Joe would ask questions like 'Daddy, why'd you bring him in?'" J.C. said years later.

Nearly as truculent as the men he arrested, J.C. once crashed his brand-new state-issued Plymouth headfirst into a telephone poll while chasing moonshiners at nearly eighty miles per hour. He wore a lower-body cast much of the next year.

"He was a rough, tough guy leading a wild life," Gibbs said. "He'd be on the phone at home all the while saying, 'Ya think so, huh? Well, I'll meet ya at the corner.' And he'd come home beat up from a fistfight."

Joe Jackson Gibbs shared his father's taste for mayhem.

"Joe was always a little bit mischievous growing up," his mother, Winnie, said in 1983. "But he never had any trouble with the law."

J.C.'s boss lost the 1954 local sheriff election and—"because we were starving to death in Asheville"—he followed his brothers west and moved his wife and two children to California. Around the same time that Joe Gibbs discovered football and girls, in particular his future wife, Pat, the fifteen-year-old at Santa Fe High School found another equally challenging hobby: cars. Although sitting behind the wheel once landed him in juvenile hall—as a sixteen-year-old driving a few friends around Gibbs grazed a boy on a bicycle—drag racing consumed his free time away from the football field.

"He got hooked up with a couple of older guys who were drag racing at the time and he got very, very hooked on it," said his high school friend and Redskins tight end coach Rennie Simmons. "I think it was just a challenge to build something and then go out and beat somebody with it."

In a Los Angeles garage owned by the Sandoval Brothers, Gibbs rebuilt broken-down cars. His first was a 1933 Ford Victoria that he souped up with a Cadillac engine. He did the same with a 1927 Model

T and also put a Corvette engine in his 1937 Chevy. With his rehab projects complete, Gibbs drove to one of three places in Los Angeles County: Clock's drive-in, either in Downey or Whittier, or Scot's, a hamburger joint at the intersection of Imperial Highway and Paramount Boulevard. At those spots, he found competition and took on the locals with the same passion as his favorite racer, Don Prudhomme.

Aided by world land speed record holder Gary Gabelich, Gibbs worked his way up from hot rods to gas coupes, then gas dragsters, and finally a top-fueler that Simmons helped him build.

"We won a few races, I know that," Gibbs said. "I probably ran about 140 to 150 in the gas dragster. The top-fuelers were running about 180 then, but we never really got ours going. We only ran it twice: once out at San Fernando and then Fontana, where we blew the motor on our first run."

Gibbs's time at those not-always-legal drag strips in Long Beach, San Fernando, Famosa, and Pomona exposed him to a few unsavory situations, as did his days as a student at San Diego State. As an upperclassman, he and four friends rented a house in Mission Valley, which they called "the Farm." Believing "if you have a farm, you should have farm animals," Gibbs and his pals acquired two pigs, which they forgot to feed. The hogs escaped and began wandering along nearby Highway 80.

"I was studying for an exam and watching television, and all of a sudden there was a bulletin that the Humane Society had blocked Highway 80," Gibbs remembered. "I looked up, and out from behind this concrete column I could see this pig sticking his face out and there's eight guys chasing him."

"I never went back [to the Farm]," he said. "I'm glad I didn't sign my real name to the lease."

As a pledge in Sigma Chi—a "John Belushi–type fraternity," according to fellow Aztec and later the Redskins' special teams coach Wayne Sevier—Gibbs found more trouble. He and a few pals "had stolen some hubcaps and car batteries, and even cheated on tests." And in true Animal House fashion Gibbs was nearly expelled from school, albeit for brawling, not poor grades or debauchery.

"I got to the fight late," Rennie Simmons said. "But I remember two Marines were on the ground and Joe didn't have a scratch on him. [Don] Coryell had to vouch for him."

After graduating and serving for three years on Coryell's staff, Gibbs joined Bill Peterson at Florida State, leaving behind San Diego State, his dragster, and eventually his rebellious ways. He later conceded, "A part of me died the day I sold those cars."

"Obviously, I have not lived a perfect life," he once said.

In 1972, while on Frank Broyles's staff at Arkansas, Gibbs met George Tharel. Manager of the local J.C. Penney's and the teacher of an adult Sunday school class at the First Baptist Church of Fayetteville, Tharel became Gibbs's "spiritual father."

"It was a growing awareness," Gibbs said. "It definitely turned my life around. It was like I had been trying to grab things in life, conquer things that people said I should conquer. Once I conquered them, there was an empty feeling like 'Is this all there is?' Really, [becoming born again] was straightening out my relationship with God. I think that I recognized that there was a God since I was nine years old. But I came to know that when you recognize His presence, even though you will go through hard times and struggle, that everything will work out for the best."

That worldview would guide Gibbs for the rest of his life, and become a far greater motivation than outsmarting opposing defenses or chasing Super Bowl trophies.

Even after becoming head coach of the most popular sports team in the nation's capital, Gibbs never hid his strong faith. He fostered player-run Bible-studies group, made available to them a team chaplain, and—as he detailed at the start of training camp every year—preached three priorities to live by: "Your relationship with God. Your relationship with your family and teammates. And being the best football player you can be."

"I guarantee you," Gibbs then told his team, "if the first two priorities are not in line, you can't be your best on the field."

But Gibbs never pushed his beliefs on Redskins players. He didn't need to. Most of them, regardless of their own religious devotion, came to follow his example, rather than listen to his words.

"I didn't want to disappoint him," Charles Mann later said. "He was such a man of honor that you wanted to honor him by being a good man."

During the players' strike of 1982, Gibbs began to inspire people—both inside and far away from Redskin Park—on a much larger scale.

Despite having no one to coach, and no game plans to construct, Gibbs and his staff worked as if they did.

"He kept the staff intact, they went to work every day," Pete Cronan said. "A lot of coaches sent their staffs home. Gibbs worked as if they were going to break the strike the next day."

Still, without a game to be played on Sunday afternoons, Gibbs did have a few extra hours in his week, and he put them to good use.

While living in Tampa during his brief tenure as the Buccaneers offensive coordinator Gibbs joined his church in visiting with troubled youths and teaching them lessons from the Bible. He found the time rewarding, and upon taking the job in Washington, he vowed to continue meeting with, as they were known at the time, "delinquents." During the off-season, Gibbs and several members of his Columbia Baptist Church in Falls Church, Virginia, visited the Triangle House, an inner-city home for runaways and homeless teenagers who had become wards of the state.

And with the strike opening up his schedule in the fall of 1982, Gibbs was free to visit the small building on Sixteenth and P, to help conduct voluntary Bible studies for groups as large as sixteen: the Redskins' game films he had first brought didn't hold the kids' interest nearly as well.

"At the beginning, the kids knew that he was with the Redskins and that attracted them," said Don Murphy, one of the group's counselors and a former Redskins tryout at defensive back. "But the turnover is so great, the Redskin connection had less effect as the weeks went on. There must have been fifty different kids go through one of his classes. They wound up coming through word of mouth, not because of what Joe Gibbs represents."

By mid-November, the players' strike ended and Gibbs returned to the sidelines on Sundays in the fall, but his passion for helping the kids grew. He began conceiving a new year-round facility for needy teenagers, one that he could be more involved with.

"Maybe a farm in the country where they could have a complete program, counseling, education, jobs," he said. "The aim would be to get them ready to go out into society and be a useful citizen. I can see that happening down the road. I'm going to stay involved."

Within four years, Gibbs founded the Youth For Tomorrow program and raised $1.2 million to build the New Life Center on a 137-acre ranch in Bristow, Virginia. The thirty-some teenage boys who participated in the twelve-to-eighteen-month program, lived in dorms, studied basic high school subjects, met with counselors and social workers, and played video games, billiards, and basketball. Gibbs visited to teach lessons from the Bible, such as Saint Paul's letter to the Ephesians, which served as a guide for warding off temptation.

Gibbs didn't dedicate himself to these causes for publicity, nor did he do so to proselytize. And undertaking such an endeavor came at a great cost. Not only was his time away from football limited, but two previous business ventures ultimately turned disastrous. A failed investment in health clubs while an assistant head coach in St. Louis cost him tens of thousands of dollars in the 1970s. During the Oklahoma oil and gas boom of the 1980s, Gibbs—prompted by his bonus following the Super Bowl XVII victory—ignored his wife's advice and invested heavily in real estate. He soon owed banks roughly $1.2 million, which he did not have.

"I got on my knees. . . . I said, 'Hey, God, it's in Your hands. I'm

bankrupt. The only person who can straighten this mess out is You,'"
Gibbs said a few years later. "Now that it's over with, it's become part
of my testimony. I think I can help other young people. Most people
are going to have to deal with it sometime in their lives."

Gibbs used the lessons he learned from his failures away from
football to mentor others, particularly those at Youth For Tomorrow. He saw a "real void in our society . . . when it comes to youths
who are falling behind in school, who have difficult home environ-
ments or are in some trouble—these young people, we just don't have
anything for them."

Youth For Tomorrow prospered throughout the next several
decades, helping thousands of teenagers straighten out their lives.
Eventually, Gibbs also directed his philanthropy to adults in need.
Spurred on by once-imprisoned adviser to President Richard Nixon,
Charles Colson, Gibbs began touring the country, speaking with
hundreds of inmates, one prison at a time. With armed guards surrounding the prisoners, Gibbs offered his spiritual guidance, wis-
dom, and prayed for their rehabilitation.

"Their life is in a decision or process where they're looking for
a second chance," Gibbs later preached. "We serve a God who gives
second chances."

As head coach of the Washington Redskins, Gibbs proved to be
a forgiving patriarch, often giving troubled, misguided, or simply
unsuccessful careers second chances.

IN FEBRUARY 1978, as he debated whether or not to take the job
of general manager of the Washington Redskins, Bobby Beathard
developed serious reservations. Not only would it mean leaving his
post as director of player personnel on a dynasty—Don Shula's two-
time Super Bowl champion Miami Dolphins—for an aging team in
need of overhaul, but he'd be faced with a mammoth obstacle.

"I didn't want to follow the George Allen tradition of only

having old players, I wanted to start rebuilding through the draft," he said. "When I got there, we had no draft choices. Some people even told me I was crazy to take the job because how can you take the job when that's what you do, scout and draft, and they don't have any choices. But I thought it was a challenging opportunity, but it was a great place for football."

Beathard accepted the challenge and within five years assembled a roster that produced a Super Bowl championship, and he did so by using only two first-round draft choices. Like his predecessor, George Allen, Beathard had no problem trading away high draft choices. The two did, however, differ on the ideal compensation.

While Allen routinely dealt first- and second-round picks in exchange for veteran players, Beathard believed in turning one high pick into several later-round picks. He trusted his instincts and valued the efforts of scouts like Kirk Mee, whose grueling road trips to colleges all over the country increased the pool of players to choose from. Scouting so effectively and so thoroughly also gave Beathard and the front office a long list of undrafted college free agents to choose from once that draft ended.

Several late-round picks, undrafted free agents, and rookie cast-offs from other clubs became major contributors and even stars for the Redskins' powerful teams in 1982 and 1983. But the emergence of those players was only possible because Joe Gibbs and his staff gave those players a chance.

"It was just amazing that the coaches got what we did out of those players," Beathard said years later. "We had the agreement . . . once they get into camp there's no first-round, or twelfth-round, or free-agent kid that wasn't drafted. They are all treated the same. And they held to that, 'cause I've been with teams that said, 'Well, if he's a sixth-round draft choice he's not going to have much chance to make it.'

"And our philosophy was, until he proved he couldn't play, he was just as important as a first-round kid. And that's why we had so many of the no-names—Alvin Garrett, Darryl Grant—and all these low-round draft choices and kids that weren't drafted make our team because of the coaches. Once they were there, they all got the same chance as a first-round pick."

That approach cultivated the fine careers of Garrett, Grant, Joe Jacoby, Jeff Bostic, Charlie Brown, Neal Olkewicz, Clint Didier, Donnie Warren, and the team's captain, linebacker Mel Kaufman. But no player benefited more from the Redskins' spirit of equality than Dexter Manley, who would throughout the decade repeatedly test the limits of Joe Gibbs's forgiving nature.

Raised in Houston's Third Ward, Manley was one of four children born to Carl, a limo driver for the Tenneco Oil Company, and his wife, Jewellean, a nurse's aide at nearby Methodist Hospital. Although he looked down on the "sad-sack people" who lived in Houston's famously troubled Fifth Ward, Manley slept in a dresser drawer as a baby and then on the floor of the family's one-story house that sat atop cement blocks on Page Street.

A mischievous child who ran loose throughout the neighborhood, he set fires, snuck into funeral homes to see dead bodies, chucked sticks at animals in the local zoo, and talked incessantly just to irritate people. The frequent punishments doled out—often beatings with an electrical cord—convinced Dexter that his father favored his older brother, Reginald, a charming and good student who "was the apple of my daddy's eye."

"I was just a scared little kid," he wrote in his autobiography, *Educating Dexter.* "I'd see car headlights from the back window of our bedroom, and I would be petrified. I thought I was bad or devious—by the way my daddy treated me—and that people were coming to take me away."

Soon, there truly were people coming to take him away from the Third Ward: college football coaches. A 1976 All-American at Jack Yates High School, Manley was one of the region's most coveted prospects; two Big Eight college recruiters physically fought over him while watching him practice. Oklahoma State University head coach Jim Stanley ultimately won the sweepstakes, and by his sophomore season, Manley was starting at outside linebacker for the Cowboys. The next year, he set the school record for tackles-for-loss and forced 5 fumbles. Despite his great production against several of the nation's top programs, his NFL draft stock was saddled with baggage.

"The scouts had some questions about his character," said Manley's first agent, Joe Courrege. "I remember people telling me that he was a bad actor."

Through just a few years in Stillwater, Manley had earned that reputation.

As a freshman, he was involved in an on-campus brawl over a parking space. The next year, he was one of three players investigated by the NCAA for driving or buying new cars that had been either paid for or financed by football boosters. Manley's head coach denied the claims, saying, "I talked to Dexter, but I did not ask him where he got his car. And, besides, that's none of your business." That same year, he applied for Social Security benefits as an orphan; Manley's father recently died of cancer and his mother was incapacitated by alcoholism. Married with a young child, Derrick, Manley needed the money, but he lied on the forms—saying he had three children and was single, despite being married—and was caught. In June 1980, he pled guilty to fraud charges.

Manley's physical gifts still attracted pro scouts. Considered a freak of nature, the six-foot-four-inch 250-pounder ran the 40-yard dash in 4.55 seconds and bench-pressed 500 pounds. And although remaining academically eligible was always in question, grasping pro-style schemes did not concern the Redskins scouts and general manager.

"He didn't test well, not physical tests, but those [mental] tests we gave," recalled Bobby Beathard, who visited Stillwater to meet with Manley. "We had a doctor [Harry Wachs] that we used to give tests instead of the Wonderlic tests and all these tests for reading and math . . . that all the teams gave players.

"We devised this test that you could determine intelligence even if you're not a good reader. They were games with blocks, and tic-tac-toe, and all these different games and we finally got a kit for each of our scouts, and when we'd go to schools we'd carry it. In the spring we could test players and other teams didn't have this test, it was only for our team. They'd have to arrange blocks in a certain way, in a certain time. And Dexter could do all that. But if you asked him to read a newspaper, it was hard."

Manley couldn't read beyond a second-grade level. He had coasted through his classes by cheating and receiving grades he didn't deserve.

"[All] through my grammar, junior high, and high school, I was put back in the special ed class, and I stayed there through the third through the sixth grade," Manley told a congressional subcommittee in 1989, three years after he began regularly attending adult reading courses at the Lab School of Washington. "It was very difficult because I felt like I was normal, but at the same time, I was told a lot of different things—that I was dumb and stupid. I had a lot of rejection in my life, and there was a lot of frustration because I did not know how to read or write.

"The only thing that really made me feel good in school was athletics. That built some self-esteem and some self-worth in Dexter Manley. Other than that I had no identity. You know, as kids, we all search for some identity, and I did not have any because I felt so different. I always felt like I was the black sheep in whatever environment, whether in my family or whatever."

Manley's feeling of alienation only grew as he got older and as he became more of a football star. By the time Washington selected him in the fifth round of the 1981 draft, the burden of hiding his struggles with reading became much heavier.

"I don't ever remember him harming anyone else other than

himself, he was extremely self-destructive," said Darryl Grant, Manley's closest friend on the team. "I think one of the things that depressed him more than anything was what happened to him on an educational level and how he was pushed through schools and facilities and not being able to be as confident with reading.

"He hid a lot of that stuff, not wanting other people to know what was really going on and that's got to be a hard thing. You're trying to keep a secret that big and you're trying to function through life and now you've made it to the highest level of the profession, and you've got this big secret."

As a rookie, Manley successfully lobbied to play special teams, and his performance quickly intrigued the coaching staff. One opponent during that preseason noticed, "He was vicious, I never saw a cover man so big."

"He had the biggest smile, the best attitude," Joe Gibbs recalled. "You talk about somebody that was made for football, Dexter was made for football. He loved it."

Midway through that first season, after Coy Bacon was released, Manley won a starting job, and in the Redskins' 1982 NFC Championship Game victory over Dallas, his pass rushing became a revelation. After knocking Danny White from the game, his pressure on White's backup, Gary Hogeboom, caused the interception that Darryl Grant returned for a game-clinching touchdown. The next season, his 11 sacks were second on the team.

As the mass appeal of the defending Super Bowl champions swelled, Manley's did as well. He frequently attended weekly Tuesday Foreign Affairs events at the White House Rose Garden, mingling with Deputy Chief of Staff Mike Deaver, Secretary of State George Shultz, Alexander Haig, and Vice President George H. W. Bush. A few years later, President Reagan's secretary of defense, Caspar Weinberger, invited Manley to the Pentagon, where he was awarded a plaque that declared him the Redskins' "Secretary of Defense."

"That was real special, I came out of Houston's Third Ward and

I hadn't had any influence in politics," he said decades later. "You're standing out here and there's nothing but Caucasians. There weren't many African American folks out there, and I was a young African American out there in front of all these dignitaries. So I had great admiration for that.

"I thought, 'Well, they like me!' I would go there and the guards would know my name, when you go check in, they would know who I was. I said, 'I'm going to be a Republican!' So I became a registered Republican."

Despite earning acceptance among the Washington elite, Manley occasionally annoyed teammates and coaches, especially on the field, with his brazen, unabashed self-confidence—he guaranteed he would win the MVP prior to Super Bowl XVII. In addition to trash-talking opponents and challenging other teams' head coaches to run plays directly at him, he sometimes lost focus.

"Dexter'd get so hyped during games," said Darryl Grant. "He paid no attention in the huddle. He'd be playing up the crowd, and I'd get the call in the huddle, and he'd say, 'World!'—that's my nickname—'What's the defense?' He'd be standing there asking us, 'What's the call? What's the call?' And the offense would be about to snap the ball. He'd ask me right during the cadence, and I didn't have time to respond.

"But Dexter was there strictly to get the quarterback. Two sacks, and he'd call it a day. If he got 2 sacks on the first two plays of the game, he'd take the rest of the game off. That's what they emphasized—sacks. You may be getting blown off the line 20 yards, but if you get sacks, that's notoriety. Dexter knew that."

Off the field, he also exasperated the front office. Following his strong performance in the 1982 playoffs, Manley demanded a raise, explaining, "They are paying me pennies." During a tense negotiating session with Beathard, Gibbs, and Jack Kent Cooke, he angered the team's owner by asking for a trade. Cooke threw him out of his office, compelling Gibbs to warn Manley "you shouldn't disrespect the grandfather." He didn't heed the advice. Twice over the next three years, he publicly demanded a trade; the second time, he told the local WAVA-FM listening audience that Cooke was a "miser" for not paying him a higher salary.

"A lot of times in the past," he admitted, "I know I haven't said the right things."

That included a much-publicized incident prior to the 1982 season. Manley worked as a guard at the Fairfax County Detention Center during the off-season following his rookie year. After the job ended, he kept his badge. In November, a police officer stopped him for expired tags on his Mercedes, and Manley flashed the badge looking for some professional courtesy. A SWAT team arrived at his house and arrested Manley for impersonating an officer; threatening the police official who called Redskin Park didn't help his cause.

Manley's teammates mercilessly ribbed him for the arrest—and also for the time he showed off a brand-new black $70,000 Porsche, which he claimed to have purchased with cash, only to have a local dealership send a tow truck to Redskin Park four days into his "test drive." But they also adored him.

"He was just like a little teddy bear," said fellow defensive end Charles Mann. "He would frustrate me at times. . . . We were fierce competitors, but I love him like a brother. I would do anything for him. . . . How could you not like somebody like that? The distractions that happened, I think made us closer as a team. We didn't run from the distractions. We embraced our brother that needed our help."

Teammates, coaches, and the front office knew that Manley's innate ability to harass and sack quarterbacks improved the Redskins' chances each week, but his skills as a pass rusher were not the reason he could seemingly do no wrong.

"Not so much because of the type of player Dexter was, a lot of it was the type of person Dexter was. You really liked Dexter. He's a happy guy, always smiling. You would never think there's something bad going on in Dexter's mind," Beathard said. "You just worried about him: How can we keep him on a leash and make sure he doesn't go with the wrong people?"

Gibbs, who devoted a great deal of his precious free time to saving troubled youths, wanted to do the same for his young defensive star. He admired Manley's "big heart," and invited him to join the Gibbs family at church one Sunday. He also brought Manley to speak to the teenagers at the Triangle House, as well as the Lorton Reformatory, a prison in Virginia.

But even Gibbs—who didn't hassle the 5 O'Clock Club, looked the other way when he smelled alcohol on Russ Grimm's breath in the huddle, and in 1984 welcomed safety Tony Peters back with the team following an arrest for his part in a cocaine sale—saw the limits of his patience tested by Manley. Especially once Manley's drug and alcohol addiction began to consume him.

A few weeks after the Super Bowl XVIII loss to the Raiders, Manley's mother was diagnosed with a brain tumor. Unable to walk after the first of several surgeries, she remained in hospitals the rest of her life. Manley began drinking excessively and showing up late to team functions. During the 1985 season, Manley arrived two hours late to a team practice, after crashing his Ford Bronco into an eighteen-wheeler parked outside Redskin Park. One assistant coach present that day recalled Manley "reeked of alcohol." Manley had used cocaine for the first time the night before.

"Once I started experimenting with drugs and using drugs on a regular basis I wasn't sure what [the Redskins] knew," Manley said in 2014. "I have to be able to look in the mirror and sometimes I would look in the mirror and not be happy with that guy in the mirror because I grew up in that environment and I never used drugs until I got to the National Football League. Never. But I started experimenting with drugs in the National Football League."

Gibbs defended Manley, telling reporters, "[He] has been going through some real personal, trying times for himself. His mother's very sick . . . and he's just down now." The front office holed him up in the Dulles Marriott, to rest and hide from the press.

"I've probably had more hard and intense meetings with Dexter than with any other players," Gibbs later said. "But every time I would get upset with him, I would always think back to the good side of Dexter, the side that wanted to do right."

PRIOR TO THE START of the 1984 regular season, players and coaches were treated to a regal luncheon at the Sheraton Hotel, hosted by Jack Kent Cooke. With his customary elocution and theatrical annuncia- tion, Cooke officially welcomed everyone to the new season with an encouraging message six months after the crushing defeat in Super Bowl XVIII.

"[They] deserved to win and we deserved to lose," Cooke told his audience. "Using the words of an eighteenth-century poet, John Dryden: 'I am a little hurt, but I am not slain / Lay me down and bleed a while / Then, I'll rise and fight with you again.' Al Davis, we plan to rise and fight with you again, and this time the best team won't lose."

Two weeks into the 1984 season the Redskins were clearly not the league's top team. In consecutive losses to open the 1984 season, they allowed a combined 72 points. They recovered with a five-game winning streak that pushed them back to the top of the NFC East, and then dropped out of first place with two straight road losses to St. Louis and the Giants.

The roller-coaster season continued into November: beginning with a *Monday Night* victory over Atlanta, the Redskins won six of their final seven games to reclaim control of the division and secure a home playoff berth.

Even within that late-season resurgence, however, the Red- skins hardly resembled a two-time defending NFC Champion. In their final two regular-season games, the defense gave up 725 yards through the air and the offensive line yielded 14 combined sacks of Joe Theismann, both of which contributed to the Redskins' blowing fourth-quarter leads.

"I characterize this as a team with a lot of guts," Joe Gibbs said on the eve of their opening playoff game against Chicago. "It hasn't played as well as we might have liked at times, but it's played with guts."

Against the Bears, they lacked discipline, offensive imagination, and consistency. Chicago's famed "46-defense" recorded 7 sacks while John Riggins found little room to run. An injury to starting guard Ken Huff, a handful of long plays from the Bears' offense, and an uncharacteristic rash of seven penalties—including a costly roughing-the-punter call that prolonged a Chicago touchdown drive—also buried the Redskins during a 23–19 loss.

"Realistically, we've been dancing in a minefield all season and it all just ended Sunday," defensive coordinator Richie Petitbon said after the game.

Despite winning a Super Bowl, two conference championships, three division titles, and forty-two of their previous fifty-two games, criticism befell the head coach, specifically his play calling. When John Riggins didn't rush for 100 yards, Gibbs was blamed for being too predictable. When Joe Theismann was sacked or the passing game faltered, Gibbs was blamed for abandoning the Redskins' "bread and butter," its running game.

"Gibbs turned his back on himself when he turned away from Riggins and his Hogs in the fourth quarter Sunday," *Washington Post* columnist Thomas Boswell wrote. "Hopefully during his winter of introspection, Gibbs will rediscover his faith in his men and them in him. . . . A game or even a season might be lost without lasting damage. But not the faith—the faith in each other that lets you fail together and still take pride in the fight. Whether the Redskins will keep intact that bond of faith in mutual risk that links them remains to be seen."

The commentary bothered Gibbs, who was not shy about challenging media criticisms, most often a newspaper's choice of headline.

"I don't have to 'rediscover' faith in the players, because I've never lost it. In fact, that's the thing I hold closest to me, the thing that's most precious to me, the feeling between the players and me. I think that's the one thing we have, more than anything else—a faith in each other."

"I don't plan to abandon anything," he said. "I'm not down about this season. I'm down that we didn't go farther. We came up short, but we'll go on and do great things next year."

Boswell's column kick-started a surprisingly tumultuous off-season for the Redskins and especially Joe Gibbs, who now had to debunk far fewer "genius" labels than in previous years.

"People turn on you so fast," he said. "The only people who would hurt me are the people who have spent their life in football. And there isn't one of those people who would say that the Redskins' offense is predictable."

Gibbs's ego or self-confidence wasn't damaged by the stress, but his body was. Late in the 1984 season, he tired much more easily during his routine jogging and even felt pains in his chest. Doctors eased his mind, saying there was nothing medically wrong and declaring the short-term effects were due to stress and not enough exercise. Still, to some of those close to him, Gibbs seemed a bit different as the season wore on.

That preseason, he stunned players by storming off the field in the middle of a subpar practice and not returning. Gibbs's passion and demand for perfection were often lauded, and not seen as a concern or sign of weakness. To a few people there was, however, something unusual about Gibbs. Mark May noted that Gibbs was "more laid-back" when he first arrived in Washington. Darryl Grant said, "If there's a change in Coach Gibbs, it's in how he reacts to the pressures. The expectations are so high now."

"I've heard people say that I've changed and that's bothered me,"

Gibbs said. "Someone very close to me told me that I had changed after we won the Super Bowl and that scared me. I've tried to go back in my life and ask myself, 'Am I getting caught up in it?' because I don't want to."

But for Gibbs change was inevitable. And throughout 1985—the off-season, the preseason, and the regular season—the Washington Redskins underwent a complete makeover, seeking to keep pace with the rest of a stacked conference. Not only did the list of NFC contenders include Bill Walsh's 49ers, whom Washington barely defeated at home in the 1983 conference title game and went on to win a second Super Bowl at the end of the next season, but it also featured two far younger and far more aggressive teams, the Giants and Bears, both of whom had beaten Washington the previous season.

"It's like the theory of the dinosaur," Gibbs said that off-season, "adapt or die."

Gibbs's use of the word "dinosaur" was fitting: at the end of the 1984 season, the Redskins had the oldest roster in professional football, something he, Bobby Beathard, and the front office worked feverishly to fix.

George Starke, thirteen-year veteran and "Head Hog" of the offensive line did not survive training camp cuts. The same was true for defensive tackle Perry Brooks, kick returner Mike Nelms, and Tony McGee, the thirty-six-year-old pass rusher who couldn't overcome the effects of knee surgery. They all soon retired, as did Mark Murphy, the standout safety and one of the team's defensive leaders.

The eight-year veteran could not come to contractual terms with the team the following spring, especially after the club insisted "you'll have to prove yourself" to meet his demands. He was waived before minicamp. Speculation was that his prominent role in the union's negotiations during the 1982 players' strike hastened his contract disagreement and caused the league's other twenty-seven teams to avoid signing him.

"It's hard for a player to end his career the way he wants to," he said. "I know I can still play, but if it doesn't work out, I'll just get on with the rest of my life." Murphy soon enrolled at Georgetown University Law School—he had completed his MBA at American University two years earlier—and eventually became one of the league's most respected executives as president and CEO of the Green Bay Packers.

Another former Pro Bowler and vital member of the Redskins' Super Bowl roster had also played his final game for Washington. Wide receiver Charlie Brown skipped minicamp in May. Beset by several injuries throughout the 1984 regular season, Brown disliked his limited role in the playoff loss to Chicago. Equally displeased with his contract and sidelined by another preseason injury, Brown was traded in late August. With Alvin Garrett waived that spring and Virgil Seay released the previous November, the Smurfs' rise to fame was short-lived.

The Redskins shipped Brown to the Falcons, where his previous offensive coordinator, Dan Henning, was now the head coach. In Atlanta, he also reunited with Alvin Garrett and running back Joe Washington, who had been angered when the Redskins dealt him away in April.

"In other folks' circumstance if they had a situation where they were injured, they were always given the chance to come back," Washington said days after the trade. "I guess I'm a little disgusted with that other guys have missed whole seasons themselves and haven't been able to come back. I have been able to do it. [They] decided I was expendable. I wouldn't say I'm bitter, but I am disappointed in them."

General manager Bobby Beathard regretted dealing away the popular back, but Washington would be thirty-two years old that September and another knee injury (he had five knee surgeries during his pro career) cost him nine games the previous season. And by obtaining an extra draft choice as part of the deal with Atlanta, Beathard was able to add more youth to the roster.

"It was a tough decision to make," Beathard said. "We felt that we had to go with a younger guy."

The player Beathard preferred was George Rogers, whom the Redskins had just acquired from New Orleans in exchange for their first-round draft choice. The 1980 Heisman Trophy winner and the next spring's top overall pick, the former University of South Carolina running back had fallen out of favor with the Saints' organization. Following his All-Pro rookie season, Rogers admitted to cocaine abuse while testifying before a grand jury that investigated a teammate for drug trafficking. Rogers underwent treatment at a rehab clinic in Florida and returned to form. But during the 1984 season he started losing carries to new teammate Earl Campbell. A thorough background check assured Beathard and Gibbs that Rogers had reformed.

"He's a heck of a back, a great athlete and also a great guy," Gibbs said. "The most impressive thing to me was that almost everyone started out by saying, 'George is a great guy.'"

Tapped as the heir apparent to thirty-six-year-old John Riggins, Rogers was glad to leave behind the lousy Saints for the Redskins and the best offensive line in football. "It's a second chance for me," he said.

FOR A SECOND STRAIGHT YEAR, Washington stumbled in the early weeks of the 1985 season. The new-look Redskins were trounced (by a combined 65 points) in road losses to Dallas and Chicago, they failed to score a touchdown in a home defeat by Philadelphia, and nearly blew a 13-point lead against the feeble Houston Oilers. At the start of October, the Redskins were 1-3, with several starters injured and frustrations mounting. Reporters were quick to ask Joe Gibbs how the beginning of this season compared to his 0-5 start in 1981, his first year as head coach.

"That was brutal. . . . This is too," he muttered.

Behind a defense that now had one of the best pass rushes in the NFL—Dexter Manley tied a team record with 15 sacks that season—the Redskins climbed within one game of first place in the NFC East race, winning four of their next five. Following a 44–10 win over Atlanta, the Redskins' championship hopes were resuscitated.

"I am amazed that we are back," said center Rick Donnalley, who filled in for an injured Jeff Bostic. "We have made an excellent turnaround. I can't honestly say I expected it the whole time, especially when were 1-3. But now we're talking Super Bowl again, like we usually do."

The optimism died quickly after their rematch with Dallas. The Cowboys shut Washington out through the first three periods, and then quashed a fourth-quarter comeback by intercepting a pass by Joe Theismann on the game's final play.

"It seemed like we had to get out of a hole all day," Theismann said after the 13–7 loss. "They are playing as well as I've ever seen them in twelve years of lining up against the Cowboys."

The thirty-six-year-old quarterback, who was sacked 6 times and had several passes batted down at the line of scrimmage, had been picked off 8 times in the two losses to Dallas. Through ten games, Theismann had 8 touchdown passes and 16 interceptions. For the first time in seven years, Theismann's place as the Redskins' starting quarterback was in jeopardy.

"Joe had struggled up to that point in the season, especially the day before against Dallas," Charley Casserly recollected. "There was a discussion of whether to bench Joe and play [backup] Jay Schroeder. The decision was to stay with Joe."

Following the loss to Dallas, the Redskins hosted the New York Giants at RFK Stadium on *Monday Night Football*. With the game tied at 7 and Washington facing a first-and-ten at their own 46-yard line, Theismann handed off to John Riggins, who pitched the ball back to the quarterback. The flea-flicker didn't fool New York's top-ranked aggressive defense. The pocket collapsed around Theismann, who eluded linebacker Harry Carson, but not Lawrence Taylor. As the two-time Defensive Player of the Year brought him to the ground, Taylor's massive thigh crunched Theismann's planted right leg, just below the knee. Taylor's teammate, Gary Reasons, swooped in to secure the tackle, falling onto the pile.

Taylor—who heard Theismann yelling, "You motherfuckers broke my leg!"—frantically signaled to the Washington sideline to send out the medical staff, who rushed onto the field.

"I heard a *pow pow*, like two muzzled gunshots. It was my leg breaking. The pain was beyond my description," Theismann later recalled. "I never went into shock. I said, 'Please call my mom and dad and let them know I'm okay.' Joe Gibbs kneeled down on my right side and said, 'Joe, for six years we've been together. Joe, you've meant so much to this football team. Joe, this is a heck of a mess you've left me in.' We both chuckled."

As team trainer Bubba Tyer, team orthopedic surgeon Dr. Charles Jackson, and several others attended to Theismann, L.T. walked around the field, noticeably distraught. After several minutes Theismann was wheeled off the field—the crowd cheered and applauded—and into a tunnel where the stretcher was loaded onto an ambulance headed for Arlington Hospital. Inside, one of the D.C. Fire Department paramedics, William McLaughlin, helped Theismann remove his white #7 jersey, which McLaughlin kept, setting off a thorough investigation by the fire department, the police department's internal affairs division, and the U.S. Attorney's office. The press learned about the missing jersey when McLaughlin's wife called a Silver Spring, Maryland, novelty store to ask how much money the jersey would fetch.

"Theismann's my man," McLaughlin later said during a press conference the fire department called to apologize.

At Arlington Hospital, X-rays revealed that in addition to breaking his tibia and fibula, one of the shattered bones had sliced through the skin on his lower leg. That night, doctors performed a forty-minute surgery to set the broken bones; a follow-up procedure to close the wound was performed two days later.

The grisly injury—replayed in slow motion several times during ABC's broadcast—inspired thousands to send their best wishes to the affable quarterback, whose advertisements and endorsements gave him a national presence. The hospital received balloons, stuffed animals, candy, cards, more than one hundred arrangements of flowers, and over five hundred phone calls from fans. A spokesman told the press that Theismann asked for fans to send donations to the Children's Hospital Development Center instead of gifts and flowers. He also received get-well messages from Bears head coach Mike Ditka, 49ers head coach Bill Walsh, NFL commissioner Pete Rozelle, Secretary of Defense Caspar Weinberger, and the entire Dallas Cowboys defensive backfield.

In the nation's capital, the story trumped global politics. Several nights that week, local news stations led with the injury, not the historic peace summit in Geneva, Switzerland, which featured the first meeting of President Reagan and Soviet president Mikhail Gorbachev. Inside the walls of Capitol Hill, Theismann's leg was also an engrossing topic, and, for one member of Congress, a chance to make political hay.

Asked what role the First Lady would play in the Geneva talks, White House chief of staff Donald Regan told reporters that women didn't understand or care to follow nuclear strategy and human rights, saying "some women will, but most women—believe me, your readers for the most part if you took a poll—would rather read the human interest stuff of what happened."

Illinois's representative from the 16th district, Republican Lynn Martin, responded to Regan's comment on the floor of the House of Representatives.

"On Tuesday, I had lunch with a number of my male colleagues and their conversation, as befits those not lucky enough to be Bears fans, was about the dreadful accident that befell the quarterback of the Washington Redskins. From this, I have determined that males read sports pages and know very little about what happens—or care—in Geneva."

"That was bigger than the cold war at that time," remembered *Washington Post* writer Gary Pomerantz, who along with colleague Michael Wilbon left the press box right after Theismann's injury, got in a cab, and followed the ambulance to Arlington Hospital. "That was the magic of the Redskins. The Redskins had that unique abil- ity to unite Washington's two sectors: the political sector and that urban core. And I'm not sure anything else can do that, at least not in that kind of hyperadrenalized way where everybody was together and everybody was all in.

"So when Theismann went down and had his leg snapped in such a gruesome way by Lawrence Taylor on national TV, on the Monday night game, that's all anyone would talk about for weeks. It mattered that much."

The city consumed every piece of news they could regarding Theismann's injury. His fiancée, television actress Cathy Lee Crosby, who rushed from the owner's box with security guards to join Theis- mann in the ambulance, briefed reporters until he was healthy enough for a midweek press conference at the hospital. In a wheelchair, wear- ing an elaborately patterned kimono-like robe, Theismann addressed the media with his doctor and Crosby beside him.

Amid jokes about Joe Gibbs ripping the flea-flicker out of his playbook and assurances that his NFL career was not over, Theis- mann spoke about how the fans treated him before and after break- ing his leg.

"The criticism prior to the game was criticism I brought on myself. I wasn't having a good season. I was playing lousy football, and the fans let me know in the only way they know how," he said. "But the ovation that I got leaving that stadium. . . . It's the kind of thing I'll always remember."

During that same press conference, Theismann admitted that

out of sheer curiosity, he had watched—against his fiancée's advice—a videotape of the play that resulted in his compound fracture. He shut the television off afterward, declaring, "I don't care to see it again."

HOURS AFTER SUFFERING the most famous injury in NFL history, Joe Theismann laid on a gurney inside Arlington Hospital, waiting to be wheeled into emergency surgery. Before the anesthesia kicked in, Theismann watched, "on a little black-and-white TV they hooked up with a coat hanger for an antenna," the team he had led for the previous 71 games continue on without him.

Throughout the second quarter, the Redskins weathered the loss of their starting quarterback: at halftime the score remained 7–7. But in the third quarter, Washington grabbed the lead. Theismann's replacement, strong-armed second-year quarterback Jay Schroeder, connected on a 50-yard pass to Art Monk that set up John Riggins for a rushing touchdown.

"That certainly was a unique situation," Schroeder said. "Once I was playing, I was too busy to be nervous. But I never had any doubts about my ability and I still don't."

Schroeder's confidence remained even after the Giants pulled ahead of Washington late in the third quarter. Trailing 21–14, he engineered a ten-play drive that resulted in a field goal. After a second successful onside kick, Schroeder marched the offense 46 yards, hitting tight end Clint Didier on a slant for the go-ahead touchdown with less than nine minutes remaining. With Joe Theismann now under anesthetic and in the operating room, cornerback Vernon Dean intercepted a pass by Phil Simms to preserve a 23–21 victory.

"This game is for Joe!" someone yelled in the winning locker room.

Schroeder's fantastic performance—13 completions for 221 yards and the game-winning touchdown pass—won him both great praise from his head coach and faith from his teammates.

"For a guy who never took a snap to fill the shoes he did, it's just a feat, I still have a hard time believing it," Dave Butz said.

"Schroeder was great," Gibbs added. "When he came to the sideline, I'll tell you the man wasn't even perspiring. I think he's going to be an unusual guy."

Toward the end of the schedule, Schroeder completed 52 percent of his passes, for 1,168 yards and 4 touchdowns, as Washington went 4–1 down the stretch.

For their last game of the regular season, Washington traveled to St. Louis to play the Cardinals. A win, in addition to a San Francisco loss the next day to the Cowboys (who had already secured the NFC East title), would earn Washington the NFC's last wild card spot. The irony of actively rooting for the Cowboys was not lost on the media or Joe Gibbs, who admitted, "I don't like having to depend on the Cowboys for anything."

But first they had to defeat St. Louis on the road in the snow, and they had to do so without their starting running back. Two weeks after Joe Theismann broke his leg, John Riggins took a pounding in the loss to San Francisco and suffered dizzy spells. He would sit out the remainder of the season. In his place, George Rogers became the Redskins' feature back. And although he turned out several huge games in Riggins's absence—gaining 245 yards and 3 touchdowns in back-to-back wins—he was plagued by fumbles, including 3 in a Week Fifteen win over Cincinnati.

A week later, with a playoff chance on the line against the Cardinals, Rogers again coughed the ball up, on the first play from scrimmage.

"I was worried Coach Joe Gibbs wouldn't play me after the fumble," said Rogers, who turned the ball over 6 times that season and had already been benched once that year for fumbling. "I'm glad he did."

Gibbs not only let Rogers remain in the game, he gave him the ball on nearly half of the Redskins' offensive plays.

"Usually when he fumbles, he goes into a complete depression," Gibbs said of Rogers. "He usually goes to the bench, no one can talk to him, and he throws all his stuff down on the ground. But after he fumbled today, he came over to me and said, 'I'm gonna make up for that.'"

Rogers atoned for his fumble, totaling a team-record 206 yards rushing on 34 carries as Washington overcame an early deficit to defeat St. Louis, 27–16.

"We finished strong," Gibbs said after the Redskins' third straight win. "I hope we get another chance next week, but it's out of our hands."

The next day, however, San Francisco defeated Dallas 31–16, ensuring that Washington would miss the playoffs for the first time in four years, despite a 10-6 record.

Even Joe Gibbs could not always deliver a second chance.

CHAPTER 6

The Classic-Style Quarterback

LESS THAN a year after moving from Boston to Washington, D.C., in 1937, the Redskins won their first NFL championship, defeating George Halas's mighty Chicago Bears at Wrigley Field. Five years later, led by quarterback Sammy Baugh, they won a second title, cementing their status as one of the league's model franchises. At the same time, the team's owner, George Preston Marshall, developed a reputation of his own.

"He was widely considered one of pro football's greatest innovators," esteemed *Washington Post* sportswriter Shirley Povich wrote, "and its leading bigot."

Hailing from segregated West Virginia, Marshall considered himself a southerner and held less than progressive thoughts on race relations: a Civil War Confederate flag was among his family's most treasured possessions. In the summer of 1959, as a challenge to the emerging civil rights movement, he ordered the lyrics of the Redskins' fight song changed from "Fight for Old D.C." to "Fight for Old Dixie."

By then every other pro football franchise had already integrated their rosters to include at least one African American player. As Povich explained to his readers in 1960—a season in which Washington would win just one game—great players such as the Baltimore Colts' African American running back Lenny Moore were "ineligible for the Redskins, whose colors are burgundy, gold, and Caucasian."

An all-white Redskins roster was no coincidence.

"[Marshall] did not pretend there were no blacks good enough to make his team," wrote Andy Piascik, author of *Gridiron Gauntlet: The Story of the Men Who Integrated Pro Football in Their Own Words*. "Unlike the others, he was honest enough to admit that he simply didn't want them around."

In 1961, pressure to integrate the Redskins mounted, from the public, media, and even the federal government. Throughout that year, United States Secretary of the Interior Stewart L. Udall demanded the Redskins add an African American player. If they did not, Udall threatened to ban the team from using the federally owned National Park Service land where D.C. Stadium (later renamed RFK Stadium) had been built. Udall even hand-picked the perfect player to break the team's unofficial color ban.

"Well, through no fault of mine, [Marshall] has the first choice in the draft, and it has been customary I think. . . . . The Heisman Trophy winner is usually pretty close to the top," Udall told reporters, referring to Syracuse running back Ernie Davis. "I am no football expert. But I think [Marshall] has a very nice solution. Unfortunately, I haven't been able to go to many games locally this year. But I think he has a very nice solution that would be good for us and would be wonderful for the Washington Redskins club."

Davis, however, did not want to play for the Redskins. After they drafted him first overall, he hinted to the Associated Press that Washington wouldn't give him the contract he wanted. Shirley Povich later wrote that Davis simply didn't want to be on a team owned by George Preston Marshall, saying, "I won't play for that SOB."

To resolve the standoff, the Redskins traded Davis to the Cleveland Browns, in exchange for a lower first-round draft pick and a twenty-six-year-old African American halfback named Bobby Mitchell. The former seventh-round pick—who that season was joined by African American Redskins teammates John Nisby and Ron Hatcher—transitioned from a good runner, consistent pass catcher, and excellent return man for Cleveland into the NFL's best wide receiver. In his first three seasons with the Redskins, Mitchell twice led the league in receiving yards, once in receiving touchdowns, and was selected to the Pro Bowl each year.

"I've played Bobby many times, and it's inevitable that you're going to be beat by a great one like him," said New York Giants Pro Bowl defensive back Erich Barnes, who watched Mitchell score 2 long touchdowns in Week Seven of the 1962 season. "He can hold his own with anyone, anywhere, even on the moon. You blink your eyes and he's gone."

But total integration and the emergence of African American stars such as Mitchell, Moore, Jim Brown, Gale Sayers, O. J. Simpson, Deacon Jones, Paul Warfield, Mean Joe Greene, and others didn't exactly wash away the league's history of racial bias.

Throughout the next two decades the quarterback fraternity remained the most segregated clubs in all of sports: few black quarterbacks reached the NFL and only a handful saw playing time. By 1977, only one African American had ever started a postseason game, and a sixth-round pick was the highest any NFL team was willing to spend on an African American quarterback.

"There was a belief that blacks were not bright enough, that we didn't have the ability to lead," Marlin Briscoe said in 2004. "Most of the players in the league were white, and most were from southern schools where they never had a black teammate, let alone a quarterback. I knew that if I didn't have success, it would be a long time before someone else got the chance. People would say, 'I told you so.'"

As a rookie for the Denver Broncos, Briscoe proved himself, throwing 14 touchdown passes in five starts during the 1968 season.

"I played well enough," Briscoe later said, "that nobody could say, 'I told you so.'"

So, too, would Doug Williams.

THREE MONTHS BEFORE Rosa Park's Montgomery bus boycott, Douglas Lee Williams was born on August 9, 1955. Raised in Zachary, Louisiana, a small town fifteen miles north of Baton Rouge, Williams experienced the Deep South's racism from an early age.

"I used to see crosses burning every Friday night," he later said. "They burned a cross at each intersection. We couldn't go out of the house after dark because we didn't know what would happen."

In the daytime, however, he and his four brothers ran around outside for hours. Although they played football with a plastic Clorox bottle stuffed with a sock and enjoyed basketball—Doug admired local legend Pete Maravich and wore floppy socks similar to "the Pistol"—baseball was his true love. Doug wanted to emulate his much-older brother Robert, who pitched in the Cleveland Indians farm system. Beginning as a six-year-old in Little League he did just that: the first team Doug played for was the Zachary Indians. And by age fifteen Doug was also a phenomenal pitcher for Chaneyville High.

Robert Williams retired from the minor leagues after a shoulder injury in 1965. He returned home to teach and coach at Chaneyville. In 1970, as part of an "exchange program," he transferred to the predominantly white Central High in East Baton Rouge, becoming their first African American teacher and coach. That summer, he also took over as head coach of the local all-white American Legion summer baseball team, sponsored by Sealtest Ice Cream. Robert brought five players from Chaneyville, including Doug, onto the team.

"Even Sealtest thought that Central was [still] an all-white team, they did not know," Williams said. "All coaches had to show up for this meeting. . . . I showed up and a gentleman asked me why was I there. I told him I was there for a baseball meeting. He said, 'I think you're in the wrong place.' I said, 'No, I think I'm in the right place.' He said, 'Who are you?' I said, "I'm Robert Williams from Sealtest Ice Cream.' Boy, you could hear a rat run across that floor."

To open the season, the integrated Central team played the league's all-white defending champion. When Robert Williams's team arrived for the game, his players were told they could not take the field if a black man coached the team. The team's previous head coach, Archie McClure, was at the game and stepped in to resolve the situation.

"The guy said, 'There's no black coaches in the league,' then my daddy said, 'No, I'm the head coach, and he's my assistant coach," recalled McClure's son, Leo. "That way we were allowed to play. I hate to say it, but we were like a traveling freak show: 'Come over here and see the integrated baseball team!'"

Pitching to catcher Leo McClure, Doug Williams struck out 15 batters as Central won. The team's African American players needed to be escorted by the parents of the team's white players from Howell Park back to Zachary, "because there were people threatening to do harm to us." Later that season, at LSU Stadium, Williams struck out 18 batters in a six-inning game, giving up only 2 hits.

"He struck out every batter," Leo McClure said. "I remember the umpire asking me, he was leaning over my shoulder and he knew me, 'Leo, is he this good?' I said, 'He can throw any pitch he wants in any count.'"

As great a baseball player as Doug was, his brother Robert steered him toward football beginning in the eighth grade; he hoped to toughen his little brother up.

"Doug did not want to play football, but I forced him to play," Robert said. "I gave him a choice of either playing or whippin' me. So he knew he could not whip me so he decided he would play."

Just five feet five inches and 155 pounds at the time, Williams shed his fear of contact, and as a freshman his arm strength landed him a spot as the backup quarterback for the varsity team. After a growth spurt, he started for Chaneyville as a junior and was approached by former Grambling State University football player Adolph Byrd, who informally recruited players for the school. Grambling State was a natural fit—Robert was an alumnus, as were a handful of Williams's high school coaches, friends, and extended family members. The only other school he considered signing with was the University of Southern California. As a fourteen-year-old in 1969, Williams became a fan of the Trojans when head coach John McKay started a sophomore African American quarterback named Jimmy Jones.

"There were only two schools I wanted to play for out of high school, either Grambling or USC, mainly because of Jimmy Jones," Williams said. "Besides Jimmy Raye at Michigan State, there weren't many black quarterbacks playing at the major universities. So I was a fan of SC, mainly because of that."

But McKay and the Trojans—who won twenty-two games and a Rose Bowl with Jones—didn't recruit Williams to Southern California in 1973. Still, he relished the opportunity to play close to home and for another revered head coach, Grambling's Eddie Robinson.

"In 1973, playing quarterback was almost obsolete in the south at the Division I schools," Williams said. "They hadn't got there yet. It was schools like Southern, Grambling, Jackson State, Tennessee State, Mississippi Valley. . . . But Eddie Robinson, to me, stood out, and that was the biggest reason . . . I ended up going to Grambling."

Robinson, beginning the thirty-third year of an incredible fifty-seven-year tenure as Grambling State's head coach, redshirted his freshman recruit, but called on Williams midway through the 1974 season. An injured wrist in the first quarter against Tennessee State sent starter Joe Comeaux to the sideline and Williams onto the field. The Tigers won that day and with Williams starting their next six games Grambling State finished 10-1 and qualified for the Pelican Bowl. Against South Carolina State at Tulane Stadium, Williams threw 1 touchdown and ran for another in a 28–7 victory that clinched Robinson his fourth Black College National Championship, the annually voted-up title awarded to the nation's top team among historically black colleges or universities.

Guiding the Tigers to a 17-6 record, Williams developed into an exceptional passer over the next two seasons. Following a great 1976 season, he was given the Mutual Black Network All-American Offensive Player of the Year award during a banquet at the Americana Hotel in New York City. The next December, he hoped to return to the Big Apple to accept an even more prestigious trophy.

As a senior, the six-foot-four-inch, 218-pound quarterback led the Tigers to nine wins and a place in the first-ever Mirage Bowl. The Tigers defeated Temple University at the Tokyo Dome in Japan and ultimately claimed their second National Black College Championship in four seasons. But Williams's own personal chase with the history books attracted far more scrutiny that fall.

Thirty-four touchdown passes and a Division I–record 2,974 passing yards that season made Williams the first African American quarterback to be named a First-Team All-American by the Associated Press. National sportswriters and reporters from all three television networks (ABC, CBS, and NBC) flocked to campus to interview the player with the words "black Joe Namath" handwritten above his locker. The governor of Louisiana, Edwin Edwards, even declared October 15, 1977, as "Doug Williams Day."

His rapid rise turned him into a campus-wide superstar, but he never acted like one. Despite his success he still drove his rundown orange Volkswagen through Zachary's Main Street, still hung out at Delafosse's Barber Shop on campus, and still dated the same girl, Janice Goss, whom he called "Gossie May." At a Grambling State football banquet after the season ended, Williams accepted a trophy honoring him as the team MVP, but not before he and his brother

Mike constructed homemade trophies and presented one to each of his offensive linemen.

"He was always down-to-earth. . . . He knows where he's from, he's grounded," Williams's Grambling State teammate and decades-long friend Herb Nelson said in 2014. "Just because he was a senior or a junior he never looked down on you, he was always friendly. I remember nights when he'd come home from Zachary, his grandmother—they called her Ma B—used to make buttermilk pies and he'd share them with us. . . . He had a loving-kind heart, always."

All the national interest he received was in anticipation of the Heisman Trophy balloting: no African American quarterback had ever been in such close competition for the greatest award in college sports. When the votes were tallied in early December, Williams was not among the three finalists. Finishing fourth, Williams was not invited to New York City's Hilton Hotel, where, for the first time, the Heisman Trophy announcement was broadcast live in primetime on CBS.

"As a kid, eighteen, nineteen years old, I never believed he would get it," Herb Nelson said. "Being black, number one, being from a black college, number two. We always said if it had been a white boy who did all this he would have gotten it."

Although he missed out on the Heisman, the next spring Williams was expected to set another milestone: NFL scouts saw him as a first-round draft pick. And unlike other talented, accomplished African American college quarterbacks, Williams did not attract scouts who only wanted to switch him to another position.

Four years as a starter for Grambling State and his poise in handling the Heisman Trophy hoopla suggested Williams could make the transition from small college to the pros. And the old, tired skepticisms about an African American quarterback's inability to grasp complex NFL offenses did not seem to pollute Williams's draft stock.

"I haven't found anything that he lacks to make it in professional football," Packers longtime scout Baby Ray said that winter. "He has size, arm, and intelligence. . . . He has more self-discipline than any quarterback I've seen from the small school since, well, probably [Terry] Bradshaw. . . . He's a passer, he's not just a wind-up thrower who lets it all go and hopes it lands in the receiver's arms. He thinks out on the field. He has tremendous self-discipline and leadership. He loves the game. He's the kind you want leading your team."

The criticism he did receive—other than the concern over the level of competition he faced at Grambling State—were veiled compliments that continued throughout his professional career. Some skeptics claimed that he threw the football *too* hard.

"Code for 'We weren't smart enough, we didn't have any touch,'" Williams later explained.

Code or not, Williams's arm strength still fascinated people around the NFL.

"I'm not talking about one of the best arms in college," said former Grambling State quarterback James Harris, who tutored Williams in the off-season. "I'm talking about one of the best in football, period. There are very few guys in the pros who can throw any better."

Harris knew what it took to play quarterback in the NFL. Not only was "Shack" the highest-drafted African American quarterback of his time—the Buffalo Bills selected him in the eighth round in 1969—Harris was the only one to start an NFL playoff game, starting three for the Los Angeles Rams in 1974 and 1975.

"I knew this, being drafted in Buffalo in 1969, that's a tough job," Williams said. "But never one time did Shack ever say to me, you going to have a tough time because you're black. Never. What he always told me—and I think we both came up under a guy [Eddie Robinson] that made sure we both understood this—whatever you wanted to do, you could only do it because you were in America. America was the only place that's going to give you an opportunity to do what we were doing. He used to always say, 'Remember, if you can do it at Grambling, you can do it anywhere.'"

The Tampa Bay Buccaneers, desperately in need of a quarter-back, scouted Williams as intently as any team. During the national media storm over Williams, prior to the Heisman Trophy announce-ment, the Buccaneers director of pro personnel, Ken Herock, said, "He's the best black quarterback ever to come out of college."

Nearing the draft, Tampa Bay's head coach John McKay—the same man who entrusted his high-powered offense to Jimmy Jones nine years earlier—sent a member of his staff to evaluate the pros-pect. At Carroll High School in Monroe, where the education major was volunteering as a student-teacher, Doug Williams met Joe Gibbs, the Bucs' new, first-time offensive coordinator. In between classes and lunch with Williams and his girlfriend, Janice, at McDonald's, Gibbs administered a handful of pop quizzes to test the quarter-back's football knowledge.

"I put things on the board, then I would erase them, and I'd come back to them and he was right there," Gibbs later recalled. "When I came back, I said I think the guy's bright and works well with people."

Gibbs made the same impression on Doug Williams, who was accustomed to playing for one of the most respected men in football.

"Coach Gibbs and Coach [Eddie Robinson] had so many simi-larities when it comes to people," Williams said. "Both of them had excellent people skills. I don't think they ever met anybody that they couldn't stand up and hold a conversation with. I don't think either one of them ever was a standoff individual. They understood people; they liked people. But I also think both of them knew how to choose people, character-wise."

Convinced Williams's arm could lift the Bucs out of their his-torically awful start—they had just snapped their NFL-record twenty-six-game losing skid—Tampa Bay chose Williams with the seventeenth overall pick in that May's draft. For the expansion team that had won just two games in two seasons, Williams was seen as a savior.

"It's like Coach Rob told the press the day of the draft," Williams said in May 1978. "He told them, 'Doug's no Moses,' and I know that I can't turn water into wine. I know I can't make chicken salad out of chicken feathers. But I'm going to try my best."

A contract dispute cost Williams the first week of training camp, and as a result, the rookie fell behind in learning the Buccaneers' complicated offense. With the help of Joe Gibbs, Williams caught up.

"After each day, after meetings at night, we'd be done at 8:30, nine o'clock, and I'd follow Coach Gibbs home every night to go over the playbook," Williams remembered. "His wife, Pat, would fix dinner for us, I'm sitting there with [the Gibbs's sons] J.D. and Coy. So it was just like me being part of the family. . . . I never forgot the fact that, here's a guy that didn't know me from Adam, but he took me to his house and sat me down at his table with his wife and two boys."

Now in command of the playbook, Williams saw most of the Buccaneers' first-team snaps during the preseason and showed great promise throughout the exhibition schedule. By Week One of the regular season, Williams had clearly earned the starter's job.

"The so-called general manager of the Buccaneers, Phil Krueger, he had made a statement in the press that Doug Williams probably would not play this year, because he needed to learn the system and get accustomed to professional football," recalled Jimmie Giles, the Buccaneers tight end who played against Williams twice in college. "But it was so evident, when Doug Williams stepped on the practice field for the first time, that nobody could touch him in terms of talent and intellect that was on that field. Eddie Robinson had truly prepared this man to be a professional quarterback in the NFL. The talent was so far above everybody else's, everybody knew it."

He started ten games that season, winning four of them and twice fashioning a pair of comeback wins for the team that was slowly crawling out of the cellar. Apart from his personal stats and victories, Williams's toughness also won the rookie great respect: he fought back from a shoulder injury and a broken jaw to return to the starting lineup.

Gibbs left Tampa for San Diego prior to the 1979 season, but Williams developed into a clutch passer. He directed three fourth-quarter comebacks on the road as the Bucs captured the NFC Central division title with a 10-6 record, achieving more wins than the team's first three seasons combined. They defeated Philadelphia in the second round of the playoffs, but in the NFC Championship Game, against the Los Angeles Rams, Williams overthrew several passes and the entire Bucs offense failed to score in a 9–0 loss. A torn biceps sidelined him in the third quarter. Despite the injury and the remarkably successful season, Williams drew harsh criticism from the fans and media.

Coach John McKay vehemently defended his quarterback. "Twice, Williams called the right audible to get what we needed," McKay said. "Both times, the receiver ran another pattern—the one called in the huddle. The receiver put in his own pattern and that leaves the quarterback high and dry."

The Buccaneers returned to the playoffs in both 1981 and 1982, but Williams's tenure in Tampa Bay was never smooth despite winning twenty-four starts in a three-year span. He completed less than 50 percent of his passes, threw more interceptions than touchdowns, and became the butt of a popular joke around town, thanks to a local reporter who wrote, "They ought to send Doug Williams to Iran because he is the only man who could overthrow the Ayatollah."

Some despicable Buccaneers fans expressed their criticism by mailing Williams degrading, hateful notes, "nigger letters," as he called them.

"A number of things happened," Robert Williams later said. "I used to go to the football games and you could hear the racist slurs and people saying things. I remembered one time where he got a big box that came to his house and there was a watermelon in there. The [note inside said,] 'N—, take this and see if you can throw it.'"

Williams's claim as the franchise's quarterback took another hit once his contract expired following the 1982 season. His $120,000 salary that year was not only the lowest of any starting quarterback in the NFL, it was also lower than eighteen backup quarterbacks. The quarterback who hadn't missed a regular-season start in more than four seasons wanted a substantial raise. Hugh Culverhouse, the team's notoriously parsimonious owner, refused to meet his demands. As a restricted free agent, any team who signed Williams would have to give Tampa Bay several draft choices.

"At that time, teams owned you. If they really wanted you, they would have paid it. My guess is, they really didn't want to keep Doug because they never offered him a good-faith contract," said his leading pass catcher, All-Pro tight end Jimmie Giles. "He certainly had proven that he was a winner. He certainly had proven that he could, not only command respect, but he demanded respect on the football field. And he got it, not only from our players, from other players . . . I think people were still skeptical, they just didn't have the confidence to have a black man leading a football team. That's just the way it was."

A lengthy stalemate was destined to carry on throughout the spring and summer of 1983, but in early April of that year, fighting Culverhouse no longer mattered very much to Doug Williams.

For Easter, Williams and his wife, Janice, headed home to Zachary. With them, the recently married college sweethearts brought their eleven-week-old firstborn, Ashley. One morning, Janice woke up with a headache. A week later she was dead from complications after surgery to remove a brain tumor the size of a grapefruit.

"Suddenly, I didn't give a damn if I played another down of football or not," he said.

"He took it really hard, especially at the funeral," remembered Eddie Robinson. "They had just had the baby. They were such a lovely couple. We [Robinson and his wife, Doris,] had gone to their home and visited with them before she died. He looked like he had something snatched out of his life."

Williams's family rushed to his aid. Following the funeral, he left town for several weeks to clear his mind. His mother, Laura, and father, Robert Sr., took Ashley into their home; she lived with her grandparents throughout much of the next several years.

During his mourning, Williams and the Buccaneers remained far apart on contract terms. But as the 1983 training camp neared, Tampa Bay's director of pro personnel Ken Herock contacted Williams, who was at the Veterans Hospital in New Orleans, with his father, Robert Sr.; the World War II veteran had rheumatoid arthritis and needed surgery to amputate his leg. Williams left his family and flew to Tampa, where John McKay informed him that Culverhouse was not going to budge: $400,000 per season was his final offer. Williams, who originally sought $875,000 per season, had already agreed to come down to $600,000.

He considered signing the one-year, $400,000 deal, but general manager Phil Krueger undercut the agreement even further. After explaining to Williams, "You're not going to go to the Hall of Fame anyway," Krueger said they would take an additional $25,000 off their latest offer because Williams "hadn't been in town to help sell season tickets." Trying to dress up the offer by loading it with incentives was the final straw for Williams.

"No, Phil," he told Krueger. "I don't want any more of your 'If Money,' I've been here five years, I had no complaints, I played my behind off, I played hurt, if a guy dropped a ball, it was no problem, if a guy missed a block, it's no problem. I don't want no 'If Money.'"

Rather than remain with the franchise that refused to pay him fair-market value, Williams scorned the Buccaneers and the NFL and signed with the Oklahoma Outlaws of the newly formed United States Football League (USFL), which continued to fight for credibility. Team owner Bill Tatham Sr. welcomed Williams with a five-year, $3 million contract and a $1 million signing bonus.

"What was good for me was leaving Tampa and being [treated] the way I thought I should be . . . and going to a situation where the owners basically looked at me like family," said Williams, whose picture remains in the Tatham family house thirty years after he signed with the Outlaws. "It wasn't about football, it was about people wanting you to be part of something."

Williams also delighted in the upstart league's style of wide-open offenses as well as the opportunity to compete against great players such as Reggie White, Steve Young, Hershel Walker, and league MVP Jim Kelly. But other than a few star players scattered throughout the league, most teams lacked the depth of talent to produce consistent, quality football. The Oklahoma Outlaws were one of the league's worst teams.

In eighteen games played during the spring of 1984, Williams produced just six victories while completing less than half his passes, and throwing 15 touchdowns and 21 interceptions. Small crowds at Skelly Stadium in Tulsa forced the Outlaws to merge with the Arizona Wranglers for the following year. Again, support for the new team diminished, and after another subpar 1985 season for the Outlaws, in which Williams posted marginal statistics, the future of the team and the USFL appeared doomed. The next fall, he worked as an assistant coach for Southern University in Baton Rouge, just a few miles from where his parents cared for three-year-old Ashley, and where he was having a house built on a five-acre plot next to his sister's home.

But Joe Gibbs, Bobby Beathard, and the Washington Redskins' front office—always in search of second-chance projects—still saw value in Williams. Knowing the rival league's precarious status, they heavily scouted the USFL for players and targeted Williams in the summer of 1986. Even though Joe Gibbs was still fond of his former Tampa Bay quarterback, the Redskins' interest was based on more than loyalty; Beathard believed that "outside of Jim Kelly, we had him rated as the top quarterback in the USFL."

In August, the Redskins gave Tampa Bay a fifth-round draft choice to acquire the rights to Williams, who then signed a three-year contract with Washington. Although pleased to return to the NFL, Williams tempered his excitement. He knew that over the course of eight long, trying years, the expectations of him had changed: Joe Gibbs no longer viewed Williams the way he once did in Tampa Bay, as the quarterback around which he could build a franchise.

"They told me I would be a backup, but I'm a competitor also," he said days after arriving at the 1986 training camp. "It will be tough to sit on the side and watch the action.

"The guy that's doing the job should be playing."

"THE CLASSIC-STYLE QUARTERBACK," Joe Gibbs said in 1986, referring to Jay Schroeder. "If you drew it up, he's the way your quarterback would look."

Schroeder was six feet, four inches, 220 pounds, muscular, blond, blessed with a strong arm and excellent foot speed. Milwaukee-born and Southern-California-raised, Schroeder won a football scholarship to UCLA and a $120,000 signing bonus from the Toronto Blue Jays, who selected the catcher out of high school with the third overall pick in the 1979 MLB Draft.

Although he had memorably come off the bench to defeat archrival USC in November 1980, Schroeder gave up football after his freshman-year season in order to pursue a professional baseball career. Playing for Medicine Hat, Canada, in the Pioneer League; Florence, South Carolina, in the South Atlantic League; and Kinston, North Carolina, in the Carolina League, the outfielder/catcher/third baseman never hit over .234.

"I didn't make it in baseball because I tried to pull the sliders," he said. "It's that simple."

After hitting .206 during the 1983 Class A season (and being asked to move to pitcher) Schroeder quit baseball. Despite a four-year hiatus from competitive football, he hoped an NFL team might select him in the next spring's draft. Schroeder returned to UCLA's campus to fine-tune his passing and mechanics under the tutelage of Bruins offensive coordinator Homer Smith. To get back into football shape, he trained with his wife, Debbie, an aerobics teacher and former gymnast.

"When I left baseball, she was the receiver I practiced with," Schroeder later said. "For a good six months, she had the bruises to prove it."

Schroeder regained his sharpness as a passer and his football speed. Smith wrote letters to every NFL team requesting they come see Schroeder work out prior to the 1984 NFL Draft. Few responded to Smith, until news of Schroeder's progress circulated among scouts.

"I got very little reaction to Jay until he ran a 4.65 [in the 40-yard dash]," Smith said.

Bobby Beathard and Joe Gibbs reacted; they attended several of his workouts. His mobility reminded them of a young Joe Theismann, who had also followed an unusual path to the National Football League. The Redskins used their third-round pick on Schroeder, who was just the fourth quarterback selected in that year's draft.

"I remember Bobby working him out and coming back and raving about him and it was almost like 'Let's not even talk about this guy,'" team scout Billy Devaney said years later. "He didn't flinch, he was dying to get the guy: he thought he had all the traits to succeed as a quarterback. . . . We thought it was setting up perfect where Joe was going to play a couple of more years, Jay was going to be a developmental-type of guy."

Schroeder didn't see the field as a rookie, but with Theismann turning thirty-six years old in the fall of 1985, Washington viewed Schroeder as a promising heir apparent.

"He's a real talented guy," Gibbs told reporters during the preseason. "What he gives you is a great athlete like Joe. . . . But what I liked about him, for a guy who hasn't played very much, he is very poised. He shows no excitement. He seems to know what you're talking about."

Schroeder's growing reputation as a quick study helped save the Redskins' season after Joe Theismann's infamous injury.

"It was funny because that week leading up to it, I had a lot of people asking me if I was ready to play, between Sonny Jurgensen, Billy Kilmer, it was kind of ironic: I said I was ready to go," Schroeder said. "At halftime, Coach Gibbs and the offensive staff came to me and they said, 'What [plays] do you feel good about?' I said, 'Let's go, whatever you got.' And I think that kind of shocked them."

Schroeder was now the toast of the town. When he left the RFK Stadium locker room that evening, so many fans swarmed him that it took nearly an hour to get to his truck in the players' parking lot. The next day reporters arrived at his home, where the Schroeders were hosting their son Brian's first birthday party. A few weeks later, while Christmas shopping at a local mall, he "almost got killed" by fans who spotted him buying a snack.

Like his predecessor, Joe Theismann, Schroeder soon became a part of D.C.'s philanthropy scene. He joined the board of directors for the Ronald McDonald House, participated in the White House's Team Up Against Drugs program that spoke to high school students, assisted in a major radiothon for the Leukemia Society, and even coheadlined a star-studded fund-raiser for Joe Gibbs's Youth For Tomorrow foundation.

"Things change quickly," Schroeder said that August. "You go from being a nobody to a somebody who drives down the street causing three accidents because people are trying to see who you are. It was being in the right place at the right time for me. I'm not trying to step into anybody's shoes. I'm just trying to do my job. It's unfortunate for anyone to get hurt, but it was a good break for me."

Released from Arlington Hospital eight days after his horrific injury, Joe Theismann refused to concede that his career was over.

The Redskins' 1982 coaching staff, from left to right: (*back row*) LaVern "Torgy" Torgeson, Wayne Sevier, Dan Henning, Charley Taylor, Don Breaux, Warren "Rennie" Simmons; (*front row*) Dan Riley, Larry Peccatiello, Richie Petitbon, Joe Gibbs, Joe Bugel, Bill Hickman. August 1982. *Courtesy of the Washington Redskins*

Charter members of the Hogs, from left to right: (*back row*) Joe Jacoby, George Starke, Fred Dean, Mark May, Jeff Bostic; (*front*) Russ Grimm. November 1982. *John McDonnell* / The Washington Post *via Getty Images*

The Hogs' popularity and marketability soared following the Redskins' victory in Super Bowl XVII, and many fans started wearing Hogs T-shirts, buttons, hats, and rubber pig snouts on game day. The most celebrated group of Hogs supporters were the Hogettes, who attended games wearing dresses, women's wigs, necklaces, and handmade white leather hats. Circa 1992. *Courtesy of The Hogettes®*

Members of the 5 O'Clock Club in front of their "lodge" near Redskin Park, from left to right: (*back row*) Joe Jacoby, Ed Allen, Dave Butz, Russ Grimm, Ken Huff; (*front row*) Peter "Stretch" Williams, John Riggins, John Jenkins, William "Lego" Lamb. Circa 1984. *Photo by Nate Fine / Courtesy of Dave Butz*

John Riggins hunting near his 160-acre farm in Lawrence, Kansas. June 1983. *Ronald C. Modra*

In the locker room after Washington's 24–21 NFC Championship Game win over the 49ers, John Riggins drinks a beer. Riggins rushed for 123 yards and 2 touchdowns on 36 carries as the Redskins advanced to Super Bowl XVIII. January 8, 1984. *AP Photo / J. Scott Applewhite*

Darryl Grant steps past Tony Dorsett to score on a Cowboys pass deflected by Dexter Manley. Grant's 10-yard touchdown return midway through the fourth quarter of the NFC Championship earned Washington a 31–17 victory over Dallas and a berth in Super Bowl XVII. January 22, 1983. *Arnie Sachs / Consolidated News Photos*

Alvin Garrett, Rick "Doc" Walker, Clarence Harmon, and the other members of "The Fun Bunch" celebrate Garrett's touchdown catch late in the first half of Super Bowl XVII. The 4-yard completion tied the game at 10, but the Dolphins promptly reclaimed the lead, returning the ensuing kickoff 98 yards for a touchdown. January 30, 1983. *Walter Iooss Jr. /* Sports Illustrated */ Getty Images*

Jack Kent Cooke shows Ronald and Nancy Reagan the Vince Lombardi Trophy after Washington's 27–17 victory in Super Bowl XVII. Upon the Redskins' return to Washington from Southern California, the president and first lady greeted the Redskins on the tarmac at Dulles Airport. January 31, 1983. *Courtesy of Ronald Reagan Presidential Library*

Fans gather to cheer on the Redskins three days after Washington's win in Super Bowl XVII, the franchise's first championship game victory in forty years. Despite cold rain, an estimated 500,000 people attended the rally and parade that began in front of the District Building, continued down Constitution Avenue, and ended near the U.S. Capitol Building. February 2, 1983. *Courtesy of Kirk Mee*

Joe Theismann celebrates his touchdown pass to Alvin Garrett late in the second quarter of Super Bowl XVII at Rose Bowl Stadium. January 30, 1983. *AP Photo, File*

Trailing by 19 points late in the third quarter of Super Bowl XVIII, league MVP Joe Theismann walks off the field following a third-down sack by the Los Angeles Raiders. Theismann and the Redskins set an NFL record during that season by averaging 34 points per game, but scored only 9 in the 29-point loss to the Raiders. January 22, 1984. *AP Photo*

After suffering a gruesome broken leg in the second quarter of a *Monday Night Football* game versus the New York Giants, Joe Theismann exits the field on a stretcher as the RFK Stadium fans cheer him on. November 18, 1985. *Arnie Sachs / Consolidated News Photos*

Following the Redskins' NFC Championship Game loss to the New York Giants, Jay Schroeder exits the field at Giants Stadium with Dr. Charles Jackson (*left*) and equipment manager Jay Brunetti (*right*). In the 17–0 defeat Schroeder completed 20-of-50 attempts and suffered a concussion. January 11, 1987. *Arnie Sachs / Consolidated News Photos*

Outside Redskin Park, Washington players picket as part of a league-wide strike that started two weeks into the 1987 NFL season. The Redskins were the only team to remain completely united during the 24-day strike. September 22, 1987. *Howard Sachs / Consolidated News Photos*

Despite rarely returning punts and tearing a muscle in his chest while hurdling a would-be tackler, Darrell Green reaches the end zone for a touchdown in the third quarter of Washington's divisional playoff game against the Bears. The 50-yard punt return—only Green's sixth that season—was the difference in the Redskins 21–17 victory at Chicago's frigid Soldier Field. January 10, 1988. *Bettmann / Corbis / AP Images*

Trailing Denver 10–0 late in the first quarter of Super Bowl XXII, the Redskins lose Doug Williams to a hyperextended knee injury. Williams—the first African American quarterback to start in a Super Bowl—sat out the next two snaps but returned to lead the greatest offensive display during a single quarter in championship game history. January 31, 1988. *AP Photo / Rusty Kennedy*

Timmy Smith races past Denver's Tony Lilly for a 58-yard touchdown run in the second quarter of the Redskins' Super Bowl XXII win. In the first start of his NFL career, the rookie rushed for a Super Bowl record 204 yards on 22 carries. January 31, 1988. *AP Photo / Al Messerschmidt*

Following his MVP performance (340 yards, four touchdown passes), Doug Williams celebrates Washington's 42–10 victory in Super Bowl XXII. Behind Williams's passing and the running of Timmy Smith, the Redskins scored 35 points and gained 356 yards from scrimmage during the second quarter. January 31, 1988. *Focus on Sport / Getty Images*

President Ronald Reagan fires a pass to Ricky Sanders from the South Portico of the White House. Three days earlier, Sanders caught nine passes for 193 yards and a touchdown as Washington defeated Denver 42–10 in Super Bowl XXII. February 3, 1988. *Courtesy of Ronald Reagan Presidential Library*

A frequent visitor to the White House during his playing career in Washington, D.C., Dexter Manley (*left*) poses with West Virginia governor Gaston Caperton, art gallery owner William Doyle, and President George H. W. Bush following a ceremony honoring people who overcame learning disabilities. Manley, who recorded three sacks the previous day in a 10–3 win over Philadelphia, would be suspended by the NFL that week and never played another game for the Redskins. November 13, 1989. *AP Photo / Marcy Nighswander*

Inside Redskin Park, Bobby Beathard watches film with several members of the scouting department. From left to right: Beathard, Billy Devaney, Dick Daniels, George Saimes, Charley Casserly. July 7, 1988. *Bill Ballenberg*

Joe Gibbs diagrams one of his signature plays, the Counter Gap. Circa 1992. *AP Photo / NFL Photos*

THE POSSE

GARY CLARK   ART MONK   RICKY SANDERS

Following their historic season—in which all three recorded at least 1,000 yards receiving—Gary Clark, Art Monk, and Ricky Sanders appear on a Costacos Bros. poster. The trio's nickname, "The Posse," fit perfectly with the popular, fantastical sports poster series of the 1980s and 1990s. Circa 1990. *Courtesy of John Costacos, Inc.*

Andre Collins (55), Brad Edwards (27), Wilber Marshall (59) and Fred Stokes (60) swarm Buffalo wide receiver Andre Reed late in the second quarter of Super Bowl XXVI. Although overshadowed by their offensive teammates, Washington's defense under Joe Gibbs was frequently among the best in the NFL: in 19 games during the 1991–92 season they allowed fewer than 14 points per game and recorded three shutouts during a five-game stretch. January 26, 1992. *Rogers Photo Archive/Getty Images*

Through a hole plowed opened by Joe Jacoby (66) and Mark Schlereth (69), Gerald Riggs scores his second touchdown of Super Bowl XXVI. The two-yard rush gave Washington a 24–0 lead over Buffalo early in the third quarter. January 26, 1992. *Howard Sachs / Consolidated News Photos*

Earnest Byner (*left*) and Mark Rypien celebrate the Redskins' Super Bowl XXVI triumph. In the 37–24 victory over Buffalo, Byner scored the game's first touchdown and Rypien, the game's Most Valuable Player, threw for 292 yards and two touchdowns. January 26, 1992. *AP Photo / Greg Gibson*

Standing above the three Super Bowl trophies he produced, Joe Gibbs is reintroduced as head coach of the Redskins, eleven years after retiring from the NFL. During his second tenure, Gibbs posted a 30–34 record with two playoff appearances over four seasons. January 8, 2004. *AP Photo / Gerald Herbert*

As part of a charity benefit for the D.C. College Access Program, Joe Gibbs is roasted by several of his former players including Dexter Manley (*right*), who told the audience "I can't roast Joe Gibbs; I can only toast Joe Gibbs." September 19, 2013. *Hyon Smith*

That January, he appeared in a full-page advertisement for the Health and Tennis Corporation of America that ran in *Sports Illustrated* and other national publications. Beneath a photo of Theismann dressed in full Redskins uniform, the text read: "They're dead wrong. After 16 years in this game, I know one thing for sure. The critics don't know anything. Nobody tells me when my career is over. My doctors may mumble. The competition may hope. But I'll decide. You'll see number seven calling plays when next season opens."

Not only was Theismann hell bent on redeeming himself from a poor performance in 1985, but a financial incentive also pushed the thirty-six-year-old. According to a report by the *Washington Post*'s Christine Brennan, to cash in the $1.4 million Lloyd's of London insurance policy he took out two years earlier, Theismann had to clearly demonstrate vigorous efforts to resume his career.

But his recovery was slow. The full-leg cast remained on for months. And even though he was playing racquetball and hoped to participate in the minicamp, the Redskins did not plan to have him for the 1986 season. And he knew it.

"When you're not around, it's cut and dried," Theismann said as he watched the team practice in May. "You're not a stranger, but you're certainly not part of the team. You feel like a boy whose father doesn't have time for him."

In late July, at the start of training camp, Theismann failed the team's physical examination and—rather then retire and risk not collecting his insurance claim—he asked the Redskins to waive him. None of the other twenty-seven NFL teams wanted him, but CBS did. They hired the loquacious former MVP as a color commentator for games, pairing him with Jack Buck.

Still, he negotiated an out in the contract with CBS: he could return to the NFL, "if a miracle does occur."

"Based on what I know [in] reality, I don't think it's going to happen," he said. "If it does, it belongs in the same category as walking on water."

Although doctors still had not cleared him to play and no teams showed any interest in him, chatter about a return to the field the following year persisted throughout the 1986 season. Playing golf, tennis, and racquetball on his mended leg convinced him that his football career was most likely over.

"It hasn't gotten a whole hell of a lot better," he said in November. "I don't have movement in the ankle. I don't have the strength in the leg. It doesn't seem to want to go much further. I said it before: if you take a year off from the game, it makes it difficult to come back and play."

Theismann's longtime teammate John Riggins proved that five years earlier. He had struggled mightily in his return from sitting out the 1980 NFL season, though he did rebound to become the only player in NFL history to rush for more yards in his thirties than he did in his twenties. Riggins clinched that feat against San Francisco during Week Thirteen of the 1985 season, the game he left early due to dizziness. He recovered and Joe Gibbs offered him the chance to return to the field as a backup to George Rogers, beginning with the Redskins' final home game of the season. True to the maverick's unpredictable nature, Riggins declined.

"He only wants to go in there if he's in there to help win the game," Gibbs told reporters before Washington's matchup with Cincinnati. "He did not want to go in and just play a play. He wants to go in there if he is called on to help the team, and that's the only reason why I'd put him in there. A token appearance is not really him anyway. He doesn't need that, he doesn't want that."

Riggins's decision to stay on the sidelines late in the 1985 season did not mean he was ready to walk away from the game.

"I ain't hanging nothing up," he insisted. "If I'm retiring, the decision will come from [the Redskins' front office]. Of course, I might be wearing a different colored uniform."

Riggins would turn thirty-seven before the start of the next season, and his body had begun to break down. Late in the 1984 season, he experienced such great pain in his lower back and hips that he admitted himself to Sibley Hospital and was in traction for two days. Less than a week later, with the NFC East lead on the line against Dallas, Riggins returned to the field, carrying the ball 24 times for 111 yards and scoring the game-winning touchdown midway through the fourth quarter.

As usual, Riggins downplayed the pain, which often made walking to the bathroom in the middle of the night unbearable.

"It's been formidable," he finally admitted that December. "That's the reason I don't want to talk about it. I'm scared of looking like some jerk saying I'm out there dying for the team."

Riggins found a means of coping with the pain. And at no time was that more evident than during the annual Washington Press Club's salute to Congress in January 1985. At the black-tie banquet, Riggins—who told *People* magazine's Washington bureau chief Gerry Clifford that he was in agony and wearing a back brace—self-medicated with red wine and scotch. During a speech by ABC News's Sam Donaldson, the event's master of ceremonies, Riggins passed out underneath a table, but not before he chided Sandra Day O'Connor for leaving the banquet early. In a moment he later said would ultimately eclipse his MVP performance in Super Bowl XVII, Riggins barked at the first woman ever appointed to the United States Supreme Court, saying, "Come on, Sandy baby, loosen up. . . . You're too tight." Given the presence of so many members of the media, the quote made big news the following day.

Riggins's back continued to ache throughout the 1985 season, especially following a 30-carry, 112-yard effort against Cleveland. After that year ended, team officials believed he could not endure another season of wear-and-tear.

"It would take a miracle for John to come back," said one Redskins official.

"The truth is no matter what John has done in the past, this is a young man's game," another team official said.

In March, Riggins was released. Joe Gibbs suggested he retire, but Riggins had no intention of doing so and declared through his attorney, "I would like to issue a challenge to anybody who thinks he wants to be the starting running back to a 60-yard dash at the minicamp. I think the outcome of the competition will prove that I have not lost a step. Should my challenge go unanswered, I want everyone to know I wish the Redskins well."

The challenge was never met.

"I'll wait and see what comes along," he said. "I told Joe, 'It'd be difficult to play for another team.' Ten years here. [A] Super Bowl. This is home for me. Until my banker gives me another call, I'll stay unemployed."

The departures of Riggins and Theismann, Washington's two centerpieces since 1978, engendered great uncertainty heading into the 1986 regular season. But the slow decline of the Redskins' championship progress—losing in the Super Bowl, losing their opening playoff game a year later, then missing the postseason entirely—made for a welcomed change. And in a way, the massive turnover the Redskins had experienced rejuvenated members of the organization, especially Joe Gibbs.

"I think everybody knows this is going to be a different year for the Redskins than we've had for quite a while," he said in July. "I think of going to training camp in two ways: you're kinda sorry the summer is over, but the other side is, you're excited about starting something new, about maybe doing something great."

One reason for Gibbs's optimism was Jay Schroeder. In addition to the raw athleticism showcased during his 40-yard dash, Schroeder possessed awesome arm strength: as a minor leaguer, he won a bet by throwing a baseball over the left field fence at a stadium in Billings, Montana.

"Schroeder could throw the ball further than any quarterback I've ever been on the field with," offensive coordinator and former Dallas Cowboys quarterback Jerry Rhome said. "Schroeder could throw it 70 yards. . . . He's the only one I ever saw throw the ball that far."

Schroeder's unmatched pure ability did not guarantee him any success as the Redskins' starter to begin the 1986 regular season, but the twenty-five-year-old quarterback's strong work ethic and willingness to learn gave observers hope that he'd overcome his tremendous inexperience.

"Whenever we were practicing defense, Jay dragged Jerry Rhome over to a corner of the field," Gibbs said that summer. "He made Jerry run ups and outs and hooks, and kept throwing the ball out there until he'd mastered every pass in the game plan. He didn't just do it once. He did it all the time, week after week. Here's a backup who doesn't figure to play all year, and he's working like he's the only quarterback on the team. That's Jay."

In the first season opener to be started by a Redskins quarterback other than Joe Theismann, Billy Kilmer, or Sonny Jurgensen in twenty-two years, Schroeder's diligence yielded noticeable results. Frequently employing audibles at the line of scrimmage, Schroeder threw for 2 scores and rushed for another during a chippy, penalty-filled 41–14 victory over Philadelphia.

"I'm very surprised by the final score," Schroeder said. "I never expected to score that many points and I don't expect to score that many the next time we play."

The Redskins' offense netted only 10 points a week later against the Raiders, scoring their lone touchdown midway through the fourth quarter of a four-point win. But throughout the 1986 season Washington's offense—and, in fact, the entire team—surged toward the top of the NFC. *Sports Illustrated* noted in December that the "Washington Redskins have that Super Bowl look."

Aside from road losses to division foes Dallas and the Giants, the Redskins cruised through their midseason schedule. They won games on the strength of a resurgent George Rogers, by employing an aggressive pass rush led by All-Pro Dexter Manley, and with a secondary featuring Darrell Green, who that April won the first-ever NFL's Fastest Man competition in 105-degree Palm Desert weather. By Week Thirteen, their 11-2 record was tied for the best in football. And Jay Schroeder—named to the Pro Bowl that December—earned much of the credit.

"Right now, he is doing very well," Rhome said. "If he never got any better, he'd be just fine. But the things we're looking for is for him to be the best in the NFL. And he's not the best in the NFL yet."

During training camp, Joe Gibbs and the coaching staff aimed to take advantage of Schroeder's big arm in search of home-run plays.

"I think you change about one-third of what you do every year," Gibbs said after Schroeder threw two late touchdowns to produce an overtime victory versus Minnesota. "When you see us still in the one-back, people would say we haven't changed. But I think we've changed a lot, in the way we have adjusted in blocking schemes, in formations. We might run the same play, but we do things differently within it."

Schroeder's desire and ability to heave the ball down field often brought both excitement and points to the Washington offense. But Schroeder's refined skills as a passer and patience in the pocket gave the Redskins consistency.

"It's like a pitcher firing a fastball and bouncing it before the plate. He has to realize he doesn't have to throw every pass like a rocket," Rhome said. "He still gets impatient, but very rarely. He has learned that if a receiver gets held up, he should wait, not bail out or throw too soon."

Losses to the Giants and Denver dropped Washington out of contention for winning the NFC East (the Giants had clinched the division), but defeating Philadelphia in the final week of the regular season secured Washington a wild card berth and a 12-4 record. Reminiscent of the dominating playoff runs of a few years earlier, Washington's defense and ground game outmuscled the Rams in the opening round. The next week they dominated the defending-champion Bears in the second half to win 27–13. During the two victories, they forced a total of 10 turnovers while rushing for 272 yards.

Still, with the big personalities of Joe Theismann and John Riggins now gone, much of the praise went to the team's quarterback, whom Joe Gibbs characterized that December as "probably the most highly scrutinized individual in town next to the president." And after Washington's two high-pressure, high-stakes games, Jay Schroeder's approval rating among the fans as well as the Redskins' veteran players had soared.

"The most impressive thing about Jay is the way he handles himself," Art Monk said after the win over Chicago. "Jay takes control over things. You get the feeling he has always been there."

More than simply his personal statistics—including a team-record 4,109-passing-yard season—or the touchdown drives and wins he produced, Schroeder's poise and leadership were praised.

"If you were drawing up a quarterback, he's the type of guy you'd draw up, not only physically but mentally. Jay has that air about him that you would call athletic arrogance," Bobby Beathard said after beating Chicago. "Best of all, he'll do something wrong and take the blame for it: he'll say, 'I blew it' and not point fingers."

A week later, however, Schroeder's athletic arrogance was greatly humbled by both the Giants' defense and harsh thirty-mile-per-hour winds that constantly blew debris throughout Giants Stadium. In a 17–0 NFC Championship Game loss, Schroeder completed just 20 of 50 attempts, was sacked 4 times, and absorbed several brutal hits from a New York defense that two weeks later would lead the Giants to their first Super Bowl title. And in an ironic twist for the quarterback who had only gained the starter's job due to the nasty tackle leveled by Lawrence Taylor and Gary Reasons, Schroeder suffered a concussion late in the game when two Giants defenders shoved him headfirst into the hard, cold AstroTurf.

Joe Gibbs instructed Doug Williams to take the field and spare his franchise quarterback any further damage. Williams, who had appeared in just one game that season and attempted only one pass, jogged halfway to the huddle. Schroeder angrily waved him off, refusing to be relieved. An embarrassed Williams trotted back to the sideline, unbuckled his chin strap, and returned his helmet to a table on the bench.

"That was probably the lowest point of my life in football," Williams later remembered.

The next day at Redskin Park, Joe Gibbs conducted exit interviews with select players, aiming to wrap up the season and look toward the next one. Among those the coach spoke to was Williams, the backup quarterback he practically never used.

"I asked him, 'Could you do this again?'" Gibbs said. "This [year] was great for us, but the question is 'Was it great for you?'"

"It's kind of tough," Williams told reporters that off-season. "I came up as a starter and I've been a starter for a long time. Last year wasn't tough early in the season, but it got tough going down the stretch sitting on the sideline. At one point this year I felt like maybe I would be traded to a team where I know I would have an opportunity to be a starter. . . . I'd like to start, but what can I do?

"Jay Schroeder is the quarterback of the future here. It doesn't take a Phi Beta Kappa to figure that out."

CHAPTER 7

Gut Feelings

THE MORNING after a late-night, cross-country flight from Southern California, Doug Williams strolled into Redskin Park in great spirits. He had not played particularly well in the team's final exhibition game prior to the start of the 1987 regular season, completing just 9 of 16 passes for 96 yards with 2 interceptions. But that no longer mattered. The night before, upon landing at Dulles Airport, Joe Gibbs gave Williams fantastic news: he was being traded to the Los Angeles Raiders.

With their thirty-nine-year-old Super Bowl MVP quarterback Jim Plunkett having just failed his physical, the Raiders did not have a clear-cut starter, let alone a young, emerging star like Jay Schroeder.

"I'm happy, not so much happy to leave the Redskins, but I'm happy because now I think I got a chance to start," Williams would say later. "I went home and I made calls. . . . I told everybody that I was going to the Raiders."

Anxious to hear the details of his trip back to Los Angeles,

Williams walked into Joe Gibbs's office. The two sat down across from each other, and with a coy smile on his face, the head coach began to chuckle.

"Douglas," Gibbs said, "I changed my mind."

Williams didn't find it nearly as humorous. Eyes widened, no expression on his face, the thirty-one-year-old quarterback sat up stiffly in his chair.

"Coach, you can't change your mind."

Gibbs promptly snapped out of his apologetic, almost-sheepish mood.

"Hey," Gibbs shot back seriously, "I don't work for the Raiders. I work for the Washington Redskins."

Williams understood better than most players that above all, the NFL was a business.

"At that time, I knew exactly where he was coming from."

As Gibbs explained why he backed out of the trade, the tension dissipated.

"Coach is one of those guys always talking about a gut feeling," Williams said years later. "He said, 'I just got a feeling that somewhere along here you're going to come in here and we gonna win [the Super Bowl].' I'm sitting over here, I've just been traded, with an opportunity to make more money, opportunity to be a starter, and he's over there talking about a gut feeling. Where do you think my mind was? It wasn't on no gut feeling, I can tell you that."

Dismayed, even angered, by the news, Doug Williams remained skeptical of his head coach's divine inspiration.

"Bible was on the desk," Williams remembered. "I know he's strong spiritually, but we've got a long ways to go to get to [the Super Bowl]."

WITH THE PRO BOWL on the horizon, the concussion he received late in the 1986 NFC Championship Game loss to the Giants didn't sting Jay Schroeder for long. The husband and father of two young children enjoyed an extended vacation, first at Disney World, then in his home state of California, before spending a week in Hawaii, signing autographs, taking pictures, and casually throwing footballs to some of the league's best pass catchers.

Following the NFC's 10–6 loss to their AFC counterpart, he returned to the East Coast in order to manage his booming one-man brand. That off-season, the city's newest celebrity kicked off the opening ceremonies of the annual Fairfax County Fair, sat through a public roasting by his teammates to benefit AMC Cancer Research, signed exclusive contracts for weekly interviews with local television (WUSA-TV) and radio (WMAL-AM) stations, and even acquired partial ownership of a Falls Church restaurant that was reopening in the fall. In exchange for a percentage of the profits, he agreed to appear weekly and lend his name to the eatery—formerly called Rumours of Virginia, now renamed Jay Schroeder's All-Pro Restaurant—located in a shopping center near Highway 50.

He left the negotiations of far more substantial business dealings to his agent, Marvin Demoff.

Throughout the spring, Demoff sought a hefty raise for his client via a contract extension. Although he had planned on sitting out all team activities, in tacit protest to the $225,000 he made in 1986, Schroeder surprised the media, his teammates, and especially the team's front office by showing up at Redskins minicamp in May.

"I came out as a favor to Coach Gibbs," he told reporters. "It's a combination: it's his club and my club. It's one of those things that the team's going to be out here, and I plan to be a part of the team in the fall. . . . [Coming to minicamp] was totally up to me. The coaching staff didn't know, Bobby Beathard didn't know, Mr. Cooke didn't know. I'm here because I'm a member of this football team."

A few weeks before players were scheduled to arrive for the preseason in Carlisle, Pennsylvania, the two sides reached an agreement.

Signed in late June, the new, three-year, $2.7-million contract Schroeder signed was the highest in team history.

"Success hasn't changed me," he said. "A lot of people want to know what I've been doing, and the answer is the same thing I've always been doing. I still go to McDonald's with my little boy, and I still love being with my family more than anything else."

Entrenched as the franchise's quarterback of the future—"I think he's going to be here a long time," Gibbs told the press—Schroeder arrived at training camp ready to start the season. Laughing off teammates who playfully asked for a loan, he set about honing the finer points of playing the position. Since May he'd worked with quarterbacks coach Jerry Rhome on adding touch to his shorter passes and throwing on the run. Improving the latter became difficult given a sore left knee that required arthroscopic surgery. With rehab, a knee brace, and a scaled-back practice schedule, Schroeder's knee quickly mended and he was solid in the preseason.

By the start of the regular season, he had returned to full strength, only to be dealt a new injury.

Washington opened the 1987 schedule at home against Philadelphia, a team boasting the best defensive line in football. In addition to Reggie White, who would record 21 sacks that season, the Eagles front four included future All-Pro Clyde Simmons and rookie standout Jerome Brown. All three fit head coach Buddy Ryan's aggressive, hungry defensive strategy that had produced a Super Bowl during Ryan's tenure as defensive coordinator for the Chicago Bears.

Four and a half minutes into their matchup with the Redskins, the Eagles claimed their first victim of the year. With the rush bearing down on him, Jay Schroeder released a pass just in time to avoid a sack, but not a brutal hit from White. A badly sprained shoulder—which led to internal bleeding—sent Schroeder to the sideline, where Doug Williams searched for his helmet and threw warm-up tosses. He instantly found a rhythm, completing his first 4 passes, the last of which resulted in a touchdown to Art Monk.

"When I first got in the game it was almost like I was untouchable," Williams told NFL Films years later. "Four passes, four completions, touchdown."

A back-and-forth shootout sent the game into the fourth quarter tied at 24 before a second touchdown catch by Art Monk gave the Redskins a 34–24 victory and Doug Williams a feeling of vindication.

"I just hope some of the people who never called to give Doug Williams a chance—I hope they hurt," he said. "It's great to be in control. It's been a long time since I've been the key figure as far as the team leader and everything like that, but by the same token it's the same old feeling that it used to be. The guys had confidence in me, and that made the difference."

Williams's model of resilience and leadership—he rebounded from a third-quarter fumble-turned-touchdown to complete 17 passes for 272 yards and 2 scores—allowed Washington to survive Week One with a win, albeit an expensive one. In addition to Schroeder, Washington lost starters Russ Grimm, George Rogers, Darryl Grant, and Markus Koch to injuries. Even kicker Jess Atkinson was hurt in the win. The former Maryland Terrapin dislocated his ankle upon nailing an extra point; teammate Rich Milot accidently blocked an Eagles defender into the kicker, stirring up memories of another ghastly moment at RFK.

"That was the worst-looking football injury I've ever seen, except for Joe Theismann's leg," Milot said. "It was comparable. I wanted to throw up."

While Atkinson was rushed to Arlington Hospital, punter Steve Cox handled the field goal and extra point duties, but the front office quickly scoured the waiver wire and free agent list for a fill-in.

"Right now," Gibbs said after the win, "we're in a mess everywhere you look."

But not at quarterback. An injury to the throwing shoulder of his young, high-priced Pro Bowler did not bother Gibbs.

"That's exactly why we kept Doug," he said. "He's a veteran, a guy who gives the other players confidence. He's like Cool Hand Luke out there."

A week later in Atlanta, Cool Hand Doug again sparked the makeshift Redskins in his first NFL start since January 1983. Playing without injured middle linebacker Neal Olkewicz and outside linebacker Rich Milot, who developed a staph infection during the week, Washington fell behind late in a wacky game that featured several special teams errors, penalties, and a slew of turnovers. Trailing 14–13, Williams threw a go-ahead touchdown pass to Art Monk early in the final quarter, but the depleted Washington defense could not stop Atlanta's running game. The Falcons retook the lead, two Washington offensive series produced no points, and the Redskins fell to 1-1.

"We had some tough things happen to us," Gibbs said. "All of us share in this loss."

That spirit of unity and group identity would be thoroughly tested beginning the next day.

IN 1982, A PLAYER'S strike shortened the NFL season considerably, but the work stoppage did not derail the Redskins, who won Super Bowl XVII less than four months after play resumed. Five years later, play again came to a halt due to labor negotiations, but no one saw this interruption as déjà vu foreshadowing another Washington world championship.

The day after the Redskins' close loss in Atlanta, the NFL Players Association voted to strike. Their chief protest, among others, focused on the league's restrictive free agency policy. Unlike the 1982 strike, league owners fought back, hiring replacement players to stand in for the strikers.

Aware of the impending labor crisis, the NFL already had in place a contingency plan to avoid a mad scramble to sign players.

"In training camp there was a concept that there could be a strike," Charley Casserly said. "So the league set up a contract with players that when they were cut, they'd sign this contract, that if they came back and played in a strike—work stoppage or whatever—they could only play for your team."

That policy provided the Redskins with twenty-four players, not nearly enough to field an entire team. The week of the game versus Atlanta, Washington's front office began combing through old scouting reports, alternate leagues, and even the streets for available players.

Familiarity with the Redskins' offensive scheme made for an ideal fit, so the personnel staff placed a high priority on prospects who played for Don Coryell or Dan Henning, who had just returned to the Redskins' coaching staff after three years as the Falcons head coach. That approach yielded tight end Joe Caravello, guard and former United States Marine Phil Pettey, wide receiver Anthony Allen, and running back Lionel Vital. A seventh-round draft pick, Vital served on the Redskins' practice squad in 1985, was later released by both Washington and the Giants, played one season in the Canadian Football League, tried pro baseball, then returned home to Loreauville, Louisiana, to invest in and manage a grocery store.

"The guys inside like myself are just trying to get our names in the lights. It's the American way," Vital said. "Sitting in the grocery store, I didn't want to do that. I want to play in the NFL."

Rosters in other professional leagues were also targeted and poached. Walter Holman, a running back for the Washington Commandoes of the Arena League and once an Arizona Outlaws teammate of Doug Williams in the USFL, was signed. So was Willard Scissum, a guard who started for Bear Bryant at the University of Alabama and had been a member of the Denver Broncos and British Columbia Lions of the Canadian Football League. Just prior to joining the Redskins he was a security guard at a 7-Eleven in the tough southeast area of Washington, D.C. And Skip Lane, a cornerback from Mississippi who was working as a commercial real estate broker in Connecticut, had recently played in the CFL as well as the Italian Football League prior to joining the Redskins.

A semipro league, the Continental Interstate Football League also supplied the Redskins with a player who brought to Washington more athleticism, notoriety, and baggage than any other signee. A native of Tallahassee, Florida, Tony Robinson accepted a scholarship to the University of Tennessee in 1982. As a junior, he became the team's starting quarterback and led the proud program to seven wins and a spot in the Sun Bowl. The next year, his precise throwing (that season he completed nearly 65 percent of his passes) gave the Volunteers an upset over top-ranked Auburn and put Robinson on the cover of *Sports Illustrated*. His head coach, Johnny Majors, labeled the rail-thin, six-foot-three-inch senior "the most dynamic college quarterback since Joe Namath."

Two weeks later, in a showdown of Top 25 Southeastern Conference teams, Alabama's All-American linebacker Cornelius Bennett tackled Robinson, tearing the anterior cruciate ligament in his right knee. He missed the rest of the season, but the truly devastating blow to his future in football came the following January. In their Knoxville apartment, he and former Volunteer player Kenneth "B.B." Cooper sold cocaine to an undercover narcotics agent and were arrested. Robinson pleaded no contest and was sentenced to six years in prison, though he was only required to serve ninety days on a penal work farm in Knox County. Violating the terms of his release later sent him back to the work farm.

With his knee healed, Robinson still hoped for a professional football career, but NFL general managers had no interest in drafting or even signing to a free agent contract the convicted felon. John McGregor, however, gave him a chance. Head coach of the semipro Richmond Ravens, McGregor had spoken with Robinson's offensive coordinator at Tennessee, Walt Harris, and then visited the penal farm. Granted a work release, Robinson played well for the Ravens, and when Joe Gibbs called McGregor to ask for possible replacement players he mentioned Robinson.

"I think they were hesitant about bringing Tony in," said

McGregor, who had coached under Dan Henning in both Atlanta and at Boston College. "He was very polite, not particularly outgoing. I had no problems with him. Of course, I think you would have to understand that Tony didn't have money. That controls things a whole lot."

On McGregor's recommendation, Washington signed Robinson and his former Tennessee teammate Joe Cofer, a linebacker with tackling skills so impressive that Redskins coaches later told McGregor that "they'd never seen anybody hit harder than Joe did."

But the pickings eventually became slim, especially on the offensive line.

"I'm just going through scouting reports to find guys," Charley Casserly remembered. "This one guy was three-hundred-some pounds. That's good. But he hadn't been in one training camp and back then you averaged one hundred guys in camp for each team, this guy can't be very good. So I call up his [college] coach—I'm looking for anything—and he says they had played [Mike Wise] from Cal-Davis who the Raiders took in the [fourth] round. And he said, 'Well, he didn't do bad against him.' I said, 'That's great!' That's all I wanted to hear.

"I get the kid on the phone, you are signing these guys blindly. Guy comes up to my office, he's breathing heavy. I thought they must have put him on the treadmill. I said, 'Were you on the treadmill?' He said no. I said, 'You're breathing kind of hard.' He says, '[heavily panting] Oh . . . the steps . . . the steps.' We got no choice, we gotta have someone to practice, so we signed him."

The second labor crisis in five years was agonizing for the NFL. Jobs, television contracts, and millions of dollars were at stake with each passing day. But the free-for-all of identifying, recruiting, and signing players offered Bobby Beathard, Charley Casserly, Kirk Mee, and the entire Redskins scouting department a rare opportunity to exercise skills they had developed over a lifetime.

"I know there were some teams that I heard about that said, 'Aw, screw it,'" said Beathard. "They didn't go about it the same way. And I don't mean that braggingly. But it was a challenge, and it was fun looking back. But it was not something you'd want to have to do because the strike was a terrible thing."

NFL Players Association director Gene Upshaw officially announced the strike at halftime of the Jets-Patriots Week Two Monday night game, by which time the Redskins had signed fifty-five new players. Upon their arrival to Redskin Park for their first full practice, they were greeted by the angry, picketing "former" Redskins players, who had been barred from the facilities. Darryl Grant, Cliff Enson, and Reggie Branch attempted to block the team charter from entering, while several others pounded on the bus windows. Grant banged on the windows so hard that he cracked two. The Redskins' front office had to obtain a court injunction in order to avoid a repeat incident the next day.

That week's slate of games was canceled, but by Week Four of the season, all twenty-eight teams returned to the field. Bob Gagliano started for the 49ers, instead of Joe Montana. Kyle Mackey was under center for the Dolphins, instead of Dan Marino. Anthony Mosley carried the ball for the Bears instead of Walter Payton. And for the Redskins, Ed Rubbert—a college free agent from the University of Louisville whom Washington cut in the preseason—was the starting quarterback. Tony Robinson didn't play or even attend; according to Jerry Rhome, he was . . . unavailable.

"Tony Robinson, bless his heart, he comes up to me about fifteen minutes before [Thursday practice]," Rhome said twenty-seven years later. "He says, 'Coach, I gotta go to the bathroom.' I said, 'Hurry in there and get on back.' So he didn't come back. . . . I went around to [someone] and said, 'Go in there and get Robinson out of the dag gum bathroom.' He comes back out says, 'He's gone, his clothes are gone.' He went AWOL. . . . We didn't know what happened to him, but we were trying to find him. And they had people all over everywhere and I think the police were helping us."

Even without Robinson, who had taken a good deal of the practice snaps that week, to split the quarterback duties, Ed Rubbert and the Redskins' offense torched the St. Louis Cardinals in the first "scab" game. With dozens of Redskins picketing outside RFK Stadium, Rubbert threw 3 touchdowns as the Redskins won 28–21.

"Jerry, that was awful," Russ Grimm later told Jerry Rhome. "All we heard was yelling and screaming, and the crowd was going crazy. We were all walking up and down [picketing]. We're going, 'What's going on in there?' They're saying, 'The Redskins are bombing 'em!' By halftime, we all went home."

Anthony Allen, the former Atlanta Falcon, did most of the damage. Despite joining the team just three days earlier, Allen caught 3 long touchdown passes from Rubbert, breaking the team record with 255 receiving yards.

"They can put an asterisk by it. Fine with me," said Allen. "They can thank me first and then be mad at me, because I helped them win a division game."

Allen and the other replacement players delivered Washington a second NFC East win the following Sunday. In the Meadowlands, the Redskins pounded out 200 yards rushing against the Giants, who did not have Lawrence Taylor, Carl Banks, and Leonard Marshall to carry their top-notch defense. And for a second straight week, the defense allowed no more than 14 points, thanks in part to the coaching staff's unorthodox methods.

"It was really different coaching," Gibbs said. "In the NFL, you have a set scheme: it's 4-3, and here's the rules, and you play two-deep. I remember Richie [Petitbon] and the defensive guys did a fantastic job. We had one kid that was an unbelievable talent: guy could hit, run. He couldn't get one part of the defense down. Nothing. He was in the wrong place all the time. So eventually, what Richie and those guys did was they said, 'Look, you pay no attention to any rules. You just line up over there and go get the ball. BALL! Get the ball.' You're doing things like that rather than having a scheme."

Defeating the Giants in the Meadowlands—where the "real" Redskins had lost four straight games—didn't earn the replacement players any gratitude from their striking counterparts. Especially not from Doug Williams. He had waited more than four years to reclaim a starting job in the NFL, and it finally came with the shoulder injury to Jay Schroeder, but his chance to either win the Redskins' job or showcase his skills for another team was disappearing with each Ed Rubbert start.

"We have compromised a heck of a lot, and the owners haven't budged," he told reporters following a players-only meeting the day of the scabs game against the Giants. "It's like they just want to take everything away from us."

At the end of that meeting, held at assistant player representative Jay Schroeder's home in Great Falls, they all voted on whether or not to continue their holdout. Throughout the league several stars had crossed the picket lines, including the Steelers' Mike Webster, the Jets' Mark Gastineau, the Raiders' Howie Long, and the 49ers' Joe Montana. Doug Williams had no intention of doing so. Neither did any of his teammates.

Every striking Redskin at their team meeting voted to remain united and continue the strike. Dexter Manley didn't attend. Earlier in the day he told local radio station WWDC-FM that he was abandoning the cause, explaining, "I've just never been the type of guy that can follow." Teammates ultimately persuaded Manley not to break ranks.

"If we have to chain him to his bed, he ain't going in until we all go in," defensive tackle Dean Hamel said.

Loyalty to the NFL Players Association was a part of the Redskins players' solidarity. The union's headquarters were located in Washington, D.C., and they recognized the poor message they would send by caving to management. Doing so in the nation's capital—home to the AFL-CIO and many of the country's largest unions—also affected the decision to stay unified.

"We knew that we were the beacon on the Hill for the rest of the NFL," Charles Mann later said.

But more than any of those outside sources, one influence weighed most heavily on the Redskins' decision to stay together.

"Joe [Gibbs] said to us: 'This is out of my hands, guys. You've got to stay together,'" Jeff Bostic recalled years later. "And it's the culture he has created in and around the team that leads guys to do just what he asks, especially when you've got crazy stuff going on all around you."

Gibbs's mandate carried risk for his team's fortunes. He understood that players who crossed the picket line might create long-lasting hostility within the locker room, but he also knew these scab games would count toward the Redskins' 1987 record.

"What you're always searching for as a coach is camaraderie," Gibbs said years later. "I looked at that situation—it wasn't only me, but the whole coaching staff and all of us, as we talked it over—you realize this is going to be over at some point, because we knew the strike wasn't going to last forever. We're going to have our players back, so what's the most important thing, at that point, for us to be? We need to be together. And so we did talk long and hard about it and the players took it upon themselves to a certain extent, but what I basically said to them was, 'Look, whatever we do here, we do it together. All of us. No individuals, everybody does it together.'"

But Gibbs's authority only extended so far. And his appearance at one of the frequent players-only meetings during the strike was not well received.

"[Jeff Bostic] told me about one instance, where they were all in there together and Joe came in to basically show his support for the players' solidarity, not necessarily their causes or their requests and their demands, just the fact that they were all solid," local Fox-TV affiliate WTTG-TV's sports director Steve Buckhantz recalled years later. "And Gary Clark, who was a very vocal guy, stood up and basically told Joe to 'get the hell out of there,' and 'this is for the players only, nobody else has any business being there.' He didn't mean any disrespect to Joe, but Joe was treading that fine line of being management but he also was the coach of these players. But he was management when you came right down to it and I think that's how Gary looked at it."

Twenty-three days into the strike, the union's resolve had dwindled: 110 players abandoned the fight. Lawrence Taylor rejoined the Giants, Eric Dickerson rejoined the Rams, and in Cleveland Pro Bowl tight end Ozzie Newsome was one of sixteen players to rejoin the Browns. Only the Redskins remained united throughout the entire strike: not one Washington player crossed the picket line.

Their numbers shrinking, the union conceded defeat on October 15. But without a tentative agreement reached between the two sides, the players who had not crossed the picket lines before one p.m. the previous day were not allowed to play in the third week of replacement games. No Redskins players had reported before the strike officially ended, and as a result none of the "real" Redskins could play in the final replacement game, which would be on *Monday Night Football* against the restocked Dallas Cowboys. Randy White and Ed "Too Tall" Jones had never sided with their striking teammates, while stars Tony Dorsett, Danny White, and Mike Renfro returned before the strike officially ended.

Prior to the showdown, in the locker room of Texas Stadium, Joe Gibbs addressed his scab players, most of whom knew that after that evening they would never again play professional football.

"Think about this," he told them. "What you guys wanted was a chance to prove you that belong in the NFL. Well if we were playing just a bunch of other strike guys, what's that mean? You're going to get an unusual opportunity. You're going to be playing against some of the best football players in the NFL. And you're going to play against the Dallas Cowboys. So if you want a chance to prove that you belong up here, this is the perfect chance."

Dallas may have had a handful of Pro Bowlers and future Hall of Fame players on their side, but at least the Redskins had Tony Robinson back.

"All of a sudden, Tony Robinson walks into my office on Friday," Jerry Rhome said years later. "I go, 'Where've you been!?' And I said, 'You need to go see Joe Gibbs,' so he went in and saw Gibbs and Beathard and all that. . . . And it turns out, that he had called his sister when he went in to the locker room, because he was worried about her. And somebody had 'kidnapped' her and he took off to find her. . . . That's what he told us, and he found her and everything was all right."

Robinson had chosen an ideal time to return. Ed Rubbert badly bruised his shoulder late in the first quarter against Dallas and Joe Gibbs asked Jerry Rhome if Robinson could play.

"Have you got him ready?" Gibbs asked.

"Well, he knows two runs and four passes," Rhome answered.

"That's all?!"

"That's it, Coach."

"Well, what does he know?"

"He knows 'the Gut' and the outside runs, he knows the hitch, the go, the slant, and the double-in."

Playing what Rhome later called "backyard football," Robinson scrambled around and away from Dallas's great defensive front, completing 11 passes for 152 yards and directing Washington to 2 second-half scores. His often-improvised third-down completions along with 136 yards on 26 carries from Lionel Vital maintained Redskins' drives and kept the ball away from the Cowboys' talented offense. When Dallas did have the ball, theirs was the offense that looked like a team stocked with scabs: they allowed 5 sacks, quarterback Danny White appeared out of sync with his receivers all evening, and Tony Dorsett fumbled twice. The crowd repeatedly booed the hometown Cowboys.

Gibbs had preached unity to his striking players before and during the work stoppage, but solidarity also developed among the scab players, despite less than a month together.

"Because all those [striking players] stayed out and never crossed the line, I think it helped us, helped Gibbs and those guys put together a team that knew each other," said Redskins replacement wide receiver Joker Phillips. "A lot of teams were bringing in guys that they couldn't bring together. There were a few guys they had to put up in hotels. There were a few guys that were already on the team that had their own houses and apartments or whatever.

"Well, none of the guys that Gibbs and those guys brought in were even local, that had their own place. So everybody lived in the hotel. And I think that, in turn, made us feel like a college team. We got to know each other, we played cards at night, we ate every meal together, we went out together. It just had a college feel for all of us," added Phillips, who would later become the head coach at his alma mater, the University of Kentucky. "[Against Dallas] we all knew that this was many of our last time to put on the uniform. It was like Senior Day for all of us. You see college teams, how they play on Senior Day. . . . We all went out there and played like it was our last game on Senior Day."

With 2:37 remaining in the game and Dallas behind 13–7, the Cowboys marched from their own 7-yard line to the Redskins' 20. Washington's replacement defense then stiffened, and on fourth down, White misfired, giving Washington a 13–7 victory. Joker Phillips and long snapper Mike Wooten hoisted Joe Gibbs onto their shoulders.

"This is one of the most exhilarating nights we've had as Redskins," Gibbs told his players after the game. "This meant a lot to me, to all of us. Thank you."

The no-longer-striking Redskins—roughly thirty of whom watched the game on television at Rick "Doc" Walker's Scoreboard bar/restaurant in suburban Virginia—were not nearly as grateful. For more than three weeks they had jeered, intimidated, and denounced the replacement players. And despite the official end of the strike and the importance of a win over their division rival, many remained torn over whom to cheer for.

"I sensed they were rooting against them, even though the game meant a lot," said the *Washington Post*'s Tom Friend, whose first-ever assignment for the paper was to cover the scene at Walker's restaurant. "I think they felt obligated to root against them, but as the game wore on they were cheering and cheering and cheering. I'll never forget [Redskins cornerback] Barry Wilburn just leapt up into the air on that last stand and someone had to shout him down. He was so amped."

The third consecutive win, all against NFC East foes, put Washington alone atop the division. They had a one-game lead over Dallas and a four-game advantage over the defending-champion Giants. Seemingly just as critical to their postseason fortunes, Jay Schroeder's shoulder had healed, and he was ready to return to the lineup along with all the other Redskins for a Week Six matchup with the New York Jets.

But Schroeder missed 20 of his first 30 attempts, incurring boos from an RFK crowd that chanted, "We want the scabs!" with their team trailing 16–7 in the fourth quarter. As his accuracy improved, Schroeder produced two scoring drives in a span of six minutes and the Redskins salvaged a 17–16 win.

"We weren't real sharp out there," he admitted. "We worked all week in practice. But we got in a game situation and no one was sharp, including myself. We're going to have to go out in practice next week and get it together."

A blowout win over Buffalo the following week suggested the Redskins' offense was back on track, but in Philadelphia, Schroeder's problems returned. He threw 30 incompletions, two of which resulted in costly interceptions in a 31–27 defeat. A return to RFK for Week Nine against Detroit offered no cure for Schroeder. He overthrew several receivers who appeared open for touchdowns, lost a fumble, and was nearly picked off twice. Halfway through the second period, with the score 3–3, Gibbs yanked his starter in favor of Doug Williams. The hometown fans went wild.

"It shocked me," said tackle Mark May. "I was running out for the series and the crowd started cheering madly. I didn't understand it at first. I looked back and saw Doug, and then I looked back again and saw him running in. I was flabbergasted."

As he did in Week One, Williams took advantage of the opportunity, tossing a pair of touchdown passes before halftime. And with the defense, as well as the RFK crowd, flustering Lions' quarterback Chuck Long all afternoon, the Redskins held on for a 20–13 win.

Darrell Green snapped a season-long drought that day, recording 3 interceptions. Barry Wilburn added one as well: his fourth-quarter pick near the Redskins' goal line not only ended a deep Detroit drive, it marked the sixth consecutive (nonreplacement) game in which he intercepted a pass. And late in the fourth quarter, as Detroit neared Washington's red zone, linebacker Monte Coleman dropped Long for an 11-yard loss on third down, adding to the Redskins' league-best streak of fifty-nine straight games with a sack.

But in a city once captivated by the mid-1970s quarterback controversy over Billy Kilmer and Sonny Jurgensen, all anyone wanted to talk about was Joe Gibbs's choice to sit Jay Schroeder. And from that day until the end of the season, every quarterback-related decision Joe Gibbs made was magnified, scrutinized, and dissected.

"I may have rushed Jay back into playing after the strike," Gibbs admitted following the win over Detroit. "He's inaccurate right now. I didn't make it based on a sack. It's not based on two or three throws. It was a hard decision for me to make. I know Jay's upset about it, mad about it. But I know this is something he can come through."

Following the benching, Schroeder stood on the sideline, mostly by himself, arms folded. He granted no postgame interviews, not even to WMAL Radio, whom he was contractually obligated to speak with. Reporters who approached his locker heard him say, "You might as well forget it," as he walked away. Schroeder even skipped a public appearance at his new restaurant in Falls Church, opting to grab takeout from McDonald's. Much of the next week, he was contrite to the media, who noted his suggestively pouty "body language" after the benching.

Some inside Redskin Park had already noticed red flags surrounding Schroeder.

"Jay may have lost his focus," Charley Casserly later recalled. "He had a restaurant, maybe he was involved in too many things. Got the big contract. And that was a problem. So as time went on, there became more questions on him. And he was an inconsistent player and a lot of it had to do with fundamentals. He could throw a 50-yard pass and then bounce a 10-yard-out."

Gibbs had hoped to avoid making the switch. Earlier in the week he told reporters that he was "always reluctant to change the quarterback." But team executive Bobby Mitchell, appearing on the *Home Team Sports* television network's "Redskins Report," admitted that several players had approached Gibbs about replacing Schroeder with Williams during the loss to Philadelphia a week earlier.

"The players and some of the coaches, I think in my opinion, had gotten to Coach Gibbs, too," Williams later said. "Some things are taught and some things are caught. I think the leadership part, it's hard to pick a leader. To me, leaders just come out of nowhere. My whole life I've been that guy. From the time I was six years old, playing Little League baseball, I always played with the older guys. I've always been that guy that people would cling to from a leadership standpoint. I think it's natural. It's something you can't just expect someone to be if they don't have it in them.

"I knew this team, I watched them, was part of them. I knew who they believed in. But that wasn't for me to say. . . . I think Coach Gibbs knew, the coaches knew, [Richie] Petitbon, Emmitt Thomas, just from practice alone, you could see it."

More than anywhere else, Williams's teammates sensed it in the huddle.

"You look at Doug, and what he did down in Tampa . . . and with his personal life and what he'd gone through, you know the man has been through some ups and downs," Pro Bowl offensive tackle Joe Jacoby said years later. "You look at that and how he carries himself, and you know he's going to be calm and cool with things flying around him. And that's what Doug was. He was very calm when he got in the huddle, very even-keel voice. Not to say he didn't get fired up, but you just knew and felt that when he got in the huddle."

Williams's strong performance against Detroit convinced Gibbs to start him eight days later at RFK Stadium. On *Monday Night Football* against the Rams, special teams bungles allowed 2 Rams touchdowns and Washington fell behind 23–9 late in the second quarter. Williams then rallied his team to within 4 points, and with 1:40 remaining, he drove the offense from their own 30 to the Rams 14. Only a vicious hit from defensive back Johnnie Johnson, which knocked the game-winning touchdown pass out of Art Monk's hands—and into the arms of the Rams' LeRoy Irvin for an interception—prevented Williams from delivering another late-game comeback.

"Doug Williams was playing like he was twenty-four years old," Rams defensive end Gary Jeter said. "A couple times, I was all over him, and he wouldn't go down. One time, he brushed me off."

Williams's surprising elusiveness extended plays for Washington several times and even accounted for a rushing touchdown before halftime that narrowed the gap to 23–16. On that diving run toward the pylon, Williams tweaked his spine. He didn't miss a snap, but he aggravated the injury at practice the following Thursday. He sat out the rest of the week's practices and missed the Redskins' next game against the Giants.

"Timing's bad," Williams said. "This was the opportunity I'd been waiting for. I guess all it does is put everything in perspective, what has always happened for me. Once you get up, you're down again."

For Jay Schroeder, who had been down following his benching, the opportunity was now his. Against New York, the Redskins trailed 19–3 late in the third quarter, and then bounced back with 3 Schroeder touchdown passes to defeat their NFC East rival.

"He has a great late surge," Gibbs said of Schroeder, who finished with 331 yards passing. "I don't think I've seen anybody better late [in the game] when he has that look in his eye. The main thing is he is a mentally tough guy. For three quarters, things weren't going right, but he has the ability to keep coming back."

The victory convinced Schroeder he had deserved the starter's job once again, explaining that the "team is getting in a groove now, and we've got to keep it going." Gibbs not only agreed, he admitted regret over his earlier benching.

"I felt like that was a mistake. And I don't want to make it again," Gibbs said after the win over the Giants. "I want to have a good talk with both of them. Whichever guy I pick, there will be reasons for doing it."

The next day, Gibbs informed the press that Jay Schroeder would remain the Redskins' starter.

DOUG WILLIAMS HANDLED his benching as best he could. Fighting back tears when reporters asked him about Joe Gibbs's decision to start Jay Schroeder, Williams did not publicly lobby for the job, criticize Gibbs, or say the organization treated him unfairly.

"It was Coach Gibbs's gut feeling that the comeback Jay engineered put him over the hump," Williams told the press. "I'll pick up the pieces and go on."

Taking the high road won the praise of many Redskins fans. Hundreds felt compelled to write to him: unlike many of the racist letters he received a decade earlier in Tampa, these expressed great respect for his display of class upon the demotion.

"We admired the way you handled yourself," one read.

"We watch you on the sideline and compare the way you get

involved in the game when you're not playing with the way Jay Schroeder took it when he was benched," wrote another fan.

As the weeks passed and he watched games from the sidelines, Williams came to accept his fate as a backup for the remainder of the season.

The Schroeder-led victory over the Giants brought Washington within one game of capturing the division. They claimed the NFC East title for the first time in three years the next Sunday. George Rogers's best rushing effort in two seasons (134 yards) paved the way for a second-half comeback as the Redskins toppled the Cardinals 34–17.

"[Gibbs] is going to go with Jay unless he gets hurt," Williams told reporters after Schroeder guided the Redskins over the Cowboys the following week, the team's third consecutive divisional win. "He's his starter. . . . Coach Gibbs won't make a change again. Why? It's something I probably should keep to myself. I just think from a personal standpoint that he would not make that decision. Coach Gibbs is an easygoing, noncontroversial type of person. He doesn't like attention as far as what decision he makes. They've invested a lot in Jay. Jay is the future."

Needing wins in both of the final two regular-season games to guarantee a home playoff game, Washington lost to Miami in Week Fourteen. To host the second round of the NFC playoffs (the conferences' two wild card teams played the opening week of the playoffs), they would need to beat Minnesota in the regular-season finale and have the Chicago Bears lose to the Raiders. Playing in front of the disruptive RFK fans would be a huge boost to the Redskins' upcoming playoff run. But they wanted a convincing, decisive win over Minnesota. Despite their 10-4 record, Washington had not beaten a team with a winning record since the first week after the strike.

"I think the main thing is we're trying to get momentum," said left guard Raleigh McKenzie prior to the game against Minnesota.

Jay Schroeder was also in search of a rhythm.

The previous season, he had enjoyed one of the best games of his career against the Vikings. One week after throwing for 420 yards against the New York Giants' great pass defense, he had sliced up an equally stout Vikings defense for 378 more yards and directed a 12-point fourth-quarter comeback to force overtime. During sudden death, Schroeder's 38-yard touchdown pass to former USFL star Gary Clark gave Washington a 44–38 victory.

"Jay is a big-play guy," Gibbs said after that exhausting win. "During the game, he is very aggressive. He comes to me and says, 'Let me throw this' or 'Let me throw that.' He has confidence and great poise."

A lot had changed in a year's time.

On the first pass of his rematch with Minnesota, Schroeder was intercepted. As the *Washington Post* noted, he began to rush several throws and fall back into the "bad habits" that cost him his job several weeks before. He then threw a second interception. And when he bounced a pass to an open Ricky Sanders on third down midway through the third quarter, Joe Gibbs reneged on his late November promise. He switched quarterbacks.

"[You'd] prefer not to make a change in the last game, but at the same time I was trying to win this game," Gibbs said. "I didn't dream I would feel that way or want to do that. It's something you just do at the time, a gut feeling."

Once again, Joe Gibbs's gut had stunned Doug Williams.

"I never thought I'd be playing again, quite naturally," he said. "I didn't expect the change. I don't think Coach Gibbs expected to make it. I think he thought Jay was able to play up to his potential."

Williams completed his first pass to tight end Terry Orr, netting 23 yards as the Redskins crossed into Minnesota territory. A few plays later, he threw deep over the middle, where former USFL standout Ricky Sanders hauled in the football just inches beyond the arm of a Vikings defender. Sanders dove into the end zone to grab a 14–7 lead. A group of Redskins swarmed Doug Williams as he came to the sideline.

"Guys just gravitated to Doug," Raleigh McKenzie later said. "Doug was just a natural leader. I don't think he really understood how much of an impact he had on a lot of people. He was the reason we came together toward the end of that season and got better and believed."

Sanders's late-third-quarter touchdown triggered a shootout for the final period. The Vikings drove 80 yards to tie the score, forced a turnover on Gary Clark's bobble of a Doug Williams throw, and then scored to retake the lead. A careless interception by Williams on the ensuing drive led to a Vikings field goal, and with less than ten minutes to play, Minnesota held a 24–14 edge.

Ignoring the 2 recent interceptions, Williams drove the offense 65 yards as the Redskins cut into the deficit with a 37-yard field goal. The defense forced a punt, but with less than two minutes to play, Washington still trailed by 7 and faced a third down at their own 49-yard line. As Joe Gibbs and Doug Williams discussed play options, they received a suggestion from the most unexpected of sources: Jay Schroeder. The benched quarterback recommended running a hitch to Ricky Sanders on the game's most critical play. Sanders found a hole in the Minnesota zone and snagged a short throw from Williams. The second-year receiver streaked down the field and snuck past a defender at the goal line for a 51-yard touchdown that sent the game into overtime.

"I think, right now on our football team, the difference from six or seven weeks ago is that guys were upset before with their own personal situations," Gibbs said. "Jay's response [against Detroit], that was normal. Today what Jay did was get right there by my side, the whole time talking and talking to Doug and to me about play selection and ideas."

Once sudden death began, Sanders—who had taken on a much larger role in the offense following a knee injury to Art Monk in early December—continued to torment the Vikings. He returned the opening kickoff 36 yards and caught 2 more passes from Williams for 32 yards, setting up the game-winning field goal by Ali Haji-Sheikh.

Washington escaped the noisy Metrodome with a thrilling win that showcased an offense capable of scoring from anywhere on the field, a defense that recorded 4 sacks and 3 turnovers, and a quarterback with an intangible je ne sais quoi.

"There's just something about the guy," Sanders said. "He just sparks the team."

Still, the 27–24 victory only produced more questions and stress for Joe Gibbs. He publicly regretted the benching of Schroeder six weeks earlier, then vowed not to bench him again, only to reverse course four weeks later. Despite the comeback over Minnesota and dozens of teammates stating a preference for Williams, the quarterback controversy had not been resolved.

"We'll make our quarterback decision later," he told the press after the win. "I'm too tired to think."

CHAPTER 8

Turnabout

THE 1987 Washington Redskins regular season had been defined by the quarterback shuffling of Jay Schroeder and Doug Williams. Between Schroeder's shoulder sprain, misfires, and interceptions, Williams's back injury, Joe Gibbs's flip-flopping, and the string of fourth-quarter heroics both passers delivered, almost every week offered more drama.

So when Gibbs announced on December 30—four days after the overtime win in Minnesota—that Williams, not Schroeder, would start the postseason, the news served as a relief.

"I think everybody was excited, I know I was. Doug was a guy that rallied people around him," center Jeff Bostic recalled. "[Players] want the person that gives you the best ability to win. And certainly Jay had done that, but once he had established himself in the league . . . Unfortunately, it went from 'we' to 'me' with him. He got a new deal after '86; in '87 he came to training camp and his whole personality was different."

Despite any rise in locker-room morale gained by Gibbs's public decree, the Redskins' Super Bowl prospects were shaky, and not just because of the inconsistency and indecision surrounding their starting quarterback.

Special teams were a frequent problem for the Redskins. Longtime special teams coach Wayne Sevier—a college teammate of Gibbs's whose wife, Barbara, was Gibbs's personal secretary—left Washington for the San Diego Chargers the previous winter. At the time, Gibbs joked that "we can get by without Wayne, but I don't know about Barbara," drawing great chuckles from the press. Once the 1987 regular season started, however, Gibbs was not laughing.

Jess Atkinson's broken ankle in the season opener forced the Redskins to find a new kicker for the second time in three seasons. They settled on former New York Giant All-Pro Ali Haji-Sheikh, whose consistency dipped late in the regular season, especially in the last game against Minnesota. On the AstroTurf of the weather-free Metrodome, he missed 2 field goals from inside the red zone, including one at the end of regulation that would have avoided overtime. With Atkinson's ankle fully healed and the popular kicker ready to return, Joe Gibbs had a second personnel conundrum to solve prior to the start of the postseason.

Further complicating the timing of the field goal and extra point process, the Redskins used three different snappers that year. During the first two weeks of the season, veteran center Jeff Bostic suddenly lost his consistency and was responsible for several botched kick attempts. He was replaced by defensive tackle Darryl Grant, who later was supplanted by late-season free-agent signee David Jones.

Kickoffs and punts proved just as much of a problem that season. In the *Monday Night* loss to the Rams in Week Ten, the Redskins had a punt blocked (their fourth partial or complete block of the season), which led directly to a touchdown. That night, they also allowed the Rams' Ron Brown to return a kickoff 95 yards for a score.

"Our special teams, in particular, are killing us," Gibbs said after the 30–26 defeat.

Apoplectic over the continued miscues since Sevier's departure, Joe Gibbs turned to another old friend, Paul Lanham, who worked with Gibbs in both St. Louis and at the University of Arkansas, and had a reputation as a special teams guru. Let go from the Detroit Lions after the 1986 season, he was taking a year off from football, living in Mission Viejo, California, with his wife, Helen. An assistant under George Allen—he was the special teams coach who had to answer for rookie Joe Theismann sneaking onto the field to return punts in 1974—Lanham agreed to return to the Redskins as an unpaid consultant the day after the loss to the Rams. Alongside the team's official special teams coach, Chuck Banker, Lanham went to work on improving the Redskins' shoddy kicking game.

Another once-reliable unit, the Hogs, also underwent a major overhaul during the Redskins' 1987 season.

Largely based on the pounding Jay Schroeder and the Redskins' offense took in their 1986 NFC Championship Game loss to the New York Giants, Joe Bugel and Joe Gibbs wanted more size upfront. They moved left guard Russ Grimm to center and filled the vacancy with Raleigh McKenzie, an eleventh-round pick in 1985, who had developed into an important role player with strong pass-protection skills. The changes left Jeff Bostic as the odd man out. A former Pro Bowler and founding member of the Hogs, Bostic was ten pounds lighter than McKenzie and fifteen pounds lighter than Grimm.

Throughout the first two months of the season, he did not start on the offensive line, and because he had been replaced as the team's short-snapper, he barely saw the field for the first time since his rookie year. Bostic never publicly complained (although he did ask to be traded) even when Darrick Brilz, one of the replacement players the Redskins re-signed after the strike ended, saw more playing time. Urged by Joe Gibbs to "just be patient," Bostic remained a reserve and prepared in case he was called upon. His opportunity came in late November.

Russ Grimm, who had missed only one game in five years, sprained his knee in the Week Eight loss to Philadelphia and underwent arthroscopic knee surgery. The procedure did not keep the four-time First Team All-Pro from a hunting trip a few days later—a rifle served as one of his crutches—but it did keep him off the roster until the final week of the regular season. By that point, Jeff Bostic had reclaimed the starter's job. Bostic excelled in the late-season win over the Giants, against the same interior defensive linemen who contributed to his demotion. As the season wound down, his play only improved, and Joe Bugel insisted Bostic had returned to the form that made him an All-Pro selection in 1983.

"I mean it," Bugel said in early December. "That's why we're winning. Jeff has added a stabilizing effect. We've got all vets on the offensive line now."

But as soon as the banged-up, pieced-together offensive line gelled, injuries bogged down the Redskins' group of skill players.

The trade for running back George Rogers kept the Redskins' ground game among the best in the NFL after John Riggins's departure prior to the 1986 season. That year, Rogers rushed for 1,203 yards and led the league with 18 touchdowns. The next season, he was again a fixture in Joe Gibbs's one-back scheme, but by early December, groin, toe, and shoulder ailments slowed him enough that running backs coach Don Breaux admitted Rogers had "lost a step."

Even John Riggins piled on. During a live interview on WMAL radio, Riggins publicly bashed the running back who took his place: "[He's] not the answer as the natural guy to follow me after I left the game," Riggins told Sunny Jurgensen at halftime of the Week Thirteen game against Dallas. "We'd run plays when there were arms and legs and things hanging, dangling in the hole, and you'd go ahead and run through that stuff. In my personal opinion, George Rogers doesn't want to run through that stuff."

Rogers brushed off the reluctant retiree's comments, saying they were "probably just to get attention." He remained the Redskins' starter, but his playing time had been cut into by shifty runner Kelvin Bryant and fifth-round draft pick Timmy Smith, who did not carry the football until November. By the start of the postseason, Rogers was so banged up—his lower back now nagged him as well—he had to sit out the team's first practice of the week.

Art Monk also missed the team's first practice. The All-Pro receiver partially tore a ligament in his right knee against the Cardinals in early December. Replacement-game record-setter Anthony Allen was re-signed to fill the void. Monk held out hope of returning at some point, should the Redskins go deep in the playoffs.

"If I have to sit out and miss everything, I'm prepared for that," Monk said. "When I got injured, the next day, I thought all about how this happened to me in 1982 and I missed the Super Bowl. I said, 'Here we go again.' But that was only one day, really. I now realize that's the nature of the game and I can deal with it."

"The potential of a great team is there," Monk observed a week after the regular season ended. "But we're not playing with any consistency or cohesiveness. I can only think back to the years of the Super Bowl, when we played well and we played smart. But there also was a closeness there I haven't felt before or afterward. Once you get to the Super Bowl, the hunger just isn't there anymore. You never get the same feeling as if you've never been there before.

"I just don't feel like the team is as close as it was then. We have the perfect blend for a great team, old guys and new guys. Yet at times we played like we were unstoppable and at other times we played like we couldn't beat anybody. This is something everyone's been trying to figure out since day one."

Not every element of the Redskins needed retooling. Throughout all the chaos at quarterback, the injuries to key offensive personnel, and the poor efforts on special teams, Washington's defense had been excellent. After a poor performance in the Week Eight loss at

Philadelphia—young star quarterback Randall Cunningham befuddled the Redskins with both his legs and arm—the defense tightened up, yielding an average of just 18.8 points the rest of the way.

Dexter Manley and Charles Mann continued to harass opposing quarterbacks, combining for 18 sacks in the shortened season. Darryl Grant and Dave Butz plugged up running lanes, allowing the NFL's most underrated rotation of linebackers—Monte Coleman, Mel Kaufman, Neal Olkewicz, and Rich Milot—to limit rushing gains.

Still, as much as any unit on the team, Washington's secondary secured their NFC East title.

In the locker room after the regular-season finale, wide receiver Ricky Sanders may have drawn the biggest crowd from reporters. His second long touchdown catch of the game forced overtime, and his 68 yards in the extra period set up the game-winning field goal. But Washington might not have even reached overtime had it not been for second-year safety Alvin Walton. Just before overtime began, the former third-round choice from the University of Kansas collected his second interception of the day, ending a Minnesota drive following Sanders's game-tying touchdown in the final two minutes.

Walton had become an extremely versatile safety. Sporting a short, John Riggins–like Mohawk underneath his helmet, Walton created turnovers, contributed immensely against the run—he led the club in tackles—and even recorded 3 sacks. During the Redskins' Week Thirteen win over Dallas, John Madden declared Walton "the best strong safety in the game right now."

On any other team, Walton might have been considered a superstar. But Darrell Green, whom voters named to the Pro Bowl for the third time in four years, remained the team's defensive stud. Few teams now challenged Green and his fabled speed: frequently shutting down half of the field as well as the opponent's top receiver, he forced quarterbacks to attack the Redskins elsewhere. And repeatedly throughout the 1987 season the team's "other" cornerback, Barry Wilburn, made opposing passers pay.

Wilburn soaked up all the lessons he could from his revered teammate.

"[Darrell] Green's helped immensely," Wilburn said in December. "Since I came here, he set the standard not only with this team but throughout the league as far as cornerbacks. Just having that to compete against and watch every day and learn from, it can only help you. By him being on one side, the other corner was bound to get a lot of work because teams were usually throwing away from him. That gave me the opportunity to pick off a lot of balls."

In his first year as a full-time starter, Wilburn cashed in nine of those opportunities, leading the league in interceptions. But the timing of Wilburn's picks made him as valuable as the raw numbers. During the 20–13 win over Detroit, his late-fourth-quarter interception secured the win, but in the postgame commentary, it was upstaged by Jay Schroeder's benching. Another came deep inside Washington territory toward the end of the 24–20 defeat of Dallas. And Wilburn's final interception of the regular season, against Minnesota, swung the momentum in favor of the struggling Redskins. Already ahead 7–0 in the second period, the Vikings drove to the Redskins' 2-yard line. Minnesota's quarterback Wade Wilson forced a throw toward the goal line, which Wilburn snatched out of the air. He surged through a mass of offensive and defensive players, and despite losing his balance near midfield the cornerback completed his end zone to end zone dash for a game-changing 100-yard pick-six.

"I've done everything in football, played offense and defense, scored touchdowns," Wilburn said that evening, "but I've never run 100 yards on a big play like that when my team really needed it."

Even if Wilburn had never done *that* before, sprinting 100 yards—or close to it—on a huge stage to help his teammates pursue victory was certainly in his blood.

Wilburn's parents were Jesse Wilburn, a star college running back at Tennessee State, and Maragret Matthews, a 1956 Olympics bronze medalist in the 4 × 100-meter relay and a Tennessee State

Tigerbelles teammate of Wilma Rudolph, the track icon who became Barry's godmother. In high school, Barry Wilburn posted a 3.8 grade point average and emerged as one of the state's best football players. In 1978, the wide receiver accepted a scholarship to Ole Miss, where he would start at safety and cornerback. During his senior season, two Washington Redskins coaches visited the Oxford campus to scout one of his teammates. They remembered Wilburn the following May and selected him in the eighth round of the 1985 draft. A year later, when Darrell Green suffered an injury during a *Monday Night* game against the 49ers, Wilburn won over the coaching staff and his opponent, wide receiver Jerry Rice.

"He never gave up," said Rice, who caught 12 passes for 204 yards, but didn't score. "He got beat. But he didn't act beat. He'd hit me fair and square, then say, 'I guess it's gonna be like this all night.' He's impressive with his skill, but mostly with his attitude. Relax, and it's over. He never did. He always came back. He's a championship corner."

The next summer, Wilburn beat out the Redskins' top draft pick Brian Davis, incumbent Vernon Dean—who had led the team in interceptions in 1984 and 1985—and Tim Morris for the starter's job. And once Wilburn snared interceptions in each of his first two starts, opposing quarterbacks reluctantly tested him.

"We saw some games for the first time this year, like Atlanta, where they almost turned around and said, 'We're gonna try [throwing at] Darrell Green some,'" Joe Gibbs noted.

While unparalleled speed was Green's greatest asset, size and a physical style of play gave Wilburn a different set of advantages over opposing receivers. At six feet three inches and two hundred pounds, Wilburn could hit as well as any defensive back in the league. His approach to the game provided another useful edge.

"I think I have the type of speed that if I ran just by myself, I'd run a 4.4 or 4.5 40-yard dash," he said late in the season. "But then you've got 'scared' speed, as in scared to death of the receiver. I'll run as fast as he'll run if he's a burner. I don't care how fast he is;

that's how fast I'll run. If you timed me with a bullet at my back, I'd run pretty darn fast."

Speed had become a hot topic for discussion prior to Washington's first playoff game. Although the Redskins had Wilburn and Green, Chicago had Willie Gault.

Born in Griffin, Georgia—hometown of Barry Wilburn's mother—Gault was a member of the 1980 U.S. Olympic team that boycotted the Moscow-hosted games and he finished third in the 110-meter hurdles at the 1983 NCAA Championships. In that year's NFL Draft, Chicago selected the University of Tennessee product eighteenth overall, ten spots ahead of Darrell Green. The Bears' top receiver every year since his rookie season, Gault led the team in yards from scrimmage during Chicago's three-game playoff rout culminating with a Super Bowl in 1986.

During the 1986 NFL's Fastest Man competition, he narrowly finished second to Darrell Green. The following winter, in a playoff game at RFK Stadium, the two again squared off. Gault beat Green for a 50-yard touchdown in the first quarter, but Green bounced back. In the third quarter, with Chicago trailing 13–7, Green intercepted a pass intended for Gault. Three plays later the Redskins took the lead and surged past the Bears for a 27–13 win. The Bears-Redskins playoff rematch following the 1987 regular season set up another showdown.

"We bring out the best in each other," Gault said. "It's always an interesting confrontation."

Prior to the game, Bears head coach Mike Ditka added a new wrinkle to the Gault-Green rivalry: he announced that Gault would return kicks. Although he had once been an important special teams weapon for the Bears—he returned a kickoff 98 yards for a touchdown against Washington early in the 1985 season—Gault did not field a single kickoff for Chicago in 1987.

"I'm just trying to put a little more of a speed element back there," Ditka said that week.

Although he never mentioned it to the media, Joe Gibbs had the same idea.

January in Chicago meant frigid conditions at Soldier Field. Prior to kickoff, the temperature was minus-four degrees (minus-twenty-three with the wind chill factor). In the bitter cold, Washington fell behind 14–0 but fought back to tie the game late in the second quarter. With the cold only intensifying as the sun disappeared in the early afternoon, both team's offenses faltered, turning the ball over on consecutive possessions. Late into the scoreless third period, the Redskins' defense forced a three-and-out from Chicago, who sent out their punting unit, backed up near their own end zone. Instead of regular punt returner Eric Yarber, who fielded the Bears two earlier punts, Darrell Green lined up deep to receive Chicago's kick.

An electrifying punt returner in college—as a senior he returned two for scores, including a 96-yarder—Green saw few chances to contribute on special teams. The Redskins' coaching staff believed that starting at cornerback was enough for the rookie to handle. And once Green became an All-Pro defender capable of shutting down an opposing star all by himself, they did not want to risk his health.

"He should have been groomed and not started [on defense] that first year; had him [only] returning punts and kickoffs," director of pro personnel Kirk Mee later said. "Remember Billy 'White Shoes' Johnson? He would have been the same caliber, probably better. They did use him a couple times in preseason. First time he touched the ball he went [61] yards for a touchdown. But they had to start him [at cornerback]. They didn't want to put too much on him."

Five years later, with points at a premium in frigid weather against a great Chicago defense, Joe Gibbs turned to Green for the first time in the playoffs since the second half of Super Bowl XVIII.

"You put him back there, he was probably going to get a touchdown [or] he was probably going to get hurt," Gibbs said. "So we picked our spots, when you thought you could put him back there.

He could have been a great return guy but you always ran the risk of him getting hurt. And sure enough on that punt . . ."

Ready to field just his sixth punt of the 1987 season, the Houston native kept his hands inside a hand warmer until well after Chicago's Tommy Barnhardt punted the ball. He took them out just in time to field the kick at his own 48. Green darted toward the sideline, where he saw a considerable obstacle, Bears tight end Cap Boso, lunging at him.

"I decided that he was either going to run me out of bounds or hit me, or I would cut across the grain," Green said. "Well, I didn't really think about it. You're not so much thinking out there."

Although he had been an All-American sprinter at Texas A&I, excelling in the 50-, 100-, and 200-meter events, hurdles hadn't been his event.

While running full speed he leapt over the six-foot-four-inch, 235-pound Boso, cut back to the inside, sidestepped another would-be tackler, and raced untouched into the end zone. The Washington sideline and his ten fellow Redskins on the field were jubilant. Not Green: the hurdle had torn cartilage in his ribcage. Green returned for the next defensive series, but attempting to stay step-for-step with Willie Gault proved too painful. He sat out the remainder of the game.

"[The injury] is very sore, very painful," Redskins head trainer Bubba Tyer told the press the next day. "He just jumped out of his ribs."

Rookie Brian Davis replaced Green and surrendered a 44-yard catch to Gault, setting up a field goal that cut Washington's lead to 21–17. With some help from Barry Wilburn, however, the talented second-round pick from the University of Nebraska shut Gault out for the rest of the game.

Early in the fourth quarter, with Chicago at Washington's 14-yard line, Wilburn blanketed Gault across the end zone. When Bears quarterback Jim McMahon threw off-target toward the goal line, Wilburn broke in front of Gault and hauled in the pass. The interception ended the Bears' best, though not their last, chance to take the lead.

With less than a minute to play and Chicago nearing midfield, McMahon tossed a pass to Walter Payton on fourth-and-eight. Payton had recently announced that he would retire after the season, but as he headed upfield, "Sweetness" neared a first down that would keep the drive, the game, and his career alive. Within a yard of the marker, Payton was wrestled to the sideline, short of the first down. Barry Wilburn was credited with tackling the NFL's all-time leading rusher on the final play of his career. Margaret Matthews Wilburn enjoyed telling her son that fact after the Redskins won, 21–17.

"When you have parents like mine," Wilburn later said, "they make sure you have a sense of history."

RAISED IN LOUISIANA, a college star in the same state, and a pro in Florida, Arizona, and Oklahoma, Doug Williams had never seen weather like the Redskins faced in Chicago, let alone played in it.

Icy weather wasn't totally foreign to him. As a member of the Buccaneers in December 1982, he completed 18 passes for 204 yards and a touchdown in a loss to the Jets at Shea Stadium, where a blizzard had befallen the city that morning. And during his time with the Outlaws, the USFL's spring schedule sent him to Chicago in March for a matchup with the Blitz: at snow-covered Soldier Field, he threw 2 touchdown passes in a 17–14 victory.

But the Hoth-like scene he saw four years later when at Soldier Field was entirely different.

"Pregame, I said, 'Damn, I don't know whether I can play.' I couldn't even hold the ball," Williams recalled decades later. "The frigid weather, twenty-three-below wind chill factor, that was brutal for an ol' country boy from Louisiana. That was totally brutal."

Wearing gloves on his throwing hand for the only time in his career, Williams was tripped up by both the weather and the Bears' defense early on. Deep in Washington territory, a sack by Richard Dent caused a fumble, which the Bears converted into an early 7–0 lead. And to begin the second half, he misfired on his first six throws, one of which was intercepted near the Bears' goal line, killing a great scoring opportunity.

But in between those costly turnovers, Williams caught fire amid the frost. On consecutive possessions late in the second period, he marched the Redskins from their side of the field into the Chicago end zone. His 18-yard touchdown pass to tight end Clint Didier—a perfect throw over the middle despite linebacker Otis Wilson in his face—tied the game before halftime.

"[Williams's] second quarter was about as good as you can hope for," Joe Gibbs said. "It was superb."

The offense did not score in the second half, but 5 sacks and 3 interceptions from the defense along with Darrell Green's punt return allowed the Redskins to hang on and advance to the NFC Championship Game, where their opponent was the very familiar Minnesota Vikings.

Losing to the Redskins in overtime on the final weekend of the regular season had greatly hurt the Vikings' postseason chances, but a St. Louis loss the next day gave Minnesota the NFC's final playoff spot. They shocked the New Orleans Saints during the wild card round, then went to Candlestick Park and, in one of the greatest upsets in postseason history, thrashed the top-seeded San Francisco 49ers, who had lost only one game since the first week of the season.

Spearheaded by All-Pro lineman Chris Doleman, Minnesota's defense pounded the 49ers, convincing head coach Bill Walsh to make the unfathomable move of benching Joe Montana in favor of backup Steve Young. Nearly as surprising as the 49ers' offensive ineptitude that day was how poorly their defense fared against the Vikings. In their 36–24 win, Minnesota totaled 397 yards against the NFL's top-ranked unit.

Washington had seemingly caught a break: with the conference's top two seeds, Chicago and San Francisco, eliminated, the Redskins would now host the NFC Championship Game at RFK Stadium. But the manner in which Minnesota achieved their two road upsets cast some doubt over the Redskins' ability to prevent a third. In the wild card win over New Orleans, Pro Bowl wide receiver Anthony Carter scored 2 touchdowns and gained 222 all-purpose yards. A week later against San Francisco, the former USFL star caught 10 passes for 227 yards. Given Carter's dazzling play, the rib injury to Darrell Green—who had limited Carter to just 2 catches in the regular-season game against Minnesota—became a major story line in the days leading up to the second Vikings-Redskins game in twenty-two days.

"I think the best way is to make preparations as if Darrell won't be able to play," Joe Gibbs said midweek. "We're making plans to go ahead without him, hoping all the time that he will be able to play. Better that than to make plans, 'Hey, yes, Darrell is playing,' and then be disappointed."

By Sunday, however, Green not only returned to cover Carter (he sat out just five defensive plays), but he was again fielding punts for the Redskins. A pregame shot of novocaine helped Green fight through the pain as he stared down his fellow Pro Bowler. To aid Green, Barry Wilburn, and the rest of the secondary, against an offense that had scored fourteen times in two playoff games, the Redskins' coaching staff devised several new blitzes and defensive fronts that week.

"Our game plan against a good team like this is to mix it up," Gibbs said. "We try to make it a guessing game all the way."

The aggressive, fluctuating scheme caught Minnesota off-guard, especially on first and second down. Seven different Redskins recorded sacks of quarterback Wade Wilson, and the Vikings' running backs gained just 48 yards on 17 carries.

"They were never in the same defense two times in a row," said Minnesota's offensive line coach John Michels. "It's always surprising when you play a relatively conservative team and they do that much switching."

But Minnesota also boasted one of the NFL's most talented defenses, especially along the defensive line. And after allowing Washington a touchdown on their first possession of the game, the Vikings confounded the opposing offense. Despite beginning several drives with favorable field position, Washington did not score again in the first half, then failed to record even a single first down in the third quarter. With the score tied 7–7 late in the third period, the once-raucous crowd at RFK Stadium quieted, except for whispers of another Redskins quarterback change.

Doug Williams did not play well against the Vikings. He overthrew receivers, threw behind others, and at one point in the second half had completed just 7 of 24 passes for 69 yards. Some fans booed; others chanted, "Bring in Jay!"

"I was worried. [Schroeder] was chomping at the bit," Gibbs said. "But I wasn't going to take Doug out. It was kind of a gut feeling, and sometimes you have to go along with those. Even though Doug was struggling, he definitely never lost his poise."

Gibbs even had an opportunity to replace Williams with Schroeder and chalk up the switch to injury: midway through the third quarter, Williams scrambled for 10 yards, was tackled by the Vikings' Issiac Holt, and landed harshly on his throwing shoulder. Feeling a burning pain down his spine, Williams laid still on the ground, where he was attended by the team trainers, before gingerly walking off the field. As Schroeder threw warm-up passes along the sideline, team doctor Charles Jackson inspected Williams on the bench. Joe Gibbs then approached his quarterback.

"You can kind of tell by the look in a player's eye," Gibbs said. "He looked right at me and said, 'Hey, I'm fine.'"

Insisting that "it would have been tough to get me out of there. . . . I wasn't comin' out," Williams finally rewarded his head coach.

Following a Vikings field goal that tied the game at 10 early in the fourth quarter, Washington took possession, and on a third-and-five from their own 46, Williams spotted Gary Clark down the left sideline, two steps beyond Vikings safety Reggie Rutland. Clark hauled in the deep throw, setting Washington up at the Vikings 11-yard line.

"It was getting pretty frustrating. Not just for me, but for our entire offense," Clark said. "We're a big-play offense, and eventually we usually get to you."

Williams had shown Clark the same type of faith and trust that Joe Gibbs had shown in him. By his third NFL season, Clark developed a reputation for both huge plays and huge drops. In the second quarter, he beat defensive back Wymon Henderson to the corner of the end zone, where a perfect throw from Doug Williams waited for him. More concerned with keeping his feet in-bounds, the All-Pro receiver dropped the certain touchdown.

"With Gary Clark," said Williams, "you just keep throwing the ball in his direction and hope the next time he catches the ball."

Three plays after the 43-yard pickup, Williams again hit Clark, over the middle in the back of the end zone for the go-ahead score.

"Doug was struggling. The whole offense was struggling," Clark said. "But Doug stands in there. He's a competitor and a winner. You always have the feeling that somewhere, sometime, he's going to make a big play."

Clark's clutch grabs gave the Redskins a 17–10 lead with 5:15 remaining. On the ensuing possession, Minnesota steadily advanced from their own 33 to the Washington 12. With barely a minute remaining, Wade Wilson connected with Anthony Carter for the seventh time on the day, pushing the Vikings to the 6-yard line. Two incompletions followed, and for the second consecutive week, the Redskins' defense faced a game-defining fourth down. Joe Gibbs knelt on the ground, closed his eyes, and prayed silently.

"I was praying, but it was the right kind of prayer. I was praying for God's will, and I could have lived with it either way," he said. "Obviously I was thinking about overtime. I didn't want overtime. I think everyone was really exhausted."

A trip to the Super Bowl hanging in the balance, Wade Wilson dropped into the pocket and sent a pass to the goal line for running back Darrin Nelson, who bobbled the ball. The novocaine having long since faded, Darrell Green peeled off his coverage of Anthony Carter to crunch Nelson, preventing the running back from regaining possession.

A Doug Williams kneel-down drained the clock and 55,212 Redskins fans went wild. By now, the RFK crowd had come to expect this type of finish. For the fifth consecutive game, and the thirteenth time that season, the Redskins had competed in an excruciatingly close nail-biter that was decided by 7 points or less.

"I know it was tense out there," linebacker Mel Kaufman told the press, "but you name a game this year that wasn't tense."

"IT'S THE ULTIMATE, like going to the mountaintop, like Martin Luther King said," Doug Williams explained following the win over Minnesota. "After the Super Bowl, if I never play another down, I'll be satisfied."

The next morning, on just three hours' sleep, he appeared on ABC's *Good Morning America*, much to the delight of the network hosting Super Bowl XXII. Later that morning he served as the honorary grand marshal at a southeast D.C. parade celebrating Martin Luther King's birthday. Although he "just rode through waiving . . . and signed a few autographs" as his car drove along the streets of Anacostia, Williams proudly told a crowd of several thousand, "I'm just glad that I am going to be one part of Martin Luther King's dream."

The week off prior to the annual Super Bowl festivities allowed Williams to forget any leftover angst from his mostly poor performance against Minnesota as well as heal up from the late-game hit that sandwiched his shoulder and left him a bit woozy.

But upon arriving in Southern California on January 24, new headaches surfaced.

Williams didn't mind the hefty price he paid for fifteen family members to fly to San Diego, then stay in a posh hotel for the week; he'd waited thirty-two years to reach the Super Bowl. But the day before Washington would take on the Broncos, Williams awoke with a sharp pain in his jaw.

While the team wrapped up a final walk-through practice, Williams was in a La Jolla dentist's chair for four and a half hours, having an abscessed tooth removed via root canal. He met up with the team later that evening, but was excused from meetings. The night before the biggest game of his life, Doug Williams ate a dinner of painkillers and Hershey's Kisses.

"It was no big thing," Williams remembered.

The media circus that surrounded him that week, however, was.

Reporters hounded the first African American quarterback ever to start a Super Bowl from the moment he arrived in San Diego. For the most part, he successfully hid in his room from the gaggle camped outside the team's hotel. Only former Buccaneers teammate Jimmie Giles, who showed up to his room one night in the middle of the week, could coax him out of his seclusion for a nice dinner. Still, he was required to give formal interviews at designated places and times. He faced countless questions about "the black quarterback issue," the progress of race relations in the United States, and whether he or other black civil rights leaders such as Reverend Jesse Jackson planned to use this moment on the national stage as a "personal forum."

"I'm not playing this game for black America," he said. "I'm playing this game for the Washington Redskins."

Other questions focused on the media's role in his battling discrimination. Prior to the playoff game in Chicago famed *CBS Sports* prognosticator Jimmy "The Greek" Snyder—whom the network would fire just a week later for comments with "patently racist overtones"—had suggested that the Redskins would lose because Williams tended to choke. The subtext of his prediction suggested racism.

Repeatedly asked to comment on Snyder's recent firing, Williams told reporters, "I'm not uncomfortable about it. Why pour salt in the wound?"

Many of the other questions had been reasonable. Discrimination toward and stereotypes about black quarterbacks permeated the NFL for years and within one week Williams had become the poster child for proving those skeptics wrong.

Throughout it all, Williams handled the insanity with tremendous grace.

"No, no. I anticipated this," he said. "These people have jobs to do, stories to write and tell. People advised me of the questions that would be asked, and I spent a lot of time on the flight out here thinking about everything. I'm not interview-happy, but it hasn't bothered me."

He didn't even balk during one the most infamous moments in the history of Super Bowl media coverage. The day the Redskins arrived, Williams sat with a small group of reporters, including Butch John of the *Clarion-Ledger* (Jackson, Mississippi), who had worked the Grambling State football beat when Williams's younger brother Mike starred at quarterback.

"For about twenty minutes, Doug's getting all these questions about the significance [of Williams's race]," said John. "All these question, blah-de-blah-de-blah. Never let up. Being from the South, having covered Grambling and his brother Mike, Doug being a black quarterback was no big deal to me."

"This is what I said, verbatim: 'Doug, it's obvious you've been a black quarterback all your life. When did it start to matter?' Everybody got a pretty good laugh out of it. His answer was that it didn't matter till he got to the NFL. That answer was used in the wire services. Also, there was a little blurb—no more than a paragraph—in the San Diego paper the next day, about 'a question from a well-meaning writer.' From there, things just kind of shot out of control."

Over the next few days—and years—the story of Williams being asked "How long have you been a black quarterback?" grew into one of the game's greatest tall tales. But by Super Bowl Sunday, Williams's weeklong press interrogation was behind him. He even woke up that morning, twelve hours after his root canal, completely pain-free. Along with his fellow Redskins teammates he left the Lawrence Welk Resort in Escondido; for privacy, Joe Gibbs moved the team to that "secret" location on Saturday before a joint chapel service attended by both Redskins and Broncos players. Once inside Jack Murphy Stadium, Washington players dressed, stretched, warmed up, and then waited for the end of the *Salute to Bob Hope* pregame show featuring donkeys, camels, and thousands of performers to exit the field. At 3:18 p.m. local time, the game finally began. And for the second consecutive time, Washington limped out of the Super Bowl gate.

Denver, who had lost the previous year's Super Bowl despite leading the Giants at halftime, shut down the Redskins on the game's very first possession and needed just one offensive snap to take the lead. From the shotgun, NFL MVP John Elway heaved a bomb downfield, where wide receiver Ricky Nattiel had blown past Barry Wilburn. Nattiel made the catch at the 8-yard line and lunged into the end zone for the fastest score (1:57 into the first quarter) in Super Bowl history.

Being burned by a rookie wide receiver for a 56-yard score on the first play of the Super Bowl did nothing to discourage Barry Wilburn.

"I gave them that touchdown," he said. "They caught me sleeping. We started with a zone and I came out a little lax and he blew by me."

Matched up man-to-man with Nattiel most of the day, Wilburn immediately woke up; he allowed Nattiel only one more catch the rest of the game. But several of his Redskins teammates appeared similarly asleep at the switch during the game's opening minutes. Gary Clark, who dropped a Doug Williams pass on Washington's first series, dropped another easy grab on their next possession, forcing the Redskins to punt. A few plays later, the Redskins' defense fell for a trick play—a throwback to the quarterback—that pushed Denver into field goal range. Less than six minutes into the game, Washington trailed, 10–0.

Washington's third drive also produced no points, evoking memories of the nightmarish Super Bowl start four years earlier against the Los Angeles Raiders. The ominous flashbacks only intensified on the next series when Doug Williams took the snap on a first-and-ten from his own 35.

The natural grass at San Diego's Jack Murphy Stadium was unusually slick that day. Eight regular-season Chargers home games, six San Diego State Aztecs games, December's Holiday Bowl between Iowa and Wyoming, the San Diego Padres eighty-one home games, and the stadium's irritating trespassers—opossums, skunks, cottontail rabbits, squirrels, cats, and pigeons—persuaded the Super Bowl's resident turf-expert, George Toma, to plant new grass.

Despite the expensive grounds-keeping and dry conditions throughout the week, players on both sides complained about the surface. Many scrambled to change from regular-spiked cleats to longer spikes.

"The field was very slippery," Charles Mann said. "The field was young grass and it was very low-cut. We didn't want to lose a one-on-one battle because of a slip, so therefore most of the guys changed cleats."

Doug Williams didn't change his. He hadn't brought a longer-spiked pair. Standing tall in the pocket as the first quarter wound down, he didn't seem to need them: he completed 2 passes, including a 20-yarder that converted a third-and-eleven deep in his own territory. But on the next play, Williams dropped back to pass and steadied himself by planting his right leg into the ground. His foot coasted on the slippery surface and he buckled like a prizefighter who had just been delivered the knockout blow. Williams rolled around on the ground, stood back up, limped around behind the huddle, only to drop back onto the grass. Several minutes passed while the training staff examined him on the field.

"I didn't know if I would be able to play another down," Williams recalled.

Jay Schroeder took his place in the Washington huddle. The quarterback, who spent most of his homecoming to Southern California imitating John Elway for the Redskins defense in practice, didn't fare much better than Williams. A sack and another dropped pass forced Washington to punt again. On the sideline, Doug Williams conversed with the doctors, carefully applied weight to his leg, then lightly jogged and jumped around. From high above the field, in the coach's box, assistant coach Jerry Rhome called down to Williams on the team's in-game phone system to check on his quarterback.

"Jerry, they'd have to cut off both my legs for me not to go back out there," he told Rhome.

Perseverance had been one of his hallmarks during a long career. As a rookie, Williams returned to the lineup following a broken jaw late in the 1978 season, and he rebounded from a mangled biceps in the playoffs to return as the starter the next year. He'd played with a back injury in the Redskins' regular-season loss to the Rams. And fighting through intense shoulder pain, Williams threw the touchdown pass that defeated Minnesota in the NFC Championship Game.

Aside from his grit, pride, and dedication to his teammates, a more specific urge propelled Williams to retake the field: he did not want Jay Schroeder to play.

"I wouldn't have cared who the backup was that day, I wanted to finish the game," he said. "But if I could not have finished the game, I certainly would have preferred [third-string quarterback Mark Rypien] going in if it had come down to that. Because the year before we played the Giants for the NFC Championship Game, Schroeder had gotten hit hard, knocked woozy, barely getting off the ground. . . . Schroeder waved me off. It was an embarrassing time for me . . . and I never forgot it."

While Williams further tested his knee's readiness, the rest of the bewildered starting offense walked to the sideline following a fourth consecutive fruitless series. In the two weeks leading up to the Super Bowl, Joe Gibbs and his offensive staff had prepared for the relatively basic, unnuanced 3-4 defense that Denver employed all season. But on game day, the Broncos unveiled a new, exotic, 46-style scheme with several stunts specifically designed for Washington. The surprise and confusion that it caused the Redskins' offense greatly contributed to their anemic start. In search of answers, Joe Gibbs approached the Hogs.

"It's the only time Joe ever came over to the offensive line during the game for knowledge," Jeff Bostic said years later. "He goes, 'What's going on up front?'"

Bostic grabbed a nearby dry-erase board, sketched out Denver's unexpected alignment against the Redskins' formation, and awaited instructions. Gibbs, whose reputation for on-the-fly thinking and second-half adjustments had already become famous, then applied his greatest skill in the season's biggest game.

"He puts his finger beside his face, and goes, 'Okay, here's what were going to do.' That quick! He said when 'We get the ball back, we're going to run a hitch, get some momentum,'" Bostic said. "'Then we're going to run the 40/50 Gut . . . after we finish running the Gut, we'll run the counter and ball 'em up inside.' . . . He had the ability for people to feed him information and to almost instantaneously make changes to his offense."

Armed with a new game plan and given a few extra moments for his knee to recover during the quarter change, Doug Williams returned to the field when the Redskins regained possession less than a minute into the second period. From his own 20-yard line, Williams lined up behind Bostic, surveyed the defense, and recognized press coverage from cornerback Mark Haynes on Ricky Sanders. As prescribed by the coaching staff, Williams changed the play at the line of scrimmage: instead of the short 5-yard hitch, he would throw a deep fade to Sanders. Williams shouted out the audible "Charlie 10," gave Sanders a subtle head-nod, and took the snap. Backing into the pocket, Williams planted on his gimpy right knee and uncorked a long pass downfield.

The hero of the regular-season victory over Minnesota and the team's leading receiver against Chicago, Ricky Sanders had been practically invisible in the NFC Championship Game rematch, not catching a single pass. Early in his Super Bowl debut Sanders was all too visible, but for the wrong reasons. Deep in his own territory, he fumbled the kickoff following Denver's first-quarter field goal; teammate Ravin Caldwell averted disaster by falling on the ball. Minutes later, on a reverse, he was tackled for a 4-yard loss. And after making his first grab of the day, a 9-yard pickup, he dropped an easy pass with plenty of open field in front of him.

As most of his teammates had, Sanders found the turf at Jack Murphy Stadium a serious problem.

"I was slipping all over the place," he said. "I just couldn't get my footing. I couldn't get upfield like I wanted to."

Fed up, he changed to longer-spiked cleats in the middle of the opening quarter. And as Doug Williams prepared to execute the Charlie 10 audible, "Slick Rick" used his improved traction to elude Mark Haynes. Well beyond the former Pro Bowl cornerback, Sanders caught the football over his right shoulder just before midfield and burst down the sideline for an 80-yard touchdown, matching the longest pass completion in Super Bowl history.

"[Haynes] came up and he hit me in the chest but I slipped him," Sanders remembered. "And 80 yards later, touchdown. That was the start of it."

Denver went three-and-out on their next series and five snaps later, the Redskins were back in the Broncos' end zone. On third-and-one at the opponent's 27, Doug Williams flicked another lobbed pass beyond the secondary, where Gary Clark had shook defensive back Steve Wilson. Clark dove to make the catch right at the goal line.

"I think more than anything, I'll remember their second touchdown," Denver's Jim Ryan said that evening. "We had a delayed blitz on, and I was the guy blitzing, and I was coming clean. Then, as soon as I get my hands on Williams, he gets that pass off. I don't know how, but he gets it off. Now that rattled me. Made me think, maybe this thing is not going to go my way."

Washington had gone from being behind 10 points—a Super Bowl deficit no team had previously ever overcome—to ahead 14–10 in the span of six offensive plays.

And there were still ten minutes and fifteen seconds remaining in the second quarter.

JOE GIBBS LOVED to tinker. Every week his strategies for attacking defenses changed.

"We never ran the same game plan for sixteen weeks," remembered quarterback Mark Rypien, an inactive member of the Super Bowl XXII roster. "If we ran the same game plan for sixteen weeks, we probably would have been 1-15. We changed things all the time."

Throughout the 1987 season, Gibbs's penchant for "gut feeling" adjustments repeatedly seeped into his lineups. In addition to the game of musical chairs he played with Jay Schroeder and Doug Williams, and shuffling the middle of his offensive line, he toyed with his special teams by bringing in Paul Lanham, switching long snappers and holders, and inserting Darrell Green as a punt returner against the Bears.

Gibbs, however, saved his greatest lineup alteration for the Super Bowl.

George Rogers's litany of injuries did not heal during the playoffs. Against the Bears, he rushed for 13 yards on 6 attempts. After being stuffed on a fourth-down attempt early in the game, he only carried the ball once more, scoring a touchdown from 3 yards out in the second quarter. The next week, he gained 26 yards against Minnesota, only to reinjure his ankle and miss much of the second half. And although he missed portions of practice throughout the week in San Diego, aggravated the injury on Wednesday, and was "a little iffy," according to Joe Gibbs, Rogers announced that he would start the Super Bowl. Expected to occasionally relieve Rogers were Kelvin Bryant as well as Timmy Smith, who had rushed for 138 yards on 29 carries during the two playoff victories.

"My role is the same as it's always been," Smith told the *Washington Post* two days before the Super Bowl. "I'll be in the background."

Smith had been in the background much of his rookie season. The five-foot-eleven-inch 215-pounder appeared in only four regular-season games. The longest of his 29 runs in those four games was for just 15 yards. Smith didn't mind: he was just happy to be on an NFL roster.

An all-state basketball player and All-American running back at Hobbs High School in New Mexico, Smith met with dozens of recruiters from Oklahoma, Texas, Texas A&M, Baylor, and other powerhouse programs following his 312-yard, 5-touchdown performance in a defeat of Monterrey High in Lubbock, Texas. Nearing the time to select his college choice, he moved into a motel for two weeks just to find some peace. Following his older brother to Texas Tech, Smith led the Red Raiders in rushing during both his freshman and sophomore seasons, but a promising career was derailed by injuries beginning his junior year. Against New Mexico State he rushed for a 42-yard touchdown, celebrated in the end zone, and was clobbered from behind by a defender. The "cheap shot" tore cartilage in his knee, later requiring surgery to repair the damage.

Although he came back and played near the end of that season, prior to the start of his senior year a teammate fell on him in practice, dislocating his ankle. Hospitalized, he needed a pin and metal plate permanently inserted into his foot. Set to return late in the year, he reinjured the ankle playing pickup basketball and underwent another surgery.

"I never thought I'd play again," he said.

Two significant lower-body injuries and the hefty gut he gained due to prolonged inactivity scared off nearly every team prior to the 1987 NFL Draft. But Redskins general manager Bobby Beathard, who always stopped in Lubbock during his Texas trips, heard about Smith from the Red Raiders' coaches and became intrigued.

"One of the coaches told me, 'Well, we have a running back here that's really probably better than all these guys, but he's been [injured]," recalled Beathard, who then watched film of Smith as a junior and even during spring practices. "I think I went clear back to his high school, to call the high school coaches, to talk about him. He was one of the top kids in New Mexico. He was just an amazing running back. And I looked at the old things, and I guess some scouts just didn't pay much attention to going back and looking at that. But boy, he was really something."

Prior to selecting him in the fifth round of the 1987 draft, Beathard met with Timmy Smith in his hometown of Hobbs and arranged for the team doctors to inspect his ankle. Although he was given a clean bill of health on his ankle, Smith arrived at minicamp ten pounds overweight. Beathard ordered him to "stop eating."

"Bobby Beathard is always on me," he later said. "I think he sees the talent deep down. I think he's trying to push me into being the best running back I can be."

Smith followed Beathard's advice and arrived at training camp in fine shape. With the help of veteran George Rogers, who let the rookie live with him and drive his car—"George would give you the shirt off his back . . . he took me under his wing"—Smith led the Redskins in rushing during the 1987 preseason. When the regular season opened, however, the only carries he saw were as a running back for the Redskins' scout team.

"I was just waiting on an opportunity, that's all you can do," Smith said decades later. "We really helped the defense out by giving them the best look we could possibly give them for any running back we'd be going up against. And that definitely helped me out when it came time for me to get in there and to play, because I figured if I can run on our defense, I can pretty much run on anybody's defense."

Smith received his first action in the Redskins' Week Seven blowout victory over Buffalo, carrying the ball 7 times for 54 yards. He saw several more attempts late in the season, and once the playoffs began and George Rogers's many ailments tightened up in the harsh Chicago weather, Smith carried the load for the Redskins, even if he was not their official starter.

"I don't think I deserve to start," Smith said prior to the playoff win over Minnesota, a game in which he led all rushers with 72 yards. "I think George deserves to be in there. It's too late [in the season] to put me in there right now. I think my time will come."

To his astonishment, Smith's time came just minutes before the start of Super Bowl XXII.

Although George Rogers's name would be called during the ceremonial pregame introductions, Timmy Smith would start against Denver. Running backs coach Don Breaux did not inform the rookie until the Redskins stood in the tunnel, preparing to run on the field.

"We wanted him to enjoy his trip over here," assistant head coach Joe Bugel said. "We told him he'd play five, six plays in [the game]. We didn't want to have to throw a smoke bomb to get him out of the locker room."

Flabbergasted and breaking out into a cold sweat, Smith tried to calm his nerves by mentally reviewing all his plays, but his mind went blank. Only a pep talk from Doug Williams shocked him back into coherence.

"Hey, Timmy," Williams told him. "This is my first Super Bowl. If you fuck it up, I'm gonna kick your ass."

"That's when my plays started coming back to me," Smith said years later.

Smith carried the football on the first play from scrimmage, gaining 4 yards. But during Washington's dismal, scoreless first period, he found few holes, collecting just 9 yards on 5 carries. The one play in which he did find daylight, an off-tackle run for 25 yards, was wiped out by a holding call.

Everything changed when the first quarter ended.

Although Doug Williams's touchdown passes had grabbed Washington the lead just six offensive plays after trailing 10–0, Timmy Smith, the Hogs, and Joe Gibbs's creativity transformed Super Bowl XXII from a great comeback story into the most devastating turnaround in NFL championship game history.

The halfback counter remained a central play in the Redskins' arsenal long after John Riggins had retired. George Rogers ran it effectively in his three seasons as the team's workhorse, but Timmy Smith possessed instincts and quickness that made the play seem tailor-made for him. Dubbed "the Cutback King" by tackle Mark May and his fellow Hogs, Smith's penchant for running to the side opposite the play's designed direction often picked up extra yards. A defense's over-pursuit and aggressiveness sometimes left the "backside" of the play wide open for a runner to attack.

In the Super Bowl against Denver, however, the play of the Redskins' offensive line—having adjusted to the Broncos' new schemes—meant Smith didn't need to cut back. He saw huge gaps to run through, right where the play had been intended, especially when the Redskins ran 60 Counter Gap from their own 42-yard line early in the second quarter. Handed the ball from Williams, Smith raced through an enormous hole plowed open by Raleigh McKenzie and Joe Jacoby, who had pulled from the backside.

With a full head of steam and no defender within five feet of him as he broke free of the line of scrimmage, Smith outran Denver's

defensive backs Tony Lilly and Steve Wilson to the end zone for a
58-yard touchdown.

"I close my eyes and the only thing I can see is Joe Jacoby and
Raleigh McKenzie pulling in front of me and nothing left ahead of
me but hole," Smith said years later.

On their next series, Washington didn't run the ball. Nevertheless, Counter Gap still produced another touchdown. Following an
incompletion and a 10-yard strike to Sanders, Williams faked a handoff to Smith. The entire Denver defense bit on the action that had
produced Smith's touchdown just minutes earlier. Williams stood
alone in the pocket and heaved a pass downfield for a wide-open
Ricky Sanders, who caught the ball and easily crossed the goal line.

His team ahead 28–10, barely ten minutes after falling behind
10–0, Joe Gibbs let his habitual tinkering run wild.

"We must have run that Counter Gap maybe twenty-five
times in the game," Jerry Rhome remembered. "And what was
great about what Joe Gibbs and those coaches were doing—Don
Breaux and Rennie Simmons and Joe Bugel—they had about six
different ways to run it. One guy in motion, then this guy doing
it, then the back would do it. We just kept changing. We had about
five or six different ways to run that play. . . . And they were all
with different motion-looks. And that's what Gibbs was a master
at. He was a master at formation motions and the system allowed
us to do all that."

Given the ball back by way of a Barry Wilburn interception just before the two-minute warning, the Redskins' offense
promptly turned a Counter Gap run, with Mark May and R. C.
Thielemann pulling, into a 43-yard gain as Smith crossed into
Denver territory. From there, two consecutive Ricky Sanders
receptions picked up 28 total yards, and pushed Washington to
the Broncos 8-yard line. With halftime approaching, Doug Williams found tight end Clint Didier in the back left corner of the
end zone for yet another score.

Less than fourteen minutes had rolled off the second period game clock and Washington had scored 5 touchdowns. It was the greatest offensive display during a single quarter in NFL history: 35 points, 356 total yards, 228 passing yards, 128 rushing yards.

Halftime finally came for the Broncos—rookie Brian Davis intercepted a John Elway pass to close out the period—and both teams headed for their respective locker rooms. While there, Redskins team doctor Charles Jackson drained fluid from Doug Williams's fast-swelling knee.

But with the score 35–10, the final two quarters became an afterthought. With the outcome all but a certainty, little drama remained for ABC's viewing audience. Those who did stay tuned after the end of a wholesome halftime show featuring Chubby Checker and Radio City Music Hall Rockettes were treated to more Super Bowl landmarks.

Following a sloppy, scoreless third quarter—Washington missed a field goal and Doug Williams threw an interception—the Redskins' running game continued to trample the Denver defense.

"Them boys upfront: best blocking and execution you're ever going to see," Williams said a quarter century later. "We ran a play called 50 Bang where the tight end comes in and traps the tackle. And I just turned and handed the ball up the gut. I've never seen a hole that big in my life in a game. A freight train could have ran up that."

Timmy Smith played the role of runaway steam engine.

"Everybody says the holes were pretty big [but] I still had to run, I still had to outrun the safety, I still had to outrun the linebackers, you still have to do your part," he recalled. "The linemen were very experienced, they communicated, they did their job. . . . You couldn't ask for better linemen than those guys. That defense was not ready for those linemen."

The once-obscure running back scored his second touchdown of the day early in the fourth quarter, capping off a drive in which he gained 43 yards on 3 rushes. He opened up the next series with 4 more carries, gaining 22 more yards to put him over 200 total yards—enough to reclaim the single-game Super Bowl rushing crown for the Redskins, blowing past the 191-yard mark that Marcus Allen set against Washington in Super Bowl XVIII to eclipse John Riggins's record.

"[Joe Gibbs] took me out with about seven minutes left in the game," Smith half complained. "I felt like I could've run all day long. I felt like I could've gotten 300 yards out there."

In any other Super Bowl, Smith's 2-touchdown, 22-carry, 204-yard performance likely would have earned him a landslide win in the media's Most Valuable Player vote. And if not Smith, Ricky Sanders would have been a deserving MVP, setting a Super Bowl record with 193 receiving yards and 235 all-purpose yards. But as the final two minutes wore down, the public address announcer delivered obvious news: Doug Williams, who tied one Super Bowl record with 4 touchdown passes and set another with 340 yards passing, received the award.

No longer would he be known as "Doug Williams, the first black quarterback in Super Bowl history." From that day on he would forever carry the title of "Super Bowl MVP."

"All week long, the importance of being a black quarterback was thrown around," he said. "But before I got here I knew one thing: I wasn't the quarterback of the Redskins because I was black. There were a lot of TV sets turned on today. A lot of people will start to see me as a role model. . . . But the most important thing is to be able to play well and still be a role model. That's what we did today."

When the game clock reached all zeroes the victorious Redskins, led by Williams—who became the second player to deliver the famous post–Super Bowl "I'm going to Disneyland" pitch—eventually walked off the field. Champagne and championship gear circulated the Redskins' locker room while reporters surrounded Williams, Timmy Smith, Ricky Sanders, and the rest of the winners.

Even Joe Gibbs enjoyed himself, as well as the thought of a few nights away from the couch in his office.

"I'll be staying at home for a while now, I'll be sleeping there," Joe Gibbs said. "I'll probably go skiing with my boys, but right now, I'm really looking forward to tonight back at the hotel. It'll be nice not to have to worry about a game tomorrow. I just might stay up all night."

Gibbs celebrated with his family, players, coaches, and boisterous Redskins fans at a victory party inside San Diego's Hyatt Islandia Hotel: his return to San Diego, where he lived, played, and worked for several years, was a great success. But the MVP of Washington's 42–10 win in Super Bowl XXII was nowhere to be found.

Groggy from medicine to ease the pain in his knee and tired from four quarters of football, hours of postgame questions, and the previous day's root canal—unable to sleep, he awoke at four a.m. to review his playbook for several hours—Doug Williams had no energy left. Throughout his triumphant evening, Williams stayed in his hotel room with family and called his father, who watched the game in Zachary from his wheelchair. Then the MVP unhooked his constantly ringing phone.

The only person allowed into the room, other than immediate family, was Williams's former college coach, Eddie Robinson, who put Williams's achievement in perspective.

"He said it was like Joe Louis knocking out Max Schmeling," Williams remembered. "He said that's what you did today. He told me, 'You will never understand, until you get older, the impact.' And I didn't, because I did what I was supposed to do as a player. But Coach being who he is, an older guy, understood being African American and some of the things you have to overcome and the impact that a Jackie Robinson and a Joe Louis and a Jesse Owens and a Wilma Rudolph has had on this country, from an African American standpoint."

Although ecstatic for his close friend and one of his prized pupils' momentous success, Robinson couldn't help but think about the other great football players he'd coached.

"This is the performance he gave us for four years," he told a reporter that evening, referring to Williams's tenure at Grambling. "It's just a different scenario. I'm not excited about the way he played, because I knew he could play this way. I'm excited that he got to this game and did this, because it's the ultimate for a football player.

"We've had a lot of people who could have done this at Grambling. But they haven't been given the chance."

CHAPTER 9

Ushered Out

"**THE MOST** satisfying victory of my sports career," a greatly pleased Jack Kent Cooke told reporters the night of his win over Denver. "It's better than winning the NBA championship with the Lakers, better than the thirty-three-game winning streak, and better than anything." Better, certainly, than the $3,300 won by his chestnut gelding, Redskin Chief, during Saturday's race at Golden Gate Fields in Berkeley, California.

Cooke had always demanded the best from his sports ventures, but the tempestuous owner's personal life was under siege in early 1988. The previous October, the seventy-five-year-old filed for divorce from his third wife, thirty-one-year-old Suzanne Martin, who would give birth to their child while Cooke was with the Redskins in Southern California. Already responsible for paying the largest divorce settlement in American history—costing him $42 million and ultimately ownership of the Los Angeles Lakers in 1979—Cooke prepared for another contentious, highly public legal battle.

He explored again selling off one of his largest assets. In August 1988, the *Wall Street Journal* reported that Cooke sought $1.9 billion for his CableVision television empire. He did not, however, consider putting his beloved Redskins up for sale, especially given the efforts he'd made to build a new stadium.

Just three days after the Redskins' Super Bowl win, Cooke announced that the city had until June 30 to deliver a proposal for building a new stadium.

"Failing that," Cooke told local WJLA-TV, "it's going to be necessary for us to go to one of the surrounding counties and say, 'We've exhausted every means of keeping the stadium in D.C. We are now awaiting bids from each of the counties to determine which is the best one for us to move to.' "

Built twenty-eight years earlier and cherished by the Redskins' fans whose celebrations often shook the foundations of the bleachers, RFK Stadium was not deteriorating. But even though the Redskins had sold out every home game (excluding the lone replacement game) since 1966, the third-smallest capacity (55,750 seats) stadium in the NFL meant Cooke claimed to lose roughly $4 million per season on the team.

"The Redskins are a very expensive hobby," he said in February. "Until we get a new stadium, they will never turn a profit."

Cooke dreamt of a 75,000-capacity domed stadium with a retractable roof, possibly located in Loudoun County, Virginia, near Dulles Airport. To counter, D.C. mayor Marion Barry's administration suggested a 78,000-capacity, open-air venue to be built next to the current stadium. Both plans recognized the importance of increasing the stadium's capacity by at least 20,000, but the key to making the Redskins solvent were luxury skyboxes that could be leased out for tens of thousands of dollars per year. The city proposed 250; Cooke wanted 300. At RFK, there was only one luxury box: Cooke's.

Located in the mezzanine, in between the press box and general mezzanine seating, the owner's box looked over the 40-yard line. Not nearly as lavish and elaborate as the skyboxes that would later become commonplace, Cooke's box featured three rows of seats, each occupied according to the fastidious owner's specifications.

"It was like a seated dinner party," recalled George Will, the *Washington Post* columnist who Cooke frequently invited along with his son, Jon. "It wasn't random."

Neither was an invitation from Cooke. Prospective guests received a phone call and later a formal note requesting they arrive an hour before game time. In Lot 5, they valeted their cars, received seating assignments from a parking attendant, and then rode an elevator up to the Lombardi Room, where they drank cocktails and ate hors d'oeuvres prior to kickoff and again at halftime. Once the game began, they crossed a rickety catwalk to the owner's box and sat in cozy Naugahyde chairs.

Most mingled about, chatting, ordering more drinks or food from roaming waitresses, and casually watching the action. But not Cooke.

Seated in the first row on the far left, flanked by a television, a telephone, and oftentimes *CBS News* correspondent Lesley Stahl, Cooke unabashedly expressed his emotions. Not only did he passionately root for his team, he did not approve of guests supporting the opposition: during a game against Dallas, Virginia governor Charles Robb had to hush his wife, Lynda Bird Johnson Robb—the daughter of the late president Lyndon Johnson of Texas—from applauding a play that benefitted the Cowboys.

"Jack would get very intense," remembered Stahl, who attended games with her husband, writer Aaron Latham. "Jack would sit way over in the front row by himself, and the socializing was done by everybody else because he was really concentrating on the game. And if [the Redskins] did well he would scream, and if they didn't he'd sit there quietly. But he did very little schmoozing during the game."

In between Cooke's cheers or protests, he would occasionally chide the team's general manager—"He would snap at him during the games, in front of everybody, and everybody would tense up," Stahl recalled—criticizing bad plays or decisions from his on-the-field employees.

"The box was crazy," Bobby Beathard remembered. "I would always . . . give him an excuse to get out of the box, because I didn't want to sit in the box. I wanted to sit in the coaching booth, behind the coaches."

As the Redskins became perennial Super Bowl contenders, however, many high-profile faces did want to be in the owner's box. More important, they wanted to be seen sitting in the owner's box.

"Washington is a town of transients, people who have come here from elsewhere," George Will said. "Mostly they are not transients, really, because they never go home, they circulate Washington, a great many of them. But because it is a city of people from elsewhere, they sort of need [to be] socialized into this cosmopolitan city, and the Redskins helped."

Even before Cooke moved east and made himself very visible to the fans, the owner's box—called "the President's Box" during Edward Bennett Williams's tenure as Redskins president—was a place to be seen. In 1981, famed sportswriter Red Smith noted that the box had been "long considered one of the real seats of power in Washington." But Cooke's individuality and the success of the Redskins throughout the decade boosted his and the team's profile.

"Getting a seat in Jack Kent Cooke's box was very highly sought after, sort of like you had made it even [if] you might have been secretary of state. Being in Jack Kent Cooke's box for a football game when they were winning, it was a big deal," longtime *Washington Post* beat writer Paul Attner remembered. "We could see the box from the press box at RFK and we'd check it out all the time: Who's in there this time? [*Washington Post* executive editor] Ben Bradlee and Sally Quinn! That was a big thing to get a ticket to get into Jack Kent Cooke's box. But he was above playing Washington politics and being part of the society. Out in Middleburg [Virginia] he did his own little thing socially."

Cooke's box—which he had expanded to forty-six seats, then later sixty-four seats—became a Who's Who of D.C.'s political figures and prominent journalists. The group of regulars featured a remarkably eclectic mix of Democrats and Republicans, conservatives and liberals: George Will, Lesley Stahl and Aaron Latham, columnists Carl Rowan and Bill Safire, Senators Eugene McCarthy and Paul Laxalt, Lyndon Johnson's chief of staff Lloyd Hand, Virginia governor Charles Robb, and the Shriver family, who once brought with them Arnold Schwarzenegger. Less frequent guests included Ted Koppel, Sam Donaldson, Alan Cranston, Senators George McGovern and John Warner, Larry King—both the playwright and the journalist—as well as former CIA director Richard Helms. Wearing a Native American war bonnet to Cooke's box for the 1982 NFC Championship Game against Dallas, Helms remarked, "Iran? Iraq? It's the damn Cowboys I'm worried about."

Cooke's guest lists also included several members of Ronald Reagan's administration, including Secretary of Agriculture John Block, Secretary of State James Baker, Attorney General Edwin Meese, Chief of Staff Donald Regan, and Vice President George H. W. Bush. And on multiple occasions—once following a speech to the RFK crowd promoting her "Just Say No to Drugs" campaign before a 1988 game against the Giants—Nancy Reagan also sat in Cooke's box. The president, however, never did.

Still, as he had following their victory in 1983, Reagan did personally congratulate the Redskins upon winning Super Bowl XXII. Instead of meeting the team on the tarmac at Dulles, he invited them to the White House three days later. But before their trip to 1600 Pennsylvania Avenue, Redskins players and coaches were met by six hundred thousand people in front of the District Building. Amid freezing temperatures, fans gathered on rooftops, looked through open apartment building windows, stood atop benches, hung from traffic lights, trees, and D.C. landmarks just to catch a glimpse of the champions. Snapping the wooden barriers at the base of the dais, rowdy spectators—thirty-one people were arrested and two dozen others required minor medical treatment—rushed the stage as players appeared.

"I haven't seen it like this since the hostages came back," said Mike Davis, an official for the city council chairman.

In addition to John Warner, Congressman Steny Hoyer (D-MD), and Washington, D.C., mayor Marion Barry—who warned the advancing fans, "Somebody's going to get hurt," and urged "Come on, back up, back up, take two steps back"—Joe Gibbs, Dave Butz, and other Redskins stars addressed the crowd.

The most exuberant, most raucous cheers, however, were "We want Doug! We want Doug!" People wanted to see and hear from Doug Williams, who limped to the microphone on crutches; his hyperextended knee still ached.

"I consider myself a real, real lucky person," Williams told the crowd. "Three years ago, there was only one football team that gave me an opportunity to play and that was the Washington Redskins."

Williams's humility that day—he insisted that the game's MVP award "could have been given to a lot of people"—and the grace he showed when he was benched in favor of Jay Schroeder won over Redskins fans just as much as his tremendous play that season did. And to the African American community the outcome of Super Bowl XXII signified a watershed moment.

"There probably isn't an African American sports fan in America who doesn't remember where he was on that day," former *Sports Illustrated* managing editor Roy S. Johnson said years later. "Just as we remember where we were when Martin Luther King was killed, where we were when the Civil Rights Act was passed."

But within the Washington, D.C., area, Williams's triumph carried a special meaning. By 1988, the nation's capital was in crisis, with no segment harder hit than the city's African American population.

"White flight" robbed the city of its tax base. The crack epidemic was surging, and "black-on-black" violence would soon plunge the city toward the title "murder capital of America."

The city's once-promising mayor, former civil rights leader Marion Barry, not only struggled to remedy the growing problems, but rumors about his own drug and alcohol abuse had already surfaced.

Even the sports world was not immune. The heart-wrenching death of D.C. metro area hero Len Bias—the University of Maryland All-American basketball player who overdosed on cocaine two days after being selected second overall by the Boston Celtics in the 1986 NBA Draft—disillusioned the entire region.

"All of this pride, all of this connection, everyone looking up to [Len Bias] because he's representing many African Americans in D.C.—and then he dies," said Dr. Charles Ross, the University of Mississippi's Director of African American Studies. "It was almost like, to those black folks in D.C., that he's one of them . . . and they can't get themselves together, they're not winners. . . .

"So I think Doug Williams came along at a time when many African Americans needed a hero," Ross observed. "As the [1987] football season continued to move forward . . . and they get to the Super Bowl, all of this optimism now can be shifted to him. . . . Doug Williams really resuscitated that hero component that people were looking for."

The day after the Redskins' championship rally, Williams visited Howard University, the historically black school located in the Shaw neighborhood of Washington, D.C. At Burr Gymnasium, 2,500 students, faculty, and local citizens attended "Doug Day" to see Williams, who spoke to the crowd for forty minutes. Over constant flashbulbs clicking, shouts of his name, and thunderous applause, Williams discussed his similar education at Grambling State, overcoming aches and pains, the media scrutiny he faced, and his performance against Denver. Some of the loudest cheers came upon mention of the scary knee injury he suffered just minutes before rewriting the Super Bowl record books during the game's second quarter.

"When you fell down . . . and hurt your leg, we went down, too," D.C. Council member and civil rights activist Frank Smith Jr. told Williams in front of the crowd. "And when you rose up, we rose with you."

FOLLOWING THE RALLY IN front of the District Building, the Redskins' Super Bowl XXII championship celebration continued into the afternoon. Players and coaches boarded four two-car Tourmobiles headed for the White House. Tinted windows saddened many in the crowd, but several players popped their heads out in the cold temperatures. Employing the same nine-block parade route used for presidential inaugurations, the procession arrived at the White House around two p.m.

Soon, they gathered on a stage in the south portico, and listened as the president congratulated the team, tossed out a few jokes—saying the Redskins' Super Bowl performance "gave new meaning to the term 'Capital offense' "—then singled out Doug Williams, who "recently showed the world how to overcome adversity and did it with style and grace."

On crutches, Doug Williams hobbled to the podium and acknowledged, "This is a long ways from Zachary [Louisiana]." Williams then handed the president an engraved, signed football. To receive his gift, however, Reagan had to carry out one of Joe Gibbs's signature plays: Trips Right, Fake Zoom, Larry Crisscross.

"Where's Ricky Sanders?" Reagan yelled out.

"Here he comes," Williams replied.

Sanders, the Redskins' leading receiver in the Super Bowl, darted across the lawn in front of the stage. Reagan fired a short pass to Sanders, who caught the ball in perfect stride to complete the carefully planned charade. Prior to the ceremony, as Sanders and teammate Clarence Verdin explored the White House, Joe Gibbs pulled Sanders aside, asking him to appear on cue when the president called his name.

"Here I am in a suit, street shoes on," he remembered years later. "He threw a good pass. It might have been wobbly, but I wasn't going to drop it. . . . Coach Gibbs said, 'It's President Reagan's birthday, so when you catch the ball, run up to President Reagan and say 'Happy birthday, sir.' So I caught it, went up, gave him the ball, and [said] 'Happy birthday, sir.' "

Reagan, who turned seventy-seven later in the week, was not the only one to receive a birthday acknowledgment onstage that afternoon. Dexter Manley celebrated his thirtieth birthday the previous day, and in the middle of his short speech, the president wished him "a happy belated birthday."

After Sanders's catch, Manley returned the favor. Breaking with the prescribed protocol of the event, Manley loudly shouted out his support for Reagan, whose second term would expire the following January.

"I came up with a solution, that we're going to renegotiate the president's contract for four more years," he said.

The public endorsement elicited both a roar from the crowd as well as an invitation to Reagan's birthday party from Chief of Staff Donald Regan.

For many of his teammates, the day had been a political whirlwind. But Manley, a frequent White House visitor and proud registered Republican, was more than comfortable in the presence of powerful politicians. Earlier in the day, while at the District Building, he grabbed the telephone on Mayor Marion Barry's desk. Referencing the vice president's much-publicized evasiveness during a recent interview with Dan Rather over his role in the Iran-Contra affair, Manley shouted into the receiver, "Hey, Mr. President, this is the mayor, Mayor Manley. If George Bush doesn't answer those questions, I'll come over and answer them."

Only the hundreds of thousands of fans that madly cheered when he held the Lombardi Trophy out the window of the team bus as it passed down Pennsylvania Avenue caused the Redskins' Secretary of Defense to flinch. "Thank God I'm not a movie star. What if I was The Boss, Bruce Springsteen? I felt like him today," he said. "I've been mobbed before, but today was great. It was hard to have humility today. It's good to be humble, but it was hard today."

As he had been the last time the Redskins won the World Championship, Dexter Manley was an essential part of a Washington defense that secured a Super Bowl victory. In the playoffs, against the Bears and head coach Mike Ditka—who said Manley "has the IQ of a grapefruit"—the double teams Manley saw from Chicago's offensive line freed the rest of the defense to collect 5 sacks.

A week later, in the NFC Championship, Manley recorded 1.5 sacks against the Vikings' All-Pro tackle Gary Zimmerman, then added another 1.5 sacks of league MVP John Elway in the Super Bowl.

"We thought Dexter played his best ball of the season in the playoffs," defensive coordinator Richie Petitbon said.

A knee injury and the players' strike had contributed to an inconsistent 1987 regular season and Manley's lowest sack totals in five years. But once the playoffs began, his strength and quickness off the snap returned and he became nearly impossible to contain. By then, so too had his drug use.

Manley's battles with alcohol became national news the previous season. The week of Washington's 1986 playoff game against the Rams, he overslept due to a colossal hangover, missed practice, and received both a $1,000 fine and a warning from Joe Gibbs: "Dexter, you're going to wind up in the gutter."

Instead, Manley entered the Hazelden Foundation's alcohol rehabilitation facility following a cocaine binge in March. He came home so sick that his wife called an ambulance. While in rehab, he swore off alcohol and vowed to attend Alcoholics Anonymous meetings after he left. He felt ashamed for hurting and embarrassing the people around him, including his ten-year-old son, Derrick, who learned of his father's problems one day in school.

"Now, all the dumb stuff will have to stop," he said in May 1987. "It's time for Dexter Manley to grow up."

But during those thirty days in Hazelden he ignored the drug addiction he'd carried for years. Team officials, however, could not. On game days, he popped Sudafed tablets before kickoff, a trick former Cowboys linebacker Thomas "Hollywood" Henderson taught him.

"I started taking three, four, five Sudafeds before a game and I'd be hyped up, wired up," he recalled. "One of our team physicians told me, 'You can't keep going up and down like that.' Eventually if you're gonna keep using Sudafed, eventually you're going to go to your drug of choice."

Manley's preferred vice was cocaine. He came to practices still high on coke from the night before: sweating, hyper, paranoid. When the 1987 regular season ended, with the overtime win in Minnesota, he went on a cocaine binge and failed a drug test the team administered him. Manley pleaded with team officials to administer a second drug test, which he apparently passed. He abstained from drugs again until the night after the NFC Championship Game, leading to another failed drug test the week of Super Bowl XXII. Nevertheless Manley—whose regular drug dealer came to San Diego that week—played on game day.

"Shoot, I took the test five days before the game," he wrote later. "They *had* to have known and had to have covered it up. How do I know? Well, I got a letter from the commissioner's office early that next off-season, saying I had flunked a test at the Super Bowl. The thing was, the league wasn't involved with my drug testing during the Super Bowl. So the Redskins probably knew I was dirty and waited to tell the league."

The league office eventually suspended Manley for thirty days, beginning with the start of the next year's training camp. He was eligible to return for the start of the regular season.

"I think, obviously, he means a lot to us," Joe Gibbs told reporters in Carlisle. "We've missed him. He's been a part of what we've done around here. We need him back and we want him back."

Throughout the decade, drug abuse saturated the NFL: that summer alone, sixteen other players were suspended, including Giants great Lawrence Taylor. All but one—the Patriots' Tony Collins, who was considered a repeat offender—were dealt the same thirty-day suspension as Manley.

"I think we're getting their attention this summer," commissioner Pete Rozelle said after issuing the suspension for Manley and six others. "They realize it's embarrassing to be out for thirty days."

The bender that led to Manley's stay at Hazelden meant he reached "Step 1" of the league's newly enacted drug policy. Failing a drug test the next year pushed him into "Step 2." Another positive test would result in a lifetime ban, although players were allowed to apply for reinstatement after one year.

"I'm just going to comply with what the commissioner wants me to do and that's basically it," Manley said. "I know what the situation was and I know that everything is behind me."

It wasn't.

In Week Nine of the 1989 season, Manley tortured the Philadelphia Eagles. He forced a fumble and recorded 3 sacks of the elusive Randall Cunningham, the last of which came in the final two minutes on fourth down, preserving Washington's 10–3 victory. He would never again play another snap for the Washington Redskins.

A few weeks earlier, Manley—no longer attending AA meetings but frequently being drug tested several times per week—skipped his weekly segment on WTTG Channel Five's sports report to use cocaine in a local Holiday Inn. He failed his next urine analysis. Five days after the win in Philadelphia—and three days after meeting with President George H. W. Bush during a White House ceremony honoring people who overcame learning disabilities—news broke that Manley was to be permanently banned from the NFL.

"We did more than anyone knows to try to help him," Joe Gibbs said. "Everybody gets disgusted to a certain extent. There are two sides to this. You feel for Dexter, you want him to be able to whip this. He's meant a lot to us, provided a lot of thrills and fun. You remember all the good things. But then, you are disgusted. We work very hard to be the right kind of team for our community. There's a lesson in this."

Unfortunately for Gibbs, two of his most promising young talents did not learn from Manley's cautionary tale.

Timmy Smith's record-setting performance in Super Bowl XXII made him an overnight star. Following the team parade and the trip to the White House, Smith appeared on NBC's *Late Night with David Letterman*. In addition to reenacting his Super Bowl end zone celebration—the "Cabbage Patch" punctuated by spinning the football on the ground—Smith told Letterman about nearly fainting before kickoff and how he came to be a football player.

"I went to a basketball [high] school," he told the host. "The coach wanted us to run two miles a day. I didn't want to do that, so I played football."

"And you only have to play one game a year!" Letterman replied.

Over the next few months, he was honored by the New Mexico Senate, received "preliminary feelers" from Coca-Cola and McDonald's for endorsements, and successfully negotiated a new contract featuring a substantial raise in his base salary with several incentives. That summer, running backs coach Don Breaux also publicly declared the 220-pound Smith the Redskins' starting running back after the team had released George Rogers.

"We're concerned we don't have that big, strong running back we've had in the past," Breaux said. "But 220 is pretty darn big. I think everyone wants Timmy Smith to stay healthy sixteen games and carry the load."

After showing up at minicamp in May overweight—"he looked like he'd just come from a party," Charles Mann recalled—Smith got back into the coaches' good graces by arriving at training camp early to work out with the rookies and free agents. In the hot sun of Carlisle he quickly lost five pounds, easily won the starting job, and despite 2 fumbles looked fantastic in the team's preseason finale against Atlanta, rushing for 99 yards and 2 touchdowns.

"We have to put last season away," he said prior to Washington's opening game. "We've got a tough schedule ahead and we have to go in with our heads straight. The most important thing now is to know the defense and play accordingly. The Giants have a great team and one of the best defenses. I'll be ready for them."

Throughout the first month of the 1988 season, Smith picked up where he left off in Super Bowl XXII. Against both the Giants and Eagles—two of the top defenses in the league that year—he reached the 100-yard rushing mark as the Redskins jumped out to a 2-1 start.

But his production dropped substantially, and he admitted, "It's tough for me to go in there and try and do what I did in the Super Bowl." In addition to being ejected from a game for shoving a referee, ball security suddenly became a major concern, greatly irritating the front office and coaching staff.

As the season progressed, Kelvin Bryant and rookie Jamie Morris received nearly all of the Redskins' snaps. Only a brief injury to Bryant put Smith back into the lineup. In the second half of the 1988 season, relegated mostly to short-yardage and goal-line duties, Smith rushed for just a combined 106 yards— just over half as many as his record-setting effort in Super Bowl XXII.

"Timmy had so much talent," Doug Williams said, "but I think Timmy was just like a lot of young guys—even today—really don't understand the price you pay to get there and the price to stay there. . . . It was a lot of things, but the most important thing, he didn't come back ready to play.

"I can remember the last play that Timmy ran as a Washington

Redskin. That was '80 Truck,' against the [San Francisco 49ers]. It was fourth down and about two. We called time-out. And 80 Truck, it's constructed to stay outside no matter what happened, because all the blocking is inside. And I told Timmy, 'Timmy, we're running 80 Truck, I don't give a shit what happens, come hell or high water, stay outside. Stay outside.' And Timmy always had this knack of cutting back. Man, I turned and handed to Timmy, and Timmy started [outside] and BOOM! Timmy lost a yard. Timmy never played again."

In the locker room following the final game of the 1988 season, both Joe Gibbs and Bobby Beathard admitted that Morris— fresh off a 45-carry, 152-yard performance—would open training camp as the presumptive starter. Smith would be fighting for a roster spot.

"He didn't [have a good season]," Bobby Beathard said in December. "It was a disappointment. [After the Super Bowl] maybe football wasn't a top priority. His preparation was a disappointment. . . . His reputation has never been as a hard worker."

Smith's reputation had also been tainted by the company he kept.

"Bobby [Beathard] told me about some concerns they had that he was partying too much and thought he was probably using the white stuff," his agent, Steve Endicott, later said. "But when it came down to it, he always had a good excuse: 'I'm not partying as much as they say; it's all okay, there's no problems.' I don't know if he had a drug problem. I'm not saying he was an addict, but I do know he spent a lot of money."

Seven weeks after the season ended, the twenty-five-year-old's career in Washington was over: the Redskins chose not to prevent him from becoming an unrestricted free agent. The Phoenix Cardinals planned on signing him until he twice failed a physical following off-season knee surgery. The San Diego Chargers, who hired Redskins offensive coordinator Dan Henning as their head coach that year, signed him late the next summer only to cut him prior to the start of the season.

"He was seen with a drug dealer," a member of the Chargers told *Sports Illustrated* in 1991. "Henning said, 'That scared the hell out of us.' Timmy didn't have football smarts. He wasn't focused on the job at hand. He was worried about what was going on that night."

"Steve Ortmayer, the director of player personnel, said I'd been seen with a drug dealer," Smith later said. "I'd seen this guy after practice one day, and he asked me if I had a roommate. If not, he said, I could move in with him. I told him I already had a place. Some people on the team saw me shake his hand. The next day, the Chargers made me take a drug test."

Smith didn't play football in 1989. The next year he received a final shot at resurrecting his career, signing with Dallas late in the summer. He was cut after one game—Cowboys rookie Emmitt Smith took his spot in the lineup—and he began working at a health club in Dallas.

"It's amazing, you know," he later said. "You look at it, and the guys who are doing drugs, they don't catch them. . . . I don't do it. I don't even know what the stuff looks like. Yet once some rumor starts, everybody's sure I do. It sticks with you, like a hole in your back, and I couldn't get it off of me."

Smith never once (publicly) failed a drug test. Fifteen years later, however, he would serve time in a federal prison for conspiracy to distribute cocaine.

Although Smith was not arrested for or charged with any crime during his playing career, the same could not be said about the Redskins' other breakout star of the 1987 season.

Like Timmy Smith, Barry Wilburn cashed in on a superb year that culminated with Super Bowl glory. After accepting the Washington Touchdown Club's Player of the Year award, he flew home to Tennessee. Along with a hero's welcome, he received the Professional Athlete of the Year award from the Vanguard Club—who had honored his mother with a lifetime achievement award the previous fall—at a banquet in downtown Memphis. That summer, the free agent cornerback signed a new deal with Washington, worth more than three times (roughly $300,000 per season) what he made the previous year.

Despite a knee injury that cost him the first six games of the season, Wilburn led Washington in interceptions again in 1988. The next year, seeking to take advantage of his size and hitting ability, the Redskins moved him to free safety.

"If you drew up a free safety, that's who you'd draw up," Gibbs said that fall. "He's a rangy guy with good speed and size. I hope he'll respond to this."

But in September, Wilburn was late to a team meeting prior to the Redskins' exhibition game with New Orleans, giving the team cause to drug test him. The results came back positive for cocaine and the league began testing him every week. He failed another test in late October and was suspended. After three weeks of rehab, Wilburn returned to practice, but his career as a Washington Redskin would soon be over. In March 1990, he was arrested for driving while intoxicated and driving with a suspended license. Washington released him a few weeks later.

"It was the same year that Dexter Manley tested positive and the same year that Marion Barry . . . had drug problems," Wilburn later said.

"It was a bad year to test positive."

LOSING FIVE OF THEIR final six games cost Gibbs's 1988 team far more than a shot at defending their Super Bowl title. In addition to missing the playoffs, their 7-9 record marked the worst campaign in the Joe Gibbs era. Little changed at the start of the next year as Washington lost their first two games, both at home, to NFC East opponents, the Giants and Eagles. But a road trip to Dallas sparked a three-game winning streak and by Week Nine, they had climbed back to a .500 record. And with the 0-8 Cowboys coming into RFK—for the first time ever without Tom Landry as their head coach—the Redskins appeared guaranteed a fifth win. Gibbs saw it differently.

"I firmly believe that Dallas is a much better team than when we played them the first time," he said three days before kickoff. "They can beat us."

That's exactly what happened. On a crisp evening, the fourteen-point underdog Cowboys, led by rookie head coach Jimmy Johnson, kept Washington's turnover-prone offense out of the end zone during a 13–3 victory, Dallas's only win of the entire 1989 season.

"The low point of my nine years here," Gibbs later said.

For his players, the loss had been just as deflating.

"It would be hard to overestimate the effect of that game," Jeff Bostic said. "A lot of people were very, very upset."

Even before that awful home loss, many Redskins were irate.

Three weeks earlier, after a narrow loss to the Giants, a players-only meeting was held. At a storage warehouse next to the team's practice field, over pizza, beer, and soft drinks, players aired their grievances. One player told the *Washington Post*'s Redskins beat writer Tom Friend that the meeting "was nothing. Just a get-together, a social function." But others expressed their frustrations with coaches who "have told certain players to tone it down; don't do this, don't do that." Joe Gibbs had recently complained to the press about "stupid mistakes and penalties" that greatly contributed to the frustrating season.

"There was a coup d'état, a rebellion, a mini-rebellion against Gibbs in 1989," Friend recalled years later. "They thought he was this Bible-thumper who was having them play a little too cautious. They were instructed over and over not to get penalized for late hits and to never retaliate to cheap shots, and they were done with it. They called a players-only meeting in mid-October before a game against Tampa, and the message—particularly from the defensive players—was, 'Fuck Gibbs.' They were sick of getting pushed around by the Giants and Eagles, and decided they were going to body-slam people after the whistle if need be. I remember a player telling me, 'Everybody wants us on their schedule; everybody wants to play the Redskins.'

"Honestly, part of me felt this was the beginning of the end of the Gibbs era. I thought he'd potentially lost the team for good, and, when I wrote about the meeting in the *Post*, his reaction almost bordered on paranoid. Publicly, he said, 'I'm glad they had [the meeting]; it's their team, too.' But truth was, he was steaming. You always knew he was mad when he'd grit his teeth when he spoke. And in a team meeting with the players before the Tampa game, he sat the players down and demanded to know who had ripped him to me. He wanted the player or players to raise their hand. He wanted the person to own it. Nobody did. The point was, he may have said it was their team, too, but it was his, and how dare someone question him. So, trust me, 1989 ended up not being a coup d'état. It just reaffirmed to Gibbs that if you didn't like him and wanted to play dirty, go play for Buddy Ryan."

Just a few weeks after the much-publicized players' meeting, Dexter Manley and Barry Wilburn would both fail drug tests and be suspended. Losing two defensive stars to scandals, and facing another losing season, left Gibbs—whose father had passed away the previous month—emotionally drained and mentally exhausted. As the end of the season neared, he considered retiring.

"There's been a chance for two years," he said in early December. "I'm just being honest about it. I don't anticipate it happening, but I'm honestly answering the question. . . . We won a Super Bowl, and I was excited about the way we finished the season and the way we came from behind. That made the decision for me. The next year, we go 7-9. . . . Seriously, that could've been one where you say, 'Hey, we finished on a downer, I'm tired, I don't want to do this anymore.' But I didn't feel that at all on either one of those, and this one? I think how we finish this year will have a lot to say about how I feel. But I always do this."

Despite the tensions, speculation, and disappointment, the Redskins managed to right the ship. They pounded the Bears and Cardinals in the two weeks after Thanksgiving, closed out their home schedule with a win over San Diego, and then overcame a 17-point second-half deficit to beat Atlanta. In the regular-season finale, the Redskins flew cross-country to Seattle and stomped the Seahawks, 29–0.

The turnaround—not unlike the one following the 0-5 start to the 1981 season—lifted Gibbs's spirits. In mid-January, he vowed to return for a tenth season.

"It's all go," he said while scouting players at the Senior Bowl in Mobile, Alabama. "I think it's the way everything wound up; the family feels good about it. I didn't anticipate a change. I was excited about the way we finished, but that's not all of it. It's more just everything. I enjoyed the way we finished and I enjoyed the team."

"[They'll] have to usher me out. . . . I don't think I will ever change on that. I mean it would take something happening to change me, and probably that will never happen. I still feel good about what I'm doing."

DESPITE THEIR EXHILARATING end-of-the-season surge to finish a respectable 10-6, the 1989 Redskins earned another dubious record. One year after posting the only losing season of Joe Gibbs's head coaching career, Washington failed to reach the postseason for the second straight season, another first under Gibbs.

But the Redskins did at least produce an encouraging milestone that year, one that rewrote more than just the team's record books. Art Monk, Gary Clark, and Ricky Sanders each gained 1,000 yards receiving that season. Although Chargers teammates John Jefferson, Charlie Joiner, and tight end Kellen Winslow had all reached that mark in 1980—Joe Gibbs's last year as San Diego's offensive coordinator—Monk, Clark, and Sanders were the first trio of wide receivers in NFL history to achieve the feat.

Clark's 9 catches in the final game against Seattle had clinched him the team lead in both yards and touchdown grabs. The two-time Pro Bowler stood just five feet, nine inches and was naturally considered a throwback to the Smurfs who were so popular just a few years earlier. But other than height, the product of Pulaski High School in southwestern Virginia shared little in common with the cute, happy-go-lucky cartoon characters.

"The guy with all the fire," Doug Williams said. "Pound for pound the toughest SOB I ever seen in my life was Gary Clark."

The all-time leading receiver at Division I-AA James Madison University, Clark had been the sixth overall selection by the Jacksonville Bulls of the USFL in 1984. Turning down a $12,000-per-year teaching job in his hometown for a pro football contract worth several times that amount—enough for him to buy himself a cream-colored 1980 Mercedes and his parents a new split-level house—he became the team's top receiving threat.

"We've even got some guys that are smaller than he is," Bulls head coach Lindy Infante said in the summer of 1984. "We nicknamed our receivers the Fraggles because they aren't even as big as the Redskins' Smurfs."

Clark led the Bulls in receiving during the 1984 season, but after the franchise lost more than $9 million during its first two seasons, they looked to cut their $4.6 million payroll. Midway through a disappointing season, Clark was one of the first players that Bulls general manager Larry Csonka released.

"It happened on May 1, I'll always remember that: I got fired on my birthday," he said. "It was the best thing that could have happened to me."

Within two weeks, the Redskins brought him in for a workout: in the middle of tense contract negotiations with star Charlie Brown, they signed Clark and put him to work as a kick returner.

Washington dealt away Brown in late August and Clark climbed the depth chart. Coaches liked his quickness, hands, and dedication: living in a townhouse in Harrisonburg, Virginia, so he could finish his degree at James Madison, he drove ninety minutes to and from practice every day.

A month into his first season, Clark gained a starting role, and despite the shakeup at quarterback with Joe Theismann's broken leg later that year, he found a chemistry with Jay Schroeder. During Schroeder's Pro Bowl season of 1986, Clark caught more passes for more yards and more touchdowns than any player on the team.

As much as any measureable—yards, receptions, height, 40-yard-dash time—Clark's grittiness endeared him to teammates. He refused to miss practices due to injuries and routinely carried out the lesson his father taught him: "Son, if you go across the middle, you're going to get hit anyhow, so you might as well catch the ball."

"He's gutsy," Russ Grimm said. "You send him across the middle, and he'll get his head tore off three times in a row, and the fourth time he'll still go out there and run the same kind of route. He's that kind of player."

Amid the quarterback-shuffling between Schroeder and Doug Williams, Clark remained one of the league's most explosive receivers. In 1987, he was named to the Associated Press's All-Pro team and caught decisive touchdowns in both the NFC Championship Game and Super Bowl XXII.

"Never saw a guy that could elude a defensive back," Doug Williams said. "I never seen a defensive back get his hand on Gary. He was like a snake. He had no backbone. Gary could do some things that you can't coach."

The Redskins did not have to give up anything to sign Clark: they had chosen him in the NFL's supplemental draft of USFL players. Ricky Sanders, however, cost Washington a third-round pick.

The collapse of the USFL in 1986 bolstered needy rosters around the league. The Buffalo Bills landed Jim Kelly, the Tampa

Bay Buccaneers received Steve Young, and the Dallas Cowboys finally had Herschel Walker. The Redskins also benefitted from the USFL's mass exodus. In addition to acquiring Doug Williams from Tampa Bay, Washington brought in speedy receiver Clarence Verdin and former USFL MVP Kelvin Bryant, whom the team had used a seventh-round pick on three years earlier in the hopes that he'd eventually play in the NFL.

But Bobby Beathard still wanted more.

A pole vault, long jump, and hurdles star at Belton High, Ricky Sanders became one of the best running backs in the history of Southwest Texas State University, where he starred for back-to-back Division II national championship teams. In 1984, he signed with the USFL's Houston Gamblers and moved to wide receiver as part of offensive coordinator Mouse Davis's prolific Run-and-Shoot offense, orchestrated by quarterback Jim Kelly. That year, he caught the second most passes of any player in the league: only teammate Richard Johnson caught more passes than Sanders during his first season in the USFL. A year later, knee surgery sidelined him for weeks and teammate Clarence Verdin became the Gamblers' second receiving option. The Redskins had selected Verdin in the supplemental draft and scouted several Gamblers games throughout the season. But Sanders caught the eye of Bobby Beathard, who had seen Sanders play in college during one of the general manager's many trips to Texas.

"Some people ridiculed the USFL, and it wasn't a great league because it didn't have any depth," said Beathard. "Most of the guys in it were cut from teams in the NFL. But there were some terrific players. We drafted most of the guys we picked up from the USFL either in the regular draft or the supplemental draft. So we made sure we could check on them while they were playing in the other league."

"We had one of our people stay on top of it. He broke down the films. He graded the players. He kept us up to date on how they were doing. When we looked ahead, we tried to figure out how and where these players could help us. A lot of our planning for the future was done around how and when we might be able to get these guys," Beathard said. "Ricky played in Houston with the Gamblers and Jim Kelly. We watched him because we were looking at Verdin. We thought Sanders was terrific. He caught a bunch of balls that first year with Kelly. But New England had his rights."

Beathard paid the Patriots' asking price of a future third-round draft choice, and in August 1986 Sanders joined Gary Clark, Kelvin Bryant, and Doug Williams as newcomers to Redskins training camp. Rarely thrown to in his rookie season, Sanders saw his playing time greatly increase the next year following a pep talk from offensive coordinator Dan Henning: "Get your act together and begin competing for one of the top two wide receiver spots on this team."

He scored the winning touchdown in the Jay Schroeder–led comeback victory over the New York Giants, thrashed the Minnesota Vikings in the final game of the regular season, then rewrote the Super Bowl record for receiving yards against Denver. His 193 receiving yards broke the mark Pittsburgh Steeler Lynn Swann set in Super Bowl X, a game Sanders watched as a fifteen-year-old Cowboys fan born in Texas.

"I've always dreamed of days like this," he said that night. "I've always watched Super Bowls and watched the super receivers like Lynn Swann and to break his record is a lifetime dream."

Sanders's dream came true partly at the expense of his teammate Art Monk.

A knee injury sidelined Monk at the end of the 1987 regular season and for Washington's first two playoff games. He returned for Super Bowl XXII, and although he caught only one pass—a 40-yarder in the first quarter—the win was long overdue for the thirty-year-old, who missed Super Bowl XVII with a broken foot and caught just one pass a year later in the loss to the Raiders.

His relationship with the two Redskins receivers who bested

Denver for 248 yards and 3 touchdowns on 12 catches made the outcome of Super Bowl XXII even more meaningful. Not only had Monk mentored Sanders and Clark since their arrival in Washington two years earlier, he'd become very close to them.

"They were three of the tightest receivers I've ever been around," Doug Williams said. "They hung together, talked together, had fun together, played together, and congratulated each other."

Two years before Clark and Sanders arrived in Washington, Monk caught a league-record 106 passes. As the focal point of the Redskins' passing attack, he frequently attracted multiple defenders toward him, freeing up his teammates in the opposition's secondary.

"Art's my best friend on the team. He's great on the field and off. He's helped me from Day One," Clark said in 1986. "He draws so much double coverage, which means single coverage for me, and that's the best you can expect."

In Monk's absence during the 1987 season and playoffs, Clark and Sanders carried the Washington passing attack on their own. Upon Monk's return to the lineup, beginning with the aerial onslaught against the Broncos in the Super Bowl, they became the best trio of pass catchers in the NFL, each averaging over 1,000 yards receiving in 1988 and 1989.

As had nearly every Redskins subgroup before them, the threesome promoted a catchy nickname. Dubbed "the Posse" by Gary Clark's father, they had T-shirts printed up that read "Posse—Monk, Clark, and Sanders: There's no escape."

"We've got three great wide receivers, so we got together and decided to do something to get some publicity," Sanders said. "So when you interview us, you have to interview all three of us."

Sanders and Clark chose Monk as the Posse's official spokesman. His selection was a strange choice: he spoke infrequently to the press and had recently begun a self-imposed media embargo.

"It's just my nature—I'm not very outspoken," he said in August 1989. "I'm quiet, I stay to myself most of the time, and I don't like a lot of distractions. I just like to come out and do my job and stay behind the scenes, so to speak."

Monk also said very little inside the Redskins' locker room. One of the few times he did, prior to a game against Miami, it astonished many of his teammates, including tight end Ron Middleton, who said, "I bet I can count on both hands the number of words I've heard him say in the three years that I've been here." But Monk's low-key, seemingly aloof persona only masked a deep compulsion to excel.

"I played with two of the best receivers in the history of the NFL and that's Art Monk and Jerry Rice. And it's funny how they both did it very similar," recalled Charles Mann, who would later play for the San Francisco 49ers in his final NFL season. "I remember leaving the facility—that's what they called it in San Francisco—one night and that was after ice, and lifting weights, and I was walking out the back gate and Jerry was still jogging around the perimeter of the whole field. This was about two hours after practice. They just work when people aren't watching . . . and Art was the same way. He would be at George Mason University in the off-season at nine o'clock every morning. You didn't have to call him and say, 'Hey, Art, are you gonna work out today? I want to be with you.' Art was there Monday through Friday at nine a.m. in the morning."

"He was very particular about his uniform. He would cut that towel, that little piece that would hang out and fix it, didn't like stuff tight on his arms. It was anal-particular. I went shopping with him one time, he was trying to buy some jeans. He found a pair that fit him and we were still there for another two hours. And he ended up not buying the pants. He was particular about stuff. Today [2014] he's a graphic designer, that's what he got his degree in. So he would rather be in a room with nobody talking to him on his computer. He would do all the documents for a company, and if the line was a little bit off-center or the font wasn't exactly right it would drive him nuts. And oh, by the way, he's color-blind!

"So the man is particular about how he wears something, what he wears, and the colors that he puts together, and he's color-blind! He's an amazing guy that's very particular about things. He played sixteen years in the league because of the way he took care. His routes were meticulous, like his designing on the graphic design—very meticulous."

Redskins owner Jack Kent Cooke once compared the immensely skilled yet obsessive, even reclusive, talent to New York Yankees legend Joe DiMaggio, saying Monk was also "a quiet, gentlemanly man who spoke in subtones." On the diamond, DiMaggio's clutch, reliable play had carried the Yankees to years of dominance; on the gridiron, Monk did the same for the Redskins.

"He's our leader," said wide receivers coach Charley Taylor, the former Redskin whose team records Monk would surpass. "In every group, you need one sparkplug, a guy the others are measured against. For us, that's Monk. He helps our young guys because he's one of the best ever."

Monk also did so because when he was a young guy, one of the Redskins' top veterans helped him.

Although he possessed obvious athletic gifts that made him an All-American wide receiver at Syracuse University, Monk had not expected to be drafted, let alone be a first-round choice of the Redskins in 1980. During each of his first two NFL seasons, he posted excellent individual statistics, but his game was still very raw. Apart from Monk's inability to lose defensive backs in bump-and-run coverage, rookie head coach Joe Gibbs believed, "He also has difficulty getting in and out of a move. He makes the move and then sometimes he's a little slow going from there."

"I'm a little disappointed in myself about this season," he said late in 1981, after leading the team with 894 yards receiving. "I haven't played as well as I wanted to. . . . I know I can get better. I know what I have to improve on. It's just a matter of getting to work and doing it."

Monk's humility and modesty held him back. With the aid of his teammate and Arlington, Virginia, neighbor, running back Terry Metcalf, Monk shed any self-doubt.

"I worked him like a slave," said Metcalf. "He lacked some confidence a little bit. So I saw that and I was like, 'Man, what are you doing!?' You're six-three, 215 pounds, you run a 4.3, you bench press 300-some pounds. Why are you letting these little defensive backs hold you? They shouldn't be able to hold you. You should bust them in the head and keep going!' In game situations, not necessarily *in* the game, I would always talk to him about utilizing what he had.

"Even when we played basketball . . . Art could play, but he didn't think he could play. But that was another way for me to motivate him: shoot the ball, play basketball! And then me and him would play racquetball, and we'd play like ten games, besides riding bikes and running. I was always knocking on his door: 'Get up, let's go!' Because I was a workaholic. And I don't know if Art really knew at that juncture in his career what it really took. . . . I knew the potential Art had."

Blending his remarkable athleticism, newfound confidence, and innate attention to detail, Monk emerged as one of the top receivers in the NFL, regardless of the somewhat pejorative "possession receiver" label he was slapped with. As intrepid over the middle as Gary Clark and as dangerous on the outside as Ricky Sanders, Monk led the Redskins in receptions during the 1989 season: his 86 grabs that year tied for third in the NFL. Still, he didn't receive a trip to the Pro Bowl. Neither did Gary Clark or Ricky Sanders.

"You guys want my four-letter word opinion? Well, I better not give it," Doug Williams told reporters after the Pro Bowl rosters were announced. "What a disgrace. It just goes to show you there are some people who deserve to go and some people who are a joke."

Williams was beyond disillusioned by the end of the 1989 season.

All had seemingly gone right for Williams after his MVP performance in Super Bowl XXII. In the six months that followed, Doug Williams Day was celebrated in his hometown of Zachary, he received a new $3.5 million contract, and the Redskins traded Jay Schroeder to the Los Angeles Raiders. But the next season everything started to fall apart.

Off to a 2-1 start early in the 1988 season, and eight days removed from a 430-yard performance in a late-game win over Pittsburgh, Williams suddenly experienced pain, not in his jaw, but in his stomach. Following a full practice and then lifting weights the next morning, the pain increased. That evening he was admitted to Arlington Hospital to undergo an appendectomy. Doctors expected him to miss at least four weeks. After his parents, and his wife, Lisa, Williams called Joe Gibbs to apologize.

He returned in Week Eight, but beginning with an awful performance in November against Chicago—during which the fans at RFK booed him—Williams lost his grip on the starter's job. Joe Gibbs benched him in the loss to the Bears and then again prior to a game against Cleveland.

"Doug was a little tired and a little worn out," Gibbs said. "It's been a grinding four weeks for him."

Two weeks later, in a flashback to the previous season, Williams—who had left the team on Friday to fly to Zachary and witness the birth of his son Adrian—came off the bench against Philadelphia. Enduring several brutal hits from the Eagles' defense, including one that split his tongue and another that badly bruised his shoulder, a battered Williams rallied the Redskins from nine points behind. The 20–19 win kept Washington's slim playoff hopes alive.

Williams started the Redskins' final two games, but the beating he'd absorbed that year and during his eleven seasons had caught up with him. More so than his shoulder, his jaw, his biceps, or his back, the thirty-four-year-old's left knee, the one hurt in his MVP performance against Denver, pained him.

"The agony on his face tells it all. . . . We thought he had really hurt himself really, really bad," Gary Clark said years later while watching footage of Williams's Super Bowl injury. "Come to find out, he really did hurt himself bad. It probably was something that within the next two years would end his career."

Committed to rehabbing his knee and strengthening his frame, Williams had a $30,000 weight room and gym built in his backyard. But while running on his treadmill during the summer he irritated his hamstring and tests revealed nerve root damage in his leg. Traction, jogging, and swimming did not improve the injury and, unable to participate in training camp, he underwent more tests that revealed a herniated disk in his back. Surgery to repair the disk sidelined him for the first eight games of the 1989 season.

As it had been for several Redskins, that year was a tumultuous one for Doug Williams away from the field. He went through a very public, very ugly divorce from his second wife. Redskins management also told Williams they were not required to pay his hefty salary because he injured himself training at home: they only decided to pay him after he threatened to file a grievance with the players' union. And on November 1, one month after Joe Gibbs's father died, Robert Williams Sr. passed away from bone cancer.

"I was working late in my office and Doug called me around midnight and asked if he could come by and talk," Gibbs said. "I didn't mind because I was staying up late anyway. We talked for about thirty minutes. He told me his dad was sick, but that he would want him to play. I like to look into players' eyes when determining just how much a player wants to play, and Doug had this burning desire in his eyes to play. I haven't said much to Doug since his surgery. I didn't want to rush him or pressure him into coming back. I'll admit I was pessimistic about his chances. . . . I was sitting in my office that night, trying to think of everything that would help this team, and Doug called. I think things happened the way they were supposed to happen."

The next day, persuaded by another gut feeling, Gibbs publicly named Williams the starter.

Williams's return to the field came in Week Nine against the

0-8 Cowboys. He threw 2 interceptions in the embarrassing home loss to Dallas. A week later in Philadelphia, behind an offensive line featuring four new starters—the Hogs also took a beating in 1989—Williams guided the Redskins to a 10–3 win. His daring completion to tight end Jimmie Johnson, in the face of an all-out Buddy Ryan–devised blitz, set up the game's only touchdown.

"Most veteran quarterbacks with four new linemen wouldn't have enough guts to play the way he did," Gibbs said. "But Doug showed great poise."

The victory was his last start as an NFL quarterback.

Despite a blindside blow from Eagles defensive end Clyde Simmons, Williams played the entire afternoon against Philadelphia, which also turned out to be Dexter Manley's final game in a Washington uniform. But the day after, Williams's back was too sore to practice. He sat out the Redskins' next two games, played briefly in two more, and expected another heart-to-heart with Joe Gibbs during the off-season.

"You don't have to be a Phi Beta Kappa to know what will be talked about," Williams said in December. "It'll be about young quarterbacks, salaries, pay cuts. It's easy to figure."

In late March, after the Redskins chose not to protect him from the NFL's Plan B free agency, Williams left Zachary for a sit-down with Gibbs at Redskin Park.

"I've been thinking about this a long time," Gibbs told him. "It's been on my mind for weeks. We've had a lot of good times. Remember 1987: I sat right here and said I didn't want to trade you to the Raiders because I thought you were going to help us win the championship. We got that Super Bowl ring, didn't we? And you've overcome so many things here, I think we've made the complete cycle."

"Douglas, I've decided to go with the younger guys," he continued. "I feel if we're going to go anywhere, it's going to be with the young guys. And I wouldn't enjoy the idea of coaching you as the backup or third-teamer. I couldn't face you in meetings. It wouldn't be fair to you after all you've done."

Williams accepted the news . . . until Gibbs let him know that the Redskins planned to sign eleven-year-veteran quarterback Jeff Rutledge.

"I was going to take a pay cut if I had to," he said twenty-five years later. "Then he told me he was signing Jeff Rutledge and that kind of stirred me up a little bit. I said, 'Coach, you're going to go with the young guys'—at that time, Jeff Rutledge was almost as old as I was—'let me say this, Coach. A banged-up Doug Williams is better than a healthy Jeff Rutledge any day.'"

"He just shook his head and he said, 'Are we good? Friends?' I said, 'Coach. Not right now. Maybe down the road.'"

APART FROM A WORKOUT for the Los Angeles Raiders, no other NFL teams showed serious interest in Doug Williams after the Redskins released him in the spring of 1990. He returned home to Zachary, Louisiana, where he played golf, fished with friends, mowed the lawn, and even took his daughter Ashley to an M.C. Hammer concert.

Although "content with my life right now," Williams decided, "This is the time to do something else." Having turned down college jobs at Virginia State and Long Beach State, Williams strongly pursued the $32,000-per-year head coaching and athletic director job at Pointe Coupee Central High School, located fifty minutes from Zachary.

"I grew up wanting to be a high school football coach," he said in early January 1991.

Later that month, the Pointe Coupee Parish School Board approved his hiring, but before receiving the good news, Williams traveled to Mobile, Alabama. For his 254 yards passing and 21 completions—including the game-winning toss to Florida Gator

Wes Chandler—in the 1978 Senior Bowl, the Grambling State star was to be inducted in the Senior Bowl Hall of Fame along with Morten Andersen, James Brooks, Weeb Ewbank, and former Redskins teammate Dave Butz.

Several members of the Redskins' coaching staff and scouting department were also in Mobile that week to survey the incoming class of rookies. One of those days, at a Senior Bowl event, Williams ran into Don Breaux. The Redskins' running backs coach told Williams that Joe Gibbs wanted to chat with him that evening in his hotel room.

"I think that in itself spoke volumes of who Coach was," Williams said years later. "Two years ago he had cut me. He didn't have to say 'I want to talk to Doug.'"

Greeted by the familiar "Douuuuug-laaaaas" upon entering Gibbs's room, Williams shook hands, hugged, and exchanged pleasantries with his former coach. The two reconciled—"from that day on we had a tremendous relationship"—and Williams thanked Gibbs for the opportunity he received years earlier, but before doing so, they discussed the elephant in the room.

"He proceeded to tell me why he had to cut me," Williams said.

"The reason why," Gibbs told him, "was that city loved Doug Williams. I'm going with the young guy. If [he] does not play well, everybody erupts and says, 'We want Doug! We want Doug!' I did not want [him] to have to deal with that."

That young guy whom Gibbs wanted to protect from Williams's giant shadow was Mark Rypien.

CHAPTER 10

Genius

ON MAY 6, 1989, reporters rushed to Redskin Park for a press conference. After eleven years of service, 105 victories, and two Super Bowl titles, Bobby Beathard was stepping down as Washington's general manager. An avid surfer, the fifty-two-year-old missed riding the waves every morning and wanted to see more of his aging parents who lived in Southern California.

Beathard's longtime lieutenant, Charley Casserly, took command of Redskins personnel.

A graduate of Springfield College, Casserly had been a teacher and head coach at nearby Minnechaug (Massachusetts) High in 1977 when he wrote a letter to Washington Redskins head coach George Allen. Receiving a positive response from his coaching hero, the twenty-eight-year-old drove from Western Massachusetts to Redskin Park in a 1969 Chevy Nova with 120,000 miles and a busted driver's-side door. A few months after a Lyndon Johnson–esque interview—it was partly conducted across the bathroom stall in the coach's locker room—Allen hired Casserly for an unpaid internship. His assignments included fetching Allen's milk shakes on road trips, answering phones, and breaking the news to players who had been cut from training camp. When Bobby Beathard assumed command after Allen's firing, Casserly landed a role as a college scout within the organization: his encouragement of twenty-two-year-old Joe Jacoby helped Washington land a future perennial Pro Bowler. Within six years, Casserly became assistant general manager and the natural successor to Beathard.

"Virtually everything I learned in football I learned from Bobby. I couldn't have had a better teacher in football than Bobby," he said at his introductory press conference. "If you're going to replace a legend, you'd rather have Jack Kent Cooke and Joe Gibbs on your side than any other two people in this league.

"What's next?" he added. "Roll up my sleeves and go to work."

To satisfy the local fans' lofty annual expectations, Casserly had a lot of work to do: his first two years in command saw a great deal of change to the Redskins' personnel, partly by the team's own design, partly not. Defensive staples Dave Butz, Mel Kaufman, and Neal Olkewicz retired, and former All-Pros Dexter Manley and Barry Wilburn departed due to their substance abuse problems. Those moves, as well as several intentional changes to the roster—parting ways with Doug Williams, Timmy Smith, Darryl Grant, and original Hog Mark May—meant Casserly had a list of important holes to fill.

But Casserly, who chiefly assembled the undefeated strike team in 1987, quickly restocked the Redskins.

Utilizing the new Plan B free agency—enacted in February 1989, it freed teams from the requirement of compensating a player's former team—Casserly collected veterans who became starters or critical role players, especially on the defensive side of the ball. Between 1990 and 1991, the Redskins signed defensive tackle Jumpy Geathers, safeties Brad Edwards and Danny Copeland, as well as three-time Super Bowl champion linebacker Matt Millen, a veteran renowned for stopping the run. Casserly told Millen, "The reason we're signing you is, I want somebody that comes off the bus that's won a game against the Giants."

"I think the draft is becoming a little bit less important than it used to be," Casserly said. "The Plan B system has changed things around, and I really believe you can now improve your team every year by using the draft, Plan B, and trades."

Savvy decisions on draft day further fortified the Redskins' offense, defense, and special teams. Second-round selection Andre Collins became a starter at inside linebacker while running back Ricky Ervins filled the vacant third-down role left open by the retirement of Kelvin Bryant. And Brian Mitchell, a quarterback from the University of Southwestern Louisiana, selected in the fifth round of the 1989 draft, became a vital part of the offense and a Pro Bowl kick and punt returner, and would eventually retire as the NFL's all-time leader in return yards.

Casserly's personality and approach to running the personnel department largely differed from his predecessor. "They were night and day, but it was a perfect relationship," scout Billy Devaney said in 2014. "Charley is the consummate, structured, organized, detail. He's always on, he's always working. Bobby is certainly more loose, not as structured. I don't want to say 'fly by the seat of his pants,' because that would be a discredit to Bobby, because it was much more than that, but he was much more loose than Charley. . . . I know Bobby had tremendous respect for Charley and his work ethic and his intelligence and the same goes with Casserly."

Less willing than Beathard to deal away high draft choices in exchange for multiple later picks, Casserly approached draft day decisions in a way that signaled a significant change to the Redskins' internal workings. Joe Gibbs even acknowledged prior to the 1990 draft, "There's definitely some differences with Charley, differences that I'd rather not talk about. . . . Charley is doing it his way, and it's a different way."

"The draft is my responsibility, and I have the final say," Casserly said that spring. "There will always be disagreements. Bobby and Joe disagreed on things, but there were also a lot of agreements. Look at all the games we won. The bottom line is we all want to win."

Although Beathard had cited personal reasons for departing Washington, rumors circulated that he and Gibbs were engaged in a power struggle. Both men denied any discord: "No, no way," Beathard said at his outgoing press conference. But after eight years, the hierarchy had changed.

"Bobby hired Joe, so it wasn't a case that Bobby *appeared* to have final say; Bobby *had* final say for sure," Devaney said. "Then eventually, just what happens naturally, the more success the Redskins had, Gibbs started to get more confident in his evaluation abilities. And I think we reached a point where we had a pretty good team. Bobby looked at it like, 'I think we need some changes, we're starting to get a little bit old.' Joe was like, 'Hey, we've got a good thing going, we don't have to make as many changes as you're talking about.' I think just philosophically, they started to see the team itself a little bit different, but it wasn't a power struggle, per se."

Beathard, who traveled throughout the country every year in search of hidden gems on college teams, wanted to see the young prospects he'd discovered get opportunities to play. Gibbs's top priority was to win games and win now.

"Mike Oliphant was a running back whom Beathard loved, he was like Darrell Green all over again," *Washington Post* beat writer Tom Friend recalled. "He was a typical Beathard guy: small school, great speed, a guy that he felt like could be the next third-down back out of the backfield, a guy who could be an explosive player."

A semipro running back who enrolled at Division III University of Puget Sound, the five-foot-nine-inch Oliphant was selected by Washington in the third round of the 1988 draft. His talent fascinated Beathard, who said Oliphant was "an exciting player, he could do everything." Fumbles early in his rookie season, however, cost him opportunities to carry the ball as the season wore on.

"I think Gibbs just didn't want to play the guy," Tom Friend said. "I think that was it; he didn't trust him and that sort of ignited it at the end there. I find it hard to believe that a guy like Mike Oliphant could break those two up, but that was the last straw between those two from what I was told."

"I know Bobby was frustrated," Casserly said in April 1990. "He saw [in games] only one guy we drafted last year and he didn't like that."

Just two weeks before he stepped down, Beathard executed his last two deals as general manager of the Washington Redskins. On draft day 1989, he traded Washington's second-round pick and the following year's first-round pick to the Atlanta Falcons in exchange for former All-Pro running back Gerald Riggs. Three hours later, he shipped Mike Oliphant to the Cleveland Browns in exchange for twenty-six-year-old running back Earnest Byner.

"I'm on a high right now," Gibbs told the press upon completion of the deals. "I'm really excited about what we've done today."

Riggs and Byner—both desperate for the type of second chances that Joe Gibbs and the Redskins had granted so many players before them—were just as excited.

Riggs, a first-round pick in 1982, had been one of the NFL's finest runners during the middle of the decade. In the scheme utilized by former Redskins offensive coordinator Dan Henning, Riggs carried the ball more times than anyone in the NFL and averaged 96 yards per game between 1984 and 1986. But Henning was fired following the 1986 season, and after a third straight Pro Bowl season the next year, Riggs's production slowed down. He missed seven games in 1988 and was criticized for not playing through hip and knee injuries.

With Riggs's role diminished and his replacement, John Settle, being named to the Pro Bowl in 1988, the Falcons looked to trade the franchise's all-time leading rusher. They found an eager partner in the Redskins, who ranked twenty-fifth in rushing the previous year, had cut Timmy Smith, and were concerned about Kelvin Bryant's injured knee.

"It was easier to trade [the draft picks] when I looked over at Joe, and Joe was crying because we didn't have a running back," Beathard said on draft day.

Gibbs had long been fascinated by Riggs, who had three 100-yard rushing games against Washington. And because Riggs played for Dan Henning, he knew the switch to Washington's offense would be smooth.

"Forty Gut, Sixty Gut, Twenty Gut, I know all that stuff," Riggs told the *Washington Post*. "It'll be like getting up and sleepwalking."

Gibbs, like everyone else in town, recognized that Riggs was built like John Riggins and possessed speed comparable to the Diesel.

"I don't know if I can make the fans up there forget about John Riggins," Riggs told the press hours after the trade, "but I will try and make them remember Gerald Riggs."

The other running back Washington acquired the same day, Earnest Byner, was all too memorable in Cleveland.

Fifteen months earlier, in the final minutes of the 1987 AFC Championship Game, Cleveland trailed Denver, 38–31. Facing second-and-six at the Broncos' 8-yard line, the Browns neared the game-tying score. Byner took the handoff from Bernie Kosar, slashed through the Broncos' defense, easily picked up the first down, and appeared headed to the goal line until Denver's defensive back Jeremiah Castille knocked the ball out of the running back's hands. The Broncos pounced on the fumble and sealed a trip to Super Bowl XXII.

Prior that day, Byner had been known as one of the game's most complete running backs. A week before the loss, he combined for 158 yards on 27 touches and scored 2 touchdowns in a playoff win over

Indianapolis. But in the wake of "the Fumble," all that goodwill—including Byner's 2 touchdowns, 67 yards rushing, and 7 receptions for 120 yards against Denver—vanished.

The next season Byner racked up more than 1,000 total yards and excelled in the passing game: he led the Browns in receptions and scored a pair of touchdowns in the Week Sixteen victory that clinched a playoff berth. But ball security continued to haunt Byner, who coughed the ball up five times that season. Strangers started to yell "Fumble!" at him on the streets or in restaurants and shopping malls; a United States serviceman even pointed out Byner's misfortune during the player's family vacation in Germany. After a loss to Warren Moon's Houston Oilers in the wild card round, Byner and the Browns looked to part ways.

"I guess some people in Cleveland used me as a scapegoat for not getting into the Super Bowl," he said after the Redskins acquired him. "I believe my overall contributions here have been positive, and I don't think the Browns would be where they are without me."

Byner split the running back duties with Gerald Riggs during that 1989 season with the Redskins. A year later, with Gerald Riggs hampered greatly by a foot injury, he reemerged as a top back, rushing for a career-high 1,219 yards and leading the NFL in carries to receive his first Pro Bowl nomination.

Still, leaving Cleveland for Washington, did not relieve Byner of the ignominy he'd been carrying ever since that cold January day in Denver three years earlier.

"That fumble is something I have to live with," he said. "You don't forget things like that, and it seems people won't let me forget it."

Byner's burden became even heavier that season during a game against the Giants, whom the Redskins had not defeated in nearly three years. On the road, Washington fell behind 14–0, but cut the deficit to just 4 late in the third quarter. With seven minutes remaining, the offense advanced to the Giants 3-yard line, where Redskins reserve quarterback Stan Humphries fired a pass to Byner in the end zone. The ball bounced right off Byner's chest and into the arms of Giants defender Greg Jackson.

"The guy has laid his guts on the line, blocking in the goal line and everything else. Hey, he dropped a pass. I've called bad plays. We've had guys who've made bad punts, we've had missed tackles. It's just something that happened," Joe Gibbs said. "The only way you can't make those mistakes is not to be in there. This guy has played great in big games. If you're in there enough, there's probably going to be some things happen to you. A couple of things have happened to him at tough times that got a lot of attention focused on him. I feel bad for him because of that. Hey, that's the life he lives and we all live in the NFL."

Byner, who had been praised for addressing reporters in the aftermath of the Fumble, ducked out of the locker room to avoid the press.

"I messed up the game again for us," Byner recalled years later. "I always took it personal, I always put it on my shoulders. The way I played, if I played well and we lost then I should have done something else. If I played not so well and we won, then I still wanted to play better. I always wanted to try and get better. That's always been the way I approached it. Going back to that game, when that happened, again the onus was on me, I always put the onus on me, even though I knew damn well that no one play loses or wins a game. It's a cumulative effect that wins or loses a game. Sometimes it's more spiritual than we realize."

Outside Giants Stadium that evening in East Rutherford, New Jersey, Byner looked up at the heavens and asked aloud, "What am I doing wrong?" He found an answer of sorts later that week. In the middle of practice, teammate defensive lineman Tim Johnson approached Byner and quoted to him a Bible verse, Second Corinthians 5:17: "Therefore, if any man be in Christ, he's a new creature. Old things are passed away. Behold all things become new."

"Really?" Byner asked Johnson. "I can start over new?"

In the coming weeks, Byner rediscovered the Baptist beliefs he'd been raised with—"I grew up in a religious family, and I strayed away"—and began attending Bible studies classes with many teammates. On December 1, in a Jacuzzi at Darrell Green's home, he was baptized by a local reverend.

Born again in religion, Byner was also revived on the football field. As the Redskins fought for a playoff berth late in the 1990 season, the twenty-eight-year-old enjoyed the greatest individual stretch of his career. In Washington's final seven games, he averaged 26 carries and 110 yards and scored 5 touchdowns, including 3 in a victory over Miami, the day after the Jacuzzi baptism.

"A team needs a leader at the running back position, and Earnest has become that leader," Gibbs said prior to the postseason. "He's an overachiever, just like our team, and the guys believe he'll do everything it takes to get the yards and help us win."

REDSKINS PLAYERS HAD A nickname for Mark Rypien: the Sweater.

The Canadian-born quarterback spent both the 1986 and 1987 NFL seasons as a member of the organization, but on game days, he did not put on a jersey, helmet, or shoulder pads; he wore the same white "Redskins" sweater virtually every week. He was only active for the 1987 home victory over the Giants, the week after Doug Williams briefly injured his back in the *Monday Night* loss to the Rams.

"Last couple years, [the Redskins] have been great to me," said Rypien, who earned an $18,000 bonus as a member of the Super Bowl championship roster. "They've made me some money. But I feel like I should be up on a post office wall with a sign saying 'Wanted!' for stealing Mr. Cooke's money."

Rypien had been a prizerecruit to Jim Walden's Washington State University Cougars but injuries sidetracked his development. As a redshirt freshman in 1982, a torn knee—an injury that would hamper his mobility for years to come—did not prevent him from claiming the Cougars' starting job a year later. Breaking his clavicle two games into that season, however, so frustrated the sophomore that he left school, went home to Spokane, and vowed to give up on football and pursue a baseball career at another school.

"I came home, I was depressed where my football career was headed," he said. "So I withdrew from school for a week or two, until Coach Walden came down and said, 'You're going to be fine, everything's going to be all right. Come back here.' But I was going to go play baseball with my brother at [Creighton University]."

He returned to Pullman, started every game for the Cougars as both a junior and senior, and was fantastic in the Senior Bowl. Several coaches and scouts worked him out as the 1986 NFL Draft approached. Among them was the Redskins' Jerry Rhome.

"Bobby [Beathard] was always finding players," Rhome remembered. "So he sent me and Charley [Casserly] out to Washington State to look at films, to work out Rypien. . . . We looked at ten games, sat there all day long and looked at Rypien, all ten games. . . . I said, 'This kid is big, strong, he's accurate. We can improve him. I think he can play.'"

Rhome invited Rypien to an informal workout combine in Cheney, Washington, at Eastern Washington University's athletic field house, which contained an indoor practice field as well as a basketball court.

"We started throwing," Rhome said. "And Rypien had a cannon. He's firing the ball and all that. Right off the bat: his feet. He wasn't very quick. . . . So at the very end, this is what did it. I said to the Eastern Washington quarterback, 'Drop back from the free throw line right here and throw it for the goal down there and see if you can throw it in the bucket.' He throws it and it lands between the free throw line and the bucket on the ground. This is about sixty yards. And so I said, 'Okay, Mark, you take a shot.' He rattled the board, on the line. He went back and fired it and it hit the backboard and BAAAAAAAAAANGGGGGG! And I turned around, and I went, 'That's a pretty good throw.' And that Eastern Washington quarterback, his eyes were [lit up]. And Rypien goes, 'I can throw it further than that.' "

Rhome left—but not before telling Rypien to jump rope to improve his foot speed—flew back to Washington, D.C., and informed Beathard and Casserly that the prospect had potential. The Redskins, skeptical about Joe Theismann's leg and not yet convinced of Jay Schroeder's abilities, selected Rypien in the sixth round.

During minicamp and the preseason, Rypien diligently practiced his footwork, but the club's early August acquisition of Doug Williams meant only one roster spot remained. Rypien won the job, besting fan-favorite Babe Laufenberg, but reaggravated the knee injury he suffered in college. Pain from the bone fragments in the patellar tendon did not improve, and prior to Week One he was placed on injured reserve. With Laufenberg released and signed by the New Orleans Saints, All-Pro guard and former Southmoreland (Pennsylvania) High School quarterback Russ Grimm served as Washington's emergency, third-string quarterback for the season-opener against Philadelphia.

Rypien was on injured reserve throughout the 1986 season, returned the next year, then injured his back in the preseason. Aside from the one-week appearance on the active roster late that season, Rypien again watched every Redskins game that year wearing his trademark sweater.

Even without a chance to participate in team practices or games, Rypien developed his skills considerably during two years as a professional. He improved his footwork under Jerry Rhome's tutelage, mastered Joe Gibbs's complicated offensive terminology and schemes, and even found a wife while on the sidelines. Rypien noticed a Redskins cheerleader named Annette; the two secretly dated, were soon married, and welcomed a baby girl in October 1988. But he had worked too hard, waited too long, to waste another season on the sidelines.

"Jerry Rhome worked with Rypien every day," Doug Williams recalled. "He'd be over there on the turf field, he worked the living dogs out of Rip."

At minicamp in May 1988, Rypien told reporters, "No way, there's no IR this year. . . . Just give me a chance to get out there." The trade of Jay Schroeder to the Raiders followed by Doug Williams's emergency appendectomy in late September granted Rypien that chance. In his first NFL appearance, Rypien completed 26 of 41 attempts and threw for 303 yards and 3 touchdowns against the Cardinals. Although a sack-fumble returned for a touchdown in the game's final minute ended Washington's shot at a win, Rypien pleased the coaches.

"Mark isn't the reason we lost. He's the reason we almost won," quarterbacks coach Dan Henning said. "He did a job. If you looked at this game without a final score, you'd say that he can be a good quarterback and win for us."

One week after Rypien's touchdown passes nearly lifted Washington to a comeback over the Giants, he notched his first win in Dallas, then avenged his earlier loss by lighting up the Cardinals at RFK. In his first four starts, Rypien threw 12 touchdowns, just 2 interceptions, completed 60 percent of his passes, and averaged 269 yards passing per game.

Bruised ribs late in the victory over Phoenix (the franchise relocated from St. Louis in 1988) sidelined Rypien in the middle of the season and returned Doug Williams to the starting job: a back-and-forth quarterback shuffling reminiscent of the Williams-Schroeder episode continued throughout the season. Williams's back ailments the following summer made Rypien the Redskins' starter at the beginning of the 1989 campaign. Again, he posted excellent numbers: through seven games, he had 13 touchdown passes and ranked third in the NFL in passing yards as Washington led the NFL in total offense.

"He was a fantastic deep thrower, that's one of the most important things to coaches," Gibbs said. "You can work so hard and how many times do you actually get somebody open deep? Not very often: five, six times a game. You better not miss them. That guy didn't miss 'em. . . . That guy was aggressive, man. When he saw deep, he was going for it."

But for all the points and yards Rypien accounted for—he supplied Gary Clark, Ricky Sanders, and Art Monk the ball during their record-setting season—his mistakes occasionally cost the Redskins.

During Washington's 4-4 start, Rypien had thrown 9 interceptions, fumbled 11 times, and was criticized for holding on to the ball too long in the pocket. He was so angry at himself for 2 fumbles and 2 interceptions in a 42–37 loss to Philadelphia (a game in which the Redskins wasted a 20-point lead) that he skipped an invitation to dinner at the home of Vice President Dan Quayle.

"I guess I left him hanging," he said. "I was so emotionally and physically drained that I just wanted to be alone."

Within a month, Rypien reclaimed the starter's role and although Washington missed the playoffs, the Redskins won the final five games of the 1989 season, during which time they averaged more than 30 points per game. The late-season turnaround and Rypien's work ethic convinced Gibbs and the front office that he could be the club's franchise quarterback.

"He had the perfect football mind in that, I don't know what Mark's IQ is, [but] I just know that for a football player—and I coached several—he was outstanding from a mental standpoint," Gibbs said. "For instance, you're in meetings, you can kind of tell if guys are hooked up with you. You look at their eyes, some guys are dozing off. This guy, he'd sit in the front row and his eyes were [wide open]. And even if I would mumble a question, he'd go 'Zero coverage!' He was so intent on football and was geared that way that he absorbed it. . . . It was really a pleasure coaching him."

Several of his teammates saw in Rypien traits similar to the MVP of Super Bowl XXII, Doug Williams.

"He wasn't too much of a talker," guard Raleigh McKenzie said. "But we did know that he liked football, he was just a tough guy.

He wasn't fast, he wasn't a good runner. But he would run, and he would try to run over somebody to just to get that first down. So we would fight for him. He was just a blue-collar guy. He was almost just like us linemen."

Rypien's toughness was never in question. As far back as his freshman year of college, he'd fought through injuries, and as an NFL rookie, he battled through persistent pain in his knee just to make the Redskins' roster. And in 1990, after his left knee buckled in a game against Dallas and surgery to the damaged ligaments kept him out for six games, he returned to the field to throw 4 touchdowns in a win over New Orleans. Protecting the football, however, was proving far more injurious to both his claim to the starter's job and the Redskins' offense.

He threw 11 interceptions in the Redskins' final six games, leading to occasional boos from the RFK faithful. Still, Washington won four of those games to finish the 1990 regular season at 10-6: Earnest Byner's late-season resurgence allowed them to qualify for the postseason for the first time since their march toward Super Bowl XXII. In a rematch of that season's infamous "Body Bag Game," in which nine Redskins players sustained injuries, Rypien threw 2 touchdown passes to produce a 20–6 upset of the Philadelphia Eagles in the wild card round. A week later Washington faced the dynastic San Francisco 49ers. Playing on a sore ankle—he took a pain-killing injection prior to kickoff—Rypien threw 3 interceptions. The first two ended drives deep in San Francisco territory while the third was returned for a game-clinching touchdown. Throughout the 28–10 defeat, Rypien appeared lost and indecisive.

"He didn't look confident," 49ers linebacker Matt Millen later said. "He didn't look like a guy in control."

Gibbs backed Rypien after the loss, explaining, "He's still learning and growing. . . . Yes, he's our starter." But both Gibbs and Rypien knew that to remain the quarterback of the Washington Redskins he would need to deliver something he hadn't.

"Let's face it," Gibbs said in 1990. "He's going to be judged here with the Redskins if he can win a Super Bowl because that's what other quarterbacks here have done."

Although Rypien's inconsistencies were certainly the most well-documented problems facing the Redskins, they faced a handful of other concerns entering the 1991 regular season. In addition to the advancing age of several of the team's longest-tenured veterans—Darrell Green, Joe Jacoby, Russ Grimm, Jeff Bostic, Art Monk, Monte Coleman, and Charles Mann were all over thirty years old—they played in the toughest division in the NFL. The Giants won that year's Super Bowl, Philadelphia was a frequent playoff team led by Reggie White on defense and Randall Cunningham on offense, Dallas had restocked their roster with talent by trading away star running back Herschel Walker, and Phoenix Cardinals head coach Joe Bugel knew Washington better than anyone in the NFL.

Joe Gibbs was shocked to learn at the start of training camp in 1991 that two national magazines, *Sports Illustrated* and *Playboy*, predicted the Redskins to reach Super Bowl XXVI.

"I don't see how anybody could pick us," he said. "It doesn't make sense."

Three losses in four preseason games further sapped the credibility of those forecasts and only added to the uncertainty surrounding the Redskins on the eve of the regular season.

"I'm not worried about any one thing," Joe Gibbs said after finishing his first losing preseason schedule in nine years. "I'm worried about everything. I look across the board and see enough questions that it would be hard to be real optimistic. For people to start talking about the Super Bowl is ridiculous. Maybe I have to do a better job of talking about our problems."

WHEN HE OWNED MINOR league baseball's Toronto Maple Leafs, Jack Kent Cooke struck up a friendship with one of big league baseball's greatest minds, Branch Rickey. In the late 1950s, Rickey's dream of a third professional baseball circuit to contend with the majors, the Continental League, took shape and Cooke became the league's vice president. Cooke greatly admired the former Brooklyn Dodgers president who had brought Jackie Robinson to Major League Baseball in 1947.

"The only man Jack revered more than himself was Branch Rickey," fellow Canadian sports owner Harry Ornest said years later. "Jack loved the English language, and he felt Rickey used it better than anyone he'd ever met. Jack used words like 'bloody,' 'nincompoop,' and 'balderdash' because Rickey did."

Although Cooke left professional baseball in 1964, one year before Rickey passed away, he would enlighten his employees for decades with lessons from "the Mahatma."

"Branch Rickey was a big influence on him; [he] always told us Branch Rickey stories," said Charley Casserly. "Two of Rickey's tenets that he told me were, Rickey believed in numbers: multiple farm teams. Cooke believed in numbers; we all believed in numbers. That's why we always went to camp with a lot of guys, why we always had a high injured-reserve list. We had a farm team all the time. Cooke believed in that from Branch Rickey. It cost money to do that. Not a lot, but it cost money. [Also] Bobby went on the road scouting, I went on the road scouting. Branch Rickey, once a week, went out on the road scouting, to stay sharp with his skills. Goes back to Cooke and Branch Rickey, understanding what he's asking, what we want to do.

"Cooke was an experienced sports owner who was very demanding, accountability was big, but he let you do your job," Casserly said. "He never told you who to cut, never told you who to trade for, never told you who to take."

But Cooke certainly let his Redskins employees know when he was displeased. And he often expressed his concerns or provided suggestions without any hesitation. He called Gibbs and Beathard out to his farm for a tongue-lashing during the Redskins 0-5 start of 1981. Requiring notification of all trades and draft selections, Cooke became livid when he learned the team had chosen Brian Mitchell, a five-foot-ten-inch college quarterback, in the fifth round. He calmed down upon learning that the coaching staff intended for Mitchell to play running back. And from his VIP-filled owner's box, Cooke even offered in-game advice.

"Mr. Cooke wanted me there. And if there was something in the game he didn't like, sometimes he'd say, 'You get down there and tell those coaches to change this!'" Bobby Beathard recalled. "Well, I'm not going to go down and tell the coaches. So I'd go leave the box and go down and sit with the coaches for a while and then come back up and [he'd] say, 'Did you tell them what I said?' And I say, 'Yea, I told them everything.'"

Joe Gibbs found escaping Cooke's scrutiny much more difficult. The morning after game day, Gibbs would talk to the owner on the phone to discuss the previous day's results.

"Now, if we won the game, it wasn't too bad," a member of the Redskins' organization said. "One time, [Gibbs] came in the meeting and said something like, 'Boy, I dreaded that phone call,' or 'I'm glad that's over.'

"Even though Gibbs was highly respected there's one guy that even Gibbs is a little bit nervous about, and that's Jack Kent Cooke. That's only natural: everyone's afraid of Jack Kent Cooke, I don't care who you were. He put the fear of God in everybody; I don't care if you're the trainer or the equipment man or the head coach."

Joe Gibbs knew that better than anyone.

"I had great respect for Mr. Cooke," Gibbs said. "But at the same time, my heart rate would go up sometimes when I see Mr. Cooke or if he called me up and said, 'I need to see you in Middleburg,' all the way out there, I got armpits down to my waist."

At least one time, however, Gibbs stood up to his domineering boss's reprimand.

Two days after the 1991 Redskins concluded their discouraging 1-3 preseason with a 13–9 loss to the previously winless Jets, Cooke tracked down Gibbs at Redskin Park.

"I'm sitting in the office, and he never came unannounced—we always knew Mr. Cooke was coming because everybody would baton down the hatches. All of a sudden they came in the office there and said, 'Hey, Mr. Cooke wants to see you out on the field.'"

"Hey, Mr. Cooke, how you doing?" Gibbs said.

"Fine, I want to talk to you about something," Cooke said. "I think we've made some real mistakes here. We're too loyal, we got too many old guys."

After nearly a decade at the helm of one of the league's most prominent franchises, Joe Gibbs had become well-known for his overt religious zeal as well as his encouragement of players to explore and develop their own faith. And players on other teams knew of the successful head coach's strong devotion: at least twelve of the Plan B free agents that joined the Redskins between 1989 and 1991 were labeled "devout Christians." Several other Redskins players, who happened to be religious, also remained on the roster far longer than expected.

"Gibbs is so sincere about religion that he has trouble believing that some players who claim to be religious are phonies," a team insider told the *Washingtonian* in the summer of 1992. "He can be naive, thinking that because a person goes the religious route, you eliminate his faults. . . . Nobody could understand why [backup running back Keith Griffin] stayed on the team as long as he did. Maybe it was because he's religious. He was an all-around super kid, very smart, but he just wasn't that talented."

Some players simply claimed to be devout—regularly attending Bible sessions or meeting with the team chaplain—because they saw religion as a way to impress Gibbs and possibly save their job.

"A lot of guys carried Bibles around, thinking it was going to get them in good favor," Brian Mitchell recalled years later. "But ultimately, Joe Gibbs wanted football players. He wants you to be a great human being, a great individual, a great Christian. But if you're not a great football player, then he's not going to keep you on his football team."

Genuine or not, by the early 1990s, the Redskins were the most outwardly religious team in the NFL, "a squad where almost half of the players consider themselves born-again Christians." And with each season that did not result in a Super Bowl title, grumblings about questionable personnel decision-making conflated *religious* players with *veteran* players, those whom Jack Kent Cooke suggested Gibbs was showing too much loyalty.

Surprised, but accepting of the owner's concerns, Gibbs listened politely to Cooke outside the practice field that cold morning in September 1991.

"He is reading me the riot act, which was okay. And then all of a sudden he hit my hot button because he said, 'You take that Jimmy Johnson, now he has built that thing the right way.' And boy, I start in on him, and it's one of the few times I ever lost my cool."

Cooke, now the surprised one, shot back at Gibbs, who had thrown his jacket on the ground in anger. He asked the coach to calm down and suggested they go into the office and discuss the issue further over a coffee.

"We go up there and talk that whole thing over," Gibbs said decades later. "So then the season starts, and he never said another word about that ever again! I always laughed at Mr. Cooke, because he would say things to you, and if they came true, then he was back in your face. And if they didn't: 'I'll never mention that again!'"

Cooke never again questioned Gibbs about his "old" players or suggested he emulate Dallas head coach Jimmy Johnson because the next week, Washington opened the 1991 season with the most lopsided win in team history, defeating the Detroit Lions 45–0. A week later, in Dallas against Johnson's up-and-coming Cowboys, the Redskins overcame an 11-point deficit to claim a 33–31 victory over their rival.

"We're going back and forth, back and forth," Earnest Byner recalled of the Dallas matchup. "We ended up coming back, winning that game. Richie Petitbon came into the locker room, and he recognized it. He said, 'We going to the Super Bowl, fellas.' Second game of the year."

Washington's defensive coordinator had been around long enough to know a great team when he saw it. A four-time Pro Bowl safety for George Halas's Bears, Petitbon won an NFL championship in 1963; he picked off Y. A. Tittle in Chicago's 14–10 title game win over the Giants. Petitbon then left one Hall of Fame head coach for another. Traded to the Los Angeles Rams in 1969, he played two seasons for George Allen's Rams and followed him to Washington in 1971. Although injured early the next season, the thirty-four-year-old was a member of Allen's "Over the Hill Gang" that reached Super Bowl VII.

The New Orleans native retired after that season, joined the Houston Oilers' staff for a few years, and then returned to Washington as a defensive backs coach in 1978. Upon Joe Gibbs's hiring, Petitbon was promoted to defensive coordinator.

Just as Gibbs had done with his offensive staff, Petitbon hired defensive coaches he'd previously worked with. As Houston's secondary coach, Petitbon met Larry Peccatiello, once a lieutenant in the army's 101st Airborne division, who oversaw the Oilers' linebacking corps. "Pec" took the same position on Gibbs's staff. Two-time NFL champion for the Detroit Lions in 1952 and 1953, LaVern Torgeson had been an assistant coach on the Rams and Redskins teams that Petitbon played on. Petitbon gave "Torgy," a two-time Pro Bowler for Washington in the mid-1950s, command of the Redskins' defensive line. In 1986, Emmitt Thomas, a five-time Pro Bowl cornerback for the Kansas City Chiefs, also joined the defensive staff.

"We worked absolutely great together," said Peccatiello, who along with Thomas watched games from the coaches' box while

Petitbon and Torgy remained on the sideline. "We really put [the game plan] in altogether, and knew on game day exactly what we wanted to call, where our calls would be."

Beginning in 1981, the Redskins' defense became one of the most consistent in the NFL. For the next ten years, utilizing a dizzying variety of schemes, coverages, and blitzes, they ranked in the top ten for yards allowed four times and finished eleventh or better in points surrendered eight times.

"I'm a big baseball fan," Petitbon said years later. "I would describe our defense as a pitcher who has about five pitches that he can throw for strikes anytime he wants. That was our defense. We were a multiple defense. We had the ability to change, and change often, and figure out what the opponent's offensive game plan was against us that day and be able adjust to stop what they were doing to us."

But the Bears' famed 46 Defense, the Lawrence Taylor–led Giants, and a San Francisco 49ers unit that produced four Super Bowl titles in nine years, all garnered much more praise. Washington's defense even played second fiddle on their own team. Darrell Green's speed and Dexter Manley's pass rushing—only surpassed by his brash, yet oddly likable personality—gave Washington two individual stars on the defensive side of the ball. But as a group, the defense was grossly overshadowed by Joe Theismann, John Riggins, Doug Williams, the Posse, the Smurfs, the Fun Bunch, and even the Hogs, the usually nameless, faceless collection of offensive linemen.

"I think because I coached offense and we had the success we had, I always felt like when we came out of all that, when it was all said and done, the defense didn't get the credit they deserved," Gibbs said in 2014. "Those guys did it. I can't take any credit for our defense, the way those guys played."

From the day he was hired as head coach, Joe Gibbs, who never worked solely on the defensive side of the ball in his twenty-seven years as a coach, trusted the defensive staff that he and Bobby Beathard assembled.

"He could have any say he wanted, but he chose not to," Peccatiello said. "He didn't interfere in anything we did. I'm sure if we had
screwed it up, he'd have a lot to say. But I guess he was comfortable
with how things were going."

And while there had been frequent turnover on Gibbs's offensive
staff—Joe Bugel, Jerry Rhome, and Dan Henning (twice) all left to
take promotions on other teams—the same three defensive assistants
remained in Washington a decade after their arrival in 1981. That
consistency, and the trust they'd earned, allowed Gibbs to devote
nearly all his time to the offense.

"Your defense, I've always felt like led you, it leads you, to Super
Bowls. Your special teams is the heart of your team, then the offense
is supposed to finish their part off," Gibbs said. "Defense leads you,
and so our defensive staff there deserves so much of the credit for
what happened over those eleven years. Richie, Pec, and Torgy: very,
very bright guys.

"My strength has always been offense, so I felt like that's where
I needed to work. So that's how we were geared. I stayed over at the
offense and worked with everyone over there. We had Wayne Sevier,
who was an unbelievable special teams coach, and then you had the
defensive staff that we had that ran the show on the defense. So lots
of times I got a lot of credit when it should have gone to those guys."

In 1983, during their blistering march toward a second consecutive NFC Championship, the Redskins' defense forced an NFL-
record 61 turnovers, amassed 51 sacks, and limited opposing teams to
an NFL-low 81 rushing yards per game. But that defense repeatedly
bungled pass coverages. "The Pearl Harbor Crew" finished dead last
in the league with 248 yards passing per game. Eight years later, with
Darrell Green the only remaining starter from the Super Bowl XVIII
team, the Redskins' defense was once again the best in the NFL.

Several Plan B free agents that the front office added—defensive
linemen Fred Stokes and Jumpy Geathers, as well as safeties
Brad Edwards and Danny Copeland—restocked the defense with

starters or key contributors who came to Washington at relatively low prices. Outside linebacker Wilber Marshall, however, did not come cheap.

A critical member of the Bears' 46 Defense, Marshall and Chicago could not agree on a new contract after the 1988 season and the Redskins promptly signed the All-Pro to a five-year, $6 million offer sheet. The Bears could have matched the deal but they chose not to and received the Redskins' first-round picks each of the next two years as compensation. Marshall became the first free agent in eleven years to switch teams.

Renowned for being "fast enough to cover wide receivers and certainly strong enough to bench press one," Marshall started every game at right (or weak side) linebacker for Washington beginning in his first year. But during spring practices in 1991, the defensive staff flip-flopped him and second-year outside linebacker Andre Collins, who as a rookie finished second on the team with 6 sacks but did not match up well against physical tight ends.

"We decided to make the change because we thought tight ends muscled Collins around a bit last year," Richie Petitbon said in May. "We think Wilber is stronger and better off on the left side, and we think Andre will be better working in open space rather than being over the tight end. I don't know if they are happy or sad about the switch, but it doesn't matter. This move will be better for the team, and that's all that matters."

Marshall's move to left, or strong side linebacker, meant he would occasionally be replaced in passing downs and have fewer chances to play freely in open space, both of which greatly angered the team's highest-paid defender. During training camp, the *Houston Chronicle* even reported that the Redskins offered Marshall to the Oilers in exchange for defensive end Sean Jones. But once the season began, Marshall—whose 5 interceptions that season would tie Darrell Green for the team-high—could not argue with the results.

Two weeks after shutting out the Lions at home, Washington blanked Phoenix at RFK. Marshall intercepted two Cardinals passes that day, returning the second for a 54-yard touchdown. Back home against Philadelphia in Week Five, Andre Collins intercepted a bobbled pass during the fourth quarter, preserving yet another shutout. Through three home games, the Redskins did not give up a single point, a feat no team had achieved since the 1934 Detroit Lions.

"The key has been that we've been able to put pressure on the quarterback with just the front four," Charles Mann said in early October. "That way you don't lose anything in the secondary and they can focus on covering the pass. I'm not going to say this is the best defense I've ever been a part of, but it's the earliest a defense has played this well together. We know how to play with each other, and that's a little surprising considering all the changes we've made. It's amazing when you think about it."

The defense's spectacular showing early in the 1991 season was matched by Washington's brilliantly versatile offense.

Six days after besting the Eagles' spectacular pass rush for a 23–0 home victory on *Monday Night Football*, the Redskins topped the Bears in Chicago, 20–7, then torched the Cleveland Browns and rookie head coach Bill Belichick—whose Giants defense had repeatedly stonewalled Washington in previous years—for 6 offensive touchdowns. Following a pair of narrow, low-scoring wins, including a 13-point, second-half comeback win in New York against the defending Super Bowl champion Giants, the Redskins' offense again lit up the scoreboard.

Home against the Falcons for Week Eleven, Washington scored a post-merger team-record 56 points and racked up 559 yards of offense. The 39-point blowout prompted Atlanta to play rookie third-string quarterback Brett Favre, who attempted his first four passes as a pro: two were intercepted, the second of which was returned for a touchdown by linebacker Andre Collins. The next week in Pittsburgh, they put up 41 more points on the Steelers and soon-to-retire head coach Chuck Noll. In consecutive games the Redskins had scored 12 offensive touchdowns and gained 1,021 yards. And quarterback Mark Rypien—who had thrown for 767 yards, 8 touchdowns, and zero interceptions—was at the center of the explosion.

Rypien's contract had expired after his erratic 1990 season. A restricted free agent—meaning that any other team which signed him would have to grant Washington considerable draft-day compensation—he could not come to terms with the team the following spring. Rypien attended the team's May minicamp, but did not show up to Dickinson College for the start of training camp, prompting Jack Kent Cooke to give Rypien a message during an interview with WTTG-TV: "I think you're a bloody idiot if you don't come soon."

Ten days into the holdout, Rypien decided to "roll the dice." In the hopes that 1991 would greatly improve his bargaining power the next spring, he signed a one-year contract and arrived at training camp in Carlisle, Pennsylvania.

"At that era of football, Redskins people really loved their players, but they didn't like when their players thought they were better than the community or the team. But that was the only leverage you had," Rypien said in 2014. "I came back, first time I walked on the field I got booed by my own fans."

Redskins fans did not boo Mark Rypien once the 1991 regular season began.

In the blowout of Detroit, he completed 15 of 19 attempts and led Washington's offense to 5 touchdowns in the first three quarters before Joe Gibbs rested him and several starters with less than seven minutes remaining. As Rypien exited the field, fans at RFK gave him a standing ovation.

"We hit just about everything we ran," he told the press. "I needed this. We needed this. You want to get off on a good foot, and everyone executed real well. We have a right to be proud, but it's just one game."

The question marks that surrounded Rypien during the previous two years quickly faded that fall. Throughout the season he continued to throw an extraordinarily accurate deep ball—hitting on 8 touchdown passes of 47 yards or longer, including 6 to Gary Clark—but it was Rypien's improved ball security and decision-making that carried Washington's offense. During the regular season he threw just 11 interceptions and lost just 5 fumbles to go along with conference-bests in yards (3,564) and touchdown passes (28).

Rypien's most incredible statistic, however, belonged as much to the Redskins' offensive line as it did to their Pro Bowl quarterback. By the end of Washington's nineteen-game regular-season and playoff schedule, the less-than-fleet-footed passer was sacked just 7 times. (Many Redskins starters sat out the second half of their Week Seventeen matchup with the Eagles, who twice sacked second-string quarterback Jeff Rutledge.)

"We did a lot with Mark, a lot of audible, packages where he could audible, and as a consequence, if you go back and study him, here's what will really come up about him: hard to sack," Joe Gibbs said. "Because he knew where every outlet was, he knew where he was exposed, and he got rid of that ball."

Rypien's decisiveness paired with Washington's blocking upfront kept defenders from bringing down the quarterback in all but five games that year.

Due to injury, retirement, and free agency, the only two original members of the Hogs to start were Jeff Bostic and Joe Jacoby. Russ Grimm, whose achy knees convinced him to announce that 1991 would be his final season, became the line's utility player, filling in at guard, center, tackle, and as a third tight end on goal-line and short-yardage situations. Against Philadelphia in Week Five, Grimm pushed off a defender, drew an offensive pass interference penalty, then dropped a 7-yard touchdown pass from Mark Rypien.

"It was a gallant effort on his part," said an amused Joe Gibbs. "I guess this means they have to cover him now."

Even without Grimm, Mark May, and "Boss Hog" Joe Bugel, the newer, younger Hogs upheld the tradition of excellence well into the new decade.

Under second-year offensive line coach Jim Hanifan—who served on the same St. Louis Cardinals staff as Joe Gibbs and used far less harsh language than his predecessor Joe Bugel—the Redskins' revamped offensive line pounded defenses. In addition to the historic protection of Rypien, Washington's running game in 1991 returned to a level not seen since John Riggins's prime. For the first time since 1983, the Redskins led the NFL in rushing attempts.

"They're the epitome of what offensive linemen should be," Hanifan said. "They're enjoyable to coach, and they've risen to the occasion in pressure-type situations."

Left tackle Jim Lachey faced those high-pressure situations nearly every week. Acquired in the deal that sent Jay Schroeder to the Raiders, Lachey developed into one of the best linemen in the NFL. Frequently neutralizing future Hall of Famers Reggie White and Lawrence Taylor in matchups twice a year convinced Joe Gibbs that Lachey was "one of the top two tackles in the NFL."

"He's blessed with all the things you'd like to have—the size, the quickness, the speed," said Hanifan. "But what sets him apart . . . is that he really enjoys playing the game. The game is fun to him."

Trading a disgruntled backup quarterback for a twenty-five-year-old blindside tackle who was soon selected to three consecutive All-Pro teams proved to be one of Bobby Beathard's shrewdest moves. His final draft as Redskins general manager also landed the Redskins an invaluable offensive lineman who fit in with the Hogs.

"I wasn't on anybody's radar," Mark Schlereth recalled. "I had so many injuries that the University of Idaho essentially retired me."

Following his junior season, the defensive lineman for the Division I-AA Vandals persuaded the coaching staff to let him finish his career despite nasty injuries to his knee and elbow. Moving to guard, he survived his senior season—Idaho won a school record eleven games—and impressed Redskins defensive line coach Torgy Torgeson and scout Billy Devaney, who visited the Moscow, Idaho, campus to work out Schlereth's teammate, Marvin Washington. Thinking he might be a "diamond in the rough," Torgy and Devaney informed Bobby Beathard and Joe Bugel, who personally worked out Schlereth a week later.

The Redskins selected Schlereth in the tenth round of the 1989 draft, and by his third season the first native Alaskan to play in the NFL started every game and won a spot in the Pro Bowl. The team's veteran offensive linemen mentored the hard worker, who possessed great natural strength.

"When I became a starter we all watched extra film together," Schlereth said. "They taught me how to study film and how to study guys. They were instrumental in the development of my career."

The Hogs took an instant liking to the good-natured youngster. Before training camp—when veterans routinely haze rookies—Russ Grimm informed Schlereth that he didn't have to carry anyone's shoulder pads or sing his college fight song for the team dinner, if Grimm wasn't in attendance, "and I never come to dinner, I always go out and have a few beers."

"One night at dinner, they started banging on the glass and Monte Coleman said, 'Hey, Rook, stand up, it's your turn to sing.' And I said, 'Well, I'd gladly do it, but Russ told me I can't sing unless he's present at dinner,'" Schlereth recalled. "And Monte looks over the room and Russ isn't there, and he says, 'Okay, sit down.' And that was it. There was never a question. That's how much respect that team had for the Hogs."

JUST THE FOURTH TEAM since the 1970 merger to begin the season 11-0, the Redskins sparked whispers of an undefeated, untied season late in 1991. And with their ability to crush opponents—through eleven games, they had recorded six victories by 23 points or more—they looked invincible. Until the second quarter of their Week Twelve visit from the resurgent Dallas Cowboys.

Cornerback Martin Mayhew's interception-turned-touchdown in the first quarter gave Washington a 7–0 advantage, which they soon squandered. Owning time of possession—they controlled the clock for nearly eighteen minutes longer and ran 25 more offensive plays than Washington—Dallas leaned on budding superstars running back Emmitt Smith and wide receiver Michael Irvin to take the lead, prolong drives, and preserve a 24–21 victory.

"It's just a hunch, but I don't think we're gonna go undefeated anymore," linebacker Matt Millen joked after the loss. "It was nice while it lasted and you hate to lose, but it was just one of those days. You have to keep it in perspective. . . . We're out here sixteen weeks. We're out to get to the playoffs and go to the Super Bowl. All those are still out there, they're all still attainable. All the things that got us here are still there. Guys have been here before. We've lost before, and we'll win again."

The Redskins instantly bounced back over the next month. A decisive road win over the Rams in Los Angeles earned Joe Gibbs a fifth NFC East crown. In Week Fifteen, 20 unanswered points against Joe Bugel's lowly Phoenix Cardinals overcame a 14–0 half-time deficit and clinched Washington both the top seed and home-field advantage throughout the NFC playoffs.

And with a 34–17 win over the Giants in Week Sixteen, Washington entered their regular-season finale against Philadelphia leading the NFL in fewest points surrendered. The Redskins lost the meaningless game, giving up 24 points (one score came on an interception returned for a touchdown) to finish the season ranked second in total points allowed. The 22 points that Washington scored, however, did secure their place as the highest scoring team that year, even though they settled for 6 field goal attempts and scored just 1 touchdown.

Still, that day—in which many starters did not play all four quarters—followed by the team's much-deserved postseason bye, did nothing to hinder the Redskins' offensive and defensive mastery as the calendar turned to 1992.

In their first playoff game against the Falcons, who used the run-and-shoot offense to score the fifth most points in the league that year, Washington intercepted Pro Bowl quarterback Chris Miller 4 times, recovered 2 Atlanta fumbles, and gave up just 52 total yards in the second half. Dominant on defense from the start, Washington didn't need much scoring to advance to their fifth NFC Championship Game in ten years, but managed 24 points, including 2 touchdown runs from goal-line specialist Gerald Riggs.

In another rematch with a visiting run-and-shoot team that they had demolished during the regular season, the Redskins faced the Lions with a Super Bowl berth on the line. Two early Detroit turnovers helped Washington grab a 10–0 lead. The Lions fought back, pulling within 7 late by halftime. Again, the Redskins' defense—on the strength of 3 sacks by Wilber Marshall—and three long scoring drives soon buried Detroit. Ahead 34–10 early in the fourth quarter, Washington sealed their trip to the Super Bowl when Darrell Green nabbed a poorly thrown ball by fellow Texan and former Heisman Trophy winner Andre Ware, returning the interception for a 32-yard touchdown.

"I'm going to take a while on this one," said Joe Gibbs, who didn't mind the Gatorade shower given to him by Jeff Bostic and Gary Clark. "The next two weeks I'm going to work, but I'm enjoying this. You may not get by this way again. I'm going to enjoy every minute."

Although Gibbs's offense executed his game plan—they turned the ball over only once and owned time of possession in both games—the defense shone brightest. In the two playoff games, Washington's defense allowed a total of 17 points, forced 9 turnovers, recorded 8 sacks, and didn't yield a single score in the second half.

Asked how the 1991 edition compared to Washington's previous teams, Richie Petitbon—who foresaw this team's Super Bowl destiny four months earlier—answered, "This one could be the best if we win it all."

Intended or not, Petitbon's postgame comment hinted at something no one inside Redskin Park wanted to acknowledge. Joe Gibbs's Redskins had reached this point before: NFC Champions nearing the end of a magnificent, historic, near-flawless season, and favored to finish with another Super Bowl triumph. But in "one of the toughest losses I've ever experienced in sports," Gibbs's 1983 Redskins team was clobbered by the underdog Los Angeles Raiders.

Eight years after that devastating loss, Washington was again favored (by seven points) to win the title. And again, their Super Bowl opponent, the Buffalo Bills, was a deep, playoff-hardened club loaded with All-Pros and future Hall of Famers on both sides of the ball, just as the Raiders had been in Super Bowl XVIII.

Buffalo lost the previous year's Super Bowl to the Giants due to an excruciatingly close, unsuccessful field goal attempt in the game's final seconds. They rebounded in 1991 to slash through the AFC, in a way comparable to Washington's supremacy over the NFC: by Week Twelve, as Washington's record stood at 11-0, the Bills were 10-1. Although a sharp contrast to the Redskins' measured, methodical approach, Buffalo also boasted an exceptionally balanced yet potent offense: that season, only the Redskins scored more points than the Bills, who averaged 28.6 per game.

Running a fast-paced, no-huddle offense dubbed "the K-Gun," first-team All-Pro quarterback Jim Kelly led the NFL with 33 touchdown passes. And similar to Mark Rypien, who relied on the fine trio of receivers Art Monk, Gary Clark, and Ricky Sanders, Kelly employed three steady and uniquely different pass-catchers. Veteran deep-ball threat James Lofton and durable inside-target Andre Reed each topped 1,000 yards receiving that year. But running back Thurman Thomas, who finished second on the team with 62 catches that season, was always Kelly's security blanket, both through the air and on the ground. The league's MVP in 1991, Thomas led the NFL in total yards from scrimmage for a record third straight season and was a threat to score from anywhere on the field.

Although the Bills' K-Gun electrified and thrilled football fans, head coach Marv Levy's team featured comparable talent on defense. Buffalo allowed just 21 points in two playoff games and in each of those postseason wins they knocked their opponent's starting quarterback (Denver's John Elway and Kansas City's Steve DeBerg) out of the game with an injury. With a trio of Pro Bowl linebackers, Darryl Talley, Shane Conlan, and Cornelius Bennett, one of the game's top cornerbacks in Nate Odomes, and former Defensive Player of the Year Bruce Smith, Buffalo's defense was loaded with individual talent. As *Chicago Tribune* sports columnist Don Pierson noted the week of Super Bowl XXVI, "The Redskins have stats; the Bills have stars."

But in the days leading up to the showdown at Minneapolis's Metrodome, the star of the Bills was their defensive line coach Chuck Dickerson.

Expecting the game's outcome to hinge on the matchup of Washington's elite offensive line versus the Bills' celebrated front seven, reporters asked Dickerson to break down the Hogs.

In addition to explaining that "people are still hungry; there are still kids in downtown Buffalo who didn't get toys for Christmas. Anybody who takes this too seriously is full of bull. We're here to entertain," Dickerson imitated a Hog shriek.

"Dickerson's 309 pounds jostled, his mouth contorted, his chest heaved, his head bobbled, and his eyes bugged," *Miami Herald*'s Greg Cote noted. "[Then] a sudden, loud guttural succession of low grunts and snorts [and] a high squeal careened in for good measure."

Dickerson then characterized each of the line's individuals.

Mark Schlereth ("He did a better job of finding Lawrence Taylor and handling Taylor than anyone we've seen") received genuine praise from Dickerson, as did Raleigh McKenzie, who he said was "rough and rugged. Bites and scratches. Smart."

The other Redskins' starting offensive linemen didn't get the same love from Dickerson.

He explained that Jeff Bostic was "ugly like the rest of 'em. He's somewhere eating grease right now." Jim Lachey had "great big chins falling over his chin strap. But nimble! He's like a 310-pound ballerina, he should wear a tutu under his uniform," and attributed much of his dominance to his "bad breath, which is why we're installing steel facemasks on our helmets so they won't melt."

Joe Jacoby was the focal point of Dickerson's shtick. In addition to attacking the four-time Pro Bowler's skills—"He's clumsy out of his stance. He comes up too high on pass protection. You could criticize all his techniques"—Dickerson said Jacoby was "a real Neanderthal. Slobbers a lot. Probably kicks dogs in his neighborhood."

Dickerson's attempt at insult comedy infuriated every member of the Redskins—"It wasn't funny," Jeff Bostic later said—but especially Joe Gibbs. On the Saturday night before Super Bowl XXVI, after his regular address to the team, Gibbs ended the meeting by playing a tape of Dickerson's set for the entire team.

"I don't know that I've ever seen Joe Gibbs as mad as he was that Saturday night—he was just livid," Schlereth said. "He was distraught that anybody—whether it was tongue-in-cheek or not—would ever say anything derogatory about that offensive line that had been a backbone, a staple of what had made Washington great all those years. So he was very upset by those comments. That was kind of a pep rally Saturday night before the Super Bowl on Sunday."

Dickerson wasn't the first person to bash the Hogs publicly that year: Atlanta Falcons head coach Jerry Glanville, irritated at the lack of holding penalties called against the Redskins, said "their offensive line tackles better than our secondary."

But the personal cracks against the Hogs on such a huge stage—in good fun or not—galvanized the entire team, not just the Hogs.

"You could have heard a pin drop when we walked out of that meeting," Earnest Byner recalled. "They were in for a thrashing. . . .

They talk about 'bulletin board material doesn't matter,' you're not going to play any harder. That's bull. That gave us more than enough to go in there and wax them."

WASHINGTON'S BRUTAL 1984 LOSS to the Raiders in Super Bowl XVIII was a fitting end to a horrible week in Florida. After the poor accommodations, the strategically compromised practice facility, the bad weather, John Riggins's illness, and the team's misguided bus route to Tampa Stadium, the Redskins' special teams gaffe that created an early 7–0 hole was just another in a long line of problems.

Super Bowl XXVI didn't start out quite as poorly for the Redskins. In fact, a far more disastrous opening moment befell the young Bills and specifically their top player. Thurman Thomas, who that week repeatedly talked about not receiving enough respect from the media, could not find his helmet during the opening coin toss ceremony. The team's equipment manager moved it without telling him, causing the All-Pro to miss the Bills first two offensive snaps.

Still, the Redskins endured a few early mishaps early as well. Although they sacked Jim Kelly on the first defensive series, and then intercepted him on the next, Washington went three-and-out on their first series, botched a field goal attempt nine minutes into the game, and failed to score in the first period. Furthermore, Chuck Dickerson's defensive front, not the Hogs, appeared to be the more inspired, more determined unit in the game's opening minutes.

"I remember getting hit those first couple plays of that Super Bowl on just simple three-step drops and coming over to our offensive linemen, getting after them a little bit, saying, 'Guys, what the heck's going on here, these are hitch routes?'" Rypien remembered. "They said, 'Calm down, these guys are flying on adrenaline, higher than a kite right now. Don't worry, we'll wear 'em down.' And so I believed that, and sure enough, that's exactly what happened."

As the defense continued to stymie Buffalo throughout the first half, recording 3 sacks and allowing just 63 total yards from scrimmage, the Redskins' offense clicked. Ahead 3–0 by way of a field goal early in the second quarter, Washington took advantage of a short Buffalo punt and drove to the 10-yard line. Rypien then threw a pass to the flats, where Earnest Byner turned upfield and dove to the goal line for the game's first touchdown. Two plays later, another Bills interception gave Washington great field position. A clutch third-and-nine completion to Gary Clark followed by a Ricky Ervins run set up a 1-yard touchdown plunge by Gerald Riggs. Nearing halftime, Washington led 17–0.

"One thing I appreciated about Joe Gibbs is that he never backed down from being aggressive. He didn't want to just grind it out for the rest of the game because we were only in the second quarter. While the momentum was in our favor, he wanted us to jump on top," Mark Rypien later wrote. "At halftime, we were feeling good. The offensive and defensive guys were telling each other that they were doing a great job and to keep it up."

As the players stoked their intensity during the elongated thirty-minute Super Bowl halftime period, the Redskins' staff tweaked the game plan. While Gibbs and his fellow offensive coaches pondered more aggressive strategies, their defensive counterparts did as well.

Acting on a hunch dreamt up during that afternoon's bus ride to the stadium, Larry Peccatiello suggested to Richie Petitbon a last-minute addition meant to surprise the Bills. Despite having "never practiced it," the longtime coaching duo decided to let linebacker Andre Collins blitz rather than continue to shadow Thurman Thomas, as he had during the first half.

On the first play from scrimmage following halftime, Collins attacked the middle of the Bills' line and clobbered Jim Kelly as he threw a pass over the middle. Linebacker Kurt Gouveia grabbed the off-line throw and returned the interception to the 2-yard line, where Gerald Riggs's second rushing touchdown gave Washington a commanding 24–0 lead.

"That was strictly [Peccatiello's] doing, and it was a stroke of genius," Petitbon said after the game. "If we don't make that play to start the second half, it might have been a different football game."

The Bills cut into Washington's lead with a pair of long drives that netted 10 points, but a beautiful 30-yard touchdown pass from Rypien to Gary Clark increased the score to 31–10 late in the third period. Although the Bills scored 2 late fourth-quarter touchdowns, the game was long over by then. At the end of the Redskins 37–24 win, the defense had forced 5 turnovers, limited Thurman Thomas to 13 yards on 10 carries, and yielded a miniscule 3.5 yards per play. On offense, the Redskins scored seven times—including 2 touchdown passes from Super Bowl MVP Mark Rypien—gained 417 total yards, and completed their playoff run without allowing a single sack.

"They were here to talk a good game," said Joe Jacoby. "We were here to play a good game."

Despite the Redskins' status as a touchdown favorite, many had expected the matchup to be a very close game. Buffalo possessed ample talent on both sides of the ball and nearly won the Super Bowl just one year earlier. But on game day there was no doubt about which team was better.

"If the Washington Redskins played the Buffalo Bills in the Super Bowl ten times, with two weeks to prepare, how many times would the Skins win?" *Sports Illustrated*'s Rick Telander wrote that week. "Answer: nine (ten, if Bills defensive line coach Chuck Dickerson were allowed to speak before every game)."

The victory didn't have the novelty of the Super Bowl XVII win—the franchise's first NFL title in forty years—or a signature moment such as John Riggins's unforgettable touchdown jaunt that evening in Pasadena. Nor did it feature the second-quarter miracle that the 1987 team performed in Super Bowl XXII by way of unlikely heroics from Doug Williams and Timmy Smith.

Super Bowl XXVI was actually quite boring, featuring 4 Buffalo interceptions, 6 total Bills fumbles, and lengthy, plodding Washington scoring drives.

The triumph, however, did have tremendous significance. By claiming a third Super Bowl victory in ten seasons, the Redskins cemented their place as a dynasty. In the previous eight decades, only one other franchise—the Raiders from 1976 to 1983—had won three NFL titles in a ten-year span without ever winning back-to-back championships.

In addition to validating the legacy of both Joe Gibbs and the Redskins during that era, the decisive Super Bowl triumph capped off one of the greatest single seasons in NFL history.

The 1991 Redskins won seventeen of their nineteen games—their two losses by a total of 5 points—and set a sixteen-game regular-season record by *averaging* 16.3 points more than their opponent. They never trailed once during the postseason and in three playoff wins they scored 12 touchdowns and committed only 2 turnovers while surrendering just 4 touchdowns and forcing 14 turnovers. And aside from the famed 1985 Bears, no other Super Bowl champion—not Vince Lombardi's Green Bay Packers, not the Pittsburgh Steelers or Dallas Cowboys of the 1970s, not Joe Montana's San Francisco 49ers, not Tom Brady's New England Patriots or Peyton Manning's Indianapolis Colts, and not even the undefeated 1972 Miami Dolphins—has ever matched the 1991 Redskins' 16.95-point average scoring differential (total points scored minus total points allowed divided by games) across both the regular season and postseason.

The 1991 Washington Redskins were Joe Gibbs's masterpiece: a team with a stellar passing game, a brutal running attack, the best offensive line in history, and a defense that sacked, stripped, or suffocated the opponent every week.

"We go 14 and 2 with two [close] losses to be, I think, one of the greatest football teams arguably that ever played in the history of the NFL," Mark Rypien said in 2014. "Outside that undefeated team in Miami—they didn't lose a game—we came that close to not losing a game and just dominated the heck out of people, playoffs, Super Bowl. And I don't think we get the due we deserve. And to be the leader of that I take a lot of pride in those guys and I take a lot of pride in myself and what we were able to accomplish that year. . . . We came out on top as probably one of the most dominant teams the NFL has seen and it doesn't get their right space in the history of the NFL in great seasons."

Still, none of the statistics, records, and honors that the Redskins collected during their Super Bowl XXVI coronation meant as much to Joe Gibbs as the group of men that earned them.

"This team really had great, great chemistry," Gibbs told reporters that evening. "The players had a great, great feeling for one another. From day one, I rarely got upset with our team. I very rarely had to deal with the off-the-field stuff.

"It was truly a team. It was not a bunch of stars."

CHAPTER 11

A Football Coach's Life

JOE GIBBS found his wife following Super Bowl XXVI: he didn't have to eat a late-night dinner alone in a chain restaurant, as he had following Washington's triumph in 1983. This championship celebration, however, was also not free of annoyance.

"This is a coach's life," he recalled years later. "You go that whole year, you fight through everything, you win a Super Bowl. Man, I'm looking so forward that night to just going out, have a dinner with Pat and the kids and everybody. So we climb in a limo. I'm in the back of this limo, I finally get to relax, I sit down. And two Redskins fans jerked open the door, and one them leans in and he goes, 'We gotta win it next year!' I'm thinking, 'Gimme an hour!' That's a football coach's life."

Gibbs and Pat took their annual romantic trip together following the end of the Redskins' season, but—if previous vacations were any indication—he wouldn't exactly unwind.

"The first day is always great because when you only see someone warm and soft every four days, it feels great to grab Pat and kiss her," he said. "By the second day, I get a little antsy. By the third day, I'm playing racquetball or finding someone I know to run with. The fourth day, we fight. And the fifth day we go home."

Once he returned to Redskin Park that winter, Gibbs, Charley Casserly, and the entire Redskins' organization began pursuing another championship. That off-season Washington re-signed Super Bowl MVP Mark Rypien to a long-term deal, extended the contracts of All-Pros Darrell Green and Jim Lachey, added veteran pass rusher Keith Willis via Plan B free agency, and in a draft day trade, moved up to acquire college football's top wide receiver, Heisman Trophy winner Desmond Howard.

Even with the exciting moves—a thrilled Gibbs marveled at Howard, who he said "doesn't have any flaws"—the head coach worried about another Super Bowl hangover, similar to the one Washington experienced in 1988, the worst season of his head coaching career.

"It only takes a little bit to knock you off in this thing," Gibbs told the *Washington Post*'s Ken Denlinger a week before the start of the 1992 regular season. "A shorter off-season, a tougher schedule. Also, the way others see you. Everybody plays harder against the Super Bowl winner. And the way you see yourself. It's harder to get players signed. Everybody thinks they're better. Know what I mean?

"Two things can kill a person or a team," he added. "Real adversity and real success."

DESPITE HIS ASSERTION THAT he "wasn't any good" as a varsity player for San Diego State University, Joe Gibbs was a fantastic athlete. A quarterback at Santa Fe High School, where he also started on the basketball and baseball teams and was named the school's Athlete of the Year in 1959, he moved to end in junior college. As a transfer to San Diego State he played on both sides of the ball for Don Coryell, who called him "my Little Bulldog."

Gibbs's playing days ended after his senior season in 1963, setting him on the path to a long, illustrious coaching career, but he always made time to exercise both his body and his fervent competitiveness. Racquetball eventually became his customary outlet: Pat bought him a membership to the local Jewish Community Center while they lived in St. Louis, during his tenure as an assistant with the Cardinals. He became near-obsessed with the game, practicing his backhands, forehands, and serves for hours, either before or after a long day of work at the team's facilities. As his passion for the game grew, Gibbs sought out the best competitors in the city. Gibbs even hounded St. Louis–area high school phenom Marty Hogan, who would become arguably the greatest player in the history of the sport, for a matchup. Hogan finally agreed to play at the nearby Spaulding Racquetball Club. Gibbs enticed him with an offer of a milk shake and hamburger at Denny's, awarded to the winner.

"I remember my first experience being on the court with him was that he's a real excitable guy, but didn't really strike me as being a racquet-kind of athlete," the six-time U.S. national champion said years later. "I just figured, what I was going to do was get on the court and punish him so he wouldn't call me again. We actually started playing and I can remember thinking, 'This guy is trying really hard.' So what I did, and I did this on purpose the first time I played him, to see what kind of guy he was, I refused to kill the ball. All I did was run him from side to side, up and back. I was just going to run him until he ran out of gas. And I was thoroughly amazed at how incredibly hard he tried, and tried, and tried, and tried."

The two struck up a friendship, playing a regular Friday night game, and Gibbs even invited him to a Cardinals game with Pat, J.D., and Coy. Together they traveled to tournaments in Detroit, Houston, and Milwaukee. So he could sleep after a long day of work, Gibbs taught the teenager to drive a stick shift during a road trip to Dallas.

"If you can imagine a future head coach in the NFL," Hogan remembered, "he is screaming at me as I'm a freakin' nervous punk kid trying not to grind the second gear out of the Chevy Vega that we drove, which was his car. He would yell and scream at me like I was a linebacker supposed to make a key tackle!"

At a few of those tournaments, competing in the over-thirty-five division, Gibbs upset several of the sport's top players, including Jim Austin and David Fleetwood.

"Nobody got more out of their ability to play the sport of racquetball than Joe Gibbs," Hogan said. "He always amazed me at how tough he could play people when . . . he was just so ultra-competitive. In hindsight, being the head coach, he just knows how to get the most out of himself and of people."

In 1976, Gibbs won the national over-thirty-five championships in San Diego and finished as national runner-up the following year. Although his schedule as head coach of the Washington Redskins left him fewer opportunities, he continued to play. Also an occasional jogger, Gibbs tried to remain physically fit.

But he did not eat well. He gobbled up chocolate candy while game-planning in the Sub with the rest of the coaches, loved hamburgers since his days of drag racing in Southern California, and ate ice cream every Saturday night before games along with the team. Irreparable damage to Gibbs's body had been done by that diet combined with his widely known sleep schedule: sessions in the Sub lasted until roughly three a.m. when he grabbed a few hours of sleep on a cot in his office.

"I lived by the adage 'Work like a horse, eat like a horse, and look like a horse,'" Gibbs later wrote. "My eating and sleeping habits were horrendous. I thought I could work like a maniac and catch up on my rest later. . . . I didn't notice the price I was paying while I was younger, but the ramifications for my body would later become apparent."

During the 1992 regular season, Gibbs began to worry.

Over a bowl of ice cream, the night before a critical Week Thirteen showdown against Phoenix, Gibbs—who had experienced tingling in his legs following a workout on the treadmill—confided in Jim Hanifan, his offensive line coach and friend since their time together in St. Louis.

"Did you ever see any spots around your eye?" Gibbs asked.

"No," Hanifan replied.

"Well, I do."

"You do, what?"

"I got these spots all over my eyes all the time."

"You're kidding me, who else did you tell?"

"Nobody else."

"Did you tell Pat?"

"No."

"Did you tell the trainers?"

"No."

"Did you tell our team doctor?"

"No."

"Now you're telling me? I think you ought to talk to the doctors and trainers."

The next day, after Washington hammered Joe Bugel's Cardinals 41–3, Gibbs finally told the team's medical staff. At that point, some people around Redskin Park had begun to notice that the once-tireless coach did not quite seem himself.

"I came in early a couple of times the day before a game because he was just struggling to get through the day," said Rod Dowhower, the team's offensive coordinator and Gibbs's teammate at San Diego State. "I'd just tell him, 'I'm here if you need me.' We were very worried about him. He was turning more of the details of the game plans over to us, and we were relying on him more for the guidance of what was being done that week. He just wasn't able to work the hours he was used to working."

Gibbs's struggle to finish out the 1992 regular season mirrored his team's: the Redskins wilted down the stretch.

After pounding Phoenix the day after Gibbs's ice cream confession to Jim Hanifan, Washington topped the New York Giants 28–10, improving their record to 8-5. A week later, at home against the division-leading Cowboys, the Redskins trailed by four in the final minutes. On a second-and-seven from the Dallas 5-yard line, quarterback Troy Aikman was sacked by Redskins defensive tackle Jason Buck. Behind his own goal line, Aikman dropped the ball; ruled a fumble, instant replays suggested officials should have declared it an incomplete pass because the quarterback's arm had been moving forward in an attempt to throw. The ball was picked up by Cowboys running back Emmitt Smith, who fumbled it again while trying to escape the end zone. A scramble for possession ultimately came to an end when Washington's Danny Copeland emerged with the football.

"There was kicking and shoving in there," defensive lineman Tim Johnson said. "It was ferocious. It was a blessing for Danny to get the ball. Coach Gibbs came in and the first thing we did was just pray. And then everybody screamed and yelled and let out a mountain of emotion after participating in the type of game that few of us have ever had the privilege to be a part of."

The game-winning defensive touchdown gave Washington the inside track on the conference's top wild card spot. But they lost by four points the next week in Philadelphia—Mark Rypien's touchdown pass to Gary Clark was batted away by All-Pro cornerback Eric Allen on the game's final play—and again in the regular-season finale against the Raiders. In both those narrow defeats, the Redskins uncharacteristically let second-half leads slip away. Only a Week Seventeen loss by the Green Bay Packers secured the 9-7 Redskins the NFC's final wild card spot, setting up a first-round playoff game against Minnesota.

"I'm fired up about getting in," Gibbs said. "That's your goal all year and when you get it, you feel good about it. All you can ask for is an opportunity, and we have that. You're thrilled about getting in because it means you've got a chance."

On the same field where they had bashed the Buffalo Bills the previous January, Washington smothered the Vikings, allowing just 9 first downs and 148 total yards to the NFC Central Champions. The 27–7 win sent the Redskins to San Francisco for a showdown with the top-seeded 49ers, led by quarterback Steve Young. On a sloppy day at Candlestick Park—a week of rain drenched the baseball stadium's dirt infield and the two teams combined for 8 turnovers in the mud—the Redskins fell behind by 2 touchdowns, then pulled within four at the beginning of the fourth quarter. Trailing 17–13, they forced a punt and marched deep into San Francisco territory only to let the game slip away: attempting a mud-covered handoff to Brian Mitchell, Mark Rypien fumbled the ball and Washington never again threatened to score.

"Last year was a magic carpet ride," Gibbs told the *Washington Post*'s Thomas Boswell following the loss. "This year was the toughest, hardest you could imagine. We had to fight, pull, grab every inch of the way. We'll have twelve or thirteen surgeries in the next two weeks . . . I'll remember that we hung together and took our shot. Sometimes you're prouder of the teams that go through the most adversity. . . . Through it all, somehow we got ten good [wins]. That's life up here. . . . We showed our heart. The future is bright."

DESPITE PLENTY OF RESISTANCE from the team's front office—"It messes up everything that they're sending you out here," Bobby Beathard told her—Christine Brennan covered the Redskins' beat for the *Washington Post* beginning in 1985. One of the first women to report on men's sports from inside the locker room, and the first to cover the Redskins, Brennan was ignored by some players, intimidated by others, asked out by still others, and even tolerated Jack Kent Cooke stroking her hair a few times.

"I covered three seasons of college football and also backed up the Dolphins' beat writer, so I was so comfortable and ready for all of this," recalled Brennan, who came to Washington by way of the *Miami Herald*. "There were things I was enduring as a woman that I knew I was going to endure because I endured some of them in Miami. [But] all in all my experiences were terrific. I have the most positive memories of everything covering the team."

After three years on the Washington beat, the Northwestern alum moved to the Olympics and more general sports coverage, but continued to report on the NFL and occasionally Redskins stories. So when she walked into the *Post*'s headquarters on March 5, 1993, sports editor George Solomon immediately tabbed her to track down quotes about the breaking news story that had begun to shock the city.

That morning, local WTTG-TV sports director Steve Buckhantz reported on *Fox Morning News* that Joe Gibbs was stepping down as Washington's head coach. Jim Speros, a friend and the Redskins' former assistant strength and conditioning coach, told Buckhantz the previous evening at Champions Bar in Fairfax that Gibbs was retiring. Early the following morning, Buckhantz called Charley Casserly to confirm the news.

"There was a pause and then the next thing I heard him say was 'Go with the story.' Those were his exact words," Buckhantz recalled. "And when I heard those words my heart sank into my stomach, because I knew he had just given me the go-ahead to report this story, which was going to turn the city upside-down. . . . I was stunned."

As the news began to saturate the region, Christine Brennan left the *Post*'s offices located at the corner of Fifteenth and L Street and headed south toward the White House, where the Dallas Cowboys were in town. President Bill Clinton had invited the team to town following their victory in Super Bowl XXVII. Looking to gauge a response from the members of the Redskins' archrivals, Brennan attended the celebration in the elegant East Room, which was temporarily decorated with an AstroTurf carpet and miniature goal posts.

Among the crystal chandeliers and portraits of George and Martha Washington, the recently inaugurated president praised head coach Jimmy Johnson's team, joked with players about lowering taxes, and even shook hands with Cowboys owner and fellow Arkansan Jerry Jones, who had supported Clinton's opponent in the state's 1990 race for governor. As the ceremony ended and Clinton started to exit the room, he passed the familiar group of White House reporters who badgered him with questions about the war in Bosnia, health-care reform, and the emergency unemployment benefits bill he signed the day before. Taking a chance, Brennan shouted to Clinton, "Mr. President, what do you think about Joe Gibbs retiring?"

Noticing the tall woman who had asked a somewhat unusual—and far less hazardous—question, Clinton responded: "I think Joe Gibbs is a very great football coach, and, in my lifetime, one of the best I ever saw. . . . I'm kind of sad because I just moved here, you know, and I was looking forward to going to the games and I'm a big football fan and I think he's a very gifted man. I wish him well."

"I think that just shows the nature of the day," Brennan recalled years later. "The East Room was alive, the Cowboys, of course, Washington's great rival, and yet, the news of Joe Gibbs leaving Washington was certainly the story of the day. It's rare when the celebration for a team winning the Super Bowl is upstaged, but it was upstaged that day. Joe Gibbs was front and center on everyone's mind, from every home in Washington, to everyone who's ever cheered for him, and then all the way to the East Room of the White House and the president of the United States."

The news that Gibbs was walking away spread so quickly and was so jarring—"I almost drove off the road when I heard it on the car radio," center Jeff Bostic said—that the Redskins called an impromptu press conference for later that day. The team had planned a formal announcement the following day, but that afternoon reporters gathered at Redskin Park; Joe Gibbs had to hurry back from a speaking engagement to a prayer group in Richmond to address the media.

"I need to spend some time catching up, I want to back up and try another kind of life," the fifty-two-year-old said during a tearful opening statement that included two standing ovations from players in attendance. "This is a leap of faith for me. . . . I don't know what's out there. I don't know if I can do without football. . . . This is the toughest choice I've ever faced."

The health issues that drained him late in his final season were a factor in his decision. That winter, he underwent a series of tests at the Mayo Clinic in Rochester, Minnesota, that confirmed team doctors' suspicions: Gibbs was diagnosed with Type II diabetes. Eventually, he would require insulin shots.

"I'd had an uncle that was diabetic and he died an early death and it was attributed to diabetes," he later said. "For me, when I hit bottom and they told me, 'Hey, Joe, you need to go on insulin,' that to me, I really kind of panicked."

But discovering he now had a disease that affected millions of Americans only clinched Gibbs's decision to walk away.

A full-time coach throughout his children's entire lives, Gibbs had not seen his sons, twenty-four-year-old J.D. and twenty-one-year-old Coy, nearly as much as he wanted. Between practices, games, road trips, game-planning, scouting, his role as a major D.C. celebrity, and his philanthropic interests, Gibbs was absent so much that his wife started recording audio tapes of the boys around the house so that he could listen to them in his car on the way to and from Redskin Park.

"There was a feeling among quite a few of the players that, here, Gibbs was talking about the importance of God and then family," *Washington Post* beat writer Gary Pomerantz remembered. "But there he was spending those nights on the couch in his office rather than going home to *his* family. And a number of players did comment on that to me and they saw it as hypocritical. But Joe wanted to win. And early in his career, when I was there, [Tom] Landry loomed as not only his great rival, but perhaps in some ways as a model. Someone who was solid and stable and had been there for a long time. And I think Joe envisioned that he would be solid and stable and be the Redskins' head coach for a very long time. And this was the only way he knew how to achieve that, by being all-in, and spending those nights on the couch in his office."

One evening during the 1992 NFL season, while Coy was home from college, Gibbs walked into his youngest son's room to say good night and was stunned to see "he was 200 pounds and had a beard. . . . I couldn't believe that was my little Coy."

"When you coach, your family has to sacrifice a lot," Gibbs said in 2014. "The one thing I second guess about the coaching thing is the time I missed with J.D. and Coy, 'cause I probably could have done that differently, spent more time with them. I didn't. I took them out a few years back and apologized to both of them and said, 'I should have done that differently.'"

Gibbs's oldest son, J.D., had already finished up his career as a defensive back at William & Mary College. He did not want to miss watching Coy, a sophomore during the spring of 1993, play linebacker for Bill Walsh's Stanford Cardinal.

"I'll get a chance to be a real husband and a real dad," he told reporters. "Hopefully, I'll find a new world out there and I'll enjoy it."

In the world that Gibbs had left behind he was a legend, the only head coach in NFL history to win three Super Bowls with three different starting quarterbacks. Upon his departure, Gibbs had as many playoff wins as Chuck Noll, more world championships than both Don Shula and Tom Landry, and a higher winning percentage than Bill Walsh and Paul Brown.

Still, none of the statistics, records, and honors that the Redskins collected during their dynasty meant as much to Washington's players as the man who led them.

"[What] a gracious opportunity we have all had to have been able to play for Coach Gibbs," Mark Rypien said the day of Gibbs's retirement announcement. "You could say he was part of the Lombardi era, and he was like what they say about Lombardi in this way: he not only taught us X's and O's, but we learned plenty from him about life away from football by the example of class and humility he always showed us. He touched our lives."

AS HE FORMALLY ANNOUNCED his departure from the Washington Redskins, Joe Gibbs made a curious observation about the state of the game he'd been a part of for twenty years.

"This league is geared to pull the top teams down," he said. "I think consistency, being able to keep the coaching staff together and be in there competing for the title nearly every year, is the thing that I will remember most."

Although Joe Bugel and Dan Henning (twice) had left Washington in previous years to become head coaches elsewhere, Gibbs kept his staff largely intact despite the franchise's great success. The same had been true about the Redskins' roster: during Gibbs's tenure, no player who left the Redskins to play for another team did so by their own choice. Without an unrestricted free agency system, players did not have a realistic chance of signing elsewhere, unless that new team was willing to compensate Washington with draft choices.

For that reason the organization was able to keep the players they wanted to retain. And without a salary cap to limit the franchise's payroll—and because Jack Kent Cooke wanted to win—the Redskins paid their players enough to keep them happy. Stars like Dexter Manley, Darrell Green, Mark Rypien, Jim Lachey, Ricky Sanders, Darryl Grant, Barry Wilburn, Mike Nelms, and many more skipped the start of training camp or threatened to do so as part of a contract holdout. But they had no real alternative (other than retire like John Riggins), and all eventually agreed to new deals. And if the two sides could not reach an agreement, at least Washington had the option of trading the player and receiving something in return.

That all changed four days before Joe Gibbs took the podium at the team's new lavish Redskin Park in Ashburn, Virginia. In January, the NFL and its Players Association had agreed to a seven-year collective-bargaining agreement that instituted unrestricted free agency as well as a league-mandated salary cap, which took effect the next year.

The free agent signing period began on March 1, 1993, and in that first month, few teams were hit harder by the new setup than the Redskins. Gary Clark, the four-time Pro Bowler and Washington's leading receiver in four of the previous seven seasons, signed with Phoenix.

The Wild West of free agency did not just sap the Redskins offense. Cornerback Martin Mayhew and defensive linemen Fred Stokes and Jumpy Geathers also left for new teams. And Wilber Marshall, who challenged his "franchise player" tag in court that spring, joined the Oilers in August. Exacerbating the loss of several key players—while the shock of Joe Gibbs's retirement still persisted—was Washington's failure to sign any big-name free agents of their own, most notably All-Pro defensive end Reggie White.

"No one can say we were right or someone else was wrong," general manager Charley Casserly said in July. "We were in a tough situation and dealt with each player. If we lost a player, we tried to sign a better one. This new labor agreement was designed to restrict the best teams. We couldn't sign anyone until we lost someone, and a lot of teams with smaller payrolls could offer more. There was a minimum they had to get up to. But we did have a budget and a plan, and let's see how everything turns out. I know that right now I'm excited. Our coaches are excited. We've got a good team and we're ready to go. Judge us by our season."

Amid an off-season of unprecedented upheaval, the Redskins maintained some continuity. They re-signed a few of their own unrestricted free agents, including defensive lineman Tim Johnson, linebacker Kurt Gouveia, defensive backs Brad Edwards and Danny Copeland, and the team's all-time leading receiver, Art Monk. And apart from Joe Gibbs, the entire coaching staff remained together, with one significant alteration: the no-nonsense, pragmatic longtime assistant, Richie Petitbon, assumed the role of head coach.

Strongly endorsed by Joe Gibbs, Petitbon was immediately promoted by an organization that wanted a seamless transition.

"I don't want anything to go wrong, and I don't think this man will let anything go wrong," Jack Kent Cooke declared. "All he will do is continue the tradition of winning with the Redskins. Think about it. It's exactly the same team. He's going to continue to exercise his control over the defensive corps. Instead of Joe listening to Don Breaux and Rod Dowhower about the offense, it will be Dowhower who will talk to Breaux. The work ethic is there with Richie. If he doesn't work like that, God help him. But he'll do it."

Petitbon's tenure as head coach featured the most auspicious start imaginable. In Week One of the 1993 season, the Redskins clobbered the defending Super Bowl champion Cowboys.

Behind a defense that forced 4 turnovers, Washington held their archrival to just 16 points, and in their first game in fourteen years without Joe Gibbs in charge, the Redskins' offense was perfectly balanced. They rushed for 171 yards, did not give up a sack, and scored 5 touchdowns. A 99-yard touchdown drive during the third quarter clinched the victory.

"The one thing we didn't want to really do was to put everything in this game and be emotionally drained if it didn't work out," said Mark Rypien, who threw 3 touchdown passes and completed

12 straight passes at one point. "We didn't make any mistakes, and that's the reason we won the game."

Mistakes, however, coupled with a string of bad luck, befell the Redskins nearly every other week of the 1993 season.

Washington lost their next six games, yielding an average of 28 points per game, turning the ball over a total of 17 times, and scoring more than 10 points just once during the franchise's longest losing streak since 1963. Significant injuries to Mark Rypien, Charles Mann, Jim Lachey, Mark Schlereth—who suffered through a frightening viral infection—Joe Jacoby, Andre Collins, and Eric Williams robbed Washington of both talented, experienced starters and several respected on-the-field leaders.

Richie Petitbon became the scapegoat for Washington's horrific season: *USA Today* anointed the head coach with a 2-6 record as the league's "biggest flop" at the season's midway point.

"I really took offense. I think that's totally unfair," said Carl Banks, a recent free agent signee from the Giants. "I think a lot of factors have come into play here. He's not dropping passes. He's not missing tackles. He's got some injuries. I think it was totally unfair to say he's the biggest flop because he's not. He knows what he wants to get done. He has the respect of his players. It's up to the players to realize what our situation is and to get it done. Richie's a very competitive guy. He's putting us in some great positions to make plays. He's calling good defenses for us. It's a situation where we have to execute."

In December, the Redskins hit rock bottom. Against the New York Jets, Washington endured their first home shutout in nearly fourteen years. Once a model offensive genius, the Redskins collected just 7 first downs and 150 total yards in the loss. Two weeks later, after a 38-3 loss in Dallas—the most one-sided outcome in the thirty-four-year history of the epic rivalry—a squabble between the Players Union and a handful of its players nearly caused the Redskins to forfeit their last game of the season against Minnesota. In protest of the new collective-bargaining agreement, thirty-five Redskins players did not pay their dues and in late December, arbitrator Herbert Fishgold ruled that the team had to suspend them all. If they did, Washington would not have been able to dress the required minimum players (forty-two) to take the field. The franchise avoided that embarrassment when United States District Court Judge Joyce Hens Green refused to order the suspensions. The Redskins' entire active roster was present to lose to the Vikings, 14–9.

"We were all so happy for Richie that he was the head coach and how well deserving it was that he became the head coach," Jim Hanifan recalled. "He had all this stuff happen to him. It was like a voodoo doll puncture. There was a curse going against Richie. Not only did we lose certain players by the nature of the game, we also wound up getting guys hurt. We had so many fellas hurt that I remember at the end of the year, half the guys, you would not know who they were. You'd have to say, 'I'm sorry, what's your first name?' And the guy's starting for you. That's how bad it was that year."

At the end of the franchise's worst regular season in thirty years the Redskins reluctantly fired Richie Petitbon: "This is one of the unhappiest days of my life," Jack Kent Cooke acknowledged at Petitbon's outgoing press conference.

"I don't think anybody liked to get fired," said Petitbon, who in the years before taking over for Joe Gibbs had turned down several head coaching interviews to remain in Washington. "You'd have to be some kind of nut. But when you get into this business, as a player, you have to be prepared to be cut. As a coach, you have to be prepared to be fired. That's the nature of the business.

"It's not an easy business . . . but let me say this: it's better than having a job. I don't think I've had a job in my life. Be that as it may. I'm happy with the profession that I've chosen, and I think it's been good to me. No regrets."

To replace him, the Redskins hired Norv Turner, the Dallas Cowboys' star offensive coordinator, fresh off a second consecutive

Super Bowl win. But that off-season, the mass exodus from Washington and the subsequent crumbling of the Redskins' dynasty that had begun a year earlier climaxed under Turner.

In addition to letting go of much of the coaching staff—Don Breaux, Rod Dowhower, Larry Peccatiello, Torgy Torgeson, and Wayne Sevier—free agent Ricky Sanders signed with the Falcons and Earnest Byner returned to Cleveland.

Just as menacing to the franchise's hopes of preserving the glory years for one more season was the salary cap. No longer were teams able to pay (or overpay) every aging veteran that might help a club. So-called "cap casualties" during the spring of 1994, as the organization attempted to cut salary, included Charles Mann, Super Bowl hero Mark Rypien, and the last remaining member of the Redskins' "Posse" of wide receivers, Art Monk. All three signed new deals elsewhere.

A few other expendable cornerstones of the now financially handcuffed franchise opted to simply walk away from the game. The last two original members of the Hogs, Jeff Bostic and Joe Jacoby—whose wife, Irene, explained that after thirteen NFL seasons, "He can't walk, he can't get out of bed"—both retired rather than limp along at a grueling job earning less than they believed themselves to be worth.

"Jeff and I have talked about going up [to training camp] and sitting on the balcony of one of those houses overlooking the practice field," Jacoby said upon announcing his retirement. "Maybe we'll throw beer cans at the guys."

At least in some form, the 5 O'Clock Club would still carry on.

Epilogue

JOE GIBBS did not stay retired for long.

Eating much healthier, running several times a week, and catching up on decades of missed sleep eased his doctors' concerns. He even found time to see Coy play football at Stanford, take a vacation to Jamaica with his wife, and finish building their vacation home on Fawn Lake in Virginia.

But within weeks of leaving the Redskins, his life was as hectic and busy as ever.

Although he had changed a great deal—professionally, financially, spiritually—since his teenage days of rebuilding hot rods and top-fuelers in dingy Southern California garages, Gibbs still loved restoring, collecting, and racing cars. And throughout 1991 he purchased Chevrolets from Motorsports mogul Rick Hendrick, lined up corporate sponsors, assembled a staff and crew, and signed rising star Dale Jarrett as a driver.

Free from his draining schedule as an NFL head coach, he could now focus on building up Joe Gibbs Racing, headquartered first in Charlotte, then in Huntersville, North Carolina, a hundred miles east of where his father chased down bootleggers and moonshiners fifty years earlier.

In the months after his retirement from the Redskins, he frequently traveled the country to see his teams race, then returned to Charlotte to meet with his executives, crews, drivers, and sponsors.

"I got in on the red-eye this morning, and I'm leaving here at 7:30," he told one reporter in April 1993. "I'm on such a wild schedule. I'm on the run. I've got a 9:30 business meeting, then Shell, Interstate—my responsibility to these sponsors. Then I go to chapel service. I run from one to the other, then the race starts. It's a very tough thing."

Gibbs's exhausting schedule was quickly rewarded. Building on Dale Jarrett's surprise win at the Daytona 500 in February 1993, his drivers won forty-seven races between 1993 and 2005 and three Winston/Nextel Cup championships during the same period. With J.D. as president beginning in 1997, Joe Gibbs Racing is annually one of the top teams in the sport, featuring several of the premier drivers in both the Sprint Cup and the Nationwide series.

Despite growing his NASCAR empire, Gibbs remained a relevant figure in professional football. The year after retiring, he appeared weekly on WTOP-AM to discuss the state of the Redskins and, from 1993 to 1997, Gibbs worked as a studio analyst for NBC's weekly NFL television coverage. His name often popped up as the ideal candidate for teams in search of a head coach (especially the expansion Carolina Panthers), and in 2002 he purchased a small stake in the Atlanta Falcons. But Gibbs didn't feel the urge to return to the sidelines.

"I didn't give it much of a thought for ten and a half years," he said. "I was caught up in the racing and I just never thought that I would go back. Then kind of a wild set of circumstances: the race team was doing. J.D. was running things around here, we had a great management team—the race team's real important to me—and I felt like we had great leadership.

"Coy, my youngest came to me. He had been racing cars and he said, 'Hey, Dad, I think I might want to go back into coaching.' So I started thinking about that and I said, 'I spent all this time with J.D. building the race team, Coy came out of school later, haven't spent as much time with him. Now he's talking about coaching, something I spent my life in, and I'm not gonna be there, for me to help him with his coaching career.'"

In December 2003, Gibbs considered a comeback. And given the state of the Redskins' franchise at the time, his interest in returning enthralled beleaguered Redskins' owner Daniel Snyder.

At the age of eighty-four, Jack Kent Cooke, the Redskins' majority owner for twenty-three years, passed away from a heart attack on April 6, 1997.

For years, Cooke had explicitly stated that the team would remain within the family. In 1992, he told the *Washington Post*, "I want to be buried in a burgundy and gold coffin. And when I'm gone, someone named Cooke is going to run the team. And when he's gone, someone else named Cooke is going to run the team."

But, never one for convention, Cooke left instructions in his will to auction off the team and the new $250 million stadium located in Landover (Maryland), which was renamed in his honor. Selling the team, he believed, would net far more money to establish the Jack Kent Cooke Foundation, a charity that would fund scholarships. John Kent Cooke—the Redskins' executive vice president during the franchise's three Super Bowl triumphs and an outstanding facilitator between the team's owner and its football minds—had hoped to buy the team, but he was outbid. In July 1999 Snyder purchased the Redskins for $800 million.

"I bid $750 million, which I was led to believe by my advisers and my lawyers . . . was going to be very competitive," John Kent Cooke said. "But it was a fait accompli. I was the runner-up."

Snyder, a thirty-five-year-old communications mogul from Silver Spring, quickly developed a reputation as an owner who believed in extravagant spending and bold, risky personnel choices.

Less than a year after Washington made the 1999 playoffs—the franchise's first postseason appearance since Joe Gibbs's retirement—Snyder fired head coach Norv Turner. He soon installed highly respected, successful, veteran head coach Marty Schottenheimer, whom he then fired after one 8-8 season in order to make an even bigger splash: luring the University of Florida's Steve Spurrier to the NFL. The brash college football icon—as well as Washington's increasingly impatient fans—suffered through two embarrassing losing seasons.

Nearly as crippling to the team's fortunes, Washington threw tens of millions of dollars at high-priced free agents. Beginning with the 2000 signing of the rival Cowboys' Deion Sanders ($56 million over seven years) who would retire after one season, Washington gave enormous contracts to veterans such as quarterback Jeff George, linebacker Jeremiah Trotter, safety Mark Carrier, defensive linemen Regan Upshaw, Brandon Noble, and thirty-seven-year-old Bruce Smith. None of them produced the way Washington had hoped and only Smith lasted more than two years.

Through five full seasons with Snyder as the Redskins' owner, Washington's record stood at 38-42 with four consecutive playoffless campaigns. So when Joe Gibbs put out a feeler to a well-connected Washington, D.C., friend—immediately after Steve Spurrier resigned—Snyder flew his private jet to Concord (North Carolina) near Charlotte and met with Gibbs in an airport conference room. Gibbs then sat his wife down in the family's library, pulled out a detailed list recounting the many positives in their lives, and read it to her.

"I got down at number six, and I said, 'What do you think about coaching again?'" he said in 2014. "And I can remember clear as a bell, she went like this: 'You're gonna ruin your good name!'"

Others shared Pat Gibbs's concerns upon learning that Gibbs and Snyder agreed to a five-year, $28.5 million contract on January 7, 2004. Sixty-three years old and managing his diabetes daily,

Gibbs was considered less likely to spend countless late nights in the Sub game-planning. Changes to the game—free agency, a salary cap, the two-point conversion, radio transmitters inside the quarterback's helmet, coach-prompted instant replay challenges, as well an exponential growth in media scrutiny—also suggested Gibbs was ill-equipped for the "new" NFL. Changes to the players posed another potential problem. Substantial rises in salaries, even the league minimum, made challenging players much more difficult: no longer could Gibbs and his assistants scare players with the threat of "you'll be selling insurance!" if their play didn't improve.

But plenty of people around town, especially those who had lived through the Redskins' championship days of the 1980s, delighted in the news.

"[This] is Joe Gibbs, this isn't a coach. This is God," longtime *Washington Post* columnist and cohost of ESPN's *Pardon the Interruption*, Tony Kornheiser, wrote the day Gibbs was officially hired. "I was out in the streets yesterday afternoon . . . and everywhere I went, folks asked me the same question, word for word, prayerfully, 'Is it true?'

" 'I think so,' I said.

"You should have seen the looks on their faces at the thought that Joe Gibbs was coming back. Beatific, I tell you. For the football fan in Washington this is, literally and figuratively, the Second Coming."

Reminiscent of his dreadful season as a rookie head coach twenty-four years earlier, the Redskins opened 2004 with a 1-4 record. At 6-10, Washington finished tied for last place in the division—a dubious distinction he had previously never experienced—and scored the second-fewest points of any team in the league that year. The troublesome trend continued into his second season back, as Washington's record sat below .500 for the second straight Thanksgiving.

"Gibbs has his bronze bust in Canton and those three Super

Bowl trophies at Redskin Park," *Washington Post* columnist Thomas Boswell wrote after Washington lost at home in overtime to fall to 5-6. "But, each week, as his team finds some new heart-cracking way to lose, the new facts on the ground become clearer. That was then. This is now. And the two are very different."

But victories in their final five games—the last three against division rivals Dallas, New York, and Philadelphia—gave Washington a wild card berth and just the second postseason appearance since Gibbs's retirement twelve years earlier. The manner in which Gibbs fashioned his team only made the franchise's turnaround more meaningful to their loyal, starved fans.

Employing many of the same offensive philosophies, terminology, and coaches—Don Breaux, Rennie Simmons, Joe Bugel, as well as Earnest Byner as a running backs coach—the 2005 Redskins made for an eerie parallel to the dynasty that had begun a quarter century earlier.

The quarterback was a veteran castoff with bad knees, thirty-five-year-old former Jaguar Mark Brunell. The centerpiece of the offense was Clinton Portis, who resembled John Riggins in more ways than just great speed and powerful running. The Pro Bowler was loved for his quirky, light-hearted humor, which included dressing up in outrageous costumes and acting out different "personalities" for his press conferences. Rather than running back Clinton Portis, reporters addressed "Bro Sweets," "Southeast Jerome," "Sherriff Gonna Getcha," and "Dolemite Jenkins" about the ball carrier who averaged 22 carries and just under 100 yards per game in 2005.

Even the offensive line included a holdover from the Hogs; in his twentieth and final season, guard Ray Brown mentored a young group of linemen, similar to how Russ Grimm, Joe Jacoby, and Jeff Bostic mentored him from 1989 to 1993.

But the most talented and dynamic player on the Redskins' roster was second-year safety Sean Taylor. One of the very first personnel decisions Gibbs and his staff made after retaking the job was to use the team's top draft pick, fifth overall, on the Miami Hurricane's defensive back with amazing strength and speed. Taylor—who was born four weeks before the Redskins drafted Darrell Green—became the team's premier playmaker, creating turnovers and delivering big hits.

"God made certain people to play football," Gibbs once said. "He was one of them."

In the 2005 wild card round, first-quarter touchdowns by both Portis and Taylor lifted the Redskins to a 17–10 road upset of Tampa Bay, setting up a trip to Seattle to face the top-seeded Seahawks. After more than three quarters of offensive futility, a touchdown pass from Brunell to Santana Moss, followed by a fumble on the ensuing kickoff gave Washington the ball down by just seven with less than twelve minutes to play.

"When we got that fumble, I was sure we were going to get it tied up," Redskins defensive end Phillip Daniels said.

A missed Washington field goal and a lengthy Seahawks scoring drive ended the Redskins' comeback bid, but Joe Gibbs's resurrection of the franchise was progressing. He was starting to find, train, and develop the right players for his system, both on and off the field.

"I told them I couldn't be any prouder of them and how hard they fought today," Gibbs said. "We certainly accomplished a lot this year. . . . Our goal is to keep everybody together. We have a lot to do here to try and get ready for next year and continue to add to our football team and to continue to build something. I know that we have the right kind of character and the right kind of players to build around."

Gibbs's team stumbled to a 5-11 record the next year, and late in the 2007 season, again fell below .500. Disappointment over the club's 5-6 record turned to tragedy in late November, when Sean Taylor was murdered in his home during a burglary. His death, followed by a season-ending knee injury to starting quarterback

Jason Campbell, seemingly closed the door on Washington's play-off hopes.

"Joe did a magnificent job of keeping the team focused on the games," recalled Redskins offensive coordinator Al Saunders, a fellow protégé of both John McKay and Don Coryell. "Leadership always comes to the forefront in very, very difficult times and it couldn't have been any more difficult for the players and for the organization. But the way it was handled by the leadership of the organization at that time, Dan Snyder and Joe Gibbs, was just phenomenal."

Rallying behind the leadership of Gibbs, Taylor's close friends, Clinton Portis and Santana Moss, as well as unheralded veteran quarterback Todd Collins—who hadn't started a game in over ten seasons—Washington won their final four games to claim an improbable wild card berth. Ahead by one point early in the fourth quarter against the Seahawks and their hostile home crowd, the Redskins gave up 3 touchdowns and fell, 31–14.

Two days later, Gibbs retired from the Redskins.

"It was the toughest [season] for me," he admitted at his outgoing press conference. "When you go through a season like that, for a while it's kind of hard to regrasp reality."

Gibbs did not deliver Washington a fourth Super Bowl title; he didn't even deliver to Redskins fans an NFC East crown, something he had done five times during his first tenure. By the towering standards he set two decades earlier, Gibbs's twent-first-century run—without Jack Kent Cooke, without Bobby Beathard or Charley Casserly, and without the same reliable, autonomous defensive staff—was considered lackluster, even a failure.

"The songs that [John] Lennon and [Paul] McCartney wrote together are better than any of the songs Lennon or McCartney wrote separately," Tony Kornheiser said in 2014. "There's magic of people working together, a lot of things changed. It was just really different the second time around. He was older, and I don't think he was nearly as hungry."

But given the misery that came before his return, and the misery that would immediately follow, Gibbs's second term in office was a triumph. Not only did he return meaningful football games to D.C. in December and January and awaken a slumbering, uninspired fan base, but he once again proved himself the master of adaptability. Despite a twelve-year hiatus, during which time the game changed drastically, Joe Gibbs made the Redskins a championship contender.

"I thought it was going to be a tough transition, but if anybody could do it, Joe could do it, because Joe was successful at whatever Joe touches," Charles Mann said in 2014. "In those four years he went to the playoffs twice. He was successful in today's standards. In his standards? No. But in today's standards? Absolutely."

AS HE HAD THE first time he retired from coaching, sixty-seven-year-old Joe Gibbs went right back to work. He resumed the day-to-day operation of Joe Gibbs Racing as well as his counseling of troubled people in need of second chances. In addition to further developing and strengthening his Youth For Tomorrow program, Gibbs expanded his scope to include adults. By 2010, he was sharing with hundreds of prisoners the personal stories and messages in his book *Game Plan for Life*, released the previous year.

"I tell people this is the most important thing that was ever shared with me, is what I'm sharing with you, today," he said. "And that is I believe life is a game and we compare it to football. Gotta have a head coach and the only head coach I see that we can have is God. . . . Does He care about us? Yes He cares about us, like I cared about my players."

On September 19, 2013, a handful of those players gathered at Lansdowne Resort in Leesburg, Virginia, to show their coach just how much they appreciated him. As part of a fund-raising event for the D.C. College Access Program, *CBS Sports'* James Brown and ESPN's Michael Wilbon organized and cohosted a roast of Joe Gibbs.

Among those who took part in the celebration were Joe Theismann, Doug Williams, John Riggins, Jeff Bostic, and Clinton Portis, players who together had been a member of every single Redskins' team coached by Joe Gibbs, from his first season in 1981 to his last in 2007.

Ignoring the inherent irony of the event—"Roasting Joe Gibbs in Washington, D.C., that would be the equivalent of roasting Jesus Christ in the Holy Land," Bostic declared—each speaker lobbed anecdotes and good-natured barbs at the Washington icon. Bostic cracked up the crowd with his impression of the coach's high-pitched, animated squeal, Williams told the story of how a "gut feeling" nixed his trade to the Raiders in 1987, and they all chided Gibbs for his distinctive, squeaky-clean language.

"He was just on a wonderful, natural high, smiling, jovial, like a little kid," James Brown, the evening's master of ceremonies, recalled. "And he truly got a kick out of sitting there while all of his ex-players are roasting him. The teasing was rooted in fun, kidding him about his idiosyncrasies . . . but, the air of reverence, love, and respect was unmistakable. It was quite apparent that Joe Gibbs poured all of who he was and is into his players."

Dexter Manley—sitting on the dais beside Bostic, Riggins, Williams, Theismann, and the rest—laughed along with the crowd. But when his time came, he couldn't bring himself to participate in the ribbing.

"Well, I want to just say thanks for having me," he told the audience. "But I can't roast Joe Gibbs; I can only toast Joe Gibbs.

"I've gone through the rain, the wind, and the storm," said Manley, who occasionally did motivational speaking and provided weekly Redskins commentary for local WTOP-FM radio.

On November 19, 1990—the same day that the NFL lifted his lifetime ban—Manley was released by the Washington Redskins. Joe Gibbs thought he'd benefit from a "fresh start somewhere else."

Manley caught on with Joe Bugel's Phoenix Cardinals for the remainder of that season, then recorded 6.5 sacks for the Tampa Bay

Buccaneers in 1991. But late that year, he rubbed a fingertip full of cocaine on his gums, and then snorted a bump into each nostril. He failed his urine analysis—Manley was being tested three times per week—and was permanently banned from the NFL, with no chance of reinstatement. Three seasons in the Canadian Football League kept his professional career afloat, but his personal life was a mess.

Following a November 1994 arrest for possessing crack cocaine during an undercover police investigation, Manley entered the Betty Ford Clinic in Rancho Mirage, California, just after Thanksgiving, but disruptive behavior—throwing milk crates at the staff—cut his stay short. He was transferred to the Anacapa by the Sea facility in nearby Ventura County, where he was later asked to leave after fighting with another patient.

Unable to kick his addiction, recently divorced from his wife, and homeless—he reportedly slept underneath the bleachers at his high school's football field or at the nearby Thurgood Marshall School of Law—Manley began to contemplate suicide. In February 1995, while in Houston, he called his friend Steve Buckhantz, the D.C. sports anchor who years earlier hosted a weekly show with Manley on WTTG-TV.

"He was distraught and he was in a bad way, and was talking about when he dies he wants his ashes to be spread at RFK Stadium and these crazy things," Buckhantz remembered years later. "And he said to me, 'I think at some point it's just time to go.' And he sounded crazy. . . . I was really concerned for his well-being."

Buckhantz called the Houston police to check on his friend. Officers traced the call Buckhantz received to a La Quinta Motel located on the southwest side of the city, and upon entering Manley's room, they found a pipe and four rocks of crack on the bed. They arrested Manley and took him to Harris County Jail, where he was held without bond for more than two weeks. In early March, as Manley sat in cellblock 8D2, he was informed that he had a visitor.

"They wouldn't tell me who it was," Manley recalled. "So I had to go to the visiting room. You know it's somebody special because they put [me] in a nice orange suit, starched and everything. I'm wondering who's gonna come through that door. I was all chained up to a chair. And I'll be darned, it was Joe Gibbs."

Gibbs had flown from North Carolina to Houston when he heard about Manley's plight. That morning he walked into the Harris County Courthouse docket call, approached the bench, and introduced himself to State District Judge Doug Shaver: he hoped to see Manley and personally show his support. Taken to a nearby holding cell, Gibbs found the former star with whom he hadn't spoken in five years, and said, "I'm here because I always knew you were a good man, that you had a good heart."

"This is the first time I felt he was close to me," Manley told a reporter the next week. "It's like Bill Parcells always loved L.T. [Lawrence Taylor]. I lost my father when I was seventeen. This was like a father coming to talk to his son."

Each man wiped away tears, then reminisced about the old days and Manley's favorite defensive front, 43 Jet. Before leaving, Gibbs knelt down and prayed with him.

"And from that point on I decided that I gotta make a change in my life. Of course, the demons kept calling me and from time to time I would go in and out," said Manley, who was arrested four months later on another drug charge and sentenced to two years in federal prison, but has been sober since June 17, 2006. "I never forgot that experience. Joe Gibbs took the time to come see me and kneel down and pray with me while I was incarcerated."

"Joe Gibbs used to always talk about having long-lasting relationships with some of his players, before and after [football]. And I'll be darned, it came true."

Acknowledgments

Interviews gave this book the authority and authenticity required to paint a full portrait of the Redskins' unprecedented championship run from 1981 to 1992. That era of professional football in Washington, D.C., spanned more than a decade and included hundreds of people, not just the players and coaches but also members of the team's front office, scouting department, medical staff, as well as journalists, and even the fans. Speaking with as many as possible was essential.

Each person I interviewed is named on pages 355–56, and they deserve my endless appreciation. So, too, do those who helped arrange these interviews. Thanks so much to Ken Coffey, Jeff Bostic, Tom Friend, Khaleelah PoRome, Will Kiss, Daniel Sampson, Aaron Popkey, Jamie Fritz, Sandy Sedlak, Kevin L. Trainor, Alex Riethmiller, Elizabeth Malia Calhoun, Katrina Walker, Clay Henry, Timothy Bourret, Jon Wheeler, Shelley Binegar, Linda Townsend, Patrick Creamer, Sarah Walton, Vic Carucci, Brooke Gard, April Edwards, and Cindy Mangum. I also owe special gratitude to Casey Beathard, Chris Helein, and Kirk Mee.

In addition to the wonderful interview subjects I spoke with, I used many other research tools to uncover interesting, forgotten, and obscure facts and people. Lauren Rasmussen and Robert Ray at San Diego State University, Chris Willis at NFL Films, Joseph Miller at the DeKalb County Library in Decatur (Georgia), and Coach David Sedmak provided assistance in their own areas of expertise.

Peter Hubbard, the brilliant executive editor at William Morrow, was equally essential to telling this story accurately, but also with the best possible "narrative arc." Peter's exceptional team—Nick Amphlett, Rachel Meyers, Ivan Kenneally, Kyran Cassidy, Laurie McGee, Diane Shanley, Kaitlin Harri, Katie Steinberg—refined this book better than I could have possibly imagined.

Together, everyone at William Morrow has provided invaluable assistance in the creation and polishing of this book. But more so than any one person, my literary agent deserves my thanks. Without Farley Chase, this book would never have existed. He took a chance on me and this idea and substantially improved the project in the early stages.

Ironically enough, just two weeks after Farley and I began *this* enterprise, the two greatest enterprises I've ever been associated with—my sons, Aaron and Benjamin—also came into my life. Along with their mother, my loyal and compassionate wife, Sarah, they instantly became both the motivation and linchpin behind this book. I wanted to do them proud with this book, and I hope I have.

Adam Lazarus
June 2015

Notes

ORIGINAL INTERVIEWS CONDUCTED

Paul Attner

Hank Bauer

Bobby Beathard

Jack Bechta

Bill Bell

Secretary John Block

Senator John Boozman

Jeff Bostic

Joe Bostic

James Brown

Christine Brennan

Frank Broyles

Steve Buckhantz

Joe Bugel

Dave Butz

Dave Butz Jr.

Earnest Byner

Louis Campbell

Charley Casserly

John Kent Cooke

Ken Coffey

Pete Cronan

Billy Devaney

Brad Edwards

Ricky Ervins

Tom Friend

Joe Gibbs

Jimmie Giles

Darryl Grant

Russ Grimm

Lloyd Hand

Jim Hanifan

Frank Herzog

Marty Hogan

Harold Horton

Dr. Charles Jackson

Joe Jacoby
Merv Johnson
Dave Kindred
Mike Kirkland
Markus Koch
Tony Kornheiser
Aaron Latham
Todd Liebenstein
Charles Mann
Dexter Manley
Leo McClure
John McDonnell
John McGregor
Raleigh McKenzie
Kirk Mee
Edwin Meese
Brian Mitchell
Mark Moseley
Mark Murphy
Terry Metcalf
Santana Moss
Herbert Nelson
Neal Olkewicz
Larry Peccatiello
Richie Petitbon
Joker Phillips
Gary Pomerantz
Jerry Rhome
Dan Riley

Gerald Riggs
Governor Charles Robb
Tony Robinson
George Rogers
Dr. Charles Ross
Mark Rypien
Ricky Sanders
Al Saunders
Mark Schlereth
Donnie Schoenmann
Jay Schroeder
Len Shapiro
Judge Doug Shaver
Warren "Rennie" Simmons
Timmy Smith
Jim Speros
Lesley Stahl
Joe Theismann
R. C. Thielemann
Michael Torbert
LaVern "Torgy" Torgeson
Bubba Tyer
Michael Wilbon
George F. Will
Doug Williams
Robert Williams
Steve Wilson
Ernie Zampese

AUTHOR'S NOTE

ix **"disparaging to Native Americans":** Darren Rovell, "Patent Office: Redskins 'Disparaging,'" ESPN.com, June 18, 2014.

x **"If I were the owner . . .":** Theresa Vargas and Annys Shin, "President Obama Says, 'I'd Think About Changing' Name of Washington Redskins," *Washington Post*, Oct. 5, 2013.

x   **"were blinded by the mercury . . .":** "The State Dinner," *The West Wing,* Episode 1.7, Original Airdate, Nov. 10, 1999.

x   **"It's our history . . .":** Ibid.

PROLOGUE: MARCH 1981

xiii   **"I have resigned my position . . .":** "A Football Life: John Riggins," NFL Films, Nov. 21, 2012.

xiii   **"You need to get . . .":** Joe Gibbs, Nov. 4, 2014.

xiv   **"For some reason . . .":** Paul Attner, "New Riggins Tune: 'Desire' the Issue,"*Washington Post,* Aug. 23, 1980.

xiv   **"I took the whole year . . .":** Dave Kindred, "Riggins: Stationary, but Elusive," *Washington Post,* Jan. 27, 1983.

xiv   **"When I left . . .":** Ibid.

xiv   **"Everybody in Lawrence . . .":** Joe Gibbs, Nov. 4, 2014.

xv   **"a barn with seven stalls . . .":** Paul Zimmerman, "They Bought His Act Hook, Line and Sinker," *Sports Illustrated,* Sept. 1, 1983.

xv   **"Right away I knew . . .":** Joe Gibbs, Nov. 4, 2014.

xv   **"I meet him . . .":** "A Football Life: John Riggins."

xv   **"every down":** Joe Gibbs, Nov. 4, 2014.

xv   **"I'm not getting anything . . .":** Ibid.

xv   **"You need to get me . . .":** Ibid.

1. JOE WHO?

2   **"We were in other . . .":** John Kent Cooke, June 18, 2014.

2   **"The reason he was . . .":** Ibid.

3   **"In those meetings, Jack Pardee . . .":** Ibid.

3   **"I can't stay with . . .":** Paul Zimmerman, "Smartest Man in the NFL," *Sports Illustrated,* Aug. 29, 1988.

4   **"They did a great job . . .":** Bobby Beathard, May 28, 2014.

4   **"It became apparent . . .":** "Power Struggle Costs Pardee Job as Redskin Coach," *Chicago Tribune,* Jan. 6, 1981.

4   **"What [Cooke] was hoping . . .":** Bobby Beathard, Dec. 19, 2014.

4   **"I've got the right guy . . .":** Ibid.

5   **"Who in the heck is . . .":** Bobby Beathard, May 28, 2014.

6   **"Get up here . . .":** John Ed Bradley, "Joe Gibbs Is a Wild and Crazy Guy," *Washington Post,* Sept. 4, 1988.

6   **"I had never felt . . ."**: Joe Gibbs with Jerry Jenkins, *Fourth and One* (Nashville, TN: Thomas Nelson, 1991), p. 15.

6   **"with as much intensity . . ."**: Richard Justice, "Redskins' Best Calls Come from Team at Top," *Washington Post*, Jan. 19, 1992.

6   **"Joe and I were both . . ."**: Leonard Shapiro, "The Ride of a Lifetime," *Washington Post*, May 21, 2000.

6   **"I was forty years old . . ."**: Gibbs with Jenkins, *Fourth and One*, p. 11.

6   **"all the gear they . . ."**: Dave Kindred, "Carolina Sheriff's Son on Football Odyssey," *Washington Post*, Jan. 13, 1981.

7   **"Probably because I . . ."**: Dave Distel, "Coryell Knew What He Had in Joe Gibbs," *Los Angeles Times*, Jan. 30, 1988.

7   **"He was a tough guy . . ."**: Bill Bell, July 12, 2014.

7   **"I was interested in . . ."**: Distel, "Coryell Knew."

7   **"I'd drive Madden on . . ."**: Tom Friend, "Gibbs Recalls No. 1 on Brink of No. 100," *Washington Post*, Dec. 8, 1989.

8   **"pair up in threes . . ."**: Jim Crosby, "Coach Pete's 50th Anniversary," *Tallahassee Magazine*, Sept.–Oct. 2010.

8   **"Bill Peterson was totally . . ."**: Tom Callahan, "The Motor's Running and It's Not Close to Quitting Time," *Washington Post*, Aug. 27, 1991.

9   **In addition to . . . "hot receiver"**: Florida State University 2012 Football Media Guide, p. 117.

9   **"You think of 'Air Coryell' . . ."**: " 'Football Genius' Don Coryell Remembered," SDSU Video, Youtube.com, accessed July 16, 2014.

10   **"John McKay: Extremely bright . . ."**: Callahan, "The Motor's Running."

10   **"A lot of coaches . . ."**: Harold Horton, July 22, 2014.

10   **"Frank Broyles was . . ."**: Callahan, "The Motor's Running."

11   **"[Gibbs] was really very . . ."**: Senator John Boozman, July 30, 2014.

11   **"The referees had to . . ."**: Ibid.

12   **"You want the best . . ."**: Distel, "Coryell Knew."

12   **"Even in those early . . ."**: Terry Metcalf, July 15, 2014.

13   **"Joe, I don't think . . ."**: Mark Kreidler, "Tampa Debacle Taught Gibbs the Value of Keeping It Simple," *San Diego Union*, Jan. 31, 1988.

13   **"I'm here to tell you . . ."**: Ibid.

13   Once the **"miserable"** season . . . : Ibid.

13   **"had to get Joe"**: Distel, "Coryell Knew."

13   **"It's an attitude . . .":** Vic Carucci, "Coryell's Attacking Offense Mirrored His Attitude on Game, Life," NFL.com, July 2, 2010.

14   **"He showed tremendous . . .":** Dennis Georgatos, "Coryell Finds That There Is More to Life Than Football," *Los Angeles Times*, Dec. 7, 1986.

14   **"Our greatest day would be . . .":** Carucci, "Coryell's Attacking Offense."

15   **"San Diego has a super . . .":** Dave Distel, "This Season Chargers Put Off Uncorking Joy," *Los Angeles Times*, Dec. 24, 1980.

15   **"I loved that team . . .":** Gibbs with Jenkins, *Fourth and One*, p. 12.

15   **Described . . . as "stylish and articulate . . .":** Paul Attner and Dave Kindred, "Redskins Like Ability to Instill Confidence," *Washington Post*, Jan. 13, 1981.

16   **Jack Kent Cooke . . . "fun for the fans":** Ibid.

16   **"like Christmas and New Year's . . .":** Ibid.

16   **"If there is one thing . . .":** "Redskins Name Gibbs as Coach," *Los Angeles Times*, Jan. 14, 1981.

16   **"I feel a tremendous sense . . .":** Ibid.

16   **compared to a "CIA [background] check":** John Ed Bradley, "Joe Gibbs Is a Wild and Crazy Guy," *Washington Post*, Sept. 4, 1988.

18   **"Everything I had heard . . .":** Bobby Beathard, May 28, 2014.

18   **"Everybody didn't know . . .":** Terry Metcalf, July 15, 2014.

18   **"I want you down at . . .":** Bobby Beathard, May 28, 2014.

19   **"Boy he chewed me out":** Ibid.

19   **"Mr. Cooke has this book . . .":** Leonard Shapiro, "The Ride of a Lifetime," *Washington Post*, May 21, 2000.

19   **"I'm getting letters from . . .":** Ibid.

19   **"You're going to turn . . .":** Justice, "Redskins' Best Calls."

19   **"Dad said to me . . .":** Mike Wise, "Burgundy & Old Pain," *Washington Post*, Oct. 21, 2009.

20   **"I told myself . . .":** Justice, "Redskins' Best Calls."

20   **"He kept his cool . . .":** Paul Attner, "1st Lesson for Gibbs: Making the Best of the Worst of Times," *Washington Post*, Nov. 15, 1981.

20   **"Injuries are no excuse . . .":** "Statistics Don't Tell Tale of Gibbs's Winless 'Skins," *Harrisonburg (VA) Daily News-Record*, Sept. 29, 1981.

21   **Injuries had been . . . "because . . .":** Frank Litsky, "Redskins Share Giants' Woe," *New York Times*, Sept. 11, 1981.

21   **"This is the hardest thing . . .":** "Statistics Don't Tell Tale."

21   **"I can't imagine a worse . . .":** Attner, "1st Lesson for Gibbs."

21   **"Don't forget, Yale . . .":** Red Smith, "Power, If Not Glory, Fills
       Box at Redskins' Game," *New York Times*, Oct. 6, 1981.

22   **"Go Back Home Cooke . . .":** *Washington Post*, Oct. 5, 1981, Photo
       by Richard Darcey.

22   **"For every two things . . .":** Mike Kiley, "Season's a Mistake for
       'Skins," *Chicago Tribune*, Oct. 9, 1981.

22   another **"weekly humiliation":** Ken Denlinger, "Forget Parity: This
       Team Needs Charity—and Faith," *Washington Post*, Oct. 5, 1981.

22   **"I want to remember . . .":** Bernie Miklasz, "Gibbs Could Use an
       Image," *Ottawa Citizen*, Aug. 22, 1992.

2. THE BIRTH OF A DYNASTY

23   **"He was the most stunned . . .":** Joe Theismann, Mar. 4, 2014.

24   **"I loved the city . . .":** Ibid.

24   **"he has just enough . . .":** "Redskins Obtain Theismann Rights,"
       New York Times, Jan. 26, 1974.

25   **"He knew who he was, . . .":** Gary Pomerantz, May 30, 2014.

25   **"cross between Clint Eastwood . . .":** Ray Kennedy, "A Mouth That
       Roars," *Sports Illustrated*, Oct. 6, 1980.

25   **"Evidently someone had told . . .":** Joe Theismann, Mar. 4, 2014.

25   **"You have a lot of . . .":** Ibid.

26   **"I had my doubts . . .":** Michael Madden, "The Future Is Gibbs,"
       Boston Globe, Jan. 29, 1983.

26   **"I wasn't [Joe's] quarterback":** Joe Theismann, Mar. 4, 2014.

26   **"It just so happens . . .":** Ibid.

27   **"If you have a Kellen . . .":** Michael Janofsky, "Theismann Has One
       Goal to Complete," *New York Times*, Dec. 5, 1982.

27   **"I'm bored, I'm broke . . .":** " 'Skins Riggins Reports," *Annapolis
       (MD) Capital*, June 12, 1981.

27   **"What did I miss the most?":** "For Riggins, Life in NFL Beats Life
       on the Farm," *Los Angeles Times*, June 12, 1981.

27   **"definite cash-flow problem":** Paul Zimmerman, "They Bought His
       Act Hook, Line and Sinker," *Sports Illustrated*, Sept. 1, 1983.

27   **"You didn't realize . . .":** Joe Gibbs, Nov. 4, 2014.

28   **"I really thought John . . .":** Denis Harrington, *Riggins in Motion*
       (New York: Pinnacle Books, 1985), p. 64.

28   **"Jack [Pardee] called . . .":** Zimmerman, "They Bought His Act."

28   dealing away the "egomaniac": Joe Gibbs with Ken Abraham, *Racing to Win* (Sisters, OR: Multnomah, 2002), p. 157.

28   "He showed he was . . .": Jack McCallum, "The New Redskins Get a Running Start," *Sports Illustrated*, Aug. 17, 1981.

29   "He was running ten . . .": Harrington, *Riggins in Motion*, p. 67.

29   "John Riggins looked awful . . .": Tom Friend, "Gibbs Recalls No. 1 on Brink of No. 100," *Washington Post*, Dec. 8, 1989.

29   "I don't thrive on . . .": Frank Litsky, "Riggins Keeps Stepping Out, But Always as a Team Player," *New York Times*, Jan. 30, 1983.

29   "I can't practice . . .": Cooper Rollow, "Redskins' Riggins Is Really Raring to Go," *Chicago Tribune*, Aug. 31, 1983.

29   "I think the coaches . . .": Paul Attner, "Gibbs Has Become a Riggins Fan," *Washington Post*, Nov. 20, 1981.

30   "I have to run . . .": Harrington, *Riggins in Motion*, p. 71.

30   "You know, Coach . . .": Mike Wise, "With Cerrato's Announcement, They Rise or Fall Together," *Washington Post*, Oct. 24, 2009.

31   "When I first got here . . .": Madden, "The Future Is Gibbs."

31   "I came from Houston . . .": Ibid.

31   "You have to have . . .": Ibid.

32   "This was the first time . . .": Paul Attner, "Gibbs Tries More Runs, Wins First," *Washington Post*, Oct. 12, 1981.

32   "This is a different . . .": "Redskins Finally Get a Victory," *Harrisonburg (VA) Daily News-Record*, Oct. 12, 1981.

32   "Things are a lot . . .": Paul Attner, "Christmas at Redskin Park," *Washington Post*, Oct. 13, 1981.

32   "We've heard about . . .": "So on to the Super Bowl," *Washington Post*, Oct. 13, 1981.

33   "Clearly," the member . . . : Ibid.

33   "To win here . . .": Paul Attner, "Moseley's 48-Yard Kick Wins in Overtime, 30-27," *Washington Post*, Nov. 16, 1981.

33   "Who would have thought . . .": Paul Attner, "9-7 Mark Is Needed—Gibbs," *Washington Post*, Nov. 17, 1981.

34   "The kids made fun . . .": John Feinstein, "There's Joy Again in Being a Redskin," *Washington Post*, Nov. 5, 1981.

34   Mark May, had become "tired . . .": Ibid.

34   "We'd drive home . . .": Glen Macnow, "Joe Gibbs Is a Worker and a Winner," *Philadelphia Inquirer*, Dec. 22, 1991.

34   "there's great optimism . . .": *Sports Illustrated*, Sept. 1, 1982.

35   Riggins's "muscles were . . .": Paul Attner, "Riggins: Strength of '79 in Fall of '82," *Washington Post*, Sept. 10, 1982.

35   "I knew that next . . .": Terry Metcalf, July 15, 2014.

36   "[The owners are] not . . .": Robert Markus, "Stop Action—NFL Strikes," *Chicago Tribune*, Sept. 21, 1982.

36   "It was hard . . .": Mark Murphy, July 11, 2014.

36   "Grabbing a bunch . . .": "Vermeil Defends Players' Right to Strike, Won't Coach Scabs," *Frederick (MD) News Post*, Sept. 21, 1982.

37   "I guess I'll do . . .": Len Pasquarelli, "Lengthy Strike Has Mostly Been Forgotten," ESPN.com, Sept. 21, 2007.

37   "It was the first time . . .": Joe Theismann with Dave Kindred, *Theismann* (Chicago: Contemporary Books, 1987), pp. 111, 113.

37   "I am very pessimistic": Paul Attner, "Gibbs Thinks NFL Season Is Over," *Washington Post*, Nov. 10, 1982.

38   "I feel good that . . .": Paul Attner, "Gibbs Ready for Players," *Washington Post*, Nov. 17, 1982.

38   "There is something . . .": Paul Attner, "Secondary Intercepts 4 in 13-9 Win," *Washington Post*, Nov. 29, 1982.

39   "the damn Cowboys": David Elfin, *Washington Redskins: The Complete Illustrated History* (Minneapolis: MVP Books, 2011), p. 63.

39   "We really can't stand Dallas": Paul Attner, "Cowboys Give Redskins First Defeat," *Washington Post*, Dec. 6, 1982.

40   The "Super Bowl Tournament": "How the Season Will Work," *Chicago Tribune*, Nov. 18, 1982.

40   "I'm really getting down . . .": Dave Kindred, "Riggins Off and Running, and So Are the Redskins," *Washington Post*, Jan. 16, 1983.

40   "Thank God we have . . .": Paul Attner, "Redskins Win in a Riggins Runaway, 21-7," *Washington Post*, Jan. 16, 1983.

41   "In my memory . . .": Frank Herzog, Feb. 18, 2015.

41   "John's a living representation . . .": Kindred, "Riggins Off and Running."

41   Chants of "We want Dallas": Denis Collins, "From Cold Line to Hog Heaven," *Washington Post*, Jan. 16, 1983.

42   "We were angry at . . .": Darryl Grant, June 19, 2014.

42   "The fans were screaming . . .": Ibid.

43   "We changed some stuff . . .": Paul Attner, "Respect: Redskins 31, Cowboys 17," *Washington Post*, Jan. 23, 1983.

43 **"I went up to John . . .":** Gordon Edes, "The Day the Computer Broke," *Los Angeles Times*, Jan. 23, 1983.

43 **"I've been around the NFL . . .":** Mark Murphy, July 11, 2014.

44 **"This is the most exciting . . .":** Charley Casserly, June 19, 2014.

44 **"Of course Dexter doesn't . . .":** Darryl Grant, June 19, 2014.

44 **chanted "We beat Dallas":** Dave Kindred, "Pigs and 'Pokes, and Celebration," *Washington Post*, Jan. 23, 1983.

45 **"I just want to . . .":** "From the President, Words of Good Cheer," *Washington Post*, Jan. 23, 1983.

45 **"This has been a . . .":** Ibid.

45 **"This was the way . . .":** Attner, "Respect."

45 **"The Super Bowls are great . . .":** Mark Murphy, July 11, 2014.

45 **"I think this is . . .":** Paul Attner, "Gibbs, Team Are Hoping Against Hype," *Washington Post*, Jan. 26, 1983.

46 **"I was ready to pack . . .":** Attner, "Respect."

46 **"I've waited a long time . . .":** Edes, "The Day the Computer Broke."

46 **"If you're a public . . .":** Leigh Montville, "Riggins Says His Piece— If You Can Hear Him," *Boston Globe*, Jan. 27, 1983.

46 **"We hit the town . . .":** Steve Daley, "Redskin Copycats Run to Catch Up," *Chicago Tribune*, Feb. 1, 1983.

46 **It wasn't the ideal attire . . . :** "A Rainy Super Bowl," *Chicago Tribune*, Jan. 29, 1983.

47 **"I wouldn't call . . .":** Litsky, "Riggins Keeps Stepping Out."

47 **"In our first couple . . .":** Joe Jacoby, edited by Danny Peary, *The Game of Their Lives* (New York: Macmillan, 1997), p. 238.

48 **"I almost swallowed . . .":** " 'Skins Stop Miami Run," *Winchester Star*, Jan. 31, 1983.

48 **"The coaches were . . .":** Paul Attner, "Dolphins Fall, 27-17, to Record 166 Yards," *Washington Post*, Jan. 31, 1983.

48 **"Hey, [Buges,] let's stop . . .":** John Clayton, "Stop Fancy Stuff, Hogs Told Coach," *Pittsburgh Press*, Jan. 31, 1983.

49 **"We're not the smartest . . .":** Ibid.

49 **"There comes a time . . .":** Gerald Eskenazi, "Redskins' Winning Gamble," *New York Times*, Jan. 31, 1983.

49 **"I seriously needed . . .":** Theismann with Kindred, *Theismann*, p. 123.

50 **"You can't have eleven . . .":** Eskenazi, "Redskins' Winning Gamble."

50 "I was tiptoeing . . .": Ibid.

50 "I felt that was . . .": Ray Didinger, "Big John Smash Hit in Drummer Boy Role," *Reading Eagle,* Jan. 31, 1983.

51 "He said he just . . .": Leonard Shapiro, "Precise Presentiment and Perfect Performance," *Washington Post,* Jan. 31, 1983.

51 "Two years ago . . .": Didinger, "Big John Smash Hit."

51 "at least for tonight . . .": Attner, "Dolphins Fall."

51 "I can still walk away": Ibid.

3. HOG HEAVEN

53 "Dad knew [former Chargers . . .] . . .": John Kent Cooke, June 18, 2014.

53 "It was dreadful . . .": Ibid.

53 "You got a pretty good . . .": Leonard Shapiro, "Dolphins: No Surprises, No Excuses," *Washington Post,* Feb. 1, 1983.

53 "I lost her": Paul Attner, "Gibbs Loses His Wife, Forgets Celebration Site," *Washington Post,* Feb. 1, 1983.

53 "During the week . . .": Ibid.

54 "Everyone was saying . . .": Curt Brown, "Gibbs remains Redskins' quiet cornerstone," *Minneapolis Star Tribune,* Jan. 27, 1992.

54 "I haven't been to bed . . .": Dave Anderson, "For Joe Gibbs, a Matter of Respect," *New York Times,* Feb. 1, 1983.

54 "[I'm] a very average . . .": Paul Attner, "Midst Glory, Gibbs Warns of 'Monster'," *Washington Post,* Feb. 1, 1983.

54 "Can I have your . . .": Anderson, "For Joe Gibbs.".

54 "I told you we . . .": Ibid.

54 "Welcome, World Champions.": "Skins Get a Capital Welcome," *Philadelphia Daily News,* Feb. 1, 1983.

55 "Congratulations," Reagan yelled . . .: Molly Moore and Judith Valante, "Reagans Welcome the Champs," *Washington Post,* Feb. 1, 1983.

55 "I don't think the day . . .": *History of the Washington Redskins,* NFL Films.

56 "I didn't reset my watch.": Blaine Harden, "500,000 Frenzied Fans Revel in the Rain for Redskins," *Washington Post,* Feb. 3, 1983.

56 "[And] I thought . . .": "Late Riggins Proves Better Than No Riggins," *Frederick (MD) News,* Feb. 3, 1983.

56   **"It's like seeing . . ."**: Irvin Molotsky, "Washington Unites to Salute Redskins," *New York Times*, Feb. 3, 1983.

57   **"We knew their tendencies"**: Will McDonough, "Lost It in the Trenches, Weary Dolphins Admit," *Boston Globe*, Jan. 31, 1983.

57   **"That's the biggest . . ."**: Paul Zimmerman, "They Bought His Act Hook, Line and Sinker," *Sports Illustrated*, Sept. 1, 1983.

57   **"From the way they . . ."**: McDonough, "Lost It in the Trenches."

58   **"Russ, of course, is . . ."**: "Russ Grimm," *Washington Post*, Aug. 7, 2010.

59   **"That was a Q-test . . ."**: Michael Torbert, Mar. 12, 2015.

59   **"They treated us like . . ."**: Ibid.

59   **"It's something we did . . ."**: Dave Anderson, "Hogs in Three-Piece Suits," *New York Times*, Jan. 19, 1984.

60   **"[Rookie offensive tackle] . . ."**: Paul Attner, "Some Redskins 'Hogging' the Victories," *Washington Post*, Nov. 27, 1982.

60   **"only perfect practice . . ."**: Ian Walker, "Giants Perfectly Happy to Practise," *Vancouver Sun*, Jan. 25, 2008.

60   **Talbert and the other "charter members"**: Michael Richman, *Redskins Encyclopedia* (Philadephia: Temple University Press, 2007), p. 339.

61   **"Riggo carried over . . ."**: Russ Grimm, Apr. 4, 2014.

61   **"Most of us were . . ."**: Joe Jacoby, Mar. 31, 2014.

61   **"I sat in [Gibbs's] office . . ."**: Jere Longman, "Redskins' Game Plan Is Simple: Hog the Ball," *Philadelphia Inquirer*, Jan. 26, 1983.

62   **"How can you pass . . ."**: Paul Attner, "Jacoby: Heavy Favorite in Early Camp Returns," *Washington Post*, July 18, 1981.

62   **"I used to yell at Mark . . ."**: Russ Grimm, Apr. 4, 2014.

63   **"I forgot who said it"**: Paul Attner, "Grimm Overachiever as a Mover of Men," *Washington Post,* Jan. 12, 1983.

63   **"Grimm makes me . . ."**: Attner, "Some Redskins 'Hogging'."

63   **"I play because . . ."**: Attner, "Grimm Overachiever."

63   **"I'm more your . . ."**: Ibid.

63   **"I would doubt . . ."**: Dave Butz, May 27, 2014.

64   **"Traffic up in D.C. . . ."**: Jeff Bostic, Mar. 24, 2014.

64   **"He opened up and . . ."**: Dave Butz, May 27, 2014.

65   **"I thought that was cool"**: Ibid.

65   **"The owner demands . . ."**: Rich Hofmann, "Gibbs Hopes to Build on Success," *Philadelphia Daily News*, Feb. 1, 1983.

65   **"I have one basic . . ."**: "Redskins Name Gibbs as Coach," *Los Angeles Times*, Jan. 14, 1981.

66 **"Obviously, we're not . . .":** Gary Pomerantz, "Gibbs's Mr. Goodbar Strategy from 'Submarine' Confounds Rivals," *Washington Post,* Oct. 27, 1983.

66 **"They had so much . . .":** Leonard Shapiro, "Dolphins: No Surprises, No Excuses," *Washington Post,* Feb. 1, 1983.

66 **"I told my players . . .":** Gerald Eskenazi, "Miami Kept Off Balance," *New York Times,* Jan. 31, 1983.

67 **"The whole counter . . .":** Tim Layden, "Don Coryell, 1924–2010," *Sports Illustrated,* July 17, 2010.

67 **"Joe and John have to be . . .":** Gary Pomerantz, " 'Counter-Trey': Redskins' Power Play Meets Goals Through a Deceiving Line," *Washington Post,* Oct. 6, 1984.

68 **"Watching a 290-pound . . .":** Ibid.

68 **"If you're a 180 . . .":** Ibid.

68 **"I guess I always . . .":** Joe Jacoby, Mar. 31, 2014.

68 **"It's a play that . . .":** Russ Grimm, Apr. 4, 2014.

69 **"I'm disappointed Riggo . . .":** Gary Pomerantz, "Redskins Win Coolly as Theismann Heats Up in Seattle, 27-17," *Washington Post,* Sept. 26, 1983.

70 **"Those TD passes . . .":** "Washington Wins in Seattle, 27-17," *Winchester Star,* Sept. 26, 1983.

70 **"Washington is the best . . .":** Pomerantz, "Redskins Win Coolly."

4. COMING UP SHORT

71 **The energetic . . . "free spirit":** Kirk Mee, June 18, 2014.

71 **"I flew all the way . . .":** Ibid.

72 **"This is the first . . .":** Ibid.

73 **"Don't let them big boys . . .":** Darrell Green's Pro Football Hall of Fame Enshrinement Ceremony transcript, Aug. 2, 2008.

73 **"My mother, bless her . . .":** Carolyn White, "Darrell Green: He Regards His Talent as a Gift from God," *USA Today,* Jan. 27, 1988.

73 **"I'm sitting there . . .":** Ron Borges, "Fast Times for Green," *Boston Globe,* Feb. 1, 1988.

73 **"grew up a little bit":** Darrell Green's Pro Football Hall of Fame Enshrinement Ceremony transcript, Aug. 2, 2008.

73 **"fastest guy in the state of Texas":** Jack Bechta, May 12, 2014.

73 **"I saw him line up for . . .":** Ibid.

74   "this kid's a hell of a player . . .": Kirk Mee, June 18, 2014.

74   "I'd never seen . . .": Bobby Beathard, May 28, 2014.

74   "They would send us . . .": Richie Petitbon, June 25, 2014.

75   "The only question was . . .": Billy Devaney, May 27, 2014.

76   "You're talking about . . .": Gary Pomerantz, "It's a Beautiful Day in Green's Neighborhood," *Washington Post*, Jan. 12, 1984.

76   "Darrell made enough . . .": Dave Kindred, "The Undressing of Darrell Green," *Washington Post*, Aug. 21, 1983.

76   "That was my fault": Darryl Grant, June 19, 2014.

77   "This missile goes by me": David Elfin, "Darrell Green Became a Redskins Icon 30 Years Ago Today," washington.cbslocal.com, Sept. 5, 2013.

77   "At the time, there wasn't . . .": Mark Murphy, July 11, 2014.

77   "that little monkey": "Reference to Garrett Not Racist, Says Cosell," *Frederick (MD) News-Post*, Sept. 7, 1983.

77   "It was kind of . . .": Neal Olkewicz, May 30, 2014.

77   "baby face": Gary Pomerantz, "Green Gains Education Rapidly," *Washington Post*, Oct. 28, 1983.

77   admittedly "itty-bitty": Harold Abend, "Green Speeds to the Hall of Fame," ESPN.com, Oct. 31, 2008.

78   "Yeah, I feel young": Pomerantz, "Green Gains Education Rapidly."

78   "sheer, unadulterated . . . ecstasy": *History of the Washington Redskins*, NFL Films.

78   "I came here tonight . . .": Dave Kindred, "RFK Glee Becomes Sadness," *Washington Post*, Sept. 6, 1983.

78   "we're not the kind . . .": Gary Pomerantz, "Redskins Take It from the Top," *Washington Post*, Aug. 28, 1983.

78   "I don't think people . . .": Ibid.

79   "Do we have respect?": Gary Pomerantz, "Redskins: In Search of Respect," *Washington Post*, Aug. 3, 1983.

79   "[the photo] was pretty ugly . . .": "For Its 50th Anniversary, 'Gentlemen's Quarterly' Salutes 'Stylish Icons,'" *Media Industry Newsletter*, Sept. 17, 2007.

79   "tell Joe, I've never seen . . .": Gary Pomerantz, "Statistics and Theismann Speak for Themselves," *Washington Post*, Nov. 5, 1983.

80   "My career has . . .": Gary Pomerantz, "Theismann: Riding High," *Washington Post*, Dec. 22, 1983.

80   **"a human spear":** Dave Kindred, "For Garrett, an End to Small Talk," *Washington Post,* Jan. 10, 1983.

81   **"It looks like he's ice skating":** Paul Attner, "Brown-Monk Act Gets Rave Reviews," *Washington Post,* Dec. 29, 1982.

81   **"cocky" Pro Bowl receiver . . . :** Gary Pomerantz, "Brown: No. 8 Closes in on the Top," *Washington Post,* Nov. 11, 1983.

81   **plate that read "All-Pro" . . . :** Ibid.

81   **"I started calling . . .":** Gary Pomerantz, "The 'Smurfs' Play Taller for Redskins," *Washington Post,* Aug. 19, 1982.

82   **"I'm Papa Smurf . . .":** Ibid.

82   **"The funny thing about it . . .":** *History of the Washington Redskins,* NFL Films.

82   **"I would go into games . . .":** Ibid.

83   **"And I was starting . . .":** Mark Kreidler, "Tampa Debacle Taught Gibbs the Value of Keeping It Simple," *San Diego Union,* Jan. 31, 1988.

84   **In what he called "probably . . .":** Jere Longman, "Redskins Do a Number (51-7) on Rams," *Philadelphia Inquirer,* Jan. 2, 1984.

84   **"We really stunk . . .":** Ken Denlinger, "Petitbon: 'We Really Stunk,'" *Washington Post,* Oct. 18, 1983.

84   **"The secondary is now . . .":** Gary Pomerantz, "Redskins' Defense Up, Cardinals Down, 45-7," *Washington Post,* Nov. 7, 1983.

84   **"Everybody knows that . . .":** Gary Pomerantz, "Redskins Get Right to the Points, 51-7," *Washington Post,* Jan. 2, 1984.

85   **"by surprise, flat-footed . . .":** Rich Roberts, "Redskins, Raiders Make Tampa Reservations," *Los Angeles Times,* Jan. 9, 1984.

85   **"There was a time . . .":** Ira Rosenfeld, " . . . The Season Continues," *Harrisonburg (VA) Daily News-Record,* Jan. 9, 1984.

85   **he declared "atrocious":** Gary Pomerantz, "After 4 Misses, Moseley Wins Game, 24-21," *Washington Post,* Jan. 9, 1984.

85   **"blindfold and a cigarette . . .":** Thomas Boswell, "Redskins Win on Late Moseley Kick," *Washington Post,* Jan. 9, 1984.

85   **"He didn't have time . . .":** Roberts, "Redskins, Raiders Make Tampa Reservations."

85   **"We were the best . . .":** Rosenfeld, " . . . The Season Continues."

86   **"could not have been caught . . .":** Rich Hofmann, "Super Powers Prevail," *Philadelphia Daily News,* Jan. 9, 1984.

86   **"If the Redskins are . . .":** Michael Wilbon, "49ers Hear the Calls, Answer with Disbelief," *Washington Post,* Jan. 9, 1984.

86 **"We're on our way . . .":** Rosenfeld, " . . . The Season Continues."

86 **"The Washington Redskins proved . . .":** Stan Goldberg, "Redskins Are Good, But They Aren't Invincible," *Frederick (MD) News-Post,* Jan. 9, 1984.

87 **"I think that team . . .":** Joe Gibbs, Nov. 4, 2014.

87 **"I thought it was . . .":** Rich Roberts, "The Redskins Go from Hog Heaven to Hogwash," *Los Angeles Times,* Jan. 23, 1984.

88 **"For some reason . . .":** Richie Petitbon, June 25, 2014.

88 **"Bad week, we had . . .":** Jeff Bostic, Mar. 24, 2014.

89 **"John Riggins, Commander . . .":** "Riggins No Clown When It Counts," *Providence Journal,* Jan. 19, 1984.

89 **"You're all probably . . .":** Jim Donaldson, " 'Skins Riggins Entertains Super Bowl Media," *Providence Journal,* Jan. 19, 1984.

89 **he was "quite exhausted . . .":** Paul Attner and Gary Pomerantz, "Riggins: Gaining 242 Yards in Two Games Left Him 'Exhausted,' " *Washington Post,* Jan. 19, 1984.

89 **"I can't help but . . .":** Ibid.

89 **"I'm just lazy . . .":** Cooper Rollow, "Riggins: I Was Set to Retire," *Chicago Tribune,* Jan. 23, 1984.

89 **"I went into his room . . .":** Dave Butz, May 27, 2014.

90 **"Reggie Kinlaw . . .":** Joe Theismann, Mar. 4, 2014.

90 **"amazed me because . . .":** Roberts, "Hog Heaven to Hogwash."

90 **"With Lester Hayes . . .":** Joe Theismann, Mar. 4, 2014.

91 **"That took away half . . .":** Dave Butz, May 27, 2014.

91 **"We always thought . . .":** David DuPree, "Redskins Beaten in All Corners," *Washington Post,* Jan. 23, 1984.

91 **"We could make excuses . . .":** David DuPree, "Redskins Nothing 'Special,' " *Washington Post,* Jan. 23, 1984.

91 **"If it was closer . . .":** Gary Pomerantz, "Raiders Dismantle Redskins, Records in Super Bowl, 38-9," *Washington Post,* Jan. 23, 1984.

92 **"I'm not a genius":** Rick Reilly, "He Rejects Genius Label," *Los Angeles Times,* Jan. 24, 1984.

92 **"That was a wonderful . . .":** "Reagan Praises Raiders," *Chicago Tribune,* Jan. 23, 1984.

92 **"I'd like to know . . .":** Ira Kaufman, "Due Credit Given Redskins at Last," *(Huntington) Daily News,* Jan. 31, 1983.

92 **"We got tired of . . .":** "Allen Spurs Raiders Past 'Skins," *Toronto Globe and Mail,* Jan. 23, 1984.

92 **That night ... "the Slaughterhouse Seven":** Rich Hofmann, "Raiders Hog-Tie Redskins," *Philadelphia Daily News*, Jan. 23, 1984.

93 **"That's bread and butter ...":** Roberts, "Hog Heaven to Hogwash."

93 **"I felt there was ...":** "Riggins Fails This Time," *Daily Intelligencer*, Jan. 23, 1984.

94 **"Joe was upset at ...":** Jerry Rhome, May 30, 2014.

94 **"With [twelve] seconds left ...":** Pomerantz, "Raiders Dismantle Redskins."

94 **"I'm at the sidelines ...":** Sam Farmer, "Theismann: From a Screen to a Scream," *Los Angeles Times*, Jan. 29, 2009.

95 **"watch for the screen":** John Ed Bradley, "Screen Became a Fizzled 'Rocket,'" *Washington Post*, Jan. 23, 1984.

95 **"If I had had ...":** John Ed Bradley, "Gibbs: Erase Memory and Move On," *Washington Post*, Feb. 15, 1984.

95 **"For one brief instant ...":** Pomerantz, "Raiders Dismantle Redskins."

96 **"He was not happy ...":** Gary Pomerantz, May 30, 2014.

96 **"True story," Gibbs said ...:** Kreidler, "Tampa Debacle Taught Gibbs."

5. SECOND CHANCES

97 **"I've never had a ...":** Ron Borges, "Gibbs Still Can Taste Bitter Defeat of '84," *Boston Globe*, Jan. 31, 1988.

97 **"We want Joe Gibbs! ...":** Charles Fishman, "Redskins Cheered by 150," *Washington Post*, Jan. 24, 1984.

97 **"I just want to ...":** Ibid.

98 **"In our Redskins family ...":** Karlyn Barker, "100,000 Fans Prove Devotion to Redskins with Lusty Welcome," *Washington Post*, Jan. 26, 1984.

98 **"to put God back ...":** T. R. Reid, "Coaches Run Joint Play to Push School Prayer," *Washington Post*, Mar. 1, 1984.

98 **"Marxist doctrine and pornographic ...":** Ibid.

98 **"the Supreme Court [had] expelled ...":** Francis X. Clines, "Reagan Criticizes House Democrats," *New York Times*, Mar. 1, 1984.

98 **"The issue of free religious ...":** James Worsham, "Senate Vote Dumps School-Prayer Plan," *Chicago Tribune*, Mar. 21, 1984.

99 "There were guys . . .": Charles Mann, June 19, 2014.

99 The closest Gibbs . . . "Coach Buns": Gary Pomerantz, "The Coach Reborn," *Washington Post*, Aug. 21, 1983.

99 "I was kind of . . .": Pete Cronan, Aug. 30, 2014.

99 so admittedly "boring": Christine Brennan, "The Joe Gibbs His Players Know: Private, First Class," *Washington Post*, Jan. 31, 1988.

99 "sitting at home with . . .": Ibid.

100 "We would bring in . . .": Pomerantz, "The Coach Reborn."

100 "He was a rough . . .": Dave Kindred, "Carolina Sheriff's Son on Football Odyssey," *Washington Post*, Jan. 13, 1981.

100 "Joe was always a little . . .": Pomerantz, "The Coach Reborn."

100 "because we were starving . . .": Kindred, "Carolina Sheriff's Son."

100 "He got hooked up . . .": Borges, "Gibbs Still Can Taste."

101 "We won a few . . .": Shav Glick, "Return to His Roots," *Los Angeles Times*, Feb. 16, 1992.

101 Believing "if you have a farm . . .": Borges, "Gibbs Still Can Taste."

101 "I was studying for . . .": Ibid.

101 "I never went back . . .": Ibid.

101 "John Belushi–type fraternity": Pomerantz, "The Coach Reborn."

101 He . . . "had stolen some . . .": Joe Gibbs with Jerry Jenkins, *Game Plan for Life* (Carol Stream, IL: Tyndale House Publishers, 2009), p. 59.

102 "I got to the fight . . .": Pomerantz, "The Coach Reborn."

102 "A part of me died . . .": Robbie Andreu, "Redskins' Joe Gibbs Takes the Plunge from Gridiron to Starting Grid," *Ottawa Citizen*, Mar. 1, 1992.

102 "Obviously, I have not . . .": Pomerantz, "The Coach Reborn."

102 Tharel became Gibbs's "spiritual father": John Ed Bradley, "Joe Gibbs Is a Wild and Crazy Guy," *Washington Post*, Sept. 4, 1988.

102 "It was a growing . . .": Pomerantz, "The Coach Reborn."

102 "Your relationship with . . .": Mark Schlereth, "Don't Lose Crucial Parts of 'The Code,' " ESPN.com, Feb. 15, 2014.

103 "I guarantee you," . . .: Ibid.

103 "I didn't want to . . .": Charles Mann, June 19, 2014.

103 "He kept the staff . . .": Pete Cronan, Aug. 30, 2014.

103 known at the time, "delinquents": Steve Marantz, " 'Skin-Deep in Success," *Boston Globe*, Jan. 12, 1983.

103 "At the beginning . . .": Paul Attner, "For Gibbs, Sundays Are Still Special Days," *Washington Post*, Oct. 11, 1982.

104 **"Maybe a farm . . .":** Ibid.

104 **"I got on my knees . . .":** Richard Justice, "Gibbs Now Open About Lows in His Life," *Washington Post,* Feb. 1, 1991.

105 **He saw a "real void . . .":** Lee Hockstader, "Gibbs Backs $2.5 Million Boys' Home," *Washington Post,* May. 3, 1984.

105 **"Their life is in . . .":** Tonya Brown, "Former NFL Coach Shares Message with Prisoners," CarolinaLive.com, Sept. 21, 2010.

105 **"I didn't want to . . .":** Bobby Beathard, May 28, 2014.

106 **"It was just amazing . . .":** Ibid.

107 **"sad-sack people":** Dexter Manley with Tom Friend, *Educating Dexter* (Nashville, TN: Rutledge Hill Press, 1992), p. 25.

107 **"was the apple of my daddy's eye":** Ibid., p. 28.

107 **"I was just a scared . . .":** Ibid., p. 26.

108 **"The scouts had some . . .":** Bill Brubaker, "Dexter Manley: Facing Realities, Testing Limits," *Washington Post,* May 10, 1987.

108 **"I talked to Dexter . . .":** "Okla. St. Under Scrutiny," *Chicago Tribune,* May 15, 1978.

108 **"He didn't test well . . .":** Bobby Beathard, May 28, 2014.

109 **"[All] through my grammar . . .":** "Eliminating Illiteracy: S. HRG. 101-260," *United States House of Representatives: Subcommittee on Education, Arts and Humanities,* May 18, 1989.

109 **"I don't ever remember . . .":** Darryl Grant, June 19, 2014.

110 **"He was vicious . . .":** Ken Denlinger, "Manley of the Redskins: Real Name Is Mayhem," *Washington Post,* Sept. 2, 1981.

110 **"He had the biggest . . .":** Joe Gibbs, Nov. 4, 2014.

110 **"That was real special . . .":** Dexter Manley, May 30, 2014.

111 **"Dexter'd get so hyped . . .":** Manley with Friend, *Educating Dexter,* pp. 151–52.

111 **"They are paying me pennies":** Gary Pomerantz, "The Maturing of Manley Grows on Redskins," *Washington Post,* Dec. 29, 1984.

111 **"you shouldn't disrespect . . .":** Manley with Friend, *Educating Dexter,* p. 22.

112 **Cooke was a "miser":** Norman Chad, "WAVA's 'Zoo' Offers Redskins Cameos, Tasteless Humor, Obnoxious Arrogance," *Washington Post,* Aug. 10, 1986.

112 **"A lot of times . . .":** Pomerantz, "The Maturing of Manley."

112 **days into his "test drive":** Pete Cronan, Aug. 30, 2014.

112 **"He was just like . . .":** Charles Mann, June 19, 2014.

112 **"Not so much because . . .":** Bobby Beathard, May 28, 2014.

113 He admired Manley's "big heart": Paul Attner, "Manley's in the Spotlight at Last—and on the Spot," *Washington Post*, Dec. 2, 1982.

113 Manley "reeked of alcohol": Manley with Friend, *Educating Dexter*, p. 170.

113 "Once I started . . .": Dexter Manley, May 30, 2014.

113 "[He] has been going . . .": Christine Brennan, "Manley Charged in Traffic Accident," *Washington Post*, Nov. 1, 1985.

114 "I've probably had . . .": Warner Hessler, "Drug Problems Cost Manley NFL Career," *Newport News (VA) Daily Press*, Nov. 19, 1989.

114 "[They] deserved to win . . .": Donald Huff, "Cooke Gives Rookies Seal of Approval," *Washington Post*, Aug. 25, 1984.

115 "I characterize this . . .": Gary Pomerantz, "Redskins' Playoffs Start with Bears," *Washington Post*, Dec. 30, 1984.

115 "Realistically, we've been dancing . . .": Gary Pomerantz, "Redskins Nurse Wounds, Praise Gibbs," *Washington Post*, Jan. 1, 1985.

115 the Redskins' "bread and butter": "Redskins: Joe Gibbs and the Evolution," *Washington Post*, Sept. 1, 1985.

115 "Gibbs turned his back . . .": Thomas Boswell, "Redskins' Future Rests on a Crisis of Judgment," *Washington Post*, Jan. 2, 1985.

116 "I don't have to . . .": "Redskins' Gibbs Angered by Criticism," *Washington Post*, Jan. 3, 1985.

116 "People turn on you . . .": Pomerantz, "Redskins Joe Gibbs and the Evolution."

116 Gibbs was "more laid-back": Ibid.

116 "If there's a change . . .": Ibid.

116 "I've heard people say . . .": Ibid.

117 "It's like the theory . . .": Ibid.

117 "you'll have to prove yourself": Christine Brennan and Leonard Shapiro, "Redskins Waiver Murphy, Safety Talking with Bills," *Washington Post*, July 13, 1985.

118 "It's hard for a player . . .": Ibid.

118 "In other folks' circumstance . . .": Gary Pomerantz, "Washington Says Little, But Anger Is Apparent," *Washington Post*, May 3, 1985.

119 "It was a tough . . .": Ibid.

119 "He's a heck of a back . . .": Christine Brennan, "Redskins Tell Rogers He Could Be the One," *Washington Post*, Apr. 27, 1985.

119 "It's a second chance . . .": Christine Brennan, "Rogers Should Earn Near $450,000, Attorney Says," *Washington Post*, Apr. 26, 1985.

119 **"That was brutal . . .":** Gary Pomerantz, "Thielemann Stands to Be Latest Loss," *Washington Post,* Oct. 1, 1985.

120 **"I am amazed that we are . . .":** Christine Brennan, "Redskins Are Thinking Playoffs, and Cowboys Are in Their Way," *Washington Post,* Nov. 10, 1985.

120 **"It seemed like we . . .":** Cooper Rollow, "Redskins Are Thrown for Loss by Cowboys," *Chicago Tribune,* Nov. 11, 1985.

120 **"Joe had struggled . . .":** Charley Casserly, June 19, 2014.

121 **"You motherfuckers . . .":** Lawrence Taylor with Steve Serby, *L.T.: Over the Edge* (New York: HarperTorch, 2003), p. 87.

121 **"I heard a *pow pow* . . .":** Ibid., pp. 87–88.

121 **"Theismann's my man":** "Theismann Says He Will Be Back Next Season," *Los Angeles Times,* Nov. 23, 1985.

122 **"some women will . . .":** "Congresswoman Reverses Regan Remark in Jest," *Boston Globe,* Nov. 22, 1985.

122 **"On Tuesday, I had lunch . . .":** Ibid.

123 **"That was bigger . . .":** Gary Pomerantz, May 30, 2014.

123 **"The criticism prior . . .":** Christine Brennan, "Theismann Anticipating '86 Return," *Washington Post,* Nov. 23, 1985.

124 **"I don't care to see . . .":** Ibid.

124 **Theismann watched, "on a little . . .":** Joe Theismann with Dave Kindred, *Theismann* (Chicago: Contemporary Books, 1987), p. 26.

124 **"That certainly was . . .":** George Usher, "Schroeder Gets Encore Chance," *Newsday,* Nov. 23, 1985.

124 **"This game is for Joe!":** Michael Wilbon and Gary Pomerantz, "Redskins' Theismann Injured, Lost for the Season," *Washington Post,* Nov. 19, 1985.

125 **"For a guy who never . . .":** Christine Brennan, "Schroeder Leads Washington, 23-21," *Washington Post,* Nov. 19, 1985.

125 **"Schroeder was great":** "Theismann Lost for the Season; Redskins Win," *Los Angeles Times,* Nov. 19, 1985.

125 **"I don't like having . . .":** Sam Smith, "Hanifan's Out; Skins Still Alive," *Chicago Tribune,* Dec. 22, 1985.

125 **"I was worried . . .":** "Rogers Keeps 'Skins' Playoff Hopes Alive," *Orlando Sentinel,* Dec. 22, 1985.

126 **"Usually when he fumbles . . .":** Smith, "Hanifan's Out."

126 **"We finished strong":** "Giants Gain Playoffs; 'Skins Stay Alive," *Chicago Daily Herald,* Dec. 22, 1985.

6. THE CLASSIC-STYLE QUARTERBACK

127 **"He was widely considered . . .":** Shirley Povich, "George Preston Marshall: No Boredom or Blacks Allowed," in *Redskins: A History of Washington's Team* (Washington, D.C..: Washington Post Books, 1997), p. 16.

127 **"Fight for Old D.C.":** "This Morning with Shirley Povich," *Washington Post*, July 26, 1959.

128 **"ineligible for the Redskins . . .":** Ibid., Sept. 26, 1960.

128 **"[Marshall] did not pretend . . .":** Andy Piascik, *Gridiron Gauntlet* (Lanham, MD: Taylor Trade Publishing, 2009), p. 5.

128 **"Well, through no fault . . .":** Dave Brady, "Marshall Given Edict by Udall," *Washington Post*, Dec. 1, 1961.

128 **"I won't play . . .":** Povich, *Redskins*, p. 17.

129 **"I've played Bobby . . .":** Dave Brady, " 'You Blink Your Eyes, Bobby Mitchell Is Gone,' " *Washington Post*, Oct. 29, 1962.

129 **"There was a belief . . .":** Phil Sheridan, "Black Quarterbacks Have Long, Controversial History in NFL," *Knight Ridder Tribune News Service*, Jan. 30, 2004.

130 **"I played well enough," . . . :** Ibid.

130 **"I used to see . . .":** Jane Leavy, "The Widening World of Doug Williams," *Washington Post*, Sept. 20, 1987.

130 **"Even Sealtest thought . . .":** Robert Williams, June 25, 2014.

131 **"The guy said . . .":** Leo McClure, Sept. 26, 2014.

131 **"because there were people . . .":** Ibid.

131 **"He struck out . . .":** Leo McClure, Sept. 26, 2014.

131 **"Doug did not want . . .":** Robert Williams, June 25, 2014.

132 **"There were only . . .":** Doug Williams, June 19, 2014.

132 **"In 1973, playing . . .":** Ibid.

133 **National sportswriters . . . "black Joe Namath":** Skip Bayless, "A Black Hope at Quarterback," *Los Angeles Times,* Nov. 23, 1977.

133 **whom he called "Gossie May":** Ibid.

134 **"He was always . . .":** Herbert Nelson, Sept. 22, 2014.

134 **"As a kid, eighteen . . .":** Ibid.

134 **"I haven't found . . .":** O. K. Davis, "Williams: The Heisman Chase," *Ruston (LA) Daily Leader*, Dec. 8, 1977.

135 **"Code for 'We weren't . . .' ":** Sam Smith, "Redskins' Williams a Survivor," *Chicago Tribune*, Jan. 6, 1988.

135 **"I'm not talking . . .":** Bayless, "A Black Hope at Quarterback."

135 **"I knew this, being drafted . . .":** Doug Williams, June 19, 2014.

136 **"He's the best black . . .":** "What They're Saying About Doug Williams," *Ruston (LA) Daily Leader,* Dec. 8, 1977.

136 **"I put things on the board . . .":** Dave Krieger, "Redskins' Williams Still Remembers Where He's From," *Chicago Tribune,* Sept. 2, 1988.

136 **"Coach Gibbs and . . .":** Doug Williams, June 19, 2014.

137 **"It's like Coach Rob . . .":** Dave Anderson, "Doug Williams Is Happy . . . But," *New York Times,* May 11, 1978.

137 **"After each day . . .":** Doug Williams, June 19, 2014.

137 **"The so-called general manager . . .":** Jimmie Giles, Sept. 29, 2014.

138 **"Twice, Wiliams called . . .":** "Bucs close to elite—McKay," *Frederick News Post,* Jan 8, 1980.

138 **"They ought to send . . .":** Bruce Keidan, "Williams's Only Wish Is to Be Winning QB," *Pittsburgh Post-Gazette,* Jan. 28, 1988.

138 **hateful notes, "nigger letters":** Krieger, "Redskins' Williams Still Remembers."

138 **"A number of things . . .":** Robert Williams, June 25, 2014.

139 **"At that time . . .":** Jimmie Giles, Sept. 29, 2014.

139 **"Suddenly, I didn't give . . .":** Brian Hewitt, "Williams Says He's Just the Starter," *Los Angeles Times,* Jan. 28, 1988.

139 **"He took it really hard . . .":** Dave Sell, "Williams: 'I Didn't Give Up,'" *Washington Post,* Aug. 15, 1986.

140 **"You're not going . . .":** Doug Williams, June 19, 2014.

140 **Williams "hadn't been in town . . .":** Ibid.

140 **"No, Phil":** Ibid.

141 **"What was good . . .":** Ibid.

141 **"It wasn't about . . .":** Doug Williams, June 19, 2014.

141 **"outside of Jim Kelly . . .":** "Redskins Acquire Rights to Doug Williams, Agree to Terms with 3 Ex-USFL Players," *Los Angeles Times,* Aug. 12, 1986.

142 **"They told me I . . .":** Sell, "Williams: 'I Didn't Give Up.'"

142 **"The classic-style quarterback":** Christine Brennan, "Schroeder Has the Tools, Does the Job," *Washington Post,* Dec. 4, 1986.

142 **"I didn't make it . . .":** Paul Zimmerman, "Lookin' Super, D.C.," *Sports Illustrated,* Dec. 1, 1986.

143 **"When I left baseball . . .":** Bob Oates, "He's Passing a 'Skin Test," *Los Angeles Times,* Sept. 13, 1986.

143 "I got very little . . .": Ron Borges, "Redskins' Schroeder Strikes Out on His Own," *Boston Globe*, Aug. 10, 1986.

143 "I remember Bobby . . .": Billy Devaney, May 27, 2014.

143 "He's a real talented . . .": Mark Heisler, "Schroeder Brings Redskins Back, 14–9," *Los Angeles Times*, Aug. 19, 1985.

144 "It was funny because . . .": Jay Schroeder, May 19, 2014.

144 "almost got killed": Jane Leavy, "Jay Schroeder and the Passing Show," *Washington Post*, Nov. 21, 1986.

144 "Things change quickly": Borges, "Redskins' Schroeder Strikes Out."

145 "They're dead wrong . . .": *Sports Illustrated*, Jan. 13, 1986, p. 42.

145 "When you're not around . . .": Christine Brennan, "At Minicamp, Theismann Was Odd Man Out," *Washington Post*, May 18, 1986.

145 "if a miracle does occur": Christine Brennan, "Theismann Is Keeping Door Open," *Washington Post*, July 30, 1986.

145 "Based on what . . .": Ibid.

146 "It hasn't gotten . . .": Norman Chad, "Theismann: Mind Willing, Leg Too Weak," *Washington Post*, Nov. 27, 1986.

146 "He only wants to go . . .": Christine Brennan, "Goodbye, But Is It Farewell?" *Washington Post*, Dec. 15, 1985.

146 "I ain't hanging . . .": Gary Reinmuth, "Angry Riggins: 'I'm Not Retiring,'" *Chicago Tribune*, Dec. 14, 1985.

147 "It's been formidable": Jane Leavy, "Owooga! Riggins on a Roll," *Washington Post*, Dec. 29, 1984.

147 "Come on, Sandy . . .": Elizabeth Kastor, "John Riggins' Big Sleep," *Washington Post*, Feb. 1, 1985.

147 "It would take . . .": Reinmuth, "Angry Riggins."

147 "The truth is . . .": Ibid.

148 "I would like to . . .": Gary Pomerantz and Bill Brubaker, "Riggins Says Redskins Have Released Him," *Washington Post*, Mar. 19, 1986.

148 "I'll wait and see . . .": Ibid.

148 "I think everybody . . .": Christine Brennan, "Today in Carlisle, Redskins Begin Their Season of Change," *Washington Post*, July 20, 1986.

148 "Schroeder could throw . . .": Jerry Rhome, May 30, 2014.

149 "Whenever we were practicing . . .": Oates, "He's Passing a 'Skin Test."

149 "I'm very surprised . . .": Bill Fleischerman, "Bryant's 2 TDs Killed the Birds Softly," *Philadelphia Daily News*, Sept. 8, 1986

149 *Sports Illustrated* noted . . . "Washington Redskins . . .":
      Zimmerman, "Lookin' Super, D.C."

150 "Right now, he . . .": Brennan, "Schroeder Has the Tools."

150 "I think you change . . .": Christine Brennan, "On Offense, the
      Redskins Think Big and Look Long," *Washington Post*, Nov. 8, 1986.

150 "It's like a pitcher . . .": Brennan, "Schroeder Has the Tools."

151 "probably the most . . .": Phil Hersh, "Schroeder: A Sudden
      Winner," *Chicago Tribune*, Jan. 2, 1987.

151 "The most impressive . . .": Phil Hersh, "Schroeder Stays Cool
      Under Fire," *Chicago Tribune*, Jan. 4, 1987.

151 "If you were drawing . . .": Hersh, "Schroeder: A Sudden Winner."

152 "That was probably . . .": Doug Williams, June 19, 2014.

152 "I asked him . . .": Christine Brennan, "Redskins Are Likely to
      Make Changes to Bolster Defense," *Washington Post*, Jan. 13, 1987.

152 "It's kind of tough": "Ex-Buc Williams restless; Wants to Start for a
      Winner," *St. Petersburg Times*, May 13, 1987.

7. GUT FEELINGS

153 "I'm happy, not . . .": Doug Williams, June 18, 2014.

154 "Douglas," Gibbs said . . . : Ibid.

154 "At that time, I knew . . .": Ibid.

154 "Coach is one . . .": Ibid.

154 "Bible was on the desk": Ibid.

155 "I came out as a favor . . .": Christine Brennan, "Schroeder Shows
      Up at Minicamp," *Washington Post*, May 12, 1987.

156 "Success hasn't changed . . .": David Ginsburg, "Schroeder's Fortunes
      on the Rise," *Harrisonburg (VA) Daily News-Record*, July 28, 1987.

156 "I think he's going . . .": "Schroeder's 3-Year Deal Pays at Least $2.7
      Million," *Frederick (MD) News-Post*, July 28, 1987.

157 "When I first got . . .": *America's Game: 1987 Redskins*, NFL Films.

157 "I just hope some . . .": "Williams Comes Off Bench to Lead
      'Skins," *Orlando Sentinel*, Sept. 14, 1987.

157 "That was the worst-looking . . .": Thomas Boswell, "Atkinson's
      Season Clouded by Injury," *Washington Post*, Sept. 14, 1987.

157 "Right now," Gibbs said: Ibid.

157 "That's exactly why . . .": Ray Didinger, "Skins' Williams: From
      Mothballs to Game Ball," *Chicago Tribune*, Sept. 15, 1987.

158 "We had some tough . . .": "Falcons Stun Redskins, 21-20," *Annapolis (MD) Capital*, Sept. 21, 1987.

158 "In training camp . . .": Charley Casserly, June 19, 2014.

159 "The guys inside . . ." : Christine Brennan and Dave Sell, "Confrontations, Defections for Redskins," *Washington Post*, Sept. 24, 1987.

160 "the most dynamic . . .": Sharon Robb, "Vols Qb Can't Stay Away from Scrapes," *South Florida Sun-Sentinel*, Oct. 12, 1985.

160 "I think they were . . .": John McGregor, July 28, 2014.

161 "they'd never seen . . .": Ibid.

161 "I'm just going through . . .": Charley Casserly, June 19, 2014.

161 "I know there were . . .": Bobby Beathard, May 28, 2014.

162 "Tony Robinson, bless . . .": Jerry Rhome, May 30, 2014.

163 "Jerry, that was awful": Ibid.

163 "They can put an asterisk . . .": Christine Brennan, "Replacement Redskins Have Their Day, 28-21," *Washington Post*, Oct. 5, 1987.

163 "It was really different . . .": Joe Gibbs, Nov. 4, 2014.

164 "We have compromised . . .": Christine Brennan, "Redskins Vote to Continue Striking," *Washington Post*, Oct. 14, 1987.

164 "I've just never been . . .": Ibid.

164 "If we have to . . .": Bob Hill, "20 Days of Wasting Time Is Costing Everyone," *South Florida Sun-Sentinel*, Oct. 11, 1987.

165 "We knew that we . . .": Charles Mann, June 19, 2014.

165 "Joe [Gibbs] said to . . .": Michael Wilbon, "When Gibbs Is at His Best," *Washington Post*, Dec. 28, 2007.

165 "What you're always . . .": Joe Gibbs, Nov. 4, 2014.

165 "[Jeff Bostic] told me . . .": Steve Buckhantz, Mar. 4, 2015.

166 "Think about this": Joe Gibbs, Nov. 4, 2014.

167 "All of a sudden . . .": Jerry Rhome, May 30, 2014.

167 "Have you got him ready?": Ibid.

167 Playing . . . "backyard football": Ibid.

168 "Because all those . . .": Joker Phillips, Nov. 20, 2014.

168 "This is one of . . .": Christine Brennan, "For Replacements, 'It Will Never Be Like This Again,'" *Washington Post*, Oct. 21, 1987.

169 "I sensed they were . . .": Tom Friend, Oct. 9, 2014.

169 "We want the scabs!": Ron Borges, "Redskins Manage to Stumble Over Jets," *Boston Globe*, Oct. 26, 1987.

169 **"We weren't real sharp . . .":** "Crowded at Top in AFC East—4 Tied for 1st," *Orlando Sentinel*, Oct. 26, 1987.

170 **"It shocked me," said tackle . . . :** Tom Friend, "Teammates Refuse to Take Sides," *Washington Post*, Nov. 16, 1987.

170 **"I may have rushed . . .":** Christine Brennan, "Quarterback Switch Creates Stir," *Washington Post*, Nov. 16, 1987.

170 **"You might as well . . .":** "Williams Replaces Schroeder, Sparks Redskins Over Lions," *Chicago Tribune*, Nov. 16, 1987.

171 **Much . . . "body language":** Christine Brennan, "Three Men and a Controversy; At Redskin Park," *Washington Post*, Nov. 22, 1987.

171 **"Jay may have lost . . .":** Charley Casserly, June 19, 2014.

171 **"always reluctant to change . . .":** Brennan, "Quarterback Switch Creates Stir."

171 **"The players and some . . .":** Doug Williams, June 19, 2014.

171 **"You look at Doug . . .":** Joe Jacoby, Mar. 31, 2014.

172 **"Doug Williams was playing . . .":** Tom Friend, "Monk's Hands-On Experiences in End Zone Are Rare Failures," *Washington Post*, Nov. 24, 1987.

172 **"Timing's bad," Williams said:** Tom Friend, "Redskins' Williams Injured, May Miss Giants Game," *Washington Post*, Nov. 27, 1987.

173 **"He has a great . . .":** George Willis, "Schroeder Bids to Reclaim Job," *Newsday*, Nov. 30, 1987.

173 **"team is getting . . .":** "Schroeder Gets Hot and Burns the Giants," *Los Angeles Times*, Nov. 30, 1987.

173 **"I felt like that . . .":** Willis, "Schroeder Bids to Reclaim Job."

173 **"It was Coach Gibbs's . . .":** Christine Brennan, "Gibbs: Schroeder Will Be Starter Against Cardinals," *Washington Post*, Dec. 1, 1987.

173 **"We admired the way . . .":** Christine Brennan, "Williams Sees His Future," *Washington Post*, Dec. 18, 1987.

173 **"We watch you . . .":** Ibid.

174 **"[Gibbs] is going to . . .":** Ibid.

174 **"I think the main . . .":** Tom Friend, "Redskins, Vikings: A Meaningful Test," *Washington Post*, Dec. 26, 1987.

175 **"Jay is a big-play . . .":** Will McDonough, "With Schroeder, Redskins Go Off the Deep End," *Boston Globe*, Nov. 4, 1986.

175 **"bad habits" that cost him:** Christine Brennan, "Gibbs Will Not Rush Naming Quarterback," *Washington Post*, Dec. 28, 1987.

175 **"[You'd] prefer not . . .":** Dennis Brackin, "For the Redskins, Quarterback Shuffle System Works," *Minneapolis Star Tribune,* Dec. 27, 1987.

175 **"I never thought . . .":** Ken Denlinger, "Gibbs: Fresh Ideas in the Crunch," *Washington Post,* Dec. 27, 1987.

176 **"Guys just gravitated . . .":** Raleigh McKenzie, Feb. 11, 2014.

176 **"I think, right now . . .":** Tom Friend, "Schroeder Gets the Hook, Then Helps Redskins Off It," *Washington Post,* Dec. 27, 1987.

177 **"There's just something . . .":** Christine Brennan, "Williams Brings Relief to Redskins, 27-24," *Washington Post,* Dec. 27, 1987.

177 **"We'll make our quarterback . . .":** Brennan, "Gibbs Will Not Rush Naming Quarterback."

8. TURNABOUT

178 **"I think everybody . . .":** Jeff Bostic, Mar. 24, 2014.

179 **"we can get by . . .":** Christine Brennan, "Sevier to Leave Redskins," *Washington Post,* Jan. 29, 1987.

180 **"Our special teams . . .":** Christine Brennan, "Redskins Can't Overcome Rams' Charge, 30-26," *Washington Post,* Nov. 24, 1987.

180 **Urged . . . "just be patient":** *America's Game: 1987 Redskins,* NFL Films.

181 **"I mean it," Bugel said:** Tom Friend, "Redskins Draw a Steady Offensive Line," *Washington Post,* Dec. 10, 1987.

181 **Rogers had "lost a step":** Tom Friend, "Rogers 'Lost a Step' But Still May Get the Chance to Run," *Washington Post,* Dec. 1, 1987.

181 **"[He's] not the answer . . .":** Tom Friend, "Rogers Says Riggins 'Ought to Keep His Mouth Shut,' " *Washington Post,* Dec. 17, 1987.

182 **"probably just to get attention":** Ibid.

182 **"If I have to sit out . . .":** Christine Brennan, "Redskins' Monk Not Optimistic on Return," *Washington Post,* Dec. 30, 1987.

182 **"The potential of a . . .":** Christine Brennan, "Redskins Still Don't Know If They're Good," *Washington Post,* Jan. 5, 1988.

183 **"the best strong safety . . .":** Tom Friend, "Clark Garners Praise for His Ability, Intensity, Attire," *Washington Post,* Dec. 14, 1987.

184 **"[Darrell] Green's helped . . .":** Robert Sansevere, "Skins' Wilburn Hopes to Corner Accolades," *Chicago Tribune,* Jan. 8, 1988.

184 **"I've done everything . . .":** "Team Has Little Faith in Cowboys," *Minneapolis Star Tribune,* Dec. 27, 1987.

185   **"He never gave up"**: Ralph Wiley, "Born to Be a Champion," *Sports Illustrated,* Aug. 8, 1988.

185   **"We saw some games ..."**: Tom Friend, "Wilburn Turns the Corner," *Washington Post,* Dec. 16, 1987.

185   **"I think I have ..."**: Ibid.

186   **"We bring out the ..."**: Mike Kiley, "Gault Matchup Adds Dash of Excitement," *Chicago Tribune,* Jan. 10, 1988.

186   **"I'm just trying to ..."**: Mike Kiley, "Ditka's Memory Racing: Gault Back for Kickoffs," *Chicago Tribune,* Jan. 7, 1988.

187   **"He should have been ..."**: Kirk Mee, June 18, 2014.

187   **"You put him back ..."**: Joe Gibbs, Nov. 4, 2014.

188   **"I decided that ..."**: Elmer Smith, "Redskins Get Much in Return from Green," *Philadelphia Daily News,* Jan. 11, 1988.

188   **"[The injury] is very ..."**: Christine Brennan, "Gibbs: Green Probably, Monk Doubtful for Vikings," *Washington Post,* Jan. 12, 1988.

189   **"When you have parents ..."**: Wiley, "Born to Be a Champion."

189   **"Pregame, I said ..."**: Doug Williams, June 19, 2014.

190   **"[Williams's] second quarter ..."**: Gary Mihoces, " 'Skins, Broncos Move on Up," *USA Today,* Jan. 11, 1988.

191   **"I think the best way ..."**: Steve Aschburner, "The Mystery," *Minneapolis Star Tribune,* Jan. 14, 1988.

191   **"Our game plan against ..."**: Steve Aschburner, "Redskins Mix Up Alignments to Win 'Critical Matchups,'" *Minneapolis Star Tribune,* Jan. 18, 1988.

191   **"They were never in ..."**: Ibid.

192   **chanted, "Bring in Jay!"**: David Steele, "Washington Closes Door on Minnesota 17-10," *St. Petersburg Times,* Jan. 18, 1988.

192   **"I was worried ..."**: Ibid.

192   **"You can kind of tell ..."**: Scott Ostler, "Why Williams? Why Wait? It Was Time," *Los Angeles Times,* Jan. 18, 1988.

192   **"it would have been ..."**: Ira Berkow, "Williams Makes His Point," *New York Times,* Jan. 18, 1988.

193   **"It was getting pretty ..."**: Robbie Andreu, "Redskins' Clark Pushes Talk About Speed to the Limit," *South Florida Sun-Sentinel,* Jan. 18, 1988.

193   **"With Gary Clark,"** ...: Jay Weiner, "Clark Comes Through with Pair of Big Catches After First-Half Flub," *Minneapolis Star Tribune,* Jan. 18, 1988.

193 "Doug was struggling . . .": Andreu, "Redskins' Clark Pushes Talk."

193 "I was praying . . .": Don Pierson, "Williams's Key Passes Foil Vikings," *Chicago Tribune*, Jan. 18, 1988.

194 "I know it was tense . . .": Christine Brennan, "Super in the Crunch: Redskins, 17-10," *Washington Post*, Jan. 18, 1988.

194 "It's the ultimate . . .": Peter Alfano, "Williams Feels Weight of Role,'" *New York Times*, Jan. 19, 1988.

194 Although he "just rode . . .": "Williams Feels Like 17," *USA Today*, Jan. 19, 1988.

194 "I'm just glad . . .": Molly Sinclair, "King Honored in 'A Day to Live the Dream,'" *Washington Post*, Jan. 19, 1988.

195 "It was no big thing": Art Levy, "Icon: Doug Williams," *Florida Trend*, Jan. 2009.

195 "the black quarterback issue": Michael Wilbon, "Questions No Match for Williams's Aplomb," *Washington Post*, Jan. 30, 1988.

195 "personal forum": Ibid.

195 "I'm not playing this . . .": Bill Parrillo, "'Skins Break Broncos for Super Bowl Title," *Providence Journal*, Feb. 1, 1988.

195 "patently racist overtones": Steve Fryer, "Snyder Tenure Quietly Ends," *Orange County Register*, Jan. 18, 1988.

196 "I'm not uncomfortable . . .": Don Pierson, "Williams Finds It Boring," *Chicago Tribune*, Jan. 27, 1988.

196 "No, no. I anticipated . . .": Wilbon, "Questions No Match."

196 "For about twenty minutes . . .": Jack Wilkinson, "Reporter Wants to Put an End to a Modern-Day Urban Legend," *Atlanta Journal-Constitution*, Jan. 25, 2000.

196 "How long have you . . .": Jim Murray, "Williams: He's Also a Quarterback," *Los Angeles Times*, Jan. 31, 1988.

197 "I gave them that . . .": "'Skins' Secondary Burned, Then Tosses Water on Broncos' Passing Attack," *Orlando Sentinel*, Feb. 1, 1988.

198 "The field was very . . .": Robert Sansevere, "Sanders Dream Day Creates Nightmare for Broncos," *Minneapolis Star Tribune*, Feb. 1, 1988.

199 "I didn't know if . . .": Leigh Montville, "Story with a Twist," *Boston Globe*, Feb. 1, 1988.

199 "Jerry, they'd have . . .": Jerry Rhome, May 30, 2014.

199 "I wouldn't have . . .": Doug Williams, Sept. 29, 2014.

200 "It's the only . . .": Jeff Bostic, Mar. 24, 2014.

200 "He puts his finger . . .": Ibid.

201 "I was slipping . . .": Dave Distel, "Sanders Pulls Switch and Gets Back on His Feet," *Los Angeles Times*, Feb. 1, 1988.

201 "[Haynes] came up . . .": Ricky Sanders, June 1, 2014.

202 "I think more than . . .": Bill Plaschke, "This One Smarts," *Los Angeles Times*, Feb. 1, 1988.

202 "We never ran . . .": Mark Rypien, Feb. 21, 2014.

203 . . . was "a little iffy": Christine Brennan, "Redskins Say Rogers Will Start," *Washington Post*, Jan. 30, 1988.

203 "My role is the same . . .": Ibid.

203 The "cheap shot" tore: Ron Borges, "Running Toward a Dream," *Boston Globe*, Jan. 31, 1988.

204 "I never thought . . .": " 'Headshot of Tim Smith . . .' He's a Tough," *St. Louis Post-Dispatch*, Jan. 29, 1988.

204 "One of the coaches . . .": Bobby Beathard, May 28, 2014.

204 ordered him to "stop eating": " 'Headshot of Tim Smith . . .' He's a Tough," *St. Louis Post-Dispatch*, Jan. 29, 1988.

204 "Bobby Beathard is always . . .": Ibid.

204 "George would give . . .": Timmy Smith, June 27, 2014.

204 "I was just waiting . . .": Ibid.

205 "I don't think I . . .": George Willis, "On a Treadmill," *Newsday*, Jan. 15, 1988.

205 "We wanted him . . .": Bob Hill, "Smith: Nothing to Fear But Fear Itself," *South Florida Sun-Sentinel*, Feb. 1, 1988.

205 "Hey, Timmy," Williams told: Doug Williams, June 19, 2014.

206 "That's when my plays . . .": Redskins.com, Redskins Chronicles, "18 Plays: The Story of Super Bowl XXII."

206 Dubbed "the Cutback King": Bob Hill, "Rushing Roulette GM's Gamble Pays," *South Florida Sun-Sentinel*, Jan. 30, 1988.

207 "I close my eyes . . .": Thomas Bonk, "Footnotes to History," *Los Angeles Times*, Jan. 27, 1993.

207 "We must have run . . .": Jerry Rhome, May 30, 2014.

208 "Them boys up front . . .": Doug Williams, June 19, 2014.

208 "Everybody says the holes . . .": Timmy Smith, June 27, 2014.

209 "[Joe Gibbs] took me out . . .": Samuel Adams, "He'll Forever Carry a Super Burden," *Denver Post*, Dec. 5, 1993.

209 "All week long . . .": Gary Mihoces and Ben Brown, "Williams Named MVP; Earns Place in Record, and History, Books," *USA Today*, Feb. 1, 1988.

209 **"I'm going to Disneyland":** Montville, "Story with a Twist."

210 **"I'll be staying at home . . .":** Earl McRae, "Gibbs's Family the Real Winners," *Ottawa Citizen*, Feb. 1, 1988.

210 **"He said it was . . .":** Doug Williams, June 19, 2014.

211 **"This is the performance . . .":** "Williams Did What Ex-Coach Expected," *Montreal Gazette*, Feb. 1, 1988.

9. USHERED OUT

212 **"The most satisfying . . .":** Leonard Shapiro and Christine Brennan, "Most Satisfying Victory," *Washington Post*, Feb. 1, 1988.

213 **"Failing that," Cook told:** John Lancaster, "Barry Mum on Cooke Threat to Move Redskins to the Suburbs," *Washington Post*, Feb. 5, 1988.

213 **"The Redskins are . . .":** "Cooke Only Profits Emotionally from Team," *Toronto Globe and Mail*, Feb. 8, 1988.

214 **"It was like a seated . . .":** George Will, Aug. 27, 2014.

214 **"Jack would get . . .":** Lesley Stahl, Aug. 11, 2014.

214 **"He would snap . . .":** Ibid.

215 **"The box was crazy . . .":** Bobby Beathard, May 28, 2014.

215 **"Washington is a town . . .":** George Will, Aug. 27, 2014.

215 **In 1981 . . . "long considered . . .":** Red Smith, "Power, If Not Glory, Fills Box at Redskins Game," *New York Times*, Oct. 6, 1981.

215 **"Getting a seat . . .":** Paul Attner, June 5, 2014.

216 **Helms remarked, "Iran? Iraq? . . .":** Dave Kindred, "The Redskins' Joe Gibbs Has Same Size Hat," *Atlanta Journal-Constitution*, Jan. 17, 1988.

217 **"I haven't seen it . . .":** "600,000 Faithful Jam Street to Hail Super Bowl Champs," *Montreal Gazette*, Feb. 4, 1988.

217 **"Somebody's going to . . .":** Marc Fisher, "Redskins Hailed in Super Rally," *Washington Post*, Feb. 4, 1988.

217 **"We want Doug! . . .":** "Washington Hails the Champions," Ben A. Franklin, *New York Times*, Feb. 4, 1988.

217 **"I consider myself . . .":** Ibid.

217 **"could have been given . . .":** Ibid.

217 **"There probably isn't . . .":** William C. Rhoden, *Third and a Mile* (New York: ESPN Books, 2007), p. 146.

218 **"All of this pride . . .":** Dr. Charles Ross, Mar. 3, 2015.

219 **"When you fell down . . .":** Courtland Milloy, "Doug Williams Scores with Howard Discourse," *Washington Post*, Feb. 5, 1988.

219 **"gave new meaning . . ."**: "Reagan, D.C. Fete Redskins," *St. Louis Post-Dispatch*, Feb. 4, 1988.

219 **"recently showed the world . . ."**: Remarks Congratulating the Washington Redskins on Winning Super Bowl XXII, Feb. 3, 1988, Public Papers of the President: Ronald Reagan.

219 **"This is a long ways . . ."**: Ibid.

219 **"Where's Ricky Sanders?"**: Ibid.

220 **"Here I am in a suit . . ."**: Ricky Sanders, June 1, 2014.

220 **"a happy belated birthday"**: Remarks Congratulating the Washington Redskins on Winning Super Bowl XXII, Feb. 3, 1988, Public Papers of the President: Ronald Reagan.

220 **"I came up with . . ."**: Ibid.

220 **"Hey, Mr. President . . ."**: "Manley Is Usual Manley," *Los Angeles Times*, Feb. 4, 1988.

221 **"Thank God I'm not . . ."**: Tom Friend, "Redskins Huddle at White House," *Washington Post*, Feb. 4, 1988.

221 **"has the IQ of a grapefruit"**: Mike Kiley, "Ditka's Memory Racing: Gault Back for Kickoffs," *Chicago Tribune*, Jan. 7, 1988.

221 **"We thought Dexter played . . ."**: Washington Redskins 1988 Press Guide, p. 92.

221 **"Dexter, you're going . . ."**: Michael Wilbon, "Manley and Washington: Once a Hero, Always . . . ," *Washington Post*, Nov. 25, 1990.

222 **"Now, all the dumb stuff . . ."**: Bill Brubaker, "Dexter Manley: Facing Realities, Testing Limits," *Washington Post*, May 10, 1987.

222 **"I started taking three . . ."**: Dexter Manley, May 30, 2014.

222 **"Shoot, I took the test . . ."**: Dexter Manley with Tom Friend, *Educating Dexter* (Nashville, TN: Rutledge Hill Press, 1992), p. 242.

223 **"I think, obviously . . ."**: "Dexter Manley's Future Now in His Own Hands," *Los Angeles Times*, Aug. 14, 1988.

223 **"I think we're getting . . ."**: Michael Wilbon, "Rozelle Defends Suspensions of 8 for Substance Abuse," *Washington Post*, Aug. 18, 1988.

223 **"I'm just going to comply . . ."**: "Dexter Manley's Future Now."

224 **"We did more than . . ."**: Christine Brennan, "Gibbs: Expulsion May Help Manley," *Washington Post*, Nov. 19, 1989.

224 **"I went to a basketball . . ."**: "Inside Corner: By Harry Readel, Sports Editor," *Roswell (NM) Daily Record*, Feb. 7, 1988.

224 **"preliminary feelers"**: Tom Friend, "These Redskins Simply Do Not Sell," *Washington Post,* Apr. 19, 1988.

224 **"We're concerned we . . ."**: Tom Friend, "Smith Opens as Starter," *Washington Post,* July 19, 1988.

225 **"he looked like . . ."**: Charles Mann, June 19, 2014.

225 **"We have to put . . ."**: Patricia Stone, "Smith Promises He'll Hang On," *Washington Post,* Aug. 28, 1988.

225 **"It's tough for me . . ."**: "Morris Promoted at Running Back," *Washington Post,* Nov. 23, 1988.

225 **"Timmy had so much . . ."**: Doug Williams, June 19, 2014.

226 **"He didn't [have . . ."**: Tom Friend, "Morris, Smith Go in Different Directions," *Washington Post,* Dec. 18, 1988.

226 **"Bobby [Beathard] told me . . ."**: Tim Kawakami, "Dash in the Pan," *Los Angeles Times,* Jan. 19, 1992.

227 **"He was seen with . . ."**: Jill Lieber, "Free-Fall from the Top," *Sports Illustrated,* Jan. 28, 1991.

227 **"Steve Ortmayer, the director . . ."**: Ibid.

227 **"It's amazing, you know"**: Lieber, "Dash in the Pan."

228 **"If you drew up . . ."**: George Willis, "Notes & Quotes," *Newsday,* Oct. 13, 1989.

228 **"It was the same . . ."**: Joanne Ireland, "A Whole New Ball Game for Ex-NFLer," *Edmonton Journal,* July 21, 1993.

229 **"I firmly believe . . ."**: "Cowboys Not an Automatic Win for Gibbs," *Winchester (VA) Star,* Nov. 3, 1989.

229 **"The low point . . ."**: Richard Justice, "No Backing Off from 'The Redskin Way,' Vows Gibbs," *Washington Post,* May 13, 1990.

229 **"It would be hard . . ."**: Ibid.

229 **"was nothing. Just . . ."**: Tom Friend, "Players Hold Meeting to Put Cards on Table," *Washington Post,* Oct. 19, 1989.

229 **"have told certain . . ."**: Tom Friend, "Redskins Decide to Play with Fire," *Washington Post,* Oct. 21, 1989.

229 **"stupid mistakes and penalties"**: Ibid.

229 **"There was a coup . . ."**: Tom Friend, Oct. 27, 2014.

230 **"There's been a . . ."**: "Gibbs to Weigh His Future After Redskins' Season," *Washington Post,* Dec. 5, 1989.

232 **"It's all go"**: Tom Friend, "Gibbs Decides to Return for 10th Season with Redskins," *Washington Post,* Jan. 18, 1990.

232 **"The guy with all . . ."**: Doug Williams, June 19, 2014.

232   **"We've even got . . .":** Kevin Record, "Taking Care of the Folks," *Harrisonburg (VA) Daily News-Record,* June 15, 1984.

232   **"It happened on . . .":** Skip Wood, "At Ease," *Harrisonburg (VA) Daily News-Record,* Nov. 23, 1985.

233   **"Son, if you go . . .":** Bill Millsaps, "Redskins' Clark Gifted, Gutsy, Modest, Too," *Richmond Times-Dispatch,* Nov. 19, 1986.

233   **"He's gutsy," Russ Grimm said:** Ibid.

233   **"Never saw a guy . . .":** Doug Williams, June 19, 2014.

234   **"Some people ridiculed . . .":** Will McDonough, "A Cache from the USFL," *Boston Globe,* Jan. 29, 1988.

235   **"Get your act together . . .":** Christine Brennan, "Backup Receivers Are Special to Redskins," *Washington Post,* Aug. 28, 1987.

235   **"I've always dreamed . . .":** Robert Sansevere, "Sanders' Dream Day Creates Nightmare for Broncos," *Minneapolis Star Tribune,* Feb. 1, 1988.

236   **"They were three . . .":** Doug Williams, June 19, 2014.

236   **"Art's my best friend . . .":** Dave Sell, "Clark Is the One at the Other End," *Washington Post,* Sept. 25, 1986.

236   **"Posse—Monk, Clark . . .":** Tom Friend, "Sanders Shows, Renegotiates a 3-Year Deal," *Washington Post,* July 25, 1989.

236   **"We've got three . . .":** Terry Larimer, "Players, Teams Aren't Helped by 80-Man Limit," *Allentown (PA) Morning Call,* July 30, 1989.

236   **"It's just my nature . . .":** Will Dunham, " 'Skins Receiver Monk Ends Silence," *New Pittsburgh Courier,* Aug. 19, 1989.

237   **"I bet I can . . .":** Vito Stellino, "The Redskins' Quiet Man," *Baltimore Sun,* Oct. 13, 1991.

237   **"I played with . . .":** Charles Mann, June 19, 2014.

238   **"a quiet, gentlemanly man . . .":** Jane Leavy, "After Record-Setting Season, Monk's Life Is Quiet, Studied," *Washington Post,* Jan. 6, 1985.

238   **"He's our leader":** Richard Justice, "Clark, Sanders: It's Better to Receive," *Washington Post,* Jan. 31, 1988.

238   **"He also has difficulty . . .":** Paul Attner, " 'Disappointed' Monk Knows How to Become a Better Receiver," *Washington Post,* Dec. 17, 1981.

238   **"I'm a little disappointed . . .":** Ibid.

239   **"I worked him like . . .":** Terry Metcalf, July 15, 2014.

239   **"You guys want my . . .":** Tom Friend, "Redskins 'Posse' Snubbed in Pro Bowl Selections," *Newport News (VA) Daily Press,* Dec. 21, 1989.

240 **"Doug was a little . . .":** Tony Kornheiser, "All-Shook-Up Redskins Fizzing to What End?" *Washington Post,* Nov. 26, 1988.

240 **"The agony on his . . .":** Redskins.com, Redskins Chronicles, "18 Plays: The Story of Super Bowl XXII."

241 **"I was working late . . .":** Warner Hessler, "Sunday Starts a Bittersweet Triumph for 'Skins QB," *Newport News (VA) Daily Press,* Nov. 2, 1989.

242 **"Most veteran quarterbacks . . .":** "Wounded Redskins Keep Eagles Grounded," *Orlando Sentinel,* Nov. 13, 1989.

242 **"You don't have . . .":** Tom Friend, "Williams Anticipates Tell-All Discussion," *Washington Post,* Dec. 24, 1989.

242 **"I've been thinking . . .":** Doug Williams with Bruce Hunter, "One Phone Call, and No More," *Washington Post,* Sept. 4, 1990.

243 **"I was going to . . .":** Doug Williams, June 19, 2014.

243 **Although "content with my life . . .":** Leonard Shapiro, "For Williams, 'Reality Is a Phone Call Away,'" *Washington Post,* Jan. 24, 1991.

243 **"I grew up wanting . . .":** "Former Redskin Williams Aims for High School Job," *Washington Post,* Jan. 9, 1991.

244 **"I think that in itself . . .":** Doug Williams, June 19, 2014.

244 **"from that day on . . .":** Ibid.

244 **"He proceeded to tell . . .":** Ibid.

244 **"The reason why . . .":** Ibid.

10. GENIUS

246 **"Virtually everything I learned . . .":** Michael Wilbon, "Charley's No Longer the Pupil," *Washington Post,* May 6, 1989.

247 **Casserly told Millen, "The reason . . .":** Charley Casserly, June 19, 2014.

247 **"I think the draft . . .":** Leonard Shapiro, "Casserly Collects on the Dues," *Washington Post,* Jan. 24, 1992.

247 **"They were night . . .":** Billy Devaney, May 27, 2014.

247 **"There's definitely some . . .":** Warner Hessler, "Redskins' GM Likes Conventional Road," *Newport News (VA) Daily Press,* Apr. 22, 1990.

248 **"The draft is my . . .":** Ibid.

248 **"No, no way," Beathard said:** Tom Friend, "Beathard to Resign as Redskins General Manager," *Washington Post,* May 5, 1989.

248 **"Bobby hired Joe . . .":** Billy Devaney, May 27, 2014.

248   "Mike Oliphant was . . .": Tom Friend, May 19, 2014.

248   "an exciting player . . .": Bobby Beathard, May 28, 2014.

249   "I think Gibbs . . .": Tom Friend, Nov. 19, 2014.

249   "I know Bobby was . . .": Richard Justice, "13 Years Later, Casserly Gets His Day," *Washington Post,* Apr. 22, 1990.

249   "I'm on a high . . .": Warner Hessler, "Redskins Go Shopping for Backs," *Newport News (VA) Daily Press,* Apr. 24, 1989.

250   "It was easier . . .": Tom Friend, "Redskins Trade for Riggs, Byner," *Washington Post,* Apr. 24, 1989.

250   "Forty Gut . . .": Ibid.

250   "I don't know . . .": Warner Hessler, "Ghost of Riggins Revived with Acquisition of Riggs," *Newport News (VA) Daily Press,* Apr. 24, 1989.

251   Strangers started to yell "Fumble!": Richard Justice, "Byner Comes to Grips with It," *Washington Post,* Aug. 23, 1990.

251   "I guess some people . . .": Hessler, "Redskins Go Shopping."

251   "That fumble is something . . .": Warner Hessler, "Byner Adds Spirit and Strength to Redskins," *Newport News (VA) Daily Press,* Dec. 20, 1990.

252   "The guy has laid . . .": Vito Stellino, "Gibbs Gives Byner Vote of Confidence," *Baltimore Sun,* Oct. 30, 1990.

252   "I messed up . . .": Earnest Byner, Mar. 20, 2014.

252   "What am I doing wrong?": Ibid.

252   "Therefore, if any man . . .": Richard Justice, "Byner's the Rock in Revitalized Ground Game," *Washington Post,* Aug. 27, 1991.

253   "Really?" Byner asked: Earnest Byner, Mar. 20, 2014.

253   "I grew up in . . .": Justice, "Byner's the Rock."

253   "A team needs . . .": Hessler, "Byner Adds Spirit and Strength."

253   "Last couple years . . .": Tom Friend, "Rypien Wants a Chance to Play—Now," *Washington Post,* May 10, 1988.

254   "I came home . . .": Mark Rypien, Feb. 21, 2014.

254   "Bobby [Beathard] was . . .": Jerry Rhome, May 30, 2014.

254   "We started throwing . . .": Ibid.

256   "Jerry Rhome worked . . .": Doug Williams, June 19, 2014.

256   "No way, there's . . .": Friend, "Rypien Wants a Chance."

256   "Mark isn't the reason . . .": Thomas Boswell, "Positively, a Good Start," *Washington Post,* Sept. 26, 1988.

256   "He was a fantastic . . .": Joe Gibbs, Nov. 4, 2014.

257   "I guess I left . . .": "Mora Says Officials Blew Call," *USA Today,* Sept. 19, 1989.

257 "He had the perfect . . .": Joe Gibbs, Nov. 4, 2014.

257 "He wasn't too much . . .": Raleigh McKenzie, Feb. 11, 2014.

258 "He didn't look confident": Ray Didinger, "Shattering the Old," *Philadelphia Daily News*, Dec. 20, 1991.

258 "He's still learning . . .": Richard Justice, "Redskins Close Book on Moderate Success Story," *Washington Post*, Jan. 14, 1991.

259 "Let's face it," Gibbs said: *America's Game: 1991 Redskins*, NFL Films.

259 "I don't see how . . .": Richard Justice, "Jacoby Leads the Injury Parade," *Washington Post*, Aug. 9, 1991.

259 "I'm not worried . . .": Richard Justice, "Quarterback, Defense Key to Season," *Washington Post*, Aug. 27, 1991.

260 "The only man . . .": Earl Gustkey, "Jiggs Was a Name Fit for a Kings' Broadcaster," *Los Angeles Times*, Apr. 10, 1997.

260 "Branch Rickey was a big . . .": Charley Casserly, June 19, 2014.

261 "Mr. Cooke wanted . . .": Bobby Beathard, May 28, 2014.

261 "Now, if we won . . .": Confidential source.

261 "I had great respect . . .": Joe Gibbs, Nov. 4, 2014.

262 "I'm sitting in . . .": Ibid.

262 "Hey, Mr. Cooke . . .": Ibid.

262 labeled "devout Christians": Randy Rieland and Michael J. Weiss, "God, Gibbs, and the Redskins," *Washingtonian*, Sept. 1992.

262 "Gibbs is so sincere . . .": Ibid.

262 "A lot of guys carried . . .": Brian Mitchell, June 18, 2014.

263 "a squad where almost . . .": Rieland and Weiss, "God, Gibbs, and the Redskins."

263 "He is reading me . . .": Joe Gibbs, Nov. 4, 2014.

263 "We go up there . . .": Ibid.

264 "We're going back . . .": Earnest Byner, Mar. 20, 2014.

264 "We worked absolutely . . .": Larry Peccatiello, June 19, 2014.

265 "I'm a big baseball . . .": Richie Petitbon, June 25, 2014.

265 "I think because . . .": Joe Gibbs, Nov. 4, 2014.

266 "He could have any . . .": Larry Peccatiello, June 19, 2014.

266 "Your defense, I've . . .": Joe Gibbs, Nov. 4, 2014.

267 "fast enough to cover . . .": Tom Friend, "Marshall Becomes Redskins' $6 Million Man," *Washington Post*, Mar. 19, 1988.

267 "We decided to make . . .": Warner Hessler, "Skins Linebacker Frustrated with Role," *Newport News (VA) Daily Press*, May. 6, 1991.

268 "The key has been . . .": Richard Justice, "New and Old Defense a Hit for Redskins," *Washington Post*, Oct. 2, 1991.

269 **"I think you're . . .":** Richard Justice, "Cooke Nudges Rypien," *Washington Post*, July 23, 1991.

269 **decided to "roll the dice":** Mark Rypien, Feb. 21, 2014.

269 **"At that era of football . . .":** Ibid.

269 **"We hit just about . . .":** Richard Justice, "Redskins Storm into '91, Blow Out Lions, 45-0," *Washington Post*, Sept. 2, 1991.

270 **"We did a lot . . .":** Joe Gibbs, Nov. 4, 2014.

270 **"It was a gallant . . .":** Paul Woody, "Grimm Sense of Humor Leaves Redskins Rolling During Victory," *Richmond Times-Dispatch*, Oct. 1, 1991.

271 **"They're the epitome . . .":** Vito Stellino, "Redskins Try to Pocket Record for Pass Protection," *Baltimore Sun*, Nov. 15, 1991.

271 **"one of the top two . . .":** "Lachey Just Getting Warmed Up," *USA Today*, Feb. 11, 1991.

271 **"He's blessed with . . .":** Ibid.

271 **"I wasn't on anybody's . . .":** Mark Schlereth, July 7, 2014.

272 **"diamond in the rough":** Ibid.

272 **"When I became a . . .":** Ibid.

272 **"and I never come . . .":** Ibid.

272 **"One night at dinner . . .":** Ibid.

273 **"It's just a hunch . . .":** Leonard Shapiro, "Redskins Not Perfect, Still Beloved," *Washington Post*, Nov. 25, 1991.

274 **"I'm going to take . . .":** Vito Stellino, "Redskins Hit an Emotional High," *Baltimore Sun*, Jan. 13, 1992.

275 **"This one could be . . .":** Warner Hessler, "Redskins Briefs," *Newport News (VA) Daily Press*, Jan. 14, 1992.

275 **"one of the toughest . . .":** "Joe Gibbs Still Has Regrets from Super Bowl XVIII Loss," *Sporting News*, Feb. 1, 2011.

276 **"The Redskins have stats . . .":** Don Pierson, "Bills-Redskins: A Match Made in NFL Heaven," *Chicago Tribune*, Jan. 26, 1992.

276 **"people are still hungry . . .":** Greg Logan, "Feeling More Like Football," *Newsday*, Jan. 26, 1992.

276 **"Dickerson's 309 pounds . . .":** Greg Cote, "Sooey—Here Piggy, Piggy Up," *Pharos-Tribune (Logansport, IN)*, Jan. 24, 1992.

276 **"He did a better job . . .":** Ken Denlinger, "Redskins' Pass Blockers Are Just Like Money in the Pocket," *Washington Post*, Jan. 25, 1992.

276 **"rough and rugged . . .":** Ibid.

277 **"ugly like the rest . . .":** Cote, "Sooey—Here Piggy, Piggy Up."

277 "great big chins . . .": Ibid.

277 "bad breath, which . . .": Ibid.

277 "He's clumsy out . . .": Denlinger, "Redskins' Pass Blockers."

277 "a real Neanderthal . . .": Cote, "Sooey—Here Piggy, Piggy Up."

277 "it wasn't funny": Gary Shelton, "Capital Performance," *St. Petersburg Times*, Jan. 27, 1992.

277 "I don't know that . . .": Mark Schlereth, July 7, 2014.

277 "their offensive line tackles . . .": Ross Newhan, "He Likes Country and Western, but He's Singing a Tear-Jerker," *Los Angeles Times*, Nov. 13, 1991.

277 "You could have . . .": Earnest Byner, Mar. 20, 2014.

278 "I remember getting . . .": Mark Rypien, Feb. 21, 2014.

279 "One thing I appreciated . . .": Mark Rypien, edited by Danny Peary, *Super Bowl: The Game of Their Lives* (New York: Macmillan, 1997), pp. 370–71.

279 Despite having "never practiced it": "No. 3 Is the Sweetest for Coach Gibbs," *Vancouver Sun*, Jan. 27, 1992.

280 "That was strictly . . .": Bob McGinn, "Superfluous Outcome," *Milwaukee Journal*, Jan. 27, 1992.

280 "They were here to . . .": Jim Souhan, "It's a Redskins Romp," *Minneapolis Star Tribune*, Jan. 27, 1992.

280 "If the Washington Redskins . . .": Rick Telander, "Superb," *Sports Illustrated*, Feb. 3, 1992.

281 "We go 14 and 2 . . .": Mark Rypien, Feb. 21, 2014.

282 "This team really had . . .": Jim Thomas, "Washington Took Systematic Approach," *St. Louis Post-Dispatch*, Jan. 28, 1992.

11. A FOOTBALL COACH'S LIFE

283 "This is a coach's . . .": Joe Gibbs, Nov. 4, 2014.

283 "The first day is . . .": Curt Brown, "Masterminds: Gibbs Worked Hard to Join Coaching Elite," *Minneapolis Star Tribune*, Jan. 21, 1992.

284 "doesn't have any flaws": Thomas George, "Extra! Extra! Redskins Get Howard, Dickerson Dealt," *New York Times*, Apr. 27, 1992.

284 "It only takes a little . . .": Ken Denlinger, "Redskins Start at Top, for Better and Worse," *Washington Post*, Aug. 30, 1992.

284 "wasn't any good": Dave Distel, "Coryell Knew What He Had in Joe Gibbs," *Los Angeles Times*, Jan. 30, 1988.

285 **"my Little Bulldog":** Bob Oates, "Joe Gibbs: Intense Fun Lover Molds a Winner in Washington," *Los Angeles Times,* Jan. 15, 1984.

285 **"I remember my first . . .":** Marty Hogan, Dec. 8, 2014.

286 **"If you can imagine . . .":** Ibid.

286 **"Nobody got more . . .":** Ibid.

286 **"I lived by the adage . . .":** Joe Gibbs with Ken Abraham, *Racing to Win* (New York: Mulnomah, 2002), p. 246.

287 **"Did you ever . . .":** Jim Hanifan, Aug. 8, 2014.

287 **"I came in early . . .":** Richard Justice, "Gibbs, Panthers: Just Talk," *Washington Post,* Oct. 30, 1993.

288 **"There was kicking . . .":** Thomas George, "Redskins' Drama Brings Curtain Down on Dallas," *New York Times,* Dec. 14, 1992.

288 **"I'm fired up . . .":** Richard Justice, "Redskins Back into Playoffs Through Minnesota," *Washington Post,* Dec. 28, 1992.

289 **"Last year was a . . .":** Thomas Boswell, "The Future Is Now," *Washington Post,* Jan. 11, 1993.

289 **"It messes up . . .":** Christine Brennan, "Who Is Christine Brennan, and Why Are Jay Schroeder and Joe Theismann and Bobby Beathard, and Jack Kent Cooke Always Yelling at Her," *Washington Post,* Jan. 24, 1988.

290 **"I covered three seasons . . .":** Christine Brennan, July 14, 2014.

290 **"There was a pause . . .":** Steve Buckhantz, Mar. 4, 2015.

291 **"Mr. President, what do you . . .":** Christine Brennan, Feb. 26, 2015.

291 **"I think Joe Gibbs . . .":** Christine Brennan and Mark Asher, "NFL Rivals Join in Chorus of Praise for 'Very Gifted Man,'" *Washington Post,* Mar. 6 1993.

291 **"I think that just . . .":** Christine Brennan, Feb. 26, 2015.

291 **"I almost drove off . . .":** Warner Hessler, "A Sad Day for 'Skins Fans," *Newport News (VA) Daily Press,* Mar. 6, 1993.

292 **"I need to spend . . .":** "Yielding to Weight of Night," Thomas Boswell, *Washington Post,* Mar. 6, 1993.

292 **"I'd had an uncle . . .":** "Joe Gibbs Will Defy Diabetes," Defy Diabetes, Youtube.com, accessed Dec. 3, 2014.

292 **"There was a feeling . . .":** Gary Pomerantz, May 30, 2014.

293 **"he was 200 pounds . . .":** Richard Justice, "The Ecstasy and the Agony," *Washington Post,* July 21, 1996.

293 **"When you coach . . .":** Joe Gibbs, Nov. 4, 2014.

293 **"I'll get a chance . . .":** Thomas George, "For Joe Gibbs, Greatest Pain Is in Leaving the Redskins," *New York Times,* Mar. 6, 1993.

294   "[What] a gracious opportunity . . .": Ibid.

294   "This league is geared . . .": George, "For Joe Gibbs, Greatest Pain."

295   "franchise player": Richard Justice, "Marshall to Press Court Battle," *Washington Post*, July 4, 1993.

295   "No one can say . . .": Richard Justice, "Redskins Ride Out Winds of Change," *Washington Post*, July 6, 1993.

296   "I don't want . . .": Leonard Shapiro, "To Cooke, Gibbs Did Right Thing," *Washington Post*, Mar. 7, 1993.

296   "The one thing . . .": Gene Wang, "Redskins Trio Dispels Doubts with Big Night," *Washington Post*, Sept. 7, 1993.

297   Richie Petitbon . . . "biggest flop": "The First-Half Highlights, Low Points," *USA Today*, Nov. 11, 1993.

297   "I really took offense . . .": Vito Stellino, "Banks Flips Over Story Calling Petitbon a Flop," *Baltimore Sun*, Nov. 15, 1993.

298   "We were all . . .": Jim Hanifan, Aug. 8, 2014.

298   "This is one of the unhappiest . . .": Richard Justice, "Redskins Dismiss Head Coach Petitbon," *Washington Post*, Jan. 5, 1994.

298   "I don't think anybody . . .": David Aldridge, "Petitbon, Redskins Exchange Their Farewells," *Washington Post*, Jan. 5, 1994.

299   "He can't walk . . .": Dave Sell, "After 13 Seasons, Jacoby Calls It Quits," *Washington Post*, July 20, 1994.

299   "Jeff and I have talked . . .": Richard Justice, "With Body Battered, Retirement Is Jake with Jacoby," *Washington Post*, July 7, 1994.

EPILOGUE

301   "football is still No. 1 . . .": Mike Dame, "General Motors May Cut Participation Next Year," *Orlando Sentinel*, July 5, 1991.

302   "I got in on . . .": Phil McCombs, "Joe Gibbs, Speeding from the Rat Race," *Washington Post*, July 7, 1993.

302   "I didn't give it . . .": Joe Gibbs, Nov. 4, 2014.

303   "I want to be buried . . .": Peter Perl, "The House of Cooke," *Washington Post*, Aug. 31, 1997.

303   "I bid $750 million . . .": Mike Wise, "Burgundy & Old Pain," *Washington Post*, Oct. 21, 2009.

304   "I got down at . . .": Ibid.

305   "you'll be selling insurance!": Charles Mann, June 19, 2014.

305 **"[This] is Joe Gibbs . . .":** Tony Kornheiser, "The Latest and Greatest," *Washington Post,* Jan. 8, 2004.

306 **"Gibbs has his bronze . . .":** Thomas Boswell, "Redskins Haunted Ghosts of Coaches Past," *Washington Post,* Nov. 28, 2005.

397 **"God made certain people . . .":** "A Football Life: Sean Taylor," NFL Films.

307 **"When we got that . . .":** Jason La Canfora, "Sunk in Seattle," *Washington Post,* Jan. 15, 2006.

307 **"I told them I couldn't . . .":** Leonard Shapiro, "Redskins' Run Is Halted," *Washington Post,* Jan. 15, 2006.

308 **"Joe did a magnificent . . .":** Al Saunders, Feb. 26, 2014.

308 **"It was the toughest . . .":** "Joe Gibbs Resigns as Redskins Coach," *Annapolis (MD) Capital,* Jan. 8, 2008.

308 **"The songs that [John] . . .":** Tony Kornheiser, Feb. 26, 2015.

309 **"I thought it was going . . .":** Charles Mann, June 19, 2014.

309 **"I tell people this is . . .":** Joe Gibbs, Nov. 4, 2014.

310 **"Roasting Joe Gibbs . . .":** Jeff Bostic, Nov. 17, 2014.

310 **"He was just on a wonderful . . .":** James Brown, Feb. 27, 2015.

310 **"Well, I want to . . .":** Dan Steinberg, "Dexter Manley's Roast of Joe Gibbs," *Washington Post: DC Sports Bog,* Sept. 26, 2013.

310 **"fresh start somewhere else":** Warner Hessler, "Manley Gets OK to Play But Redskins Give Troubled Player His Release," *Newport News (VA) Daily Press,* Nov. 20, 1990.

311 **"He was distraught . . .":** Steve Buckhantz, Mar. 4, 2015.

312 **"They wouldn't tell me . . .":** Dexter Manley, Nov. 8, 2014.

312 **"I'm here because I . . .":** Peter Finney, "Manley, Sanders Contrast in Choices," *New Orleans Times-Picayune,* Mar. 7, 1995.

312 **"This is the first time . . .":** Ibid.

312 **"And from that point . . .":** Dexter Manley, Nov. 8, 2014.

Index

About the Author

ADAM LAZARUS is a member of the Professional Football Writers of America and the author of three previous sports books, including *Best of Rivals: Joe Montana, Steve Young, and the Inside Story Behind the NFL's Greatest Quarterback Controversy*. His writing has appeared in *ESPN The Magazine*, the *Atlanta Journal-Constitution*, Bleacher Report, and *USA Today*.